This volume, the thirteenth in the National Bureau's Studies in Business Cycles, traces the effects of government policies and financial developments on changes in the nation's stock of money, which is defined as the sum of currency outside banks and commercial bank demand and time deposits held by the public. The money stock is found to display a systematic pattern of fluctuations over business cycles. These fluctuations have been influenced by a variety of forces, among which the most powerful are the federal government, the banking system, and the changing public demands for currency. This study is concerned with the effects of all of these forces and the relation of changes in the money stock to changes in prices and output. Special attention is given to gold movements and their effects on the stock of money.

As Milton Friedman says in his Foreword, Cagan "has provided basic material that no future student of the subject will be able to do without or need duplicate. . . . There does not exist any other study of conditions determining the supply of money that is remotely comparable to Cagan's in its empirical scope and thoroughness. . ."

Phillip Cagan is a Member of the Economics Department at Brown University.

DETERMINANTS AND EFFECTS OF CHANGES IN THE STOCK OF MONEY, 1875–1960

NATIONAL BUREAU OF ECONOMIC RESEARCH

Studies in Business Cycles

1. *Business Cycles: The Problem and Its Setting*, by Wesley C. Mitchell

2. *Measuring Business Cycles*, by Arthur F. Burns and Wesley C. Mitchell

3. *American Transportation in Prosperity and Depression*, by Thor Hultgren

4. *Inventories and Business Cycles, with Special Reference to Manufacturers'
   Inventories*, by Moses Abramovitz

5. *What Happens during Business Cycles: A Progress Report*,
   by Wesley C. Mitchell

6. *Personal Income during Business Cycles*, by Daniel Creamer
   with the assistance of Martin Bernstein

7. *Consumption and Business Fluctuations: A Case Study of the Shoe,
   Leather, Hide Sequence*, by Ruth P. Mack

8. *International Financial Transactions and Business Cycles*,
   by Oskar Morgenstern

9. *Federal Receipts and Expenditures During Business Cycles, 1879–1958*,
   by John M. Firestone

10. *Business Cycle Indicators:* Volume I, *Contributions to the Analysis of Current
    Business Conditions;* Volume II, *Basic Data on Cyclical Indicators*,
    edited by Geoffrey H. Moore

11. *Postwar Cycles in Manufacturers' Inventories*, by Thomas M. Stanback, Jr.

12. *A Monetary History of the United States, 1867–1960*, by Milton Friedman
    and Anna Jacobson Schwartz

13. *Determinants and Effects of Changes in the Stock of Money, 1875–1960*,
    by Phillip Cagan

PHILLIP CAGAN

BROWN UNIVERSITY

DETERMINANTS AND EFFECTS OF CHANGES IN THE STOCK OF MONEY 1875-1960

NATIONAL BUREAU OF ECONOMIC RESEARCH

NEW YORK 1965

Distributed by COLUMBIA UNIVERSITY PRESS

NEW YORK AND LONDON

Relation of the Directors to the Work and Publications of the National Bureau of Economic Research

1. The object of the National Bureau of Economic Research is to ascertain and to present to the public important economic facts and their interpretation in a scientific and impartial manner. The Board of Directors is charged with the responsibility of ensuring that the work of the National Bureau is carried on in strict conformity with this object.
2. To this end the Board of Directors shall appoint one or more Directors of Research.
3. The Director or Directors of Research shall submit to the members of the Board, or to its Executive Committee, for their formal adoption, all specific proposals concerning researches to be instituted.
4. No report shall be published until the Director or Directors of Research shall have submitted to the Board a summary drawing attention to the character of the data and their utilization in the report, the nature and treatment of the problems involved, the main conclusions, and such other information as in their opinion would serve to determine the suitability of the report for publication in accordance with the principles of the National Bureau.
5. A copy of any manuscript proposed for publication shall also be submitted to each member of the Board. For each manuscript to be so submitted a special committee shall be appointed by the President, or at his designation by the Executive Director, consisting of three Directors selected as nearly as may be one from each general division of the Board. The names of the special manuscript committee shall be stated to each Director when the summary and report described in paragraph (4) are sent to him. It shall be the duty of each member of the committee to read the manuscript. If each member of the special committee signifies his approval within thirty days, the manuscript may be published. If each member of the special committee has not signified his approval within thirty days of the transmittal of the report and manuscript, the Director of Research shall then notify each member of the Board, requesting approval or disapproval of publication, and thirty additional days shall be granted for this purpose. The manuscript shall then not be published unless at least a majority of the entire Board and a two-thirds majority of those members of the Board who shall have voted on the proposal within the time fixed for the receipt of votes on the publication proposed shall have approved.
6. No manuscript may be published, though approved by each member of the special committee, until forty-five days have elapsed from the transmittal of the summary and report. The interval is allowed for the receipt of any memorandum of dissent or reservation, together with a brief statement of his reasons, that any member may wish to express; and such memorandum of dissent or reservation shall be published with the manuscript if he so desires. Publication does not, however, imply that each member of the Board has read the manuscript, or that either members of the Board in general, or of the special committee, have passed upon its validity in every detail.
7. A copy of this resolution shall, unless otherwise determined by the Board, be printed in each copy of every National Bureau book.

(Resolution adopted October 25, 1926,
as revised February 6, 1933, and February 24, 1941)

To My Mother and Father

CONTENTS

TABLES

CHARTS

FIGURES

PREFACE

By long tradition prefaces to monetary works note the wide attention given the subject by the public. The remark is still appropriate today. Few subjects have entertained and alarmed the public for so long. A debate continuing for centuries pits the classical writers, who view money as an independent source of economic disturbance, against the critics of this view, who say money is a passive adapter to business conditions with little independent influence. Indeed, recent statements of the passive view sound much like the old real-bills doctrine propounded in the Bullion controversy over a century and a half ago. The active and passive theories of money appear to be antagonists in an unending saga: periodically one or the other side proclaims its adversary dead and laid to rest, but neither one stays buried. Hopefully the rapidly accumulating empirical work will eventually settle the matter, though my interpretation of the evidence—that money is both active and passive—obscures the sharp lines of the old debate and may please neither side.

The present work has become a collection of related but separate studies, each of which merits book-length treatment, so different are the factors affecting the various parts of the money supply in its secular and cyclical movements. Giving due attention to each part has prolonged the work, though there are still many gaps in the analysis. Drawing on the evidence of an eighty-five-year period has enlarged the work as well, but is worthwhile. Important relationships can be misjudged if studied in a few short periods because of special factors which, at short range, give an impression of dramatic impact but in a longer view lose significance. Some studies of the money stock rely too much on the unusual events of the 1930's and 1940's. The financial panic and the fluctuations in bank reserve ratios in those decades obscure the typical behavior of monetary variables and may lead to error. Comparisons with other periods lessen the danger of exaggerating the effects of some factors and missing others.

A statistical work like the present has one author responsible for the conclusions but many contributors. I have used new estimates of the U.S. money stock derived by Milton Friedman and Anna Jacobson Schwartz.[1] Their estimates are based on annual data back to 1896 compiled by the Division of Research and Statistics of the Federal Reserve System, and on nonnational bank data for the period 1875–96 prepared by David I. Fand at the Money and Banking Workshop of the University of Chicago.[2] Part of the present study was done during my association with the Workshop from 1955 to 1958, for which thanks are due to the Rockefeller Foundation for financial support.

I have benefited immeasurably at all stages of the study from the work and suggestions of Milton Friedman and Anna Schwartz. Their two volumes and this one are related, but separate, parts of the National Bureau's study of monetary influences on the economy. Through exchange of ideas and findings there is some overlap in the reports of our studies, though I hope not more than clarity requires. Mine differs from theirs in analyzing specifically and systematically the major factors affecting the determinants of the money stock, which they take up only incidentally. To draw out some implications of the findings I also discuss in Chapter 6 the effects of monetary changes on the economy. Although the conclusions reached are in general the same as those of Friedman and Schwartz, the subject is approached from a different angle. Each of the three volumes, written to stand alone, serves to supplement the others.

I wish to acknowledge also helpful suggestions from many people who commented on earlier drafts of the manuscript: Joseph Conard and Richard Selden, who served with Friedman and Schwartz on a National Bureau staff reading committee for the manuscript, Frank W. Fetter, Ilse Mintz, Geoffrey H. Moore, Jerome L. Stein, and Clark Warburton.

My debt is great to those who helped at various stages with compiling data and computing tables: at the National Bureau, Charlotte Boschan, Sophie Sakowitz, Hanna Stern, Mark Wehle, and

[1] *A Monetary History of the United States, 1867–1960*, Princeton University Press for National Bureau of Economic Research, 1963; and their forthcoming "Trends and Cycles in the Stock of Money in the United States, 1867–1960," also a National Bureau study, in preparation.

[2] "Non-National Banks Estimates: 1867–1896," unpublished Ph.D. dissertation, University of Chicago, 1954.

Tom Yu; at Chicago, Roy Elliot, George Macesich, and Lily Monheit.

Margaret T. Edgar deserves special thanks for a careful job of editing the manuscript; and H. Irving Forman, for expertly drawing the charts.

P. C.

FOREWORD

As Josh Billings wrote many years ago, "The trouble with most folks isn't so much their ignorance, as knowing so many things that ain't so." Pertinent as this remark is to economics in general, it is especially so to monetary economics. Because money is so pervasive and yet hidden, so susceptible to manipulation and yet seemingly beyond the ordinary man's control, it has attracted to itself far more than its share of "crackpots" offering easy panaceas for solving the ills of the world. And among professional economists, it has for centuries been the focus of dispute, both at the rarefied level of abstract theory and at the more mundane level of interpretation of day-to-day experience. In the process, opinion has tended to rigidify into strongly held views—on some dates precisely the opposite of those held at others—which derive their support less from carefully examined and well-organized evidence than from initial statement by great men and subsequent tiresome repetition.

It is not the least of the virtues of Phillip Cagan's monograph that it examines systematically and thoroughly many of these views in light of empirical evidence on factors affecting the quantity of money during nearly a century of United States history, and separates the propositions that "ain't so" from those that might be so from those that are so. A few specimens will document this assertion.

1. Cagan's general topic is the supply of money, so we may begin with a proposition that is almost uniformly taken for granted in current theoretical discussions of that general topic, namely, the proposition that the nominal quantity of money supplied tends to be positively related to interest rates (though, of course, the real quantity demanded tends to be negatively related). The positive effect is assumed to occur primarily through a trimming of reserve ratios by banks when the return they can get on loans and investments rises and, secondarily, through an expansion of the volume of reserves by member-bank borrowing from the Federal Reserve. Cagan examines both

channels, using evidence for both secular movements and cyclical fluctuations. He concludes that the first channel is inoperative: "Cyclical fluctuations in the reserve ratio mainly reflect business conditions, not the cost of holding reserves [interest rates], insofar as the two differ, as they often do." Though he finds some positive relation between rates of interest and member-bank borrowing, he attributes relatively little importance to this effect. Two other channels seem to him somewhat more important: effects on the demand for currency and on the division of deposits between time and demand deposits. "A rise in rates paid on time and savings deposits appears to reduce the demand for currency . . . . A rise in interest rates also induces a shift from demand to time deposits, which reduces the required reserve ratio of banks and hence the total reserve ratio. These effects produce a slight positive relation between interest rates and the money stock (defined to include time deposits)." Yet, all in all, "interest raes . . . appear to have very minor effects on the money stock."

2. A related, though far less basic, issue is the effect of changes in legal reserve requirements on the reserve ratio of the banking system. One view is that such changes will be transmitted in full to the ratio of total reserves to deposits, i.e., that what Cagan calls the "usable reserve ratio" will be unaffected. An alternative view is that changes in legal reserve requirements will affect the total reserve ratio only when usable reserves are small, that otherwise they will leave it unchanged, an increase in requirements being absorbed by a decline in the usable reserve ratio and a decrease in requirements by a rise in the usable reserve ratio. Both views can be found in the literature, and the Federal Reserve System has at times based policy on the one view and at times on the other. After examination of the evidence and consideration of various plausible interpretations, Cagan concludes that the "desired level of usable reserves . . . is usually independent of required reserves, no matter how large the usable reserve ratio may be," although the speed with which banks adjust to a change in required reserves may depend on the size of the usable reserve ratio.

3. Probably the most important issue to which the monograph contributes is the long-standing dispute about the causal relation between money and prices. Do changes in the quantity of money produce changes in the same direction in prices, as the classical economists contended for centuries? Or, as some economists have

argued in recent decades and many noneconomists for much longer,
are the price movements the result of a variety of other independent
influences, and the observed common movements in the quantity of
money a result rather than cause of the price movements? It turns out
that Cagan's examination of the source of changes in the quantity of
money yields highly relevant evidence for discriminating between these
alternatives, or, on a more sophisticated level, for indicating the role
of each.

(a) The major source of long-period changes in the quantity of
money in the United States has been changes in high-powered money,
which, until 1914, reflected mostly changes in the amount of gold.
Price rises tend to discovrage gold output and encourage gold exports
and thereby tend to reduce the quantity of high-powered money.
Conversely, price decreases tend to increase the quantity of high-
powered money. These effects show up in the data—but with a very
long lag, measured in decades rather than years. The contemporaneous
relation is precisely the opposite: price increases accompany a higher
than average rate of rise in high-powered money; price decreases, a
lower than average rate of rise.

If this variation is not coincidental, or the common result of some
unspecified third factor, it must reflect the effect of money on prices.
Cagan concludes, "The lagged reaction of the gold stock to changes in
commodity prices . . . is what makes the gold standard a poor means
of stabilizing the price level, rather than failure of gold-stock changes
to affect prices." And "to explain secular movements in prices . . . we
should look primarily to the money stock, and then secondarily to
nonmonetary factors that may also have important influence."

(b) For short-period fluctuations involving severe business contractions, the evidence is equally decisive and in the same direction.
Each such contraction is associated with a sharp decline in the rate of
monetary growth. Cagan's examination of the sources of the decline
"rules out . . . a sharp fall in business activity as the main reason."
The care with which he builds the foundation for this conclusion is
most impressive, especially his painstaking, and rather successful,
attempt to separate out the effects of banking panics from those of
severe business contractions. He concludes, "The evidence is therefore
consistent with, and, taken as a whole, impressively favors emphasis
on the decline in the rate of monetary growth as the main reason some

business contractions, regardless of what may have initiated them, became severe."

(c) For mild cycles, the evidence is no less decisive but yields a different substantive result. For these, Cagan finds clear evidence of the influence of business changes on the quantity of money. Surprisingly, in light of most of the cycle literature which emphasizes the reactions of banks and monetary authorities, cyclical fluctuations in the fraction of its money that the public holds in the form of currency account for roughly half of the cylical fluctuations in the quantity of money. These movements in the currency ratio, and also most of the less important cyclical fluctuations in the banks' reserve ratio, seem to reflect the contemporaneous movements in economic activity. Yet there is also evidence of the reverse influence of money on business. Hence, Cagan concludes that "mutual dependence" is the rule for mild cycles.

4. A by-product of Cagan's analysis of the causal relation between money and prices is his examination of the so-called Gibson paradox, the observed tendency for the long-period movements of prices and interest rates to be in the same direction. Knut Wicksell and John M. Keynes hypothesized that both movements were the common result of independent changes in the demand for loans. An increase in the demand for loans, they argued, would directly raise interest rates; indirectly, because of lagged reactions by the banking system, it would also raise the quantity of money, which, in its turn, would raise prices; and conversely for a decline in the demand for loans. Cagan demonstrates that this explanation, despite its wide acceptance—or at least repetition—is contradicted by the facts—not because there is any flaw in the theoretical reasoning but because the hypothesis requires that the major source of long-period changes in the nominal quantity of money be changes in reserve ratios, whereas in fact it has been changes in the quantity of high-powered money. One relevant fact can deprive the most rigorous chain of reasoning of explanatory value— though, I hasten to add, no assortment of facts, however numerous, have any explanatory value unless they can be organized by a theory.

Cagan considers also an alternative explanation suggested by Irving Fisher, which relies on a delayed effect of actual price changes on expectations about the future course of prices. Cagan finds that the evidence he examines neither clearly contradicts nor strongly supports that explanation. This remains one of those propositions that might be so.

Rather than adding to these examples—which the reader will find it more profitable to do for himself—let me supplement briefly Cagan's comments in his preface on the relation between his study and the two companion volumes by Anna Jacobson Schwartz and myself. All three deal with U.S. experience over the same period. All three attempt to use the factual evidence for that period and that country to illuminate the role of money in economic affairs and to test and enrich our theoretical understanding of the working of a money economy. All three use as a central element our estimates of the quantity of money. All reach compatible and, to some extent, overlapping conclusions— as is natural since the three are products of the same project and each has benefited from the others. Yet each makes its own distinctive con- tribution to the common objective.

Our *Monetary History of the United States*, already published, is primarily an analytical narrative, organized chronologically, which seeks to extract inferences about the role of money from an exami- nation of successive historical episodes. We were able to do so the better because we had access to Cagan's work and could use it as statistical underpinning for our historical account.

The special task of Cagan's monograph was, as already said, to isolate and measure the factors responsible for changes in the stock of money. In doing so, he has provided basic material that no future student of the subject will be able to do without or need duplicate—in his tables and the careful statistical calculations that underlie them, no less than in his text. There does not exist any other study of con- ditions determining the supply of money that is remotely comparable to Cagan's in its empirical scope and thoroughness, though, thanks partly to his work, this subject, like the study of money in general, is experiencing something of a boom.

Originally, we did not expect the examination of the supply of money to provide evidence on such general issues as the causal relation between money and prices. We regarded it primarily as a study that, by examining one side of the monetary problem, would provide raw material for the other studies to combine with evidence from the de- mand side. But research leads a life of its own and has no respect for initial expectations. As the earlier examples illustrate, evidence on the supply of money has turned out to yield unexpectedly powerful evidence on more general monetary relations—perhaps because it has been neglected and hence not already taken into account in the theoretical generalizations enshrined in the literature.

The monograph on *Trends and Cycles in the Stock of Money in the United States*, now in preparation, begins where Cagan leaves off, namely, with the behavior of the stock of money itself. It is a statistical analysis which seeks to find and interpret regularities in the secular and cyclical behavior of the stock of money and of monetary velocity in relation to other economic magnitudes. In addition, it gives a detailed explanation of the derivation of our estimates of the stock of money.

In contrast with our *History*, it is organized by statistical categories rather than by chronological episodes, and takes as its basic data numerical aggregates rather than qualitative events and the actions of individual human beings. In contrast with Cagan's monograph, it deals primarily with the demand for money, rather than the supply. Like the other monographs, it will unfortunately still leave for the future and for other scholars a full development of a monetary theory of the cycle which incorporates both demand and supply in an empirically meaningful way. Cagan's Appendix D is a foretaste of the most general outlines of such a development.

It is now well over a decade since the group of research studies of which this monograph is the second major product was begun at the National Bureau. In that period there has been a flourishing of monetary research in this country and abroad. This monograph, begun at a barren period, comes to fruition to join a rich and growing stream of work, to provide new material and new insights to numerous fellow workers, who will in their turn hopefully render it obsolete. It is an honor to introduce such a book to such a fellowship.

MILTON FRIEDMAN

I

THE MONEY STOCK AND ITS THREE DETERMINANTS

1. Nature and Scope of the Study

THE OBSERVATION that changes in the money stock are correlated with both secular and cyclical fluctuations in economic activity is of long standing. The covariation underlies many theories of economic disturbance and many proposals for monetary reform, though more so before the 1930's than since. It is documented and elaborated further in the recent work of Milton Friedman and Anna Jacobson Schwartz.[1] The phenomenon is too persistent to be dismissed as accidental, and it is plausible in terms of well-known economic relationships. Production and prices depend on monetary factors; and, conversely, fluctuations in general economic activity are transmitted by financial institutions to the money stock.

There are basically two ways to clarify the source of covariation between money and business activity. One is to examine the effects of changes in the money stock on business activity. These effects, though studied extensively, have proved difficult to trace. Even when large, they are likely to involve distributed lags and so to affect various parts of the economy at different times. Identifying cause and effect is then extremely difficult and hazardous. An alternative approach is to examine the factors affecting the amount of money supplied. The more they reflect fluctuations in business activity, the less reliance can be placed on the importance of money-stock effects in explaining the observed covariation—and conversely. The belief that this approach can shed light on the importance of the two directions of influence is the main motivation for the present study.

---

[1] *A Monetary History of the United States, 1867–1960*, Princeton University Press for NBER, 1963; and "Trends and Cycles in the Stock of Money in the United States, 1867–1960," their companion volume, also a National Bureau study, in preparation.

Aside from this specific purpose, a study of the factors affecting the money supply is useful to broaden our understanding of the monetary system. Most previous discussions of these factors have centered on this broader purpose and have described the institutional arrangements for issuing money. Previous studies have made only limited attempts at statistical measurement, however. The two main empirical studies for the United States—by Lauchlin Currie and James W. Angell[2] covered mainly the period from World War I to the mid-1930's, two decades of great contrasts but too short to confirm long-standing relationships. Clark Warburton has since published several articles on various aspects of the subject,[3] using data of longer coverage. More recently a growing literature has appeared on econometric studies of the behavior of banks.[4]

One reason research on the supply of and demand for money has been limited was the absence until recently of good data covering a long time span. The publication of *A Monetary History of the United States, 1867–1960,* by Friedman and Schwartz, now provides estimates for a ninety-odd year period. The present study was largely completed before estimates for the years preceding 1875 became available. It begins with that year and terminates with 1960. Some of the analysis has an earlier cutoff, however, because later data were not available at the time various tables were prepared. The estimates are annual or semiannual before 1907 and monthly thereafter. Supplementary monthly data are also available for most of the period preceding 1907 on currency outside the Treasury and on various other items used in estimating the money stock. All these series are fairly accurate, as economic data go, and allow both a more extensive and a more intensive analysis of the factors affecting the amount supplied than previously possible.

---

[2] Currie, *The Supply and Control of Money in the United States,* Harvard University Press, 1934; and Angell, *The Behavior of Money,* New York, McGraw-Hill, 1936.

[3] In particular, "The Theory of Turning Points in Business Fluctuations," *Quarterly Journal of Economics,* Nov. 1950, pp. 525–549; "The Misplaced Emphasis in Contemporary Business-Fluctuation Theory," reprinted in *Readings in Monetary Theory,* F. A. Lutz and L. W. Mints, Eds., Philadelphia, Blakiston, for American Economic Association, 1951, pp. 309–311; "Bank Reserves and Business Fluctuations," *Journal of the American Statistical Association,* Dec. 1948, pp. 547–558; "Monetary Control under the Federal Reserve Act," *Political Science Quarterly,* Dec. 1946, pp. 505–534.

[4] See, for example, A. J. Meigs, *Free Reserves and the Money Supply,* Chicago, 1962, and the references cited therein.

The money stock is defined as hand-to-hand currency plus commercial bank demand and time deposits held by all economic sectors except the Treasury and the Federal Reserve Banks and commercial banks. The present work, therefore, is largely a study of the monetary liabilities of banking institutions. The question immediately arises whether this is the most useful definition of the money stock. Previous studies have commonly used a narrower definition which includes only hand-to-hand currency and demand deposits. The main reason for including also time deposits at commercial banks in the new estimates is that they cannot be satisfactorily separated from demand deposits in the pre-1914 data and perhaps not meaningfully separated until the 1930's (see Chapter 5, section 1) and so, for purposes of comparability, were included for the later period. Another concern is whether this definition may be too narrow. A point of view expressed by the Banking School of the mid-1800's, and even earlier by others, contends that the liabilities of various nonbanking financial institutions are near-perfect moneys and should be included along with the liabilities of commercial banks. On these grounds, one should include postal savings and mutual savings deposits, perhaps also shares of savings and loan associations, and even U.S. savings bonds and Treasury bills and notes; it is difficult to know where to draw the line. Indeed, the Banking School contended that no hard-and-fast line can be drawn between money and nonmoneys. This possibility requires empirical examination. Conjectures on the characteristics of "money" do not help much, because the important consideration is market behavior, particularly the cross elasticities of demand between the various assets with respect to their comparative rates of return. The size of the cross elasticities—that is, the extent to which individuals behave as though certain assets were more or less equivalent to currency or demand deposits—and the amplitude of variations in comparative rates of return have not been determined. Since it is necessary to select a precise definition at the outset and impossible as yet to demonstrate that a broader concept of money is superior to a narrower one, this study follows the convenient definition stated at the beginning of this paragraph. The subsequent analysis may be viewed as contributing to one part of a broader study which would cover all liquid assets.

While the narrow definition of money used here may turn out, in the light of future research, to be less than perfect, it seems adequate for present purposes. It is likely to account for most of the variation in a more broadly defined money-stock variable, though long-run rates of growth will depend, of course, on which assets are included. The supply of currency and commercial bank deposits probably displays considerably greater short-run changes than the supply of most other liquid assets does.

2. Cyclical Behavior of the Rate of Change in the Money Stock

Table 1 lists the short-run cycles in the rate of change in the money stock and relates the turning points to reference cycles in general business activity on a peak-to-peak and trough-to-trough basis. There has generally been a one-to-one correspondence between the cycles in money and reference cycles. There are only two exceptions; an extra money cycle with a peak in February 1941 and trough in October 1941, which preceded a peak in June 1943 matched with the February 1945 reference peak; and no expansion during a long contraction from June 1943 to December 1948 to correspond with the reference cycle having a trough in October 1945 and a peak in November 1948. The money series consistently leads corresponding reference cycles at peaks and troughs, on the average by slightly over a quarter of a reference cycle. The amplitudes of expansions and contractions of monetary and reference cycles are also significantly correlated. These and variant measures are presented and discussed in detail by Friedman and Schwartz in their volume analyzing trends and cycles in the money stock.

The chief reason for using the rate of change in the money stock in these comparisons, rather than the quantity of money, is to eliminate the strong upward trend in the quantity, which obscures fluctuations. The results justify this procedure, for the rate-of-change series corresponds, by the usual measures, much more closely and consistently to reference cycles than the quantity of money does. With the money series in this form, however, a question arises about the meaning of its timing lead over reference cycles. The lead suggests that the effect of changes in monetary growth on business activity is largely responsible for the covariation between them. Without further evidence, however, the inference is not airtight. If the comparison were made with peaks and troughs in the rate of change in business activity, the length of the lead would undoubtedly be less, though perhaps would not disappear entirely. It is conceivable that expansions in business activity tend after a while to reduce the rate of monetary growth but that the reduction has no important feedback on business, which eventually reaches a peak a quarter cycle later and declines for wholly unrelated reasons; and similarly, for contractions and troughs. Evidence on timing, therefore, while highly suggestive, cannot be decisive on the direction of influence.

What dimensions of the variables are appropriate for comparison depends on the nature of the relationship between them, and with present knowledge no answer can be conclusive. Although the price level adjusts, at least in the long run, to the quantity of money, this does not mean that fluctuations in real output are most appropriately related to the quantity of money. Indeed, it is not implausible that different long-run rates of growth of the money stock are absorbed in the economy by corresponding differences in the rate of change in prices, while short-run variations in monetary growth mainly disturb the level of output—price changes not occurring fast enough to absorb them. The extent of the disturbance could very well depend on the size of the variation and hence imply a relation between the rate of change in money and the level of output.

Further evidence on the direction of influence is given by the correlation of amplitudes. Whatever the reason for cyclical variations in money, we should not ordinarily find a high correlation in amplitude between the phases of specific cycles in money and the corresponding phases of *subsequent* reference cycles, unless an important effect ran from the rate of change in money to business activity. We do find such a correlation, shown in Table 1. Yet, much of the correlation reflects severe business contractions and subsequent expansions, in which banking panics produced most of the decline in the money series and ending of panics produced the recovery. One might argue that the correlation can be explained by the early effect of changes in business conditions on financial institutions. In this and other ways, we cannot understand the evidence on the effects of money on business until we have examined and clarified the reverse effects of business on money.

TABLE 1

TIMING AND AMPLITUDE OF SPECIFIC CYCLES IN THE RATE OF CHANGE IN THE MONEY STOCK, 1870-1960

Specific Cycles		Matched Reference Cycles		Lead (−) or Lag (+) in Months of Specific Cycles at Matched Reference Turns		Change in Monthly Percentage Rate of Change in Money Stock Between Matched Peak and Trough Stages of Specific Cycles		Rank of Amplitude of Matched Nonwar[a] Reference Cycles	
Trough	Peak	Trough	Peak	Trough	Peak	Expansions	Succeeding Contractions	Expansions	Succeeding Contractions
					ANNUAL OR SEMIANNUAL DATA				
	July 1871		Oct. 1873		−27				
May 1877	May 1881	Mar. 1879	Mar. 1882	−22	−10	2.32	−1.82	3	6
Dec. 1883	Dec. 1885	May 1885	Mar. 1887	−17	−15	0.83	−0.49	8	17
Dec. 1887	Dec. 1889	Apr. 1888	July 1890	−4	−7	0.61	−0.58	13	11
Dec. 1890	Dec. 1891	May 1891	Jan. 1893	−5	−13	0.65	−1.43	14	4
Dec. 1892	Dec. 1894	June 1894	Dec. 1895	−18	−12	1.03	−0.89	6	7
Dec. 1895	Dec. 1898	June 1897	June 1899	−18	−6	1.74	−0.88	4	12 1/2
Dec. 1899	Dec. 1900	Dec. 1900	Sept. 1902	−12	−21	0.70	−0.73	16	12 1/2
Dec. 1903	Dec. 1904	Aug. 1904	May 1907	−8	−29	0.51	−2.05	9	5
					MONTHLY DATA				
Jan. 1908	Oct. 1908	June 1908	Jan. 1910	−5	−15	2.32	−1.15	5	15
Apr. 1910	Oct. 1911	Jan. 1912	Jan. 1913	−21	−15	0.74	−1.04	17	8
June 1913	Dec. 1916	Dec. 1914	Aug. 1918	−18	−20	2.18	−2.10		
May 1918	Dec. 1918	Mar. 1919	Jan. 1920	−10	−13	2.12	−2.55	10 1/2	3
Jan. 1921	Apr. 1922	July 1921	May 1923	−6	−13	1.71	−0.96	2	9
June 1923	July 1924	July 1924	Oct. 1926	−13	−27	0.92	−1.07	10 1/2	18
Dec. 1926	Nov. 1927	Nov. 1927	Aug. 1929	−11	−21	0.21	−2.83	12	1

(continued)

TABLE 1 (concluded)

Specific Cycles		Matched Reference Cycles		Lead (−) or Lag (+) in Months of Specific Cycles at Matched Reference Turns		Change in Monthly Percentage Rate of Change in Money Stock Between Matched Peak and Trough Stages of Specific Cycles		Rank of Amplitude of Matched Nonwar[a] Reference Cycles	
Trough	Peak	Trough	Peak	Trough	Peak	Expansions	Succeeding Contractions	Expansions	Succeeding Contractions
MONTHLY DATA									
Oct. 1931	Apr. 1936	Mar. 1933	May 1937	−17	−13	3.96	−2.04	1	2
Oct. 1937	Feb. 1941	June 1938	Feb. 1945	−8	−20	3.78[b]			
Oct. 1941	June 1943	Oct. 1945	Nov. 1948						
Jan. 1949	Nov. 1951	Oct. 1949	July 1953	−9	−20	0.77	−0.42	7	14
Sept. 1953	Feb. 1955	Aug. 1954	July 1957	−11	−29	0.26	−0.44	18	10
Dec. 1957	June 1958	Apr. 1958	May 1960	−4	−23	0.62	−0.88	15	16
Dec. 1959		Feb. 1961		−14					
Average timing									
All matched cycles				−12.0	−17.6				
1871–1907				−13.0	−15.6				
1908–1960				−11.3	−19.1				
Rank correlation coefficient with amplitude of corresponding reference cycle phase									
Nonwar reference cycles, 1879–1961 (18) excluding 1945–49						0.77	0.70		

Source: Friedman and Schwartz, "Money and Business Cycles," The State of Monetary Economics, Universities–National Bureau Conference, Review of Economics and Statistics, Suppl., Feb. 1963, pp. 32–64, Tables 1, 2, and 3, and underlying data (based on same series as in Chart 1). Rankings of reference cycles are based on an average of three trend-adjusted indexes of business activity (see Business Cycle Indicators, G. H. Moore, Ed., Princeton for NBER, Vol. I, 1961, p. 104).

[a]Largest amplitude ranked first, next largest second, and so on.

[b]Computed by suppressing extra contraction from Feb. to Oct. 1941 and treating Oct. 1937–June 1943 as a single expansion.

3. *Framework of the Analysis*

One might begin to analyze changes in the money stock by examining the behavior of its components. These can be classified in several ways. One common way is by the legal properties of moneys, distinguishing between bank money and legal-tender currency. The latter must be accepted as payment for all public and private debts. Paper currencies issued by governments and central banks do not always carry legal-tender privileges, though they do in the United States today.[5] Monetary liabilities of commercial banks (whether notes or deposits) have never carried that privilege, which is why, in order to insure the wide acceptability of checks drawn on demand deposits, banks promise to convert them immediately on request into legal tender. On the other hand, banks may require prior notice—of 30 or more days—to withdraw time deposits, though today the privilege is seldom invoked. Because of this privilege, and also because time deposits generally cannot be transferred by check, they have typically paid a higher rate of return than demand deposits have. A division of the money stock based on legal properties is, on the surface, purely descriptive and might, therefore, appear irrelevant to an analysis of the factors affecting the amount supplied. The appearance may be misleading, however, because some of these distinctions may influence the public's attitude toward different kinds of money, and differences in the demand for components of the money stock can affect the total amount supplied.

Another way to distinguish moneys is by issuer, usually the government, the central bank, and commercial banks. The latter may be further classified by the origin of their charters—national or state or, if no charter, private—and by membership in the Federal Reserve System and the Federal Deposit Insurance Corporation. These distinctions are also largely descriptive rather than analytical from the depositors' point of view, though not if a panic threatens. The distinctions mainly help analysis in so far as the various issuers behave differently in supplying money. Such differences have been important, and a classification of monetary institutions along these lines plays a major part in the subsequent analysis.

Of the many other ways of distinguishing components of the money

---

[5] Before 1933, Federal Reserve notes and Bank notes were legal tender for public but not private debts.

stock, only one other receives much attention in this study—that commonly made between commodity and paper money. Under a commodity standard, legal-tender and other paper currency is convertible into a commodity unit at a fixed rate of exchange. The commodity serves as the standard of value of the monetary unit: the U.S. dollar is defined by law as equal to so many grains of gold. The gold reserve behind Treasury and Federal Reserve monetary liabilities has at various times strongly influenced the volume of those liabilities, though less so today than before 1933, when gold coin was part of the circulating media.

The emphasis of the present study is on the behavior of the three sectors of the economy that affect the amount of money supplied—the government, the public, and the commercial banks.

The government (including the Federal Reserve Banks as a government agency) controls the issue of assets that banks use as reserves for their monetary liabilities. Such assets are called high-powered money to signify that they can serve as the base for a multiple quantity of bank deposits. When held by banks, high-powered money is not, of course, part of the stock of money held by the public. When it is not held by banks but by the public, the same term is used in recognition of its potential use by banks to expand the money stock. High-powered money therefore comprises bank reserves plus currency held by the public.

Governments have authority to define, issue, and regulate the quantity of high-powered money, but they typically delegate part of their control over the amount issued to central banks and to the suppliers of commodities used as the monetary unit, now usually gold. (The suppliers are the domestic producers of gold and the foreign-exchange dealers who import or export gold bullion, when profitable.) In the United States since the Civil War, high-powered money has included government paper issues and the stock of gold coin and bullion held by commercial banks and the public (though the last has been zero since 1934) and, since 1914, also the monetary liabilities of the Federal Reserve Banks. The latter comprise Federal Reserve currency issues and commercial bank deposits at Federal Reserve Banks which serve as bank reserves.[6]

[6] For reasons given later, national bank notes, though technically not a government issue, are also included. For a detailed discussion of the definition and derivation of high-powered money, see notes to Table F-5 for col. 1; see also Friedman and Schwartz, *A Monetary History*, Appendix B.

Under the gold standard, gold is the medium into which paper currency is convertible—at least for international payments—and acts as a reserve behind the government's monetary liabilities. The total gold stock is therefore a "super-powered" money. It seems unnecessary to formalize this distinction, however, and we may understand the term high-powered money to include gold coin *outside* the Treasury and Federal Reserve Banks, and the term total gold stock to comprise all gold coin and monetary bullion within the country (except "earmarked" gold). Gold held by the Treasury, therefore, is not counted as high-powered money outstanding, which is limited to such assets held by banks and the public, only. Changes in the total gold stock nevertheless affect the quantity of high-powered money outstanding and will be analyzed as one of the factors affecting it.

Given the quantity of high-powered money, the public and the commercial banks jointly determine its division between public holdings and bank reserves. The public determines the fraction of total money balances it wants to hold in the form of high-powered money (in the United States today this can be only paper currency); it can do so by converting currency into bank deposits and vice versa. The banking system determines the volume of monetary liabilities it is willing to create, through loans and investments, per unit of the high-powered money it holds (that is, its reserves). Although the monetary liabilities of an individual bank include deposits due to other banks, and its monetary reserves include deposits due from other banks, for the banking system as a whole these interbank deposits cancel out. If more deposits are created than the public wants to hold, banks will lose reserves as the public seeks to establish the desired relation between deposits and currency, and conversely. Adjustments of bank reserves will continue until the quantity of deposits is consistent with the quantity the public wants to hold relative to its holdings of currency. In short, banks cannot control the quantity of both their reserves and their liabilities but only the ratio of the two.

To speak of banks' monetary assets as "reserves" for deposits is figurative, of course. In a sense all bank assets stand behind the liabilities and provide security for deposits. But earning assets do not directly limit the quantity of deposits in the same way monetary reserves do. Banks can increase both loans and deposits at the same time but, in general, not both monetary reserves and deposits. We may single out high-powered monetary reserves on the grounds that banks stand ready to exchange deposits for them when requested and cannot create them; in addition, high-powered money generally satisfies legal reserve requirements, at least in the United States. These easily invoked points should not blind us, however, to our implicit assumption that high-powered monetary reserves are more important than other assets in determining the level of banks' liabilities. This is generally taken for granted, at least for the United States, when compared with possible alternative propositions, but it obviously provides only a first step in the analysis of banks' behavior affecting the money stock.

The banking system can increase or decrease the money stock, but there is nothing unique about this power. Any holder of money balances can produce effects on the money stock similar to those produced by banks (though not through creation or extinction of deposits). When banks reduce their holdings of high-powered money by making loans and thereby reduce their reserve ratio, they increase the money stock; but the public also increases the money stock (eventually) when it reduces its holdings of high-powered money in relation to deposits (assuming banks maintain the same reserve ratio).[7] Changes in the currency-money and reserve-deposit ratios, therefore, have similar effects on the money stock, though they represent high-powered balances in relation to deposits of two different sectors, the banks and the public, which view deposits differently—banks, as a liability, and the public, as an asset. The two ratios are nevertheless separated in the analysis to follow, because they behave in different ways.

The exact relation of the amount of money supplied to the behavior of the three sectors is shown by a simple identity. Denote high-powered money, which reflects the behavior of the government sector, by H. Today, as mentioned, the only kind of high-powered money held by the public (which we may understand to include individuals, businesses and all financial institutions other than commercial banks) is currency (the public does not normally hold deposits at Federal Reserve Banks or the Treasury); and all currency in circulation is part of high-powered money. Consequently, the public affects the distribution of

---

[7] The view that commercial banks alone create deposits (or produce changes in the quantity outstanding) can be misleading. It is more accurate to say that commercial banks are the sole custodians of the public's checking account deposits.

high-powered money between itself and banks by changing the ratio of currency *outside* commercial banks to the total money stock. Denote this by C/M, where $M = C + D$, the sum of currency and commercial bank deposits held by the public. Consider next the high-powered money outstanding not publicly held, namely, that held by commercial banks. Banks affect the money stock by their decisions on the level at which to maintain the ratio of high-powered money reserves to deposits. This ratio will, of course, vary from bank to bank, depending on the composition of its deposits between time and demand and on many other factors. For the moment, we may consolidate all commercial banks into one hypothetical unit and, to see the net effect on the money stock, examine the aggregate reserve-deposit ratio of the banking system. Denote this by R/D. Since all high-powered money issued is held either by the public as currency outside banks or by banks as reserves, $H = C + R$, from which we can derive the following identity:[8]

$$(1) \qquad \frac{H}{M} = \frac{C}{M} + \frac{R}{D} - \frac{C}{M}\frac{R}{D}, \text{ or}$$

$$M = \frac{H}{\dfrac{C}{M} + \dfrac{R}{D} - \dfrac{C}{M}\dfrac{R}{D}}.$$

This expresses the total money stock in terms of the quantity of high-powered money and the currency-money and reserve-deposit ratios.[9] I shall refer to the latter as the currency ratio and reserve ratio, except where the possibility of misunderstanding requires the full expression. The quantity of money is jointly determined by these three variables, as given by the above identity. The currency ratio is necessarily less than unity and the reserve ratio has always been well below unity, so that the third term on the right-hand side of the first identity above is less than either of the first two terms. In consequence, if

---

[8] Divide both sides of the preceding expression by M and then substitute $(R/D)(1 - C/M)$ for R/M.

[9] A more complicated approach that reduces to the same formula was used by J. E. Meade in "The Amount of Money and the Banking System," *Economic Journal*, Mar. 1934, pp. 77–83; reprinted in *Readings in Monetary Theory*, pp. 54–62.

Friedman and Schwartz (*A Monetary History*) express the two ratios differently as the ratio of deposits to currency and to reserves. For various reasons, it is more convenient to use the above forms here. The difference has no analytical significance.

high-powered money does not change, a rise in either ratio—with the other constant—reduces the total stock of money. Likewise, if the two ratios remain constant, a rise in high-powered money implies an increase in the money stock. The quantity of money supplied, therefore, varies inversely with the currency and reserve ratios and directly with the quantity of high-powered money.

These three variables will be referred to as the determinants of the money stock to differentiate them from its various components discussed earlier. Of course, they are only proximate determinants and serve merely as a useful breakdown of the money stock to facilitate analysis of the underlying economic factors at work. The behavior of the three determinants alone does not "explain" changes in the supply of money; the analysis must be carried considerably further. The determinants and the total money stock from 1875 to 1955 are shown in Chart 1. Details of the derivation of these series are presented in the volumes by Friedman and Schwartz cited in footnote 1, above.

The quantity of high-powered money, unlike the other two determinants of the money stock, is measured in the nominal currency unit, and the real value of a given nominal quantity is inversely proportional to prices. Price changes may keep the real quantity in equilibrium with other real variables in the economy and probably will, at least over the long run, making possible very large changes in nominal amount. The other two determinants, on the other hand, are measured as pure numbers and cannot be meaningfully deflated by an index of prices. The currency ratio can, at most, vary from zero to unity, and the nature of commercial banking imposes the same limits on the reserve ratio. Actually, these two determinants tend to stay within much narrower limits. It seems unlikely, therefore, that changes in those ratios could be the proximate source of past growth in the money stock, which has been sizable. As Chart 1 suggests and as we shall see further in the next chapter, the historical record bears out this expectation. The secular growth in the money stock has depended primarily on additions to high-powered money, though the contribution of changes in the two ratios to variations about the growth trend of the money stock has at certain times been substantial.

Identity 1 will be applied in this study to the monetary system in the United States since 1875. If we were to make the definition of high-powered money correspond strictly to legal distinctions, the identity would not apply to the period before 1935 when currency included notes issued by national banks. Such notes were a liability of the issuing bank and could not be used to fulfill legal reserve requirements of national banks;[10] on that basis, the notes were not high-powered money. Yet, they were backed in full by U.S. bonds deposited at the Treasury and could be redeemed at Treasury offices. The notes were in fact, if not in name, a Treasury issue. As a result, the notes and Treasury currency were identical as judged by their acceptability: After 1874, when the procedure for redeeming the notes was improved, the public did not distinguish between them and always readily accepted one in lieu of the other. (Before 1874, these notes were sometimes sold quoted at a small discount from greenbacks.) Banks could always convert national bank notes into Treasury currency if necessary to meet reserve requirements, and the notes could be used to satisfy public demands to convert deposits into currency. The notes served adequately as part of reserves in excess of requirements which banks kept in vault. National banks actually never held very large amounts of the notes circulating outside issuing banks; most of them were held by the public. The analysis is simplified here by focusing on their economic effects and by counting the note liabilities of national banks (and other currency not designated as lawful money) as high-powered money. This means that, before 1935 as well as after, all currency held by the public was high-powered money.

Before 1879, when the dollar was inconvertible, paper currency served as bank reserves and was accepted by the public, so that the preceding identity applies to that period too. The effect of inconvertibility, however, was to sever the fixed rate of exchange between gold and all other money and to allow the rate to fluctuate on the open market. To calculate the paper-dollar value of the gold coin in circulation, therefore, the nominal value of the gold should be raised by its open market premium over paper. Since this adjustment has a negligible effect on the figures for the total stock of money, it was not made.

Before the existence of the national banking system or, more exactly, before 1867, when state banks issued notes and so could make conversions between them and deposits interchangeably (that is, could

[10] Between Dec. 1879 and July 1882, the Comptroller of the Currency also did not count silver certificates as lawful money in figuring national banks' required reserves. Sec. 12 of the act of July 12, 1882, established silver certificates as lawful money. Subsidiary silver and minor coin have never qualified as lawful money.

issue both under the same conditions and at approximately the same cost), the situation was entirely different and the preceding identity does not apply. The public distinguished between state bank notes and deposits on the one hand, and gold on the other—as it should have, for the notes were no less liable than deposits were to depreciation through bank failures (except as the prior lien of notes on bank assets helped cut losses). For that period the three main determinants of the money stock were the stock of gold outside the Treasury, the ratio of gold held by the public to the total money stock, and the ratio of gold held by banks to their total monetary liabilities. In this formulation state bank notes are combined with deposits, and high-powered money outstanding is simply gold outside the Treasury (and possibly also greenbacks, when they were in circulation after 1862).

4. The Problem of Interdependence

High-powered money, the currency ratio, and the reserve ratio are admittedly a simple, and at the same time specific, classification of the channels through which changes occur in the money stock. Yet, if the three determinants are appropriately defined for the period under study, traditional monetary theory as well as much past research indicate that this is a useful approach. It aids in identifying and tracing effects on the money stock. This is possible, because the three determinants are not rigidly linked together through the institutional or accounting arrangements by which currency and deposits are issued. None of the determinants responds automatically to changes in the others.

This does not mean that they may not be related in their behavior, either through some economic or political effect of one on the others or through the common effects of other factors. Indeed, some interdependence is to be expected. Interdependence implies, however, that the government, the banks, and the public behave in certain ways. The postulated behavior may be confirmed or denied from analysis of the data. Later chapters present evidence bearing on many possible interrelations.

Two general sources of interdependence can be distinguished. One is indirect, arising from the dependence of the determinants on some of the same economic events. An example might be similar behavior produced by business cycles or financial panics. The second is direct, arising from the response of one sector to changes in the determinant of another sector. An example might be a higher reserve ratio when high-powered money is rising rapidly, possibly because banks do not immediately make new investments when reserves increase. Or more complicated relationships may prevail, as one between the level of the reserve ratio and the average amplitude of cyclical fluctuations in high-powered money because of the disruptive effects of such fluctuations on the money market. The latter relation would not, of course, show up in a simple correlation between the two determinants. Indirect relations present the same problems encountered in any analysis in which many variables are involved, and the patterns of cause and effect are complex. The direct relations, in addition, present a special difficulty, because they mean, in effect, that the direction of influence runs partly from the money stock to the determinants and not entirely the other way.

An important direct relation is the dependence of high-powered money on the two ratios and the money stock. Because money-stock changes affect prices and thence the balance of international payments, gold flows are set in train, which affect high-powered money; similarly, central bank operations to stabilize the economy affect high-powered money. Stated in another way, the money stock is partly dependent on prices and business activity, where changes in high-powered money are the channel for the necessary adjustments in the money stock. This relationship is discussed in more detail in later chapters.

The evidence suggests that the dependence of the money stock on prices and business activity, as well as on other variables, is strong but is neither rigid, uniform, nor immediate. An examination of the channels through which economic variables affect the money stock can, therefore, shed light on the nature and extent of their effects. Accordingly, the plan of the work is to devote a separate chapter to the factors affecting each of the three determinants, leaving to the final two chapters the task of combining the findings for each determinant into a broader view of the factors responsible for changes in the money stock. This material is preceded by an analysis in the next chapter of the relative contribution of each determinant to changes in the money stock.

2

CONTRIBUTIONS OF THE THREE DETERMINANTS TO THE RATE OF CHANGE IN THE MONEY STOCK

ALTHOUGH the three determinants of the money stock—high-powered money, the currency ratio, and the reserve ratio—are not mechanically related to each other, historically they have varied in common at certain times, and this may reflect either parallel behavior of the factors affecting the determinants or a direct relation between the determinants. Much of the covariation seems to stem from cyclical fluctuations in business activity. Yet, even in such short-run movements, the determinants display much divergence. Their effects on the money stock are therefore not the same, and an examination of the behavior of each determinant is relevant and helps to isolate the main sources of variations in the money stock.

The analysis here is based on the contribution of each determinant to the rate of change in the money stock rather than to its absolute level, for the reasons given in Chapter 1. The rate of change directly attributable to changes in each of the three determinants can be derived from formula 1 (p. 12). That formula can be expressed in terms of rates of change by first taking natural logarithms,

$$(1) \qquad \log_e M \equiv \log_e H - \log_e \left(\frac{C}{M} + \frac{R}{D} - \frac{C}{M} \frac{R}{D} \right),$$

and then differentiating with respect to time,

$$(2)$$

$$\frac{d \log_e M}{dt} \equiv \frac{d \log_e H}{dt} + \frac{M}{H} \left(1 - \frac{R}{D} \right) \frac{d\left(-\frac{C}{M} \right)}{dt} + \frac{M}{H} \left(1 - \frac{C}{M} \right) \frac{d\left(-\frac{R}{D} \right)}{dt} .$$

The left-hand side represents the rate of change in the money stock. The three terms on the right-hand side give the contribution to that rate of the rate of change in high-powered money, in the currency ratio, and in the reserve ratio, respectively.

Since the data exist only for discrete points in time, the instantaneous rates in formula 2 must be approximated by average rates over a period. The factors $(M/H)(1 - R/D)$ and $(M/H)(1 - C/M)$ in the second and third terms can also be approximated by their average values over each period for which the rates are computed or, as here for ease of computation, by an average of their values at the beginning and end of the given period. Approximating the terms in this way, however, introduces an error or "interaction" term and thereby destroys the equality. If we express the approximations to the four terms in formula 2 for a given period by m, h, c, and r, respectively, the equation may be written:

$$(3) \qquad\qquad m = h + c + r + \epsilon,$$

where ϵ is the approximation error. This error is usually small and can be ignored. We may for convenience sometimes refer to the values of m for a succession of periods as the "money series."

The contributions are discussed first in terms of secular growth and then of cyclical movements.

1. Contributions of the Determinants to Secular Growth of the Money Stock

Table 2 presents averages for the years 1875–1955 of the contributions in percentage rates of change and in relative terms. For the relatives, the contribution of each determinant was divided by the average rate of change of the money stock. Almost any other terminal dates, either a few years later or earlier, would give substantially the same results. The years encompassing U.S. participation in the two world wars have been segregated in a breakdown of the full period because of their special character. The table also gives the figures for two subperiods of about equal length before and after World War I. This is a convenient point at which to separate the earlier period, in which the monetary system depended on the gold-standard mechanism, from the later period, in which that dependence diminished.

The dominant role of high-powered money in the secular growth of the money stock, indicated by the top three lines of the table, was suggested earlier by the graph of the three determinants in Chart 1. We can now quantify the earlier impression. Increases in high-powered money accounted for nine-tenths of the growth of the money stock. The growth of high-powered money occurred chiefly through growth of the gold stock and, later, after the founding of the Federal Reserve Banks, also through credit extended by them (Chapter 3). Particularly large contributions by high-powered money (average

TABLE 2

SOURCES OF THE RATE OF CHANGE IN THE MONEY STOCK: AVERAGES
FOR SELECTED PERIODS, AUGUST 1875 TO DECEMBER 1955

Period	Average Rate Contributed[a] by: (per cent per year)				Relative Contribution[b] of: (per cent)			
	Total[c] (1)	High-Powered Money (2)	Cur-rency Ratio (3)	Reserve Ratio (4)	Total[c] (5)	High-Powered Money (6)	Cur-rency Ratio (7)	Reserve Ratio (8)
All years	5.7	5.2	0.5	0.1	100	91	9	2
War years[d]	16.0	16.3	-5.5	6.0	100	102	-34	37
Nonwar years	4.9	4.3	1.0	-0.3	100	88	20	-6
Pre-Mar. 1917	6.3	4.3	1.6	0.6	100	68	25	10
Post-Nov. 1918	3.2	4.4	0.2	-1.4	100	138	6	-44

Source: Same as for Table F-1.

[a]Computed by an approximation to formula 2 (hence the rates are compounded instantaneously). The factors in the terms for c and r were approximated by averages of the beginning and ending values of the factors for each subperiod in the table. The approximations for each subperiod were also used in computing the contributions for all years and for the post-1918 nonwar years.

[b]Cols. 1 to 4 divided by col. 1.

[c]Lines may not add exactly to total because of rounding and approximation error.

[d]Covers the two world wars, Mar. 1917-Nov. 1918 and Nov. 1941-Aug. 1945.

annual rate of 16.3 per cent) occurred during the two world wars, when government expenditures were partly financed on Federal Reserve credit; contributions were lower in the nonwar years, both in absolute and relative terms (average annual rate of 4.3). If we exclude the first few years of the Federal Reserve System, the growth of high-powered money was also considerably lower in the earlier period (from August 1875 to June 1914, not shown in the table, average annual rate of 3.7 per cent).

The contributions of the two ratios largely offset each other over most of the periods shown and so produced a combined contribution of small size. In addition, each ratio separately tended to move in different directions in successive periods. This is one reason their contributions, in absolute amount, were smaller for all years than for most of the subperiods. The currency ratio declined steadily during the pre-1917 period; it declined also during the nonwar years after 1919 but by a smaller amount than in the earlier period, primarily because of a rise during the 1930's. Its contribution to the nonwar years was therefore positive, though lower in the later than the earlier period. The declines were largely offset, however, by sharp increases during the two world wars, so that the over-all contribution of the currency ratio from 1875 to 1955, while positive, was small. The reserve ratio declined sharply after about 1900 and thereby contributed to the pre-1917 growth of the money stock. That movement was more than offset for all nonwar years by a later rise and hence a negative contribution by the reserve ratio to monetary growth during the 1930's. The subsequent decline of the reserve ratio during World War II contributed to the wartime growth of the money stock. Because neither the currency nor the reserve ratio had large declines in the post-1918 period—whereas both did earlier—the growth of the money stock was greater in the earlier period, even though the growth of high-powered money was lower.

What if either or both of the ratios had been constant? Their relative contributions then show either the fractional reduction in the growth of the money stock or the fractional increase in the growth of high-powered money, or some combination of the two, that would have occurred. The money stock alone might not have had a different growth rate if the two ratios had been constant, because there is a mutual dependence between it and high-powered money. Under the gold standard, changes in income and prices are required by the balance of international payments. Given the factors determining output and velocity of money, the change in the money stock was then a residual: what did not occur through the two ratios, occurred through high-powered money. Although the dependence was likely to be strongest under the unfettered gold standard before World War I, it also operated to some extent afterwards under the Federal Reserve System. The mutual dependence may have played a weak role in short-run movements because of long lags, but it surely had a very important role in most secular movements (see Chapter 3 for discussion of the evidence). On the other hand, the evidence on the two ratios (Chapters 4 and 5) suggests that they were not affected in the long run by the particular secular rate of growth of either the money stock or high-powered money; therefore, a different growth rate for high-powered money, however produced, would have made a corresponding difference in the growth rate of the money stock.

Aside from the complications of mutual dependence, movements in the determinants give clues to the sources of change in the rate of growth of the money stock. Many of those movements raise questions which an analysis of factors affecting each determinant will help to answer: Why did high-powered money grow on the average more slowly before the founding of the Federal Reserve System than after? (Actually, its faster growth appears to have begun around 1897, as Chart 1 shows.) To what extent was the growth rate independent of or a reaction to concurrent movements in the two ratios? Why was the steady decline in the currency ratio during earlier decades interrupted by sharp increases in the early 1930's and the two world wars? Why did the reserve ratio decline around 1900 and rise so sharply during the 1930's? The movements are discussed at length in the subsequent chapters on the determinants.

2. Contributions of the Determinants to Cyclical Movements in the Rate of Change in the Money Stock

Specific cycles in the rate of change in the money stock, derived by Friedman and Schwartz, are listed in Table 1.[1] All but a few of the expansions and contractions of specific cycles can be matched with corresponding phases of reference cycles. The cycles in the money series that do not match reference cycles have small amplitude and appear on other grounds to be spurious.[2] For this reason and also in order to analyze the cycles that correspond with business fluctuations, the unmatched phases have been suppressed in the subsequent analysis.

The specific cycles were divided into stages by the National Bureau procedure. For the monthly data since May 1907, nine stages were used; for the preceding annual and semiannual data, five stages, or fewer when a standing could be computed only by averaging adjacent stages. The stage omitted was typically VII, in brief contractions for

[1] The specific cycle dates used for the subsequent analysis are based on a slightly different earlier version of Table 1 (see notes to Table F-1).

[2] See Milton Friedman and Anna Jacobson Schwartz, "Trends and Cycles in the Stock of Money in the United States, 1867–1960," a National Bureau study, in preparation.

CHART 2

Average Contributions of the Three Determinants to Specific Cycles in the Rate of Change in the Money Stock (per cent per year)

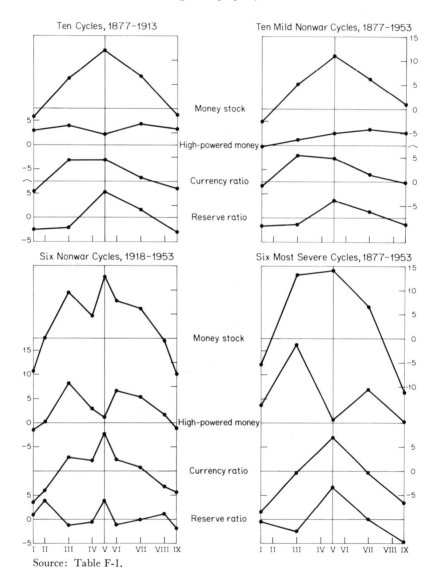

Source: Table F-1.

which the annual data available provided only a peak standing in one year and in the next a trough standing.

Specific cycles emphasize the points of highest and lowest rates of change, whereas the periods of higher and lower average rates of change may be more relevant. To allow for this possibility, Appendix A includes an analysis of step cycles, which mark off periods of higher and lower average rates of change, constituting expansion and contraction phases not further subdivided into stages. Step cycles give the same results as specific cycles do, so far as the relative importance of the three determinants is concerned.

SPECIFIC CYCLE PATTERNS

Average patterns are presented in Chart 2 for two pairs of subgroups of the nonwar cycles—a time grouping segregating the cycles before and after World War I, and an amplitude grouping segregating the cycles that are matched to mild and to the six most severe contractions in aggregate business activity. For each stage, the sum of the contributions of the determinants (the three lower series in each group in Chart 2) equals, except for the slight approximation error, the top series which shows the rate of change in the money stock. Some of the patterns lie mostly above zero because of intracyclical trend in the determinants, not eliminated. The patterns differ from patterns that would show the first differences in each ratio, because formula 2 multiplies the negative of the differences in each ratio by two positive factors to derive the ratio's contribution to the money series. Nevertheless, if the patterns shown for each ratio were inverted, they would provide a fairly good approximation to patterns of its first differences.

Chart 2 reveals a high degree of similarity among the four cycle groups in the average pattern for each determinant. The post-1918 pattern for the reserve ratio seems at first sight to differ from its earlier pattern, but that is partly due to the extra stages. If these are excluded, the pattern is more nearly the same as that for the pre-1914 group. The similarity is surprising, considering the major developments in our monetary institutions since World War I. It merits our attention in subsequent chapters as much or more than the minor changes in the cyclical behavior of the series over time. While the patterns for the later subgroup have the larger amplitude, most of the difference probably reflects the finer measurement provided by the monthly data and the greater frequency of severe cycles in the later period. One notable difference, not explained by the distribution of severe cycles over time, is the somewhat greater amplitude of fluctuation in the contribution of the reserve ratio in the earlier subgroup. It can be attributed to monetary developments since the turn of the century that have reduced fluctuations in that ratio (discussed at length in Chapter 5). Effects of those developments on the cyclical pattern of the money series over time, however, are noticeably absent. Institutional developments have affected in varying degrees the nature and relative importance of cyclical fluctuations in the three determinants but, to a much smaller degree, the pattern of fluctuations in the money series itself.

The expansions and contractions in the contributions of the two ratios roughly parallel those in the money series. The pattern for high-powered money, on the other hand, differs considerably from those of the other series. In mild cycles its pattern hardly deviates from trend, while in severe cycles it displays two steep peaks. Its large drop from stage III to stage V in severe cycles accounts for the rounded peak in the money series. From stage V to stage VII in those cycles, the decline in the patterns for the two ratios overcomes the concurrent upswing in the pattern for high-powered money and accounts for the drop in the money series. In the mild cycles, the configuration at the peak is slightly different, in that the combined contribution of high-powered money and of the currency ratio is almost constant from stage III to stage V, and the contribution of the reserve ratio alone is mainly responsible for carrying the money series to a peak.

High-powered money is largely responsible for the sharp movements of the money series in severe cycles from stage I to stage III and from stage VII to stage IX. The greater amplitude of the severe-cycle group over the mild-cycle group reflects those movements and also larger contributions of the two ratios. It should be noted that the difference in amplitude between severe and mild cycles is not an arithmetical consequence of the definition of severe cycles; these are defined on the basis of the corresponding reference cycles independently of the amplitude of variation in the money series. The average patterns for all three determinants have larger fluctuations in the severe-cycle group than in the mild-cycle group. Nevertheless, the association between the amplitude of variation in the money series from its peak to its trough stages and the severity of corresponding business contractions reflects primarily the contributions of the two ratios; high-powered money has roughly the same average contribution in the peak and trough stages.

RELATIVE CONTRIBUTIONS OF THE DETERMINANTS TO THE RATE OF CHANGE IN THE MONEY STOCK

Table 3 gives the relative contributions of the three determinants. The average contribution of each determinant, adjusted to have an

TABLE 3

RELATIVE CONTRIBUTIONS OF DETERMINANTS TO FIVE STAGES OF NONWAR SPECIFIC CYCLES IN THE TREND-ADJUSTED RATE OF CHANGE IN THE MONEY STOCK, 1877-1953
(per cent)

Specific Cycle Stage		Total[a]	High-Powered Money	Currency Ratio	Reserve Ratio
I	Trough[b]	100	23	59	18
III	Expansion	100	86	70	-54
V	Peak	100	-14	59	53
VII	Contraction	100	63	3	32
IX	Trough[b]	100	17	44	38

Source: Derived from Table F-1 after adjusting for intracyclical trend by subtracting from each series in every stage of a given cycle its average value over the five stages of that cycle.

Note: Relative contributions computed as follows: Averages of the trend-adjusted contributions of each determinant in the nonwar cycles were divided by the corresponding average for the money series. Some of the expansion and contraction stages of the pre-1907 cycles are omitted because of the limitations of the annual data.

[a]Lines may not add exactly to total because of rounding and approximation error.

[b]Stages I and IX differ only because of their respective inclusion or exclusion of stage I of the first cycle and stage IX of the last cycle, and stages I and IX of the war cycles.

average level of zero in each cycle, was divided by the corresponding average rate of change in the money stock for each of five stages of the nonwar specific cycles.[3] The measures pertain, therefore, to cyclical fluctuations about the average level. The third line shows, for example, that the currency ratio accounted, on the average, for 59 per cent of

[3] Chart 2 shows the average contribution to each stage. If we represent these after adjustment for trend by $\bar{m}_s$, $\bar{h}_s$, $\bar{c}_s$, and $\bar{r}_s$, where s denotes the stages from I to IX, the relative average contributions to each stage shown in Table 3 are $\bar{h}_s/\bar{m}_s$, $\bar{c}_s/\bar{m}_s$, $\bar{r}_s/\bar{m}_s$.

TABLE 4

RELATIVE CONTRIBUTIONS OF DETERMINANTS TO SPECIFIC CYCLES IN THE
TREND-ADJUSTED RATE OF CHANGE IN THE MONEY STOCK,
1877-1953
(per cent)

	Specific Cycles	Total[a]	High-Powered Money	Currency Ratio	Reserve Ratio
1.	All 18, 1877-1953	100	27	46	26
2.	2 war, 1913-18 and 1937-48	100	51	24	25
3.	16 nonwar, 1877-1953	100	21	53	26
4.	10, 1877-1913	100	3	48	47
5.	6, 1918-53	100	37	56	7
6.	6 most severe, 1877-1953[b]	100	25	53	22
7.	3, 1877-1913	100	19	36	45
8.	3, 1918-53	100	27	60	12
9.	10 mild, 1877-1953	100	15	52	31
10.	7, 1877-1913	100	-6	56	48
11.	3, 1918-53	100	65	44	-8

Source: Same as for Table 3.

Note: Relative contributions computed as follows: Weighted averages of
the amplitudes of the average trend-adjusted contributions of each determinant to five stages of cycles in the group were divided by the corresponding
weighted average for the money series. The weights were the fractional
number of cycles used in computing the average contributions for each stage.
The weighting is appropriate because expansion or contraction stages are
absent for some of the pre-1907 cycles due to the limitations of the annual
data.

Amplitudes were the values of the average trend-adjusted contributions to
each stage, taken positively if the same sign as the corresponding value for
the money series, and negatively if the opposite sign. The amplitudes for
the money series were simply its trend-adjusted levels without regard to
sign.

In terms of the symbols used in footnote 3, an algebraic formula of the
measure, disregarding the weights, is

$$\frac{\sum_{s} \bar{h}_s \; (\text{sign of } \bar{m}_s)}{\sum_{s} \left| \bar{m}_s \right|},$$

and similarly for $\bar{c}_s$ and $\bar{r}_s$.

[a]Lines may not add exactly to total because of rounding and approximation
error.

[b]Severe cycles are those corresponding to the six most severe business
contractions by the ranking in Table 1. Mild cycles comprise all other nonwar cycles.

the trend-adjusted rate of change in the money stock at peak stages. The three relative contributions for each stage add up to unity except for omission of the small approximation error.

The table highlights some features of the cyclical patterns evident graphically in Chart 2. First, the small contribution of high-powered money on the average to peak and trough stages; this is a reflection of its double-peak pattern, in which its contribution to stages V and IX is small, and to stage V opposite in sign to the money series. Second, the large contributions of the two ratios to the peak and trough stages, though the currency ratio contributes importantly also to the expansion stage and the reserve ratio also to the contraction stage.

The relative contribution for one or two of the determinants can be and sometimes is negative. When the contribution of a determinant for a stage has a sign opposite to the rate of change in the money stock, division of the former by the latter gives a negative number. For example, if high-powered money declines and the money stock rises, the relative contribution of high-powered money is negative, as in stage V. When the contributions of all three determinants do not have the same sign, the sign of the money series is determined by the sign of the larger contributions; the smaller contribution, if it has an opposite sign, is offset and becomes a negative relative contribution. The relative measures therefore indicate the degree of association between the contributions of each determinant and their sum, the money series.[4]

Table 3 brings out the variability of the relative contributions to cycle stages. Table 4 suppresses this variability among stages by first averaging together the contributions to the five stages. The measure in Table 4 can be interpreted as a numerical analogy of Chart 2: the trend-adjusted contributions of the determinants approximately equal the areas formed between each pattern in Chart 2 and its average level. The contributions would exactly equal these areas if Chart 2 were a bar chart instead of having lines connecting the points for each stage. Areas for each stage on the side of its average level opposite the money series areas are counted as negative contributions

---

[4] When the money series is zero, the relatives are infinite and hence undefined. Though finite, they may be very large in absolute value when the contributions are large and also of different signs, because the money series may then have a comparatively small value. Since the money series actually has no average values close to zero for the stages examined, this is not a problem.

and, on the same side, as positive contributions. To obtain a relative measure for each determinant, its contributions with appropriate sign were first weighted and summed over the five stages, then divided by the corresponding weighted sum for the money series. The weights are described in a note to the table. An alternative procedure is first to divide the contribution in each stage by the value of the money series in that stage, and then to average over the five stages. This variant, presented in Appendix A, gives largely the same results.

In terms of Table 4, the currency ratio is the proximate source of almost one-half the amplitude of all specific cycles in the money series, and high-powered money and the reserve ratio are each the source of about one-fourth. The relative contribution of high-powered money in all cycles is somewhat enlarged by the inclusion of the wartime cycles. While the contributions of all three determinants were exceptionally large during the war cycles, those of high-powered money were twice those of the two ratios, which is almost the reverse of the relative contributions of high-powered money and of the currency ratio for all cycles. The currency ratio accounts for slightly more than one-half the nonwar cycles and high-powered money, for only one-fifth; the reserve ratio has a relative contribution of one-fourth and does not differ significantly between the war- and nonwar-cycle groups. The primary importance of the currency ratio as the proximate source of all nonwar cycles in the money series holds also for most of the subgroups, while the relative contributions of the other two determinants vary considerably among the subgroups.

These results could be unduly influenced by extreme values in a few stages of particular cycles, which could swamp the typical values of many stages. That can be checked by excluding some of the extreme values. From a frequency distribution of the trend-adjusted contributions of each determinant, I selected for exclusion the three most extreme values.[5] They all occurred in severe cycles after World War I and exceeded in absolute value 25 per cent per year—a much greater rate than that of any other contribution of the determinants to the five stages of nonwar cycles. The excluded three stages were replaced by an average of the contributions of the determinants in the same

[5] One was a very large rate of increase in high-powered money during stage III of the 1918–21 specific cycle in the money series (see Table F-1). One occurred in stage IX of the 1927–31 cycle and another in stage I of the 1931–37 cycle; both stages cover the same period and contain a sharp rise in the currency ratio.

stage of the two remaining post-1918 severe cycles. The revised relatives are presented below[6] for the two subgroups mainly affected. As predictable from the nature of the exclusions, the revision raises the relative importance of the reserve ratio at the expense of high-powered money and the currency ratio (compare with Table 4). The amount of the revision, however, is not large, and any further revisions of this kind, whether or not proper, would have considerably smaller effects. Hence, extreme values do not account for the over-all results presented in Table 4.

The relative contributions of high-powered money and the reserve ratio changed appreciably over time. In the pre-1914 period, high-powered money had a small relative contribution and the two ratios were the proximate source of nearly all the cyclical variations in the money series. In the later period, the relative contributions of high-powered money and the reserve ratio were reversed. The reversal can be attributed partly to smaller fluctuations in the reserve ratio, starting around 1900 and continuing after World War I. The change in behavior of bank reserves apparently resulted from an improvement in the stability of the monetary system, which involved for commercial banks less danger from financial crises—notwithstanding the panics of 1907 and 1933. The improvement did not affect the average amplitude of fluctuations in the money series, however, which remained as large as ever until the end of World War II. While the amplitude of variations in the contribution of the reserve ratio diminished from the earlier to the later period, that of high-powered money increased and helped to maintain the cyclical amplitude of the money series. The change in behavior of high-powered money after 1914 resulted chiefly from the addition of Federal Reserve operations to changes in the gold stock—the other main source of variations in this determinant.

[6] Addendum to Table 4:

Line	Nonwar Specific Cycles	Total	High-Powered Money	Currency Ratio	Reserve Ratio
5.	6 cycles, 1918–53	100	36	51	13
6.	6 most severe cycles, 1877–1953	100	21	47	32

Source and computations are the same as for Table 4, except that contributions of the determinants to the stages listed in footnote 5 were replaced by an average of contributions to the same stage of the remaining two post-1918 severe cycles.

Surprisingly little difference in the contributions of the determinants is shown between cycles corresponding to severe and mild contractions in business activity. While the contribution of each determinant fluctuated, on the average, more in severe than in mild cycles, the increases of all three were of the same order (Chart 2). The increases reflect in part sharp reactions to banking panics, which occurred in four of the six severe cycles. Panics enlarged the amplitude of the cyclical patterns of the determinants but did not greatly alter their shape. The determinants typically rose in response to a panic reflecting, for high-powered money, gold inflows or Treasury or Federal Reserve operations; for the currency ratio, conversion of deposits into currency by the public; and for the reserve ratio, contraction of loans by the banking system. The response of high-powered money therefore typically contributed to a rise in the rate of change in the money stock, and that of the two ratios, to a fall, with the latter always predominating. The chief difference in relative contributions between mild and severe cycles is the somewhat greater value for high-powered money and lower value for the reserve ratio in severe cycles, and even that difference for the reserve ratio is entirely eliminated by the exclusion of a few extreme values.[7]

The reaction of the reserve ratio to severe cycles, however, was more pronounced than the figures indicate because of its slow response to panics. In a panic, the public demands currency immediately, which depletes bank reserves and reduces the reserve ratio. Since time is required to contract loans and sell bonds, the largest increases in the ratio come later, very often after increases in the currency ratio have subsided and after the specific cycle in the money series. Panic-induced increases in the reserve ratio therefore have often appeared in the initial stages of the subsequent specific cycle rather than the severe cycles. Without this delay, the relative contribution of the reserve ratio to the severe cycles would probably have been greater.

For severe and mild cycles separately, as well as for all nonwar cycles, high-powered money rose in importance from the earlier to the later period, and the importance of the reserve ratio declined. Both changes were much smaller for severe than for mild cycles,

[7] This can be shown by adjusting the post-1918 severe cycles for extreme values (see footnote 5). The adjusted figures for this subgroup in line 8 of Table 4, reading left to right, are 22, 54, and 23.

however, owing to the behavior of the currency ratio, which rose in importance from the earlier to the later period for severe cycles and fell in importance for mild cycles. The important differences in behavior between the two periods were therefore not characteristic of severe cycles alone, nor do they result from the accidental representation of the very severe 1929–33 contraction in the subgroup for the later period, but were even more characteristic of the mild cycles.

The diversity among individual cycles raises a question about the significance of these results, especially for small subgroups. In Appendix A the results are compared with several alternative measures to appraise the importance of particular methods of measurement. Such a comparison also reveals other characteristics of the cyclical behavior of the determinants. None of the other measures, however, contradicts the foregoing observations.

AMPLITUDE OF FLUCTUATIONS IN THE CONTRIBUTIONS OF THE DETERMINANTS

Although the relative contribution of the currency ratio was, roughly speaking, twice that of the other two determinants, the amplitude of cyclical variations in its contribution was not twice as large. The relative contributions are a function both of average amplitude and of conformity to the amplitude of the rate of change in the money stock. By the previous measures, the relative contributions of a determinant, even though individually large in amplitude, will, if half are positive and half negative, average close to zero. Table 5 gives the average amplitudes, computed as follows: The average contributions of the determinants to each of the five stages, displayed in Chart 2, were first adjusted for intracyclical trend, and the signs dropped to give absolute amounts; the data were then averaged for the five stages.

These measures of amplitude show that the contribution of the currency ratio had the largest fluctuations, but not by much. It was exceeded in amplitude by the contribution of the reserve ratio in the earlier period and almost equaled by that of high-powered money in both periods. The reserve ratio made smaller contributions in the later than in the earlier period, both absolutely and relative to the amplitude of the money series. High-powered money and the currency ratio had larger contributions in the later period, which accounts for the greater amplitude of the money series in that period.

TABLE 5

AVERAGE AMPLITUDE OF CONTRIBUTIONS OF DETERMINANTS TO SPECIFIC CYCLES
IN THE TREND-ADJUSTED RATE OF CHANGE IN THE MONEY STOCK, 1877-1953
(per cent per year)

Specific Cycles	Money Stock	High-Powered Money	Currency Ratio	Reserve Ratio
16 nonwar, 1877-1953	6.6	4.4	4.7	3.3
10, 1877-1913	5.3	2.9	3.1	3.7
6, 1918-53	8.5	6.7	6.9	2.6

Source: Same as for Table 3.
Note: Average amplitude computed as follows: The trend-adjusted contributions of each determinant in absolute value to five stages of specific cycles in the group were averaged. Symbolically,

$$\frac{\sum_{s} \sum_{c} \left| h_{sc} \right|}{\sum_{s} \sum_{c} N_{sc}} ,$$

where h is the contribution of high-powered money, N is the number of stages; the subscript c enumerates the cycles covered from 1877 to 1953 and s the five stages; and similarly for the other series.

How would cycles in the money series have been affected if any two of the determinants had been constant and only the third had made contributions? The answer is that the amplitudes of the cycles would have been reduced, though not by as much as the relative contributions suggest. Such statements implicitly assume, of course, the independence of movements in the determinants, discussed shortly.

REGULARITY OF FLUCTUATIONS IN THE CONTRIBUTIONS OF THE DETERMINANTS

One other aspect of the cyclical behavior of the series may be examined—regularity. By how much do patterns for individual cycles deviate from their average pattern? Table 6 gives such measures of regularity and their ratio to the corresponding average amplitudes in Table 5. To compute the measures, the trend-adjusted contribution of a determinant in each stage was subtracted from its average contribution in that stage among cycles. These deviations were then averaged without regard to sign. Average deviations for cycles in the money series were derived in the same way.

For all nonwar cycles together, the contributions of the reserve ratio had the smallest average deviation and hence the greatest regularity, though not as a percentage of average amplitude. The greater over-all regularity of the reserve ratio reflects its regular behavior in severe as well as mild cycles. In the severe cycles, high-powered money and the currency ratio often fluctuated violently and, as might be expected, irregularly from one cycle to the other. The main response

TABLE 6

REGULARITY OF CONTRIBUTIONS OF DETERMINANTS TO SPECIFIC CYCLES IN
THE TREND-ADJUSTED RATE OF CHANGE IN THE MONEY STOCK, 1877-1953

Specific Cycles	Average Deviation of Contributions from Stage Averages[a] (per cent per year)				Average Deviation as a Percentage of Amplitude[b]			
	Money Stock (1)	High-Powered Money (2)	Currency Ratio (3)	Reserve Ratio (4)	Money Stock (5)	High-Powered Money (6)	Currency Ratio (7)	Reserve Ratio (8)
16 nonwar, 1877-1953	4.3	4.4	4.0	2.9	65	100	85	88
10, 1877-1913	2.9	2.7	2.3	2.9	55	93	74	78
6, 1918-53	5.9	7.8	7.0	3.7	69	116	101	142
6 most severe, 1877-1953[c]	5.7	5.5	6.5	2.8	n.c.	n.c.	n.c.	n.c.
10 mild, 1877-1953[c]	2.4	3.7	2.1	2.7	n.c.	n.c.	n.c.	n.c.

Source: Same as for Table 3.
Note: n.c. = not computed.

[a]Computed as follows: Differences in absolute value between trend-adjusted contributions of each determinant to five stages of cycles in the group and average contribution of the determinant for each stage were averaged. Symbolically (see note to Table 5 for explanation of notation),

$$\frac{\sum\limits_{s} \sum\limits_{c} \left| h_{sc} - \overline{h}_{s} \right|}{\sum\limits_{s} \sum\limits_{c} N_{sc}},$$

and similarly for the other series.

[b]Cols. 1-4 divided by the corresponding cols. of Table 5.

[c]Same as Table 4.

of the reserve ratio to those cycles, as suggested earlier, occurred later during the succeeding specific cycle, always mild except in the 1930's. For the mild cycles, the currency ratio had the most regular patterns.

The contributions of the reserve ratio became less regular after World War I. In view of their reduced amplitude in the later period, the small decline in their regularity probably stemmed entirely from the greater frequency of severe cycles in the post-1918 group, which also partly explains why the contributions of the other two determinants became less regular in the later period. This explanation does not help much with high-powered money, however. The regularity measure for this determinant was less for pre-1914 cycles than for all mild cycles, and excluding severe cycles from the pre-1914 figure would reduce it. The higher figure for all mild cycles means, therefore, that the measure would be higher for mild cycles after World War I than before. Such comparisons of the contributions of the two ratios, on the other hand, suggest little change in their regularity for mild cycles before and after World War I.

The regularity of cycles in the money series reflects the regularity of cycles in the three determinants—though not additively, since movements in the determinants partly offset each other. The money series had less regularity in the latter period, in part because severe cycles were relatively more numerous, and in part because the contribution of high-powered money was less regular even in mild cycles. Since the table covers only three mild cycles for the latter period, this result cannot be taken to indicate a trend. Indeed, so far, cyclical variations in the money series since World War II have been fairly moderate.

INTERDEPENDENCE OF FLUCTUATIONS IN THE CONTRIBUTIONS OF THE DETERMINANTS

Movements in the determinants could be directly or indirectly related, as noted. We need to consider how strong such interrelations are. One indication is provided by the correlation coefficients presented in Table 7 between the contributions of the determinants. The observations are for the cycle stages covered by the preceding tables,

TABLE 7

CORRELATIONS BETWEEN THE CONTRIBUTIONS OF THE DETERMINANTS TO FIVE STAGES OF SPECIFIC CYCLES IN THE TREND-ADJUSTED RATE OF CHANGE IN THE MONEY STOCK

	Product-Moment Correlation Coefficients		
Specific Cycles	R_{hc}	R_{hr}	R_{cr}
All 18, 1877–1953	$-.33^s$	$-.20$	$.03$
16 nonwar, 1877–1953	$-.34^s$	$-.32^s$	$.07$
10, 1877–1913	$-.30$	$-.50^s$	$.15$
6, 1918–53	$-.34$	$-.30$	$.02$
6 most severe, 1877–1953[a]	$-.35$	$-.26$	$.13$
10 mild, 1877–1953[a]	$-.32^s$	$-.40^s$	$-.04$

Source: Same as for Table 3.

[s] Significantly different from zero at the .01 level.

[a] As defined in Table 4, footnote b.

usually five stages per cycle (three or four for some of the earlier cycles). The coefficients show no significant covariation between the contributions of the two ratios but do show a small but significant inverse covariation ·between their contributions and those of high-powered money. Since contributions of the two ratios to the money series are inverse to their first differences, the correlations indicate a tendency of high-powered money to move in parallel with the two ratios.

This correlation is subject to various interpretations. It may reflect a direct relation between the determinants in one or both directions or a similar response to other economic variables. Of the many possibilities, the least likely is a dependence of the two ratios on high-powered money. No evidence of it can be found in the analyses reported in later chapters. One widely alleged kind of such dependence concerns the reserve ratio: when high-powered money declines and the money market tightens, banks may be pressed for funds, and they may allow their reserve ratios to fall, at least temporarily.[8] Thus there might be an inverse relation between the contributions of high-powered money and of the reserve ratio to the money series. This implies that the reserve ratio is affected by interest rates, discussed at length in Chapter 5. Despite much attention in the literature, the relation is not supported by the data examined later.

An appealing explanation of the observed intercorrelation is that high-powered money has a direct dependence on the two ratios. As indicated in Chapter 1, the gold-standard mechanism and central-bank actions to stabilize the economy might be expected to produce such a dependence. Since this explanation implies that high-powered money depends on the *combined* contribution of the two ratios, Table 8 presents correlation coefficients between their combined contribution and that of high-powered money and—to study the relationship closely—separately for each stage of the nonwar specific cycles before and after World War I. Measuring the correlation among cycles for each stage separately avoids all spurious intracyclical covariation that exists between stages. Stages II, IV, VI, and VIII, excluded from the previous tables, are included here for the latter period. The adjustment of the data for trend used previously has been omitted here on the ground that any interdependence may apply to trend as well

[8] They may also (since 1914) apply to Federal Reserve Banks for loans, which would offset some of the contraction in high-powered money.

TABLE 8

CORRELATIONS BETWEEN THE COMBINED CONTRIBUTION OF THE CURRENCY AND
RESERVE RATIOS AND THAT OF HIGH-POWERED MONEY TO VARIOUS STAGES OF
SPECIFIC CYCLES IN THE RATE OF CHANGE IN THE MONEY STOCK

Stage of Specific Cycle	Product-Moment Correlation Coefficient		Regression Coefficient
	$R_{h,c+r}$	Level of Significance[a]	$R_{h,c+r} \dfrac{\sigma_h}{\sigma_{c+r}}$
10, 1877-1913			
Troughs[b]	−.63	.05	−.43
Expansions	−.80	.05	−.56
Peaks	−.36	n.s.	−.48
Contractions	−.88	.05	−.68
All stages	−.49	.01	−.26
6 nonwar, 1918-53			
Troughs[b]	−.66	n.s.	−.35
Expansions			
II	−.31	n.s.	−.29
III	−.97	.01	−2.32
IV	−.70	n.s.	−.99
Peaks	−.89	.05	−.53
Contractions			
VI	−.82	.05	−.93
VII	+.23	n.s.	+.80
VIII	+.69	n.s.	+.40
Stages III-VI[b]	−.74	.001	−.89
Stages VII-II[b]	−.37 (−.51)[c]	n.s. (.05)[c]	−.28 (−.25)[c]

Source: Table F-1; no adjustment for trend.

[a].05 or lower.

[b]Each trough in the cycle group included once.

[c]Excluding 1918-21 cycle.
n.s. = not significant.

as to cyclical elements in the series. The coefficients in Table 8 are generally greater than those in Table 7 because they are a weighted sum of the corresponding correlation coefficients between the contributions of high-powered money and each ratio individually.[9]

Though many are fairly high, the correlations in Table 8 for individual stages cover a small number of cycles (10 before World

[9] Specifically,

$$R_{h,c+r} = R_{h,c} \frac{\sigma_c}{\sigma_{c+r}} + R_{h,r} \frac{\sigma_r}{\sigma_{c+r}},$$

where

$$\left(\frac{\sigma_c}{\sigma_{c+r}}\right)^2 + \left(\frac{\sigma_r}{\sigma_{c+r}}\right)^2 = 1 - 2R_{c,r}\left(\frac{\sigma_c}{\sigma_{c+r}}\right)\left(\frac{\sigma_r}{\sigma_{c+r}}\right).$$

If

$$R_{c,r} \cong 0 \text{ and } \sigma_c \cong \sigma_r, \qquad R_{h,c+r} = .7R_{h,c} + .7R_{h,r}.$$

War I and 6 after), and many of the coefficients are insignificant at the 0.05 level. The significant coefficients do not occur all in the same stages of the later and earlier cycles. For the earlier cycles, the correlation is significant in all but the peak stages; for the later cycles, in stages III, V, and VI only, covering the middle part of each specific cycle in the money series (unless the 1918–21 cycle is excluded). In the bottom two lines of the table, stages of the later cycles are combined into two groups. The group of four stages III through VI has a substantially larger negative regression coefficient than the group of other stages has.

For the later cycles, the results are heavily influenced by Federal Reserve credit outstanding. It is plausible, as an explanation of the particular pattern of the correlation coefficients, that the Reserve Banks typically took more vigorous action to dampen variations in the rate of change in the money stock in its expansion and peak stages than in its contraction and trough stages. It is consistent with what is known of Federal Reserve policies during much of the 1920's and 1930's, the periods mostly covered by the calculations. After being criticized for its part in the World War I inflation, the Federal Reserve Board was for many years highly sensitive about doing anything that might contribute to inflation; its steps to counteract speculation in the 1928–29 stock market boom, for example, are well known. In contrast, the idea that vigorous monetary expansion should accompany business contractions has developed slowly and has gained wide acceptance only since World War II. The results in Table 8 throw together diverse cycles, of course, and do not distinguish possible differences in Federal Reserve behavior over the period. That the money series has displayed less fluctuation since World War II suggests that the Reserve Banks have offset the two ratios more completely since then than previously, though a detailed analysis of more postwar cycles would be necessary to confirm it.

For the pre-1914 cycles, a similar explanation would emphasize the offsetting effects of gold flows and, to a lesser extent, of Treasury operations. The regression coefficient is much lower for all stages together than for each of the stages individually, because the constant term of the regression differs among stages. This means that the offset is probably lower computed from stage-to-stage variations than from cycle-to-cycle variations for a given stage.

If we accept the regression coefficients at face value, they imply that the dampening effect of gold flows before 1914 and Federal Reserve actions thereafter did not prevent the two ratios from independently affecting the money stock.[10] For the earlier cycles, variations in the combined contribution of the two ratios were offset by one-fourth, and for the later cycles also by one-fourth in stages VII through II and by nine-tenths in stages III through VI. Hence, the Federal Reserve Banks appear to have increased the offset materially, but for one part of each specific cycle only. The fact that the offset varied in relative amount among different stages of the cycle, particularly in the later period, is perhaps one reason the contribution of high-powered money appears to be so erratic.

That the Reserve Banks were responsible, through control of high-powered money, for all variations in the money series is possible but very unlikely. If a particular pattern were to be produced in the money series through high-powered money, the desired pattern would be superimposed on the contributions of the two ratios. The contribution of high-powered money would then be composed of two parts, an offset to the two ratios and the desired pattern, and the total would not necessarily be closely related to either. Its relative contribution might even be low and the (negative) correlation with the combined contribution of the two ratios less than perfect, just as we find. But, if so, the regression coefficient would be unity or approximately so, which it is not for all stages, and the average cyclical pattern of the money series would bear little resemblance, except by accident, to the contributions of the two ratios. As shown by Chart 2, however, the patterns of their contributions and of the money series are similar.[11] We may tentatively infer that the two ratios played an important independent role in the specific cycles of the money series. As measures of that conformity, their relative average contributions are relevant;

---

[10] The regression coefficients are an understatement of the offset, only if the other factors determining high-powered money left out of the regression (defined to affect it positively) are positively correlated with the combined contribution of the two ratios. This seems unlikely for offsets due to policy, in view of the out-of-phase relation between variations in the money series and business activity.

[11] Conceivably, this could result, not from the effect of the currency ratio on the money stock, but from a dependence of the currency ratio on the money stock owing to temporary redistributions of money balances, when new money enters the economy, between sectors that maintain different currency ratios. This possibility is examined in Chapter 4 and found unimportant.

though, in view of the offsetting effects of high-powered money, the measures overstate in varying degrees the role of the two ratios.

Indeed, in view of Federal Reserve pronouncements during much of the period that it was not concerned solely with what happened to the money stock and was not to be considered fully responsible for it, the correlation coefficients for the later period may not reflect predesigned Federal Reserve policies at all. The correlations for both periods may reflect, instead, a similar response of high-powered money and the two ratios to business cycles. Such an indirect relation does not require or imply any direct dependence of the determinants on each other. Indirect relations clearly affected the regression coefficient for stage III, because deliberate offsetting movements would not produce a regression coefficient greater than unity. Although both kinds of influence imply interdependence, they lead to quite different interpretations of the sources of change in the money stock. Unfortunately, there is no simple way to measure the relative importance of the two kinds of interdependence.

Other considerations do not resolve the ambiguity of the available evidence. First, the correlation coefficients between the concurrent contributions of the two ratios in Table 7 are all virtually zero. This implies that the two were not affected in a common way by business cycles. It is therefore unlikely that either ratio and high-powered money were affected in a common way, unless possibly the effects had lags of quite different lengths. Barring that, the correlations in Table 8 seem to reflect (except stage III of the later cycles) a direct dependence of high-powered money on the two ratios.

Yet, the implication of this inference conflicts with our understanding of how such a dependence would operate. The inferred dependence might be expected to operate sluggishly and with considerable delay, which casts doubt on the foregoing interpretation of Tables 7 and 8. We may perhaps be willing to accept the implication of small delay for Federal Reserve operations in the later cycles, but what about the earlier ones? Did gold flows and Treasury actions offset *concurrently* one-fourth of the combined contribution of the two ratios? That gold flows could work so rapidly is questionable, since they respond to changes in the money stock by way of induced changes in prices and the balance of international payments. Treasury operations were too small and erratic to account all alone for the correlation. We seem to face a dilemma. If we interpret the correlations for the later period as reflecting Federal Reserve actions to offset movements in the two ratios, it seems only reasonable to attribute a corresponding role to gold flows (and in part to Treasury operations) in the earlier period.

One way to resolve the dilemma is to attribute most of the correlation in the earlier period to parallel responses of the determinants to business cycles, and just the *increase* in the degree of correlation from the earlier to the later period to Federal Reserve actions. By this interpretation, one-fourth of the contributions of high-powered money and the two ratios offset each other because of their similar responses to business cycles. In the later period, that offset seems to account for all the correlation in stages VII through II and for part—a fourth to a third—of the correlation in stages III through VI. For the latter stages, the regression coefficient suggests that Federal Reserve Banks were responsible for offsetting an additional 65 per cent or so (nine-tenths minus one-fourth) of the movements in the two ratios, though this is overstated by the large regression coefficient in stage III. The part of the coefficient in excess of unity cannot in any meaningful sense be interpreted as an intended offset and probably reflects the common effects of business cycles.

Covariation among the determinants means that some of their contributions to the money series were offset and, in a sense, were not contributions at all. There is no entirely satisfactory formula for correcting their relative contributions for interdependence. One way to make a rough adjustment, however, is to use the figures in Table 8 to delete the part of the contributions of the determinants that was offset, which leaves the money series the same, and to recompute the relative contributions with the part not offset. If we assume that the covariation always added to the combined relative contribution of the two ratios and subtracted from the relative contribution of high-powered money, we may adjust the former downward and the latter upward. This assumption probably holds for most cycle stages, but it produces some overstatement of the true correction. To the extent that the covariation reflects the common effects of business cycles, the square of the *correlation* coefficient is an estimate of the fraction offset of cyclical variations in the contributions. To the extent that the covariation reflects a response of high-powered money to the contributions of the two ratios, the *regression* coefficient is an estimate of the fraction offset of cyclical variations in the contributions of the two ratios.

In the earlier period, for which the tentative conclusion was that the covariation reflects the common effects of business cycles, we may in the foregoing manner adjust the relative contributions shown on line 4 of Table 4. The corresponding correlation coefficient in Table 8 is −0.49 and its square is 0.24. If we reduce the relative contributions of the currency and reserve ratios by 24 per cent, they both become 36 per cent. Their combined relative contribution is therefore 72 per cent (instead of 95 per cent as shown in Table 4), and the remaining 28 per cent is the contribution of high-powered money (instead of 3 per cent as shown in the table).[12]

For the later period, the conclusion was, again, that part of the cyclical variations in the contributions reflects the common effects of business cycles—perhaps one-fourth, as in the earlier period, perhaps less. If a fourth, the implied adjustment of line 5 in Table 4 lowers the relative contributions of the currency and reserve ratios to 42 and 5 per cent, respectively (from 56 and 7), and raises that of high-powered money to 53 per cent (from 37). In addition, an additional offset of about 65 per cent of the contributions of the two ratios to stages III through VI was perhaps due to actions of the Federal Reserve Banks, a total offset of nearly 90 per cent. This would further reduce the relative contributions of the two ratios in those stages to about 6 and 1 per cent, respectively, and raise that of high-powered money to 93 per cent. Although these adjustments for the earlier period do not change our previous ranking of the relative contributions of the determinants, the ranking for the later cycles is altered radically. The corrections imply that high-powered money was the primary contributor to the later cycles, and a moderate contributor to the earlier cycles, ranking

---

[12] It would understate the adjustment to estimate it as 24 per cent of the original relative contribution of high-powered money, 3 per cent, which is quite low because of the negative relative contributions of this determinant to the money series in certain stages. The procedure in the text assumes that the combined relative contribution of the two ratios was positive in all stages, which is true for the averages over the two periods discussed. Of course, the correlation coefficient is only an estimate of the average size of the correction, which theoretically is some function of the unspecified variables that produce the common fluctuations in the determinants.

A more accurate procedure than followed here would be to adjust the contributions in each stage of each cycle before computing the average relative contributions. This procedure would lend an appearance of detailed exactness to the results, however, that the general method does not justify.

third after the two ratios. While admittedly crude, the foregoing corrections may be taken as a rough (and probably exaggerated) indication of the part played by interdependence.

SUMMARY OF CONTRIBUTIONS OF THE DETERMINANTS TO CYCLICAL MOVEMENTS IN THE RATE OF CHANGE IN THE MONEY STOCK

The three proximate determinants of the money stock reflect the behavior of three sectors of the economy: high-powered money, the behavior of the government; the currency ratio, of the public; and the reserve ratio, of commercial banks. The formula presented at the beginning of this chapter defines the contribution of each determinant to the rate of change in the money stock. Although the formula can be approximated fairly closely for finite periods, there are many ways to compute the average relative contribution of the determinants over a period of time. The method adopted here was to use specific cycle stages of the money series and to compute various averages of the relative contributions. They bring out the relative importance of the channels through which cyclical variations in the money series occurred and provide a first step in identifying the factors responsible for those variations.

By these measures—and ignoring interdependence for the moment—the currency ratio is the chief contributor to specific cycles in the rate of change in the money stock, equaling the contributions of the other two determinants combined. The importance of its contributions reflects their large amplitude and their tendency to parallel those of the other two determinants; both attributes kept its contributions in conformity with the resulting cycles in the money series. The contributions of high-powered money, while just as large in amplitude, were very irregular and did not parallel the money series closely. The contributions of the reserve ratio had a fairly regular cyclical pattern but a comparatively small amplitude, though in the pre-1914 period its relative contribution rivaled that of the currency ratio.

The above statements should be amended to take account of interdependence among the contributions of the determinants. Interpretation of interdependence is hazardous, and the inferences made must be viewed as highly tentative. We found that perhaps 90 per cent of the combined contribution of the two ratios in stages III through VI of the later cycles was offset by the contribution of high-powered money, presumably in large part a result of intentional Federal Reserve policy. The erratic contribution of high-powered money in those cycles may be explained in part by that dependence. A weaker correlation for the other stages and for the earlier cycles suggests an offset of 25 per cent with the same effect but for the different reason that the determinants responded in a similar way to business cycles.

There is no entirely satisfactory way to take account quantitatively of this covariation in the measures of relative contribution. The adjustment used here suggests that, after deleting the part offset of the contributions, each of the three determinants produced about one-third of the pre-1914 specific cycles in the money series, the two ratios accounting for slightly more than high-powered money did. For the post-1918 cycles, stages VII through II and III through VI should be treated separately. For stages VII–II we found, after adjustment, that high-powered money made the largest contribution, though it and the currency ratio each produced almost half the cyclical variations in the money series, and the reserve ratio the small remainder. For stages III–VI, high-powered money was responsible for nearly all the cyclical variations in the money series.

Although the corrected figures may overemphasize, if anything, the contribution of high-powered money, they may still seem surprising, because they do not attribute all variations in the money series in the later period to high-powered money, and because they attribute an important role to the currency ratio in both periods. High-powered money dominated secular movements in the money series. Even in discussions of cyclical movements, high-powered money and the reserve ratio have generally received all the attention, while the currency ratio has been little noticed. One reason for the differential treatment is that sources of variation in high-powered money and the reserve ratio involve activities of the government and banks—both easy to discuss (and exaggerate)—whereas sources of variation in the currency ratio involve actions of innumerable holders of money and are, except in panics, obscure. While many students of the money supply have been aware of variations in the currency ratio, the present results highlight their importance, not only in panics but also for all cycles in the money series.

The emphasis on panics in discussions of the currency ratio has perhaps created the mistaken impression that the sources of change in the money series differ radically between panic cycles and mild cycles, whereas the difference is in fact small. The important differences among the cycles in the money series occur between those before and after the establishment of the Federal Reserve Banks; fluctuations in high-powered money became larger and a more important source of variation in the money series thereafter while, except for the 1930's, the reserve ratio lost much of its earlier volatility. Despite the occurrence of fewer panics after World War I, however, the cyclical behavior of the currency ratio has remained largely unchanged. In view of the changing sources of variations in the money series over time, it is remarkable that those variations have remained so similar both in amplitude and in their timing relation to reference cycles (a point taken up again in Chapter 6).

3

HIGH-POWERED MONEY

HIGH-POWERED MONEY as defined here—bank reserves and currency held by the public—is ultimately under the control of governments, which have authority to alter the conditions of issue and to change the quantity outstanding. Statutory regulations concerning money therefore play an important role in the monetary histories of most countries and in particular of the United States. This country had an inconvertible paper standard from the Civil War until 1879. It was on the gold standard from then until 1933, except for an embargo on gold exports during World War I. Since 1934 it has had the so-called gold bullion standard, which—because of the huge gold stock accumulated in excess of statutory requirements during the 1920's and 1930's—until the late 1950's allowed the government much of the freedom of an inconvertible standard. Those regulations account for much of the behavior of high-powered money in this country, though they do not alone explain the timing and amplitude of many variations associated with important economic developments. To assess the role of statutory regulations and to identify other influences, it is desirable to distinguish the various sources of change in high-powered money.

For the United States, the components of high-powered money are gold coin or certificates and other money fully backed by gold; paper money or deposit balances not secured by gold reserves but constituting a liability of the Treasury or (since 1915) of Federal Reserve Banks; and (until 1935) bank notes issued as the liability of national banks. Issue of money by the U.S. government has never been completely centralized; indeed, there have always been numerous sources of issue. They can be conveniently classified, however, into four general sources: the gold stock, Federal Reserve Banks, the Treasury, and national banks. Changes in the gold stock are determined by gold production and the balance of foreign payments. The other three are issuing agencies whose operations are sources of change in high-powered money. The Federal Reserve Banks are the only agency specifically charged with some of the responsibilities of central banking. The Treasury's operations include its cash outflow for budgetary expenditures and the management of the public debt, and inflow, including all revenues; outflow also includes silver purchases, shown separately because of the special character of silver in U.S. monetary

TABLE 9

DESCRIPTION OF SOURCES OF CHANGE IN HIGH-POWERED MONEY

By Operations of Issuing Agencies	By Changes in Monetary Assets or Liabilities
1. Gold flows (including changes in earmarkings), domestic production sold to the Treasury or coined and circulated, minus coin melted for use in the arts, or lost	1. Change in gold coin or certificates in circulation and change in the part of Treasury and Federal Reserve monetary liabilities secured by gold
2. Federal Reserve System operations: total change in Federal Reserve credit outstanding (excluding change in deposits held by foreign banks and in capital and surplus not offset by changes in fixed assets) on account of: Loans to banks Open-market operations	2. Change in Federal Reserve domestic monetary liabilities (i.e., excluding deposits held by foreign banks) minus change in FRS monetary reserves (i.e., holdings of gold and gold certificates, of Treasury currency, and of bank note liabilities of national banks)
3. Treasury operations: addition of net cash payments or subtraction of net cash receipts on account of: Budget deficits or surpluses Debt retirements or issues Deposits or withdrawals of funds at commercial banks and in miscellaneous Treasury accounts (including write-offs of discontinued currencies unredeemed and presumed lost) Cost of silver purchases and receipts from sales	3. Change in Treasury monetary liabilities (i.e., Treasury currency outstanding) minus change in high-powered monetary assets (i.e., Treasury holdings of gold, of Federal Reserve currency, of bank note liabilities of national banks, and Treasury deposits at Federal Reserve Banks)
4. Issue or retirement of notes by national banks	4. Change in bank note liabilities of national banks.

Note: Table describes high-powered money outside the Treasury and Federal Reserve Banks. For a more detailed description, see notes to Table F-5.

history. National banks issued national bank notes until 1935, under conditions set by the government. These operations covering all changes which occur in high-powered money are listed on the left-hand side of Table 9. Each corresponds to changes in a specific component of high-powered money involved in that operation, listed in the table on the right-hand side. Two or more changes may, of course, simultaneously offset each other, as in gold sterilization, when a gold in-flow is offset by Treasury sale of bonds, or in the withdrawal of Treasury deposits from commercial banks to finance Treasury expenditures.

The breakdown separates the operations of the Treasury and Federal Reserve Banks. Federal Reserve activities are essentially governmental, and for many purposes the balance sheet of the Reserve Banks could be consolidated with the accounts of the Treasury. In some important respects, however, its activities are independent of the Treasury, and separate treatment seems preferable. If Federal Reserve and Treasury operations are not consolidated, there are some transactions between the two agencies that do not involve the public, such as the sale of a bond by the Treasury directly to a Reserve Bank. The bond sale shows up on Treasury accounts as a cash receipt through the issue of debt, and on Federal Reserve Bank statements as an increase in earning assets. The transaction cancels out in terms of the change in high-powered money outstanding but still shows up in records of operations of the two agencies.

The change in high-powered money attributable to the Federal Reserve Banks is the change in the Banks' total domestic monetary liabilities not covered by monetary reserves. These liabilities include amounts extended by Reserve Banks to the Treasury (which cancel out against Treasury operations) as well as to domestic commercial banks (including, of course, loans to member banks[1]) but not to foreign banks (which do not create dollar liabilities within the United States). Monetary reserves comprise the Reserve Banks' holdings of gold and gold certificates, Treasury currency, and national bank notes, all of which stand behind and in a sense create an equal amount of Federal Reserve monetary liabilities. Changes in these liabilities can also be described by the Federal Reserve operations involved. For example, a loan to a member bank increases Federal Reserve earning assets and therefore augments high-powered money. Changes in Reserve Bank

---

[1] Some students distinguish analytically between loans to member banks and other Federal Reserve credit outstanding. (A corresponding distinction is also made from banks' point of view between borrowings and other high-powered reserves of member banks, by defining net free reserves as equal to gross reserves minus required reserves and borrowings.) The purpose of the distinction is to assess the effects of the discount rate (relative to short-term market rates) on member bank borrowings. The distinction is of doubtful value in understanding the issue of high-powered money, because other Federal Reserve credit is not—or at least need not be—independent of the volume of member bank borrowing. Indeed, open market operations presumably are intended to provide a desired total amount of credit to banks after taking account of the amount of borrowing. Whatever the amount of borrowing may be, Reserve Banks still have full control over the total amount of their credit outstanding, though in the very short run, of course, unexpected variations may occur.

CHART 3

Sources of Change in High-Powered Money, Fiscal Years, 1876–1955

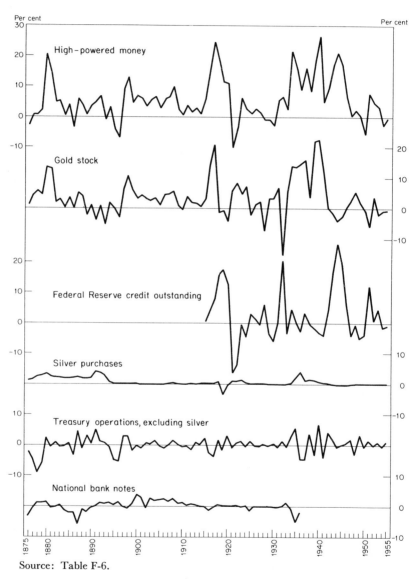

Source: Table F-6.

Note: Each source expressed as percentage of total high-powered money at beginning of fiscal year.

earning assets that do not affect their domestic monetary liabilities are excluded. Hence, an increase in assets through sale of capital stock to a new member bank or extension of deposits to foreign banks are excluded.

The definition of the change attributable to the Treasury is analogous. The Treasury operations listed in the table cover all the ways it pays out or receives money, all of which must be included to derive its net contribution to high-powered money. This source was actually derived as a residual to avoid unnecessary labor; all sources add up identically to the change in high-powered money, already computed, and any one source could be derived as a residual. As for the gold stock and note liabilities of national banks, the change in these items gives the required figure, since there are no monetary reserves behind them.[2]

Specified in this operational form, changes in high-powered money can be associated with the particular economic developments and government policies that initiated them. Part of this organization of sources of change in high-powered money is similar to a table of sources and uses of Federal Reserve credit outstanding, which appears regularly in the *Federal Reserve Bulletin*. The purpose there is different, however (changes in total high-powered money are not explicitly shown in the *Bulletin*), and there are minor differences in definition of some of the items. The scheme here helps to identify the channels through which various factors affect high-powered money. Secular and cyclical movements are distinct and are discussed separately below.

1. Secular Movements in Sources of Change in High-Powered Money

Chart 3 shows the sources of change in high-powered money outstanding for the fiscal years 1876–1955. The changes are expressed as percentages of the level of high-powered money at the beginning of the corresponding fiscal year. The data and their derivation are given in Tables F-5 and F-6. Because they show changes between two dates separated by a year (successive June 30's), these series suppress movements, however large, occurring between such dates, yet at the same

---

[2] The redemption fund for national bank notes, deposited with the Treasury, also satisfied legal reserve requirements for deposits of the issuing banks, and so is not treated as a reserve behind the notes.

time reflect in full any movement, however brief, if it spans a June 30. For example, a movement from May to June which is reversed from June to July shows up as two movements in opposite directions in adjacent years. In the chart, this gives the impression of a year-long movement reversed in the following year, whereas the whole operation covered but two months. Such reversals are especially apt to happen with Treasury operations. The Treasury might, for example, finance a deficit at the end of one fiscal year by running down its deposits at Federal Reserve Banks and then restore the deposits at the beginning of the next fiscal year with a sale of bonds. The two Treasury operations cancel out and have no effect on high-powered money, except momentarily; yet, if they occur in June and July, in the annual data they appear to have occurred over two full years. This explains part—though by no means all—of the random-like variations in the series for Treasury operations. In most periods, however, those operations were unimportant. The other series fluctuate radically at times but mostly for other reasons.

Chart 3 shows clearly that the gold stock accounted for most of the large changes in high-powered money up to World War I and shared that distinction thereafter with Federal Reserve credit outstanding. Visually, the fluctuations in these two sources are much larger than those in the others. Simple correlation coefficients quantify this impression. The gold-stock series accounted for about two-thirds of the variation in the annual percentage changes of high-powered money up to 1914 but for only about two-fifths from 1915 to 1955 (though these fractions would be lower if short-run cyclical variations were removed). Federal Reserve credit outstanding accounted for the major part of the remaining variation in the later period. The results are largely to be expected: operation of the gold-standard mechanism suggests (though not necessarily) that gold flows (or the domestic production absorbed and not exported) would produce many large changes in high-powered money; also that, even though large changes in other sources might have occurred, they would have tended to produce, before 1914 at least, offsetting gold flows. After 1914, changes in the U.S. gold stock, in percentage terms, were larger than ever, but the relative importance of gold diminished. The newly formed Federal Reserve Banks could expand or contract the quantity of high-powered money on a large scale, and on several occasions they did.

TABLE 10

SOURCES OF CHANGES IN HIGH-POWERED MONEY FOR
SELECTED PERIODS, 1876-1955

Period (fiscal years)	Total[a] (1)	AVERAGE CHANGE IN HIGH-POWERED MONEY ATTRIBUTED TO CHANGE IN: (per cent per year)				
		Monetary Gold Stock (2)	Federal Reserve Operations (3)	Treasury Operations		National Bank Notes (6)
				Silver Purchases (4)	Total, Excluding Silver (5)	
1876-81	6.0	7.1	--	2.4	-3.4	-0.1
1882-96	1.9	0.5	--	2.0	0.1	-0.7
1897-1914	5.1	3.6	--	0.1	0.2	1.2
1915-22	8.9	5.7	3.5	-0.1	-0.2	-0.1
1923-30	1.2	1.5	-0.7	0.2	0.3	-0.2
1931-40	13.0	10.3	1.6	1.1	0.6	-0.7
1941-46	12.6	0.7	11.4	0.1	0.4	--
1947-55	1.1	0.4	0.2	0.1	0.5	--

Source: Table F-6. Simple average of percentages for each year.

[a]May not equal sum of sources because of rounding.

Their main contributions were the two large expansions during World Wars I and II. Gold flows did not correct those expansions, at first or even later, as previously they would have done. Nations erected various barriers to the free adjustment of international trade during and after the two world wars by restricting the flow of gold and goods. Foreign central banks also expanded at the same time the Federal Reserve System did, which lessened the adjustment required.

While the gold stock and Federal Reserve credit outstanding accounted for the major changes in high-powered money, the other sources were not inconsequential, especially in certain periods. This is brought out by Table 10, which presents for eight periods averages of the figures graphed in Chart 3. Although the eight were selected by marking off the major movements of the series in the chart, they also correspond with major developments in U.S. monetary history:

1875-81, the prelude and return to convertibility, in which the gold stock rose as a result of government sale of bonds to build up a reserve before resumption of specie payments in 1879 and as a result of a very favorable balance of payments in the following two years

1882-96, a period of declining prices reflecting worldwide deflation, ending with several years in which gold flowed out and the government sold bonds to preserve its gold reserve and maintain convertibility

1897–1914, in which world gold stocks increased and prices rose

1915–22, in which the usual wartime expansion of the money stock came at first through gold flows and then continued because of credit extension by the newly formed Federal Reserve Banks, followed after the war by a sharp contraction of credit and collapse of prices

1923–30, a period of stability in the money stock and prices but also one of large gold imports, which reflected a disequilibrium of world trade and a weakening of the gold-standard mechanism.

1931–40, a decade of monetary expansion as a consequence of devaluation and the resulting gold inflows

1941–46, a repetition of movements in World War I, with expansion again of Federal Reserve credit outstanding and cessation of gold flows after the outbreak of hostilities

1947–55, a return to restrained growth and stability of the money stock, as the Federal Reserve Banks, at first diverted to support of the bond market, paid increasing attention thereafter to stabilizing prices

Although there was a close association in every one of the eight periods between the average change in high-powered money and in the gold stock and Federal Reserve credit outstanding, the average contributions of the other sources were in some periods fairly large. The underlying factors may best be described by a discussion of each source.

THE GOLD STOCK

Changes in the Gold-Standard Mechanism after 1914. Although gold flows have been de-emphasized in recent theoretical discussions of international adjustments and national income determination, they have important effects on the quantity of high-powered money and thus on the money stock, and cannot be disregarded. Changes in the monetary gold stock affect high-powered money directly and, as Chart 3 and Table 10 indicate for the United States, the magnitude of the effect has been substantial. To be sure, the further effect through changes in the money stock on the balance of international payments and the equilibrium of relative national price levels, though subject to the interference of other factors and therefore difficult to identify, has clearly been less important since World War I. There are several qualifications to the importance of gold even under an unrestricted gold-standard mechanism, especially concerning the speed of adjustments. Yet, granted the qualifications, changes in the gold stock have played a crucial role in long-run monetary developments before World War I and—to a lesser relative extent—since then as well.

In the long run there is a mutual dependence between the stock of gold and high-powered money. First, foreign payments made by shipments of gold produce an equal change in the quantity of high-powered money outstanding (unless offset by other sources) and may lead to further changes if the quantity is normally a multiple of the gold stock. And, second, changes in high-powered money eventually lead to changes in the stock of money and so in the level of money income and prices, which in turn affect the balance of foreign payments and so the flow of gold. Under the gold-standard mechanism, therefore, changes in high-powered money and gold flows affect each other. The money stock might respond slowly or incompletely to gold flows in the short run and still maintain a relation to them in the long run. The response may be partial and delayed, because the effects of gold flows can be moderated by central banks.[3]

The gold stock dominated long-run movements in the U.S. money stock, but was less decisive after 1914, however, than before. In the latter period, changes in the gold stock were large from time to time, indeed generally much larger than before, but they no longer predominated in determining the quantity of high-powered money. Changes in Federal Reserve credit outstanding were of equal size and frequency and, more important, were used to moderate or accentuate movements in the gold stock to suit the monetary policies of the government. Gold movements to a great extent thus lost their primary role and were important only secondarily as a factor to be considered by the government in pursuing particular goals.

During the first half of the 1920's gold flowed into the United States in large volume owing to the war-produced disequilibrium that monetary policies here and abroad had not corrected. The economic (and political) difficulties of maintaining the gold standard fell, therefore, on the foreign countries losing gold, whereas the Federal Reserve Banks did not face such difficulties and could—as they did—prevent

[3] Even before 1914 central banks appear to have viewed outflows with alarm and inflows with equanimity. See Arthur I. Bloomfield, *Monetary Policy under the International Gold Standard: 1880–1914*, Federal Reserve Bank of New York, 1959, pp. 23 ff.

the increased gold stock from expanding high-powered money commensurately. High-powered money fell during 1921–22, had a declining rate of increase during 1923–27, and fell again during 1928–30 (see Chart 3). While a bank deposit was created for each dollar of new gold domestically coined or acquired from abroad, addition to high-powered bank reserves from such deposits at banks was offset to a large extent by reduction of Federal Reserve earning assets. With that reduction, the ability of the banking system to expand credit was no greater after the receipt of gold than before.

The accumulation of gold in the early 1920's accompanied by reductions of Federal Reserve credit outstanding increased gold reserves in excess of requirements and gave the Reserve Banks freedom to expand or contract credit within wide limits to suit domestic policies, despite the absence of further growth in the gold stock during the remainder of the 1920's. There were two important instances of large gold outflows that induced the Reserve Banks to allow the money stock to contract sharply: one at the beginning of the period, 1920–21, and one at the end, 1931–32.[4] Otherwise, except for 1926, the June-to-June annual changes in Federal Reserve credit outstanding and in the gold stock tended to offset each other. Chart 3 reveals the resulting shift in the primary sources of change in high-powered money between the periods before and after 1914. In the periods before 1914, changes in the gold stock predominated. In the periods after, Federal Reserve credit has had equal or greater importance.

The United States still adhered to the formal observance of the international gold standard during the 1920's. After removal of the wartime embargo on export of gold in June 1919, there were no restrictions on the purchase, sale, or shipment of gold, and the Treasury maintained the convertibility of its currency at a fixed parity with gold. In terms of these criteria, the gold standard as traditionally practiced did not fall in this country until 1933, when the purchase and holding of gold for nonindustrial uses were prohibited. Although gold movements during the 1920's lost some of their control over high-powered money and were no longer the chief arbiter of international trade and price levels, those transgressions of the traditional responses to gold flows did not exceed the broadening prerogatives of central

[4] See Milton Friedman and Anna Jacobson Schwartz, *A Monetary History of the United States, 1867–1960*, Princeton for NBER, 1963, Chaps. 5 and 7.

banks. The transgressions complicated the problems of maintaining convertibility for countries temporarily losing gold—especially if a loss became large before it ended—but they did not portend insurmountable difficulties until the 1930's. Indeed, they seemed to adapt the standard to the new demands of freedom for domestic economic policies. One purpose of central banks was to cushion the short-run effects on the economy of gold flows; central banks were not required or expected to supplant the final authority of those flows. If it had been understood that central banks would offset gold flows temporarily but not indefinitely, and if such actions had set the conditions for a new kind of "domesticated" gold standard to be adopted and maintained in the 1930's, we should never have come to think of the 1920's as the end of an era. Yet, with hindsight, the period can be described as a prelude to suspension of the traditional gold-standard mechanism. In the few turbulent years that were to follow, the brief return to gold after World War I ended in most countries, and currencies with limited or no convertibility supplanted convertible currencies. Gold has remained the medium of international exchange and in this way has retained part of its influence—as the United States is reminded by events since the second half of the 1950's—but so far, it no longer governs so closely as it once did the quantity of nearly all the world's money.

These developments symbolize the decline of the gold-standard mechanism as a means of adjusting imbalances of international payments. Yet, as noted, changes in the gold stock since 1914 have not been smaller and have not contributed less than before to changes in the money stock. Actually, they have been larger and have contributed more in absolute amount, as Chart 3 shows—and as indeed is to be expected. Relaxing the "rules" of the gold standard while not throwing them completely out has allowed larger and more prolonged gold flows. What has happened since 1914 is that the *relative* importance of gold has declined, owing to the creation of another major source of high-powered money—Federal Reserve Banks—together with developments previously described. As a result, the ratio of high-powered money to the gold stock, shown in Chart 4, has fluctuated considerably more since 1914 than before. Even so, Treasury policies were capable of producing such fluctuations before 1914, as the 1890–99 period demonstrates; and since resumption in 1879 no large movement either up or down in this ratio has proved to be permanent.

CHART 4

*Relation Between High-Powered Money and the Gold Stock,
Annually, 1875–1955*

Ratio of High-Powered Money to the Gold Stock
(end of June)

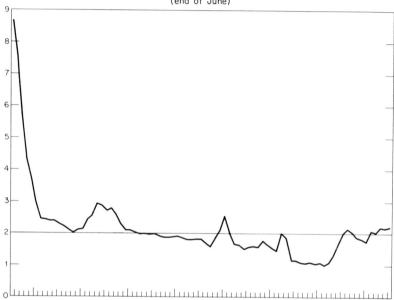

Changes in the Gold Stock (Fiscal Years) as a Percentage of
the Level of High-Powered Money at Beginning of Fiscal Year

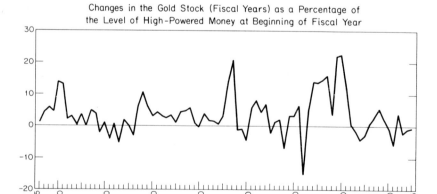

Source: Tables F-6 and F-7. The lower panel is the same as the gold-stock panel
in Chart 3.

In 1955 the ratio was 2.2, close to its average level before World War I. Throughout most of that earlier period it hovered around a level of 2, except for higher ratios in the years preceding and just after 1879, when convertibility was resumed, and the 1890's, when the Treasury experienced gold drains. The monetary developments after World War I, and particularly after the 1920's, emphasized in the foregoing paragraphs, are vividly illustrated by this chart. Before World War I the series rises considerably above 2.0 in many years but seldom falls below 1.8, while thereafter it has seldom gone much above 2.0 but has fallen considerably below that in many years, particularly in the decade following devaluation in 1934. In short, the growth of high-powered money sometimes outran that of gold in the pre–World War I period and sometimes fell short in the subsequent period—hardly ever the reverse—but in due course the imbalance has so far eventually been redressed.

Factors Affecting the Growth of the Gold Stock. Government actions have affected high-powered money and hence the growth of the U.S. monetary gold stock required to produce equilibrium under the international gold standard. Such actions therefore help to explain some of the variations in its rate of growth, particularly since 1914. Most variations, however, reflect market responses to demand-and-supply factors which are largely unrelated to changes in government policies. For purposes of discussion, all such factors can be thought of as affecting either the growth of the world monetary gold stock (representing current production not absorbed by industry and arts) or this country's share of the existing world stock. A thorough analysis would cover, under the first item, the world supply of gold from production and the nonmonetary demand for the metal; and, under the second item, the changing area of the gold standard, as countries adopted or abandoned gold, monetary substitutes for gold, the pattern of international trade and capital movements, and so on. Such analyses are not yet at hand. Much is nevertheless known, and we may identify some of the main factors by comparing the deviations from trend of the U.S. monetary gold stock with the price of gold in this country (in terms of commodities). The comparison is facilitated by the series graphed in Chart 5. The first set is the annual level and secular trend of the U.S. monetary gold stock in terms of its pre-1934 dollar value (and so shows changes in the physical stock of gold only,

CHART 5

The U.S. Monetary Gold Stock and Commodity Value of Gold,
Annually, 1875–1955

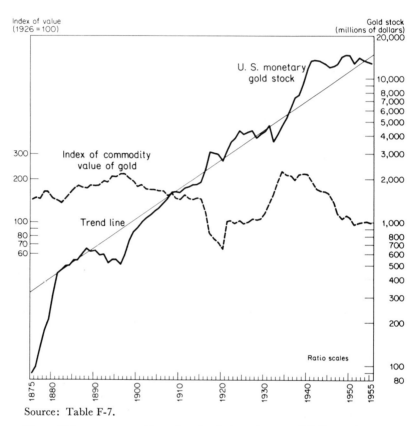

Source: Table F-7.

Note: U.S. monetary gold stock, valued throughout at $20.67 per fine ounce,
end of June figures. Commodity value of gold, based on its dollar price and dollar
prices of wholesale commodities, average of monthly data. Trend line, slope of
4.7 per cent per year (compounded continuously).

omitting changes in value due to the 1934 devaluation). The other
series (dashed line) is the commodity value of gold (which incorporates
changes in the dollar prices of both commodities and gold). Ordinarily a rise (say) in the commodity value of gold[5] will increase the
growth of the U.S. stock both by raising the rate of world production

[5] Note that changes in commodity prices (in terms of dollars) produce changes in
the value of gold (in terms of commodities) in the opposite direction.

of gold and, if the rise in value here is not matched in other countries, by attracting here part of the existing world stock; and conversely.

In addition to the two world war periods, the chart reveals four large deviations in the stock from its secular trend. Each of the four, except the first, may be divided into two submovements, one that takes the series away from the trend line, and a second that brings the series back to the trend line: 1875–81; 1889–96 and 1896–1907; 1920–24 and 1924–32; 1932–41 and 1941–55. All can be associated with important changes either in the value and therefore production of gold or in government policies affecting the gold stock.

1875–81. The U.S. Treasury accumulated a gold reserve, and in 1879 the United States returned to the gold standard. The sharp rise in the gold stock is not to be explained by changes in the commodity value of gold; although dollar prices fell in the United States during the 1870's, so also did the dollar premium on gold. The rise reflects preparations for convertibility taken by the Treasury, discussed later in this chapter in the subsection on Treasury Operations.

1889–96 AND 1896–1907. The movements reflected corresponding changes in world gold production. To understand the changes we must go back to developments in gold mining which occurred in earlier decades.

Following the opening of rich fields in California in 1848 and in Australia in 1851, no important new gold discoveries were made for some time, so that, starting in 1875 and lasting until 1887, the rate of growth in the world monetary gold stock dropped from the 8 per cent annual rate attained in the early 1850's to about 1 per cent.[6] Also, several countries adopted the gold standard in that period, which forced a wider distribution of the given supply. As a result, the commodity value of gold rose substantially from the early 1870's to the late 1890's.[7] Around 1888 world gold production began to expand again, and in a few years quite rapidly, so that output doubled by 1896–97 and almost doubled again by 1907.[8] Output reached a peak in 1912 with an annual rate of production equal to about four and a

---

[6] Based on Joseph Kitchin's estimates, *Interim Report of the Gold Delegation of the Financial Committee*, Geneva, League of Nations, Sept. 8, 1930, Table B, pp. 83–84.

[7] As gauged by British prices (see G. Warren and F. Pearson, *Prices*, New York, Wiley, 1933, pp. 74–77).

[8] See estimates of annual world production by the Director of the Mint in his *Annual Report*, 1913, p. 314.

half times that of 1878–87; the rate declined only moderately in 1913–14.

The upturn in production around 1888 was due primarily to a series of technological innovations in the purification of gold ore, which allowed profitable mining of lower-grade ores previously abandoned. The main advances involved the use of chlorine gas and of cyanide of potash in the extraction process. The chlorination process had spread widely by the mid-1870's,[9] and the cyanide process was first introduced on a large scale around 1891. The latter was the cheaper method and was soon adopted universally. That gold was soluble in a solution of cyanide of potash had long been known, but the first practical technique for utilizing cyanide to extract gold from the many substances with which it is combined in nature was not patented until 1885.[10]

There were also some important new gold discoveries in the period 1885–90 and after. The famous Transvaal fields in South Africa opened up at that time, though they did not become important until after 1890. The first of many rich deposits was found in western Australia in 1889. In the early 1890's there were also substantial increases in output partly from new discoveries and partly from opening up abandoned mines in Colorado, British Columbia, Mexico, and other parts of South and Central America. (The rich strikes along the Yukon and Klondike Rivers in Alaska first occurred late in 1896.) All together, the new fields produced a substantial increase in world output, but the earlier innovations in processing the ore provided the main stimulus. The low-grade ores in many of the new fields could not have been profitably worked by the older methods of purification, especially in the new Transvaal fields, which alone accounted for about a quarter of world output in 1900–10.[11]

It was probably no accident that those discoveries came in the late 1880's and 1890's. The commodity value of gold then was at high levels and still rising (see Chart 5). That the technological innovations for purifying gold ore were also spurred by economic incentives is a more tenuous proposition; innovations are partly inspirational, and the proverb, "necessity is the mother of invention," may not apply. Yet the proposition that it does seems credible, because the solubility of gold in cyanide of potash was already known, as noted, and great

---

[9] It was the "leading process" used in California in 1876 (see Alfred G. Lock, *Gold: Its Occurrence and Extraction*, New York, Spon, 1882, p. 186).

[10] See Edward S. Meade, *The Story of Gold*, New York, Appleton, 1909, pp. 123–133.

[11] *Annual Report*, Director of the Mint, 1911, pp. 46–47.

reductions in the cost of refining gold ore only awaited a practical application of that chemical reaction. Indeed, several similar methods were patented in this country and abroad within a few years of each other.[12]

WORLD GOLD PRODUCTION AND THE U.S. GOLD STOCK, 1873–1913. What part did gold production play in the growth of the U.S. stock during the period 1873–1913? Table 11 presents data dividing the growth of the U.S. monetary gold stock into growth of the world stock and changes in the U.S. share of the world stock. The normal share of current world production going to each gold-standard country is the ratio of its stock to the existing world stock. If the ratio does not change, the country's stock grows at the same rate as the world stock. Differences between the actual growth rates of its stock and the world stock can then be attributed to changes over time in its share of the world stock. Although the figures available on growth of the world gold stock are rough, they should suffice to bring out general movements. The growth rate of the U.S. stock, as we might expect, has fluctuated more than that of the world stock because of recurring changes in the U.S. share of the world stock. The U.S. share has also risen over time mainly because of expansion of the U.S. economy relative to that of all other gold-standard countries, making the rates in column 3 positive on the average.

The variations in these rates reflect short-run disturbances in international payments, owing to monetary developments abroad as well as to fluctuations in international trade and capital movements. The variations are not entirely suppressed, even though the table measures average rates of change between reference cycle peaks.

Because of that variation, world gold production does not completely account for the increased growth of the U.S. stock starting in 1896. In 1896–1913, compared with the preceding fourteen-year period, the annual rate of growth of the world stock rose by nearly 2 percentage points, whereas that of the U.S. stock rose by over 7 percentage points. The changes in the U.S. share from the first to the second summary period reinforced the effect of world production on the growth of the U.S. stock. The distribution of the world gold stock frequently changes, of course, even aside from short-run fluctuations. Countries expand and demand gold at different rates, and doubling the rate of growth of the world stock need not precisely or even

[12] Meade, *The Story of Gold*, p. 128.

TABLE 11

SOURCES OF SECULAR GROWTH OF THE U.S. GOLD STOCK:
AVERAGE RATES OF CHANGE BETWEEN REFERENCE
CYCLE PEAKS, 1873-1913

Peak to Peak of Successive Reference Cycles	AVERAGE RATE OF CHANGE IN U. S. MONETARY GOLD STOCK (per cent per year)		
		Attributed to:	
	Total (1)	Growth of World Gold Stock (2)	Change in U.S. Share of World Stock (3)
1873-82	17.9	1.3	16.6
1882-87	4.0	1.0	3.1
1887-90	2.6	1.4	1.1
1890-93	-2.8	1.9	-4.8
1893-96	-4.8	3.1	-7.9
1896-1900	14.4	3.7	10.7
1900-03	7.4	3.2	4.2
1903-07	6.5	3.8	2.7
1907-10	3.6	4.3	-0.7
1910-13	4.0	2.9	1.1
Summary			
1882-96	0.3	1.7	-1.4
1896-1913	7.6	3.6 (4.1)	3.9 (3.4)

Note: Rates computed between Dec. 30 figures for fiscal year reference peaks, except the 1873 peak, which is based on figures for June 30 of that year.

Source, by Column

(1): Table F-7, col. 1. Data for 1873 from Annual Report, of the Director of the Mint, 1907.

(2): Estimates of Kitchin, Interim Report of the Gold Delegation, Table B, pp. 83-84. Later studies suggest that Kitchin's figure for 1913 is too low by perhaps about $1,045 million (see C. O. Hardy, Is There Enough Gold?, Washington, Brookings, 1936, p. 207). Rates shown in parentheses are based on the revised figure and Kitchin's figure for 1896. Kitchin's 1896 figure is probably also understated, however, so the rate in parentheses in col. 2 is undoubtedly too high. The rate based on Kitchin's figures for both 1896 and 1913 may well be closer to the actual rate.

(3): Col. 1 minus col. 2; may not exactly equal the difference between figures shown for cols. 1 and 2 because of rounding.

approximately double the rate for every country. On the other hand, the disturbances behind the U.S. gold outflows during 1890–96 were not unrelated to the slow growth of the world gold stock in that and previous decades. The Baring crisis of 1890, with its subsequent international repercussions, and the domestic agitation over silver a few years later both had roots in the worldwide deflation of prices which accompanied the comparatively low output of gold. From this point of view, the increased growth of the world gold stock beginning around 1890 also removed the additional factors that produced gold outflows from the United States and then allowed the U.S. gold stock to raise its share of the world stock. Had those episodes not occurred, the average rate of growth of the U.S. stock might have been somewhat higher for 1882–96 and somewhat lower for 1896–1913, and hence closer to the world rate.

This view finds support in the response of the government to gold flows at other times. The government has often acted, in part from political pressures and in part on its own volition, to cushion their effect on the monetary system.[13] The ratio of high-powered money to the gold stock tended to be higher than usual in periods of large and prolonged gold outflows; and conversely with inflows. This can be seen by comparing the upper and lower panels of Chart 4, particularly for the rise in the ratio from 1890 to 1893 and decline after 1896, for the decline during the early 1920's and most of the 1930's, and for the sharp rise from 1931 to 1932. The government offset part of the movements in the gold stock in those periods by issuing or retiring nongold components of high-powered money. Such actions help to prolong gold movements by perpetuating the disequilibrium of foreign payments which gold flows help to correct. Changes in the U.S. share would consequently tend to parallel the swings in annual world gold production.

Whatever effects government actions had on the U.S. share of the world gold stock, all countries could not, of course, produce the same effects simultaneously, simply because every country with a rising share would force some others to have falling shares. The only movements common to all countries' gold stocks are those in world gold production not used in industry and arts; a large change in that aggregate necessarily produces a corresponding change in the growth of most countries' stocks. Considerable qualitative evidence indicates that most countries experienced first a fall in growth of their gold stocks during the 1870's and 1880's and then an upsurge sometime during the 1890's, thus corroborating our data on the world gold stock. We may, therefore, attribute the increase in the rate of growth of the gold stock in the U.S. and other countries from 1882–96 to 1896–1913 largely to changes in gold production—and these in turn to the

---

[13] Though only to a limited extent, as Chart 3 shows.

economic and technological conditions of supply—rather than to changes in their shares of the total or to nonmonetary demands for gold.

Were the factors affecting world gold production independent of other monetary variables and thus entirely exogenous? They were certainly not related to increases in aggregate output or in the aggregate demand for goods and services, which have been held responsible for the secular rise in prices from 1897 to 1914 (see Chapter 6) and so also, by implication, for the corresponding increase in the rate of change in the money stock. Such increases in aggregate output or demand would tend to raise prices and costs and thereby to discourage gold production, and not under ordinary circumstances tend to stimulate it. More likely, the deflation of prices in the decades following the Civil War, which raised the commodity value of gold, also stimulated the increase in its rate of production, as previously suggested. In that event, increased growth of the gold and money stocks in turn accounted for the upturn in prices. The effect worked slowly, however. World prices commenced a fairly steady decline in the early 1870's, while world gold production did not expand appreciably until after 1890. And when the U.S. gold stock rose sharply after 1896, the effect on the money stock was partly, though not wholly, offset by the other sources of change in high-powered money. By this interpretation, the U.S. gold stock was not an exogenous variable in that period but formed part of a closed system: the gold stock determined the long-run level of the money stock and hence commodity prices, which in turn determined the production of gold and so the level of its stock—though with a long lag, to be sure. Aside from the recognition of long lags, this is essentially the old classical theory of commodity money. It accords quite well with the evidence on long-run movements.

1920–24 AND 1924–32. The first half of the 1920's recorded the previously mentioned upheaval in international trade and finance following World War I. Thereafter, the U.S. gold stock was roughly constant up to 1931, which means it fell in relation to its secularly rising trend (see Chart 5). The halt in growth of the stock for half a decade may be explained in part by its rapid growth in the early 1920's followed by the return to convertibility and to prosperity of nations abroad, and in part by slackening of world production[14]

[14] *Banking and Monetary Statistics*, Board of Governors of the Federal Reserve System, 1943, p. 542.

associated with a value of gold almost 50 per cent lower in the 1920's than before World War I.

1932–41 AND 1941–55. The Great Depression beginning in 1929 and the international financial panic in 1931 disrupted world trade and induced governments to adopt monetary reforms of various kinds: devaluation of their currencies, exchange controls, and inflationary domestic policies. By all odds the most severe blow to the gold-standard mechanism was the general use and acceptance of national interferences with gold flows to accommodate domestic monetary policies. Of equal or greater significance for the long-run behavior of prices, however, was devaluation, which produced large increases in world gold production. In the United States the large and protracted expansion of high-powered money in the 1930's came from the steady accumulation in this country of a substantial part of the existing world gold stock and of current gold production.

Increase of the U.S. gold stock, as Chart 5 shows, commenced on a large scale even before the formal devaluation of the dollar, a step not taken until early 1934. Earlier, on March 6, 1933, convertibility had been abandoned, and on October 25 of that year the government began to purchase gold on the open market at prices above the old parity of $20.67 an ounce with a view to depreciating the value of the dollar.[15] The U.S. buying price was gradually raised and finally pegged at $35 an ounce on January 31, 1934, at which price the Treasury has since bought all gold offered (except domestic coin and scrap).[16] In Chart 3,

[15] Holders of domestic gold coin did not profit from the higher value of gold, since they had to turn it all in to the Treasury, which purchased all domestic gold coin and scrap at the old parity. Notwithstanding the nationalization of the domestic gold stock, only inconvenience prevented Americans from purchasing and holding gold to their account abroad (see R. Harrod, *The Dollar*, New York, 1954, p. 69).

Domestic producers of gold, whose exports had been banned since Mar. 1933, began to profit from a rise in value in Sept., a month before the government's buying program began. From Sept. 8 to Oct. 24 the Treasury bought gold from domestic producers at the best price available abroad and resold it in foreign markets. The increase in high-powered money from purchases thus tended to be canceled by sales abroad (the Treasury received foreign exchange from the sales, with which it could buy back the money issued for its purchases). The operation was equivalent to exporting the currently produced gold (assuming the Treasury's payments and receipts were equal); hence, high-powered money outstanding in the U.S. was not directly affected by that operation.

[16] Most Treasury purchases at the new official price have been financed by issue of gold certificates to Federal Reserve Banks and have increased high-powered money. Purchases from Oct. 25, 1933, to Jan. 30, 1934, however, at prices above the old parity price then authorized were financed by issues of 90-day debentures and so did not at the time produce increases in high-powered money (see G. G. Johnson, *The Treasury and Monetary Policy 1933–1938*, Cambridge, Mass., 1939, p. 24).

the percentage additions to the gold stock are based on the value of its physical changes; the stock figures exclude the Treasury's bookkeeping profit in 1933–34 from appreciation in the dollar value of its gold holdings purchased before devaluation, since only actual purchases of gold by the Treasury directly affect the dollar amount of high-powered money in circulation. The solid curve in Chart 5 records physical changes in the stock valued at the old parity.

Devaluation did not immediately depreciate proportionately the general purchasing power of the dollar; indeed, the $35 price, in view of the nearly 50 per cent decline in wholesale prices from 1929 to 1932, proved to be a bonanza to producers of gold throughout the decade. Prices of wholesale commodities did not until the next decade rise as high as might ordinarily be expected from such huge additions to the gold stock (considering also that offsetting changes in Federal Reserve credit outstanding were negligible). The rate of growth of the stock did not fall off until after the outbreak of World War II. Its growth first accelerated with the threat of war in 1938–39 but then stopped with the imposition of exchange controls abroad. The U.S. stock actually declined slightly during the war.

It began to grow again after the war from 1945 until 1949 and then declined moderately in most of the following years up to 1955. It increased in the next two years and then began a steady decline, still continuing in the early 1960's (not shown on charts). The post-war shift from growth to decline of the U.S. gold stock may be attributed to the resurgence of European economies from wartime setbacks and to a fall in world gold production, which reflected a value of the metal considerably reduced from the high level of the late 1930's. That the commodity value of gold had returned in the 1950's to its level in the 1920's means that the 1934 devaluation did eventually lead to much higher commodity prices, but the full outcome took two decades.

SUMMARY. The preceding discussion of the large variations in the rate of growth of the U.S. monetary gold stock has emphasized changes in the commodity value of gold as a major part of the explanation. Other factors, particularly government monetary policies, have also played an important part, though often through their effect on the value of gold. Most effects of long-run significance worked through changes in world gold production but were delayed by lags of varying duration. There are at least two reasons for long lags. First, the monetary gold stock is extremely large compared with annual additions. Second, world gold production may respond slowly to changes in the value of gold, partly because response sometimes comes through discovery of new ore fields and improved technology for refining gold ore. World price levels began to decline in the 1870's, for example, but world gold production did not rise appreciably until the 1890's. Once production started to rise, it kept rising for two decades, despite sharp price increases in gold-standard countries after 1896. The continued upsurge in output reflected newly discovered techniques and newly opened mines, both of which remained profitable despite the ensuing rise in commodity prices and mining costs. On the other hand, when the value of gold increased sharply, as with devaluation in the early 1930's, production expanded rapidly.[17]

The effect just described of the value of gold on its world production and stock shows up clearly. Although data on the world stock are increasingly incomplete after the mid-1930's, mainly because of lack of data for Russia, and cannot be easily analyzed for the whole period, data on world production are reasonably accurate for the earlier periods covered here.[18] The production data show the response to three major swings in the value of gold since the 1870's: the worldwide decline in prices after 1873, the rise after 1896 until 1920, and the sharp decline together with currency devaluations of the early 1930's. World gold output reacted with varying lags to each of the swings in the expected way and in amounts that towered over the magnitude of its short-run fluctuations and of its long-run changes in other periods.

The U.S. gold stock reflects not only world production but also comparative national price levels and other factors. The effect on it of changes in the value of gold is complicated and seems difficult to quantify. Simple correlation of the two series would not clarify the relation and for that reason has not been computed. Lack of easy quantification, however, should not lessen our recognition of the importance of these effects.

---

[17] It should be noted that the positive lagged relation between the two series in Chart 5 tends to be obscured by a strong inverse relation concurrently. The latter reflects the entirely separate effect of changes in the gold stock acting through the money stock on prices, discussed in Chapter 6.

[18] See G. Warren and F. Pearson, *Gold and Prices*, New York, Wiley, 1935, p. 121; and *Banking and Monetary Statistics*. For estimates of recent years, see W. J. Busschau, "Some Notes on Gold Production and Stocks," appendix paper to *Shall We Return to a Gold Standard Now?*, New York, National Industrial Conference Board, Studies in Business Economics No. 43, 1954.

FEDERAL RESERVE CREDIT OUTSTANDING

Unlike changes in the gold stock, changes in Federal Reserve credit outstanding cannot be associated with a short list of economic variables, for they reflect the policies of the Federal Reserve System. The policy followed at any time conceivably may link the changes in credit to particular variables, but the basis of the link will disappear when the policy is altered. When the currency is convertible into gold, at least for foreign payments, the quantity of Reserve credit outstanding will in the long run be related to the domestic gold stock. Nevertheless, the relation can be far from firm, even practically nonexistent for long periods, as in the interwar period, when the disruptions of war and depression led governments to interfere with the normal operation of the gold-standard mechanism. Thanks to an accumulation of sizable excess gold reserves during and after World War I, the Federal Reserve Board acquired great leeway in pursuing policies without regard for gold flows.

How, under those circumstances, is one to describe and interpret the Reserve System's behavior? It might at first seem sensible to suppose that the proper operation of a central bank is to produce a constant rate of growth of its credit outstanding; one might then compare the actual growth with the standard. But the Board could not and did not disregard changes in other components of high-powered money, in other determinants of the money stock, and developments in the economy at large. A policy aimed at producing a constant rate of growth of the money stock (never, of course, adopted) might or might not have been proper, but certainly a policy with that aim for Federal Reserve credit outstanding or total high-powered money would not have been. Indeed, the multitude of factors by which central bankers may be guided makes interpretation of their actions difficult, and their pronouncements have been far from explicit. There is a danger of imagining elaborate policies where none existed. Moreover, for many of the years before World War II, one is impressed with how often short-run exigencies seemed to displace longer-range considerations. In any event, the time series for Federal Reserve credit outstanding in Chart 3 is volatile and, taken in the abstract, seemingly void of any pattern that would relate it to a few other economic variables; the series only "comes to life" if we place each

movement in its historical setting. Inasmuch as many such discussions
are available elsewhere,[19] this section briefly reviews the major
developments.

The Federal Reserve System was established to prevent banking
panics like that of 1907. Designed to provide a source of emergency
reserves for commercial banks in times of stress, the System proved its
importance during its first years in this respect, but for an unexpected
purpose: to supply the wartime demand for credit which developed
soon after the Reserve Banks were organized. Their discounts created
high-powered reserves for the banking system. In 1917, Federal
Reserve credit supplemented gold inflows in expanding bank reserves
and, for the next three years, when gold was being exported, continued
the reserve expansion. The Reserve Banks did not, it should be noted,
directly finance much of the government's wartime budget deficit,
which was almost wholly covered instead by sale of U.S. bonds to
commercial banks and the public. But the Reserve Banks prevented
a large rise in the cost of borrowed money by keeping their discount
rates low and supplying at those rates most of the credit demanded.
In that way, they expanded the quantity of high-powered money
available to commercial banks for loans to businesses as well as for
investment in U.S. bonds.

For a little over a year after the end of the war the government's
war-connected expenses continued and were met by issuing short-term
certificates at low rates. The Federal Reserve Board hesitated to hinder
the Treasury's financing and did not restrict credit. Although many
people expected that the high prices of 1918 would collapse immediately after the war, there was no major decline; readjustment
to consumer-goods production was exceedingly quick, and the wartime
boom resumed. At the end of 1919, with most of the Treasury's short-
term borrowing needs out of the way, discount rates were raised to
encourage liquidation of the credit previously extended and to halt
the fall in the Reserve Banks' gold-reserve ratio. Federal Reserve
credit outstanding was nevertheless stable throughout most of 1920
and did not begin to decline until the end of that year; then it fell
drastically. The business contraction, which started a few months
after the rise in rates, reduced the demand for loans and hastened the

[19] See in particular the relevant chapters of Friedman and Schwartz, *A Monetary
History.*

subsequent liquidation of credit. The decline in business, while comparatively short, was deep.

Between the contraction of Federal Reserve credit outstanding in 1921–22 and the advent of World War II, the quantity underwent comparatively moderate cyclical fluctuations, with but one exception: a sharp increase to offset an outflow of gold in the international disturbance of 1931. Following the British suspension of convertibility on September 21, 1931, holders of dollar funds converted them into foreign exchange at a rapid rate in expectation of a similar action by the U.S. government. Most of the resulting gold outflow occurred in September and October. The Reserve Banks more than offset that loss by an expansion of credit over the fiscal year 1932 as a whole, shown in Chart 3, though not before first contracting credit sharply from November 1931 through March 1932. The contraction of credit was motivated by fear that gold reserves might otherwise fall below legal requirements and lead to suspension—apparently considered worse than the action taken.

The significance of the absence of large increases in Federal Reserve credit outstanding during the 1920's is that the Reserve Banks were not using the excess gold reserves built up during World War I to increase high-powered money outstanding. Furthermore, because of the apparently temporary nature of the large increases in the gold stock during the postwar years 1921–24, it seemed proper to prevent those flows from expanding high-powered money. They did so by offsetting decreases in Reserve Bank credit outstanding. The Reserve Banks had the resources to spare the economy the inconvenience of short-run adjustments whenever possible, and judicious management of those resources for the general welfare seemed to call for an offset to such disturbances. In some degree, too, the Reserve Board was probably sensitive to charges that it had fostered inflation by its willingness to serve the wartime financial needs of the Treasury, and it was in no mood to accept the ordinary consequences of gold flows.[20] Having accumulated excess gold reserves, the Reserve Banks could then offset outflows without encroaching upon their statutory reserve requirements. The increases in Reserve credit outstanding in

---

[20] The Board was not perturbed by the mild contractions in prices during the 1920's, even though it had been criticized severely for its part in the 1921 deflation (see H. L. Reed, *Federal Reserve Policy, 1921–1930*, New York, McGraw-Hill, 1930, pp. 31–32).

1925 and 1928, for example, almost wholly counteracted concurrent losses of gold. Nevertheless, losses were temporary during that period and were never, contrary to earlier expectations, very large, thanks in part to the continued overvaluation of the British pound and to the Reserve System's earlier policy of offsetting gold inflows. The policy worked effectively to suppress the equilibrating mechanism that would ordinarily have tended to diminish or even reverse the prevailing forces responsible for bringing gold from abroad. Because of that policy and difficulties abroad, the System had to cope mainly with embarrassing increases in the gold stock. The widely discussed decision to dampen speculation by tightening credit during the stock market boom of 1929, which shows up in a decline in high-powered money in Chart 3 for fiscal years 1929–30, required steps to counteract a sizable increase in the gold stock.

When, after 1933, gold-stock increases became enormous, the Reserve Banks allowed the increases to expand high-powered money. Although the expansion seemed desirable in view of the low state of business activity, its size soon caused concern, and in 1936–37 reserve requirements of member banks were raised to prevent possible inflationary expansion of bank loans (discussed in Chapter 5). Substantial reductions in Federal Reserve credit outstanding to offset the gold stock increases were not made, however. Instead, the Treasury sterilized the gold flows by selling bonds (discussed later under Treasury Operations).

The increases in the gold stock, at first accelerated by the unsettling events following the outbreak of World War II in Europe, were interrupted upon United States involvement. The expansion of high-powered money nevertheless continued, though the source now became Federal Reserve credit instead of changes in the gold stock. With the prospect of deficit financing by sale of government bonds, the Treasury and the Federal Reserve agreed in early 1942 that the prevailing level of interest rates, by any standard extremely low, was high enough for the government's borrowing costs. So the country waged the war at $2\frac{1}{2}$ per cent—that is, the longest-term government securities paid that rate; shorter-term, correspondingly less. Naturally, since the Treasury could not be expected to raise all the funds it needed at those rates, the Federal Reserve had in effect committed itself to make up the difference by standing ready to buy all U.S. securities offered at the agreed prices. As fully expected, those prices, which reflected interest rates reached after a decade of depression, offered yields below "the market" in the wartime years of full activity, and the Reserve Banks had to buy in heavy volume.

Yet, this episode compares favorably with that during World War I in terms of percentage increases in high-powered money. In 1917–18 the average increase per year was 21 per cent, and in 1942–45 it was 16 per cent. The direction of the difference is surprising, because the average annual federal deficit was three times as large in proportion to national income during the second war as it was during the first. Also, in the first war, U.S. bonds paid a higher rate of interest. Of the many circumstances that may be adduced to explain the difference, two seem especially important.

First, commercial banks at the start of the second war had huge usable reserves (that is, high-powered reserves above legally required amounts), which allowed banks to create, as they did, a multiple expansion of credit to purchase government bonds. From December 1940 to December 1945, of $80 billion of earning assets commercial banks added to their portfolios, about $46 billion was accounted for by the investment of usable reserves held at the beginning of the period.[21] Thus, 57.5 per cent of the increase in portfolios represented investment of usable reserves, the other remaining 42.5 per cent, investment of increases in high-powered reserves. By comparison, just before and during World War I, usable reserves were relatively low.

Second, the percentage increase per year in Federal Reserve credit outstanding was much less during the second than the first war despite the bond supports in the second. There may have been a special reason for the public's willingness to acquire and hold U.S. bonds off the market at low yields, mentioned later.

With the end of the war and of large Treasury deficits, the Federal

[21] This figure is derived by dividing usable reserves invested over the period by the total reserve ratio at the end of the period. Table F-10 shows that the total reserve ratio dropped 14.3 percentage points over the period and stood at 15.9 per cent at the end of the period. (The required reserve ratio for both member and other commercial banks was approximately the same at the end as at the beginning of the period, and so the drop in the total ratio approximates that in the usable ratio.) Table F-8 (cols. 6 and 8) shows deposits to be $51.2 billion at the beginning of the period. Hence, the amount of reserves invested by the end of the period equaled approximately $46 billion ($51.2 billion $\times$ 0.143/0.159).

Reserve Banks did not abandon the bond-support program, though several minor adjustments were allowed in the pattern of interest rates. Such continued interference with the security markets was unprecedented for peacetime. Reasons given to justify it reflected in part the desire of the government to keep down the interest burden of the federal debt and in part the belief that low interest rates would promote full employment. The deflationary aftermath of World War I and the protracted unemployment of the 1930's were still vivid memories, and measures to prevent a recurrence of such conditions seemed more important than restraint by the Federal Reserve on the postwar rise in commodity prices. Standing ready to accept all U.S. bonds at the supported price, the Reserve Banks could not, of course, also sell them in sufficient volume to restrict credit effectively.

The Reserve Banks were able, nonetheless, to make moderate reductions in their credit outstanding from mid-1946 to mid-1950, enough at least to offset concurrent additions to the gold stock and to hold the growth of high-powered money to a low rate (in fiscal year 1950, negative). That was accomplished, of course, only because holders of U.S. securities did not choose to cash in at the support prices, though it is not clear why: whether the low yields were actually competitive with the going return on alternative investments, taking into account the risk differential; or whether the guaranteed stability in selling price made U.S. bonds almost equivalent to money and thus justified their low yields by endowing them with qualities not possessed by alternative investments. Of the two alternative explanations, the second is likely to have been more important. Without the transformation of U.S. interest-bearing debt into a near money, their yields were likely to have been too low for the amount outstanding, in which case the Reserve Banks would have been obliged to buy heavily.

The dangers to monetary stability that many feared from the bond-support program arose suddenly when war erupted in Korea in June 1950, and the Reserve Banks had to underwrite an inflationary upsurge of bank credit. The consequences of the commitment to low interest rates are shown by the sharp rise in Reserve credit outstanding. For fiscal year 1951, the amount increased over $5 billion, most of which can be ascribed to the sale of U.S. securities by commercial banks. High-powered reserves so supplied to commercial banks amounted to almost one-third of the June 1950 level of their reserves, although the actual increase in reserves was considerably less because of an outflow of gold at the same time.

Those events apparently crystallized a growing dissatisfaction among Federal Reserve officials with the bond-support program, for in March 1951 they reached an "Accord" with the Treasury not to guarantee the support of U.S. bond prices, though an explicit announcement that the support program had ended was not made for another two years. The declining rate of growth of high-powered money thereafter reflects the application by the Reserve Banks of increasing restraint on monetary expansion. The policy helped achieve a roughly constant level of prices from 1952 through 1955. Federal Reserve officials were able to devote their full powers to the avowed pursuit of economic stability more or less unhindered by obligations to accommodate the credit "needs" of business and agriculture, as during the 1920's; by heavy gold flows, as during the 1930's; or by large Treasury deficits, as during both world wars.

SILVER PURCHASES

Many countries not on a silver standard make regular purchases of silver bullion for coinage; annual amounts of coins issued are typically a small fraction of the total money stock and are determined by the public's demand for them. In the United States which, since 1873, has not been on a formal bimetallic standard, such purchases have been expanded several times with the intention of raising the general price level by issue of large quantities of silver coins or paper "silver certificates" with silver bullion as backing. The required legislation has received support in Congress, usually in periods of deflation, from representatives of agricultural and silver-producing states. The effect of the silver-purchase acts was, therefore, an early counterpart on a smaller scale of recession deficits in recent decades.[22] The "silver issue" in American politics erupted for the first time in the latter 1870's and resulted in the passage of the Bland-Allison Silver Purchase Act of 1878. In 1873, Congress had discontinued the free coinage of silver dollars[23] (except for the little-used "trade dollars" for export)

---

[22] On the origin of silver-purchase legislation, see A. D. Noyes, *Forty Years of American Finance*, New York, Putnam, 1909, pp. 6–7, 35–38.

[23] Though purchase of small amounts of silver for fractional coinage continued, in particular to replace the fractional paper currency ("shinplasters") issued during the Civil War.

with not a murmur of dissent. It was three years later, in the midst of the 1873–79 depression that the action was branded the "crime of '73." U.S. prices had started to decline following the Civil War and continued to decline with preparations for resumption in 1879 and thereafter with a secular decline in world prices lasting until the mid-1890's. As already suggested, the growth of world trade and of gold use was outpacing the growth of the world gold stock and so was depressing price levels. Political leaders of western agricultural states joined forces with those of silver-producing states and territories— which had witnessed a fall of the price of silver to lower and lower levels at a time when several rich strikes were adding to its domestic output—to advocate a return to the free coinage of silver. Arresting the decline in the price of silver became the panacea for reversing the decline in all prices—a forlorn hope so long as the gold standard was maintained. Most of the silver supporters proposed, in effect, abandoning the gold standard, but the most they ever achieved was to require the Treasury to purchase silver. The only beneficiaries of the legislation were owners of silver mines.

The contribution of those purchases to the growth of high-powered money is shown in Chart 3. Under the provisions of the Bland-Allison Act, the Treasury began in March 1878 to purchase about $2 million of silver bullion a month, which slightly increased the rate of purchases for fractional coinage previously made under prior acts (in 1873, 1875, and 1876), by then tapering off. The silver movement reached its high point with the passage of the Sherman Act in 1890, which required the Treasury approximately to double its silver purchases. About the same time, the secular decline in world prices resulted in a series of large gold outflows from this country, intensified perhaps by uncertainty over future U.S. monetary policies raised by the silver issue. The decline in the Treasury's gold reserve, combined with its forced purchases of silver, proved such a threat to the continued convertibility of currency into gold that the Sherman Act was repealed in 1893, despite strong opposition by the silver forces. The repeal fanned the political fire, which blazed up during the tense Presidential election of 1896, in which the unsuccessful candidate, William Jennings Bryan, ran on a platform of unlimited free coinage of silver. Though Bryan ran again in 1900 for the Presidency on the same platform, the issue no longer agitated the nation, because events provided another solution: U.S. prices began a secular rise in 1897, following an earlier upturn in world prices, which lasted for a decade or more.

After 1893, the only silver purchases other than those for fractional coinage were made just after World War I, and then again beginning in 1934 in order to inflate the money stock—but again with the chief result of subsidizing silver production.[24] The latter purchases were fairly large until 1936 but then gradually lost importance as a percentage of high-powered money and became negligible after 1942.[25]

Aside from the direct monetary effects of silver purchases on the growth of high-powered money, they are also alleged to have impaired confidence in the dollar in the 1890's. If so, the purchases would have induced conversions of paper to gold currency, both internally and abroad, and would have contributed far more, in this way than through direct effects, to the Treasury's difficulties in maintaining the necessary gold reserve for convertibility. It seems reasonable to expect such indirect effects, and historians have unreservedly proffered this thesis with the companion implication that dishoarding of gold after Bryan's defeat greatly augmented the Treasury's reserve.[26] It is not so clear, however, how important the indirect effects were. They may have played a part in net capital imports declining and becoming net exports during the 1890's; the frequent and unfavorable comment on the silver issue in the English press is partial evidence of such an effect. There were other factors, however, which encourged a withdrawal of foreign funds, such as the blow to investors' confidence in foreign securities stemming from the Baring crisis in 1890. Furthermore, the net capital flow was outward from the United States, though declining in amount, until well after 1900, whereas the silver issue had lost importance long before. While dollar securities must have been looked upon abroad as entailing some risk of inconvertibility into gold, the size of the effect on foreign investment is unknown.[27]

---

[24] Also, sale of silver from Treasury holdings was authorized for special purposes during the two world wars.

[25] In 1963, with the open market price of silver rising, Congress repealed the silver-purchase legislation on the books since the 1930's, apparently ending a long—and costly—chapter of U.S. financial history.

[26] See, for example, D. R. Dewey, *Financial History of the United States*, New York, Longmans, 1931, p. 454; and E. W. Kemmerer, *Money: The Principles of Money and Their Exemplification*, New York, Macmillan, 1938, p. 391.

[27] For a detailed discussion, see Friedman and Schwartz, *A Monetary History*, Chap. 3.

Was there, in addition, an internal drain on the Treasury's gold reserve reflecting domestic concern over the future of the dollar? The data I have examined give evidence of such a drain but not in the way usually implied. Banks and not the public were responsible for the drain. Consider first the hoarding of gold outside banks. The ratio of gold coin and certificates to currency (including gold) held by the public actually declined from around 22 per cent in early 1890 to 19 per cent in July 1893; then, as a result of the banking panic in that year, it rose to about 25 per cent by February 1894; thereafter it declined slowly. It rose from 20.7 to 21.2 per cent from July to October of 1896, which drained about $5 million from the Treasury's gold reserve, an amount almost indistinguishable from a seasonal movement;[28] the ratio remained practically constant during the year following Bryan's defeat. According to these figures, therefore, public hoarding of gold began after the Sherman Act had been in effect for over two years and was moderate during the election campaign of 1896; nor did the public dishoard gold after the election.

The Treasury's gold reserve declined steadily after 1889, most of what it lost going abroad or to national banks. The ratio of gold specie to total vault cash of national banks rose from an average level of 27 per cent before 1892 to nearly 40 per cent by 1895–96. Although most of the increase came before repeal of the Sherman Act, the ratio continued to rise throughout 1894 and then held just under the 40 per cent level, not increasing at all during the agitation of 1896. After the defeat of Bryan, the ratio did not fall—as often implied—but rose sharply during 1897, probably because of the large gold inflows beginning in that year. The increased gold holdings before 1895 undoubtedly reflected speculation by banks on a rise in the price of

---

[28] These figures include the gold holdings of the public plus nonnational banks. It is clear, however, that those banks held relatively little, though the exact amounts are not available (see data on reporting nonnational banks in the *Annual Report* of the Comptroller of the Currency).

There is evidence of a short-lived decline of confidence in the dollar during July 1896, following Bryan's nomination. The Treasury's gold reserve fell over $10 million during the first three weeks of that month. Most of the gold went abroad. By the end of the month the reserve stood higher than at the beginning, however, helped by a transfer of gold from banks and the organization of a private exchange pool to prevent further outflows, both at the request of the government, and by a growing belief that Bryan would not win (see M. Simon, "The Hot Money Movement and the Private Exchange Pool Proposal of 1896," *Journal of Economic History*, Mar. 1960, pp. 31–50).

gold, which would occur if the Treasury suspended convertibility, though it is not clear why banks rather than the public should speculate. Banks had nothing to lose from suspension and no more to gain than the public had.[29] They were apparently not operating on behalf of their depositors, since there is no indication that the acceptance of deposits payable in gold, discontinued in 1879, was revived.[30] In any event, national banks accumulated about $50 million of gold specie from 1892 to 1894, the approximate amount of the maximum fall of the Treasury's reserve below the desired level of $100 million during that period.

Fears of currency depreciation may have been responsible for a rise in the average yield on currency bonds in 1896 compared with that on gold bonds, though the difference was only about three-tenths of a percentage point.[31] Very likely, the psychological effects of the silver agitation were not, therefore, negligible, though claims of gold hoarding by the public seem exaggerated. The data indicate, as noted above, that the decline in the Treasury's reserve can be attributed to the accumulation of gold by national banks.

TREASURY OPERATIONS, EXCLUDING
SILVER PURCHASES

These operations have generally not been used as an instrument of monetary policy in the customary sense of that term. The Treasury has seldom produced changes in high-powered money for monetary purposes. It has no mandate from Congress and used to have little

[29] Nevertheless, banks had begun to insert gold clauses in notes and mortgages in the early 1890's.

[30] An article in the New York *Tribune* (Feb. 11, 1893) states: "At some of the banks it was learned that inquiries had been made in regard to the withdrawal of depositors' balances in gold." The article then lists the rules adopted by the New York Clearing House Association on Nov. 11, 1878, prohibiting gold deposits after Dec. 31, 1878. It continues: "bankers . . . stated to the persons making the inquiries that under the rules of the Clearing House they were prohibited from opening gold accounts, and as the New York banks generally loan their money repayable in funds current at the New York Clearing House, they would expect to pay their depositors in kind. It is understood that the banks will generally take this stand."

[31] Based on my comparison of currency and gold railroad bonds (from F. R. Macauley, *Some Theoretical Problems Suggested by The Movements of Interest Rates, Bond Yields and Stock Prices*, New York, NBER, 1938, Table 1 and p. A68). Average yields on currency bonds fell by four-tenths of a percentage point from Sept. 1896 to Jan. 1897, and average yields on gold bonds fell one-tenth of a point, a difference of three-tenths of a point suggesting that the comparative yields on currency bonds had increased by that amount before Bryan's defeat in November.

flexibility in its financial operations to change the money stock. Moreover, Congress has specifically authorized the issue of each kind of currency. The only discretion the Treasury has had over amounts issued are special cases. During the Civil War, Congress authorized issue of greenbacks, within certain limits, and minor amounts of various other circulating notes as needed for expenses. The various silver purchase acts permitted the Treasury to issue silver dollars or certificates on the basis of seigniorage, that is, the profit in purchasing silver at a price lower than its value when coined.[32] The Thomas Amendment to the Farm Relief Act of 1933 authorized issue of up to $3 billion of greenbacks to retire U.S. debt outstanding, but none were ever issued and the authority was rescinded by the act of June 12, 1945. Otherwise, the Treasury, in terms of its monetary effects, has mostly functioned as a currency exchange, converting coins and paper bills on demand and issuing gold or silver dollars and certificates on the basis of its purchases of gold and silver bullion. To be sure, the Treasury is not specifically required to reissue currency when paid in, although Congress has restricted the legal retirement of certain currencies.[33] Budget surpluses or bond sales might have been used to

[32] In Chart 3 such issues are covered by Treasury operations, excluding silver; the series for silver purchases includes only their cost. Before 1934, seigniorage, after deduction of certain mint costs, has been included by Treasury accounting practice in budget receipts, the official figures for which are used in Table F-5. The table therefore understates the contribution of the budget to high-powered money (because seigniorage as received does not reduce high-powered money outstanding; when spent, usually not in the year acquired, seigniorage finances budget expenditures from the issue of new money). The table also overstates correspondingly the contribution of the residual item, miscellaneous accounts. The amounts of seigniorage have not been insignificant: under the Bland-Allison Act it was $68.6 million and under the Sherman Act, $64.3 million (see *Annual Report* of the Director of the Mint, 1906, pp. 77–78). Seigniorage from purchases under the Silver Purchase Act of 1934 has not been included in regular budget receipts (see *Annual Report* of the Secretary of the Treasury, 1935, p. 264). Sales have apparently been treated in a comparable manner. On the treatment of seigniorage, see Johnson, *The Treasury and Monetary Policy*, pp. 179–80; and D. H. Leavens, *Silver Money*, Bloomington, 1939, pp. 270–281.

[33] One example is the repeal in 1878 of the provision of the Resumption Act calling for limited retirement of greenbacks. Their circulation is still set by law at the quantity then outstanding—$346,681,016. The other examples are the Sherman Act which, until its repeal, prohibited legal retirement of Treasury notes of 1890 issued in payment for the silver purchases prescribed by the Act; and the Silver Purchase Act of 1934, which required issue of silver certificates in an amount not less than the cost of silver purchased. Those acts allowed but did not require, except the act of 1878 which did, that the notes or certificates actually be reissued when paid into the Treasury. A restriction on reissuing notes was imposed by the act of 1900, which provided that, should the Treasury's gold reserve fall below $150 million, notes presented for redemption thereafter must not be reissued until the reserve again reached that level.

withdraw Treasury currency from circulation, but such use has occurred on only three occasions, discussed below. Consequently, Treasury operations have not in the long run made a significant contribution to high-powered money. Table 10 shows their annual fluctuations also tend in most short-run periods to average close to zero.

There are only four instances of importance since 1875 in which Treasury operations, excluding silver purchases, were used as an instrument of monetary policy to affect high-powered money: (1) preparations for resumption of specie payments in 1875–79; (2) sale of bonds to augment the Treasury's gold reserve in 1895–96; (3) support of New York banks during seasonal and cyclical stringencies of credit from around 1900 to World War I; and (4) gold sterilization during 1936–38. In other years, those operations produced more or less random effects on high-powered money, as Chart 3 suggests, though monthly data, not derived, might reveal seasonal or cyclical patterns arising from the nature of Treasury budget receipts and other operations. We may look more closely at the four operations just listed.

1. During 1877–78, in order to build up its gold reserve before resumption of specie payments at the start of 1879, the Treasury sold bonds as authorized by the Resumption Act of 1875. The sources of change in high-powered money show the arithmetic of those preparations. Chart 3 and Table F-5 were derived on a fiscal-year basis, however, and need to be supplemented. In the second half of fiscal 1879, after preparations for resumption had been completed and specie payments begun, other large operations of the Treasury swamped the results of its actions before resumption. In particular, the Treasury continued refunding its war-incurred debt on a large scale after 1879, which explains the large increase in its deposits at commercial banks for that fiscal year (see Table F-5), most of which came after the end of 1878 and had nothing to do with resumption. The sources have been estimated, therefore, for the first half of fiscal 1879. Combined with figures for the preceding fiscal years back to June 1875, they are shown in Table 12.

During that period, the Treasury sold bonds for $118 million, though only $95.5 million was used specifically for purchasing gold,[34] the remainder having been issued in connection with refunding

[34] *Annual Report on the Finances*, Secretary of the Treasury, 1878, p. ix.

operations. The Treasury's gold reserve (not shown in the table) rose to $135.4 million at the end of 1878, an increase of $81.7 million over its holdings on June 30, 1875.[35] As the figures imply, about $14 million of the gold purchased was paid out again (before resumption, the Treasury was obligated to pay the interest on its bonds in gold). Bond sales provided half of the Treasury's contractionary influence on high-powered money; a budget surplus of $94 million provided the other half. The surplus and the bond sales totalled $212 million,

TABLE 12

SOURCES OF CHANGE IN HIGH-POWERED MONEY,
JUNE 30, 1875, THROUGH DECEMBER 31, 1878
(millions of dollars)

			Treasury Operations					
Total	Monetary Gold Stock	Silver Purchases	Total, Excluding Silver	Budget	Debt	Deposits at Banks	Miscel- laneous Accounts	National Bank Notes
-26	106	54	-166	-94	-118	38	8	-20

Source: Table F-5, except for June to Dec. 1878, which was derived from the same sources as the earlier figures were. Premiums received over par value of bonds sold, which are counted as a budget item in Table F-5, are here excluded from the budget and put into the debt account.

part of it absorbed by increases of Treasury deposits at banks and by changes in miscellaneous accounts, leaving the net effect on high-powered money at $166 million. Of this, silver purchases absorbed $54 million. Another $106 million purchased newly-mined and imported gold (as shown by the gold stock increase). While those purchases augmented the Treasury's reserve, they did not affect high-powered money outstanding because most of the bond sales "sterilized" the increase in the gold stock. The net remainder of Treasury operations, totaling $6 million, retired that amount of U.S. currency, which would have comprised the total reduction in high-powered money if national banks had not also retired $20 million of notes.

What the change in high-powered money would have been had the Treasury done nothing is not clear. While its contractionary

[35] *Ibid.*, 1899, p. 42; and *Annual Report*, Director of the Mint, 1907, p. 87. The net reserve at the end of 1878, that is, after deducting the quantity of gold certificates outstanding ("warehouse receipts" for gold), was $114 million and increased $77 million over the period.

influence equalled $166 million, the gold stock rose $106 million, owing in part to the Treasury's direct purchases abroad. No doubt part of the increase would have occurred anyway. Hence, if Treasury operations (excluding silver) had averaged zero, the change in high-powered money would have been augmented by at least $60 million (assuming also no change in the gold stock) and perhaps by as much as $166 million (assuming the same increase in the gold stock). On the basis of the actual quantity of high-powered money and the levels of the currency and reserve ratios at the end of 1878, this means that the money stock would have been higher by 8 to 22 per cent, if the Treasury had not acted. If the price level had been that much higher (that is, assuming the level of economic activity and the velocity of money had been the same), resumption would have been a much more precarious undertaking. In short, the Treasury's operations were not a negligible factor in the monetary adjustments of that period.[36]

2. By fiscal 1895 the Treasury's free gold reserve (that is, excluding a 100 per cent reserve for the small amount of gold certificates outstanding) had shrunk to an average end-of-month level of $89 million and threatened to fall further. Although the silver purchase clause of the Sherman Act had been repealed in 1893, further balance-of-payments deficits appeared likely in view of the declining level of prices abroad. A free gold reserve of $100 million had been considered the minimum required, and the fall below that figure was thought to undermine confidence in the government's ability to maintain convertibility and thus to intensify the drain on the reserve. Since the cash budget began to run a sizable deficit in fiscal 1894, the only way to acquire gold was to sell bonds. The Treasury had sold $59 million of bonds[37] in early 1894, but it had not even covered the budget deficit in that fiscal year, though Treasury operations (excluding silver) as a whole had slightly reduced high-powered money by virtue of changes in miscellaneous accounts. Inflationists in Congress controverted the legality of the bond sales, since the Resumption Act of 1875 did not give the Treasury specific authority to sell bonds after specie

---

[36] See also James Kindahl, "Economic Factors in Specie Resumption: The United States, 1865–79," *Journal of Political Economy*, Feb. 1961, pp. 30–48; and Friedman and Schwartz, *A Monetary History*, Chap. 2.

[37] Figures on bond sales quoted in this section include a premium over the par value of the bonds sold, which in Table F-5 is included in budget receipts in accordance with Treasury accounting practice.

payments were resumed in 1879. The courts effectively settled the issue by upholding their legality. Another sale of bonds was made in the autumn of 1894, which raised about the same amount of money as the preceding issue had and was equally unsuccessful in building up the gold reserve. The government nevertheless persisted in its course; in early 1895, selling $65 million to a syndicate on stiff terms[38]—to the indignation of the inflationists in Congress—and a year later, $111 million on open subscription. Aided by a decline in the budget deficit and, as related earlier, a general rise in world gold production, the sales raised the Treasury's gold reserve. Thereafter, the reserve generally rose, except during July 1896, through substantial inflows of gold.

The government was preoccupied with replenishing its gold reserve, but its success in stopping further drains largely depended on reducing high-powered money. Normally, the two objectives are accomplished together—selling bonds for gold to domestic buyers also retires high-powered money. To the degree that foreign buyers take the bonds, however, high-powered money is not changed, since the effect of the operation is cancelled, other things the same, by an induced importation of gold in payment for the bonds. In fiscal 1894, as noted, bond sales fell short of the budget deficit, though total Treasury operations (excluding silver) absorbed $4 million of high-powered money. Yet, as a result of concurrent silver purchases, issues of national bank notes, and gold inflows, high-powered money expanded $50 million or 3.3 per cent. In contrast, bond sales of $234 million in the following two fiscal years far exceeded a budget deficit of $67 million, and total Treasury operations (excluding silver) took $152 million of high-powered money out of circulation. Largely for these reasons, but also because of a gold outflow and despite issues of national bank notes, the total reduction in high-powered money was $170 million or 11 per cent.

The reduction was only a little more than the amount of silver purchased in the four preceding fiscal years, 1891–94,[39] and might well have been avoided in the absence of those purchases, not to

---

[38] See Noyes, *Forty Years*, Chap. X.

[39] Silver purchases in those years totalled $158.9 million (the figures in Table F-5 add to $160 million because of rounding errors), of which $3.0 million represented purchases under authority of the Bland-Allison Act of 1878, and $155.9 million, under the Sherman Act.

mention any capital exports produced by the accompanying agitation over silver.

3. In order to safeguard the public moneys, federal law circumscribes the uses and movements of Treasury funds. The Treasury's ability to change the amount of high-powered money outstanding for purposes of moderating short-run disturbances of its own or others' making in the money market is limited and was strictly so before World War I. Today, the Treasury may shift its cash holdings as desired from its vaults to commercial bank depositories (though in practice, seldom does) or may issue and retire short-term securities in order to forestall random disturbances in the money stock. Such use of short-term debt did not develop until World War I, however, and before 1907 depositing Treasury funds at banks was circumscribed by the Independent Treasury Act of 1846. To use long-term bonds for such short-run purposes was too cumbersome. Moreover, issue of long terms for other purposes than to acquire or augment the gold reserve might not have been legal; in any case, there was certainly no precedent or Congressional intent before 1907 to justify purchase or sale for other purposes. The Treasury could delay calling funds paid over by the public to Treasury accounts in national banks—a long-time practice following new bond issues, which avoided sudden large reductions in high-powered money outstanding. The Treasury could not legally increase high-powered money by depositing currency on hand at banks. Yet in 1902 and later and to some extent even before, the Treasury increased and withdrew U.S. deposits held at banks in order to alleviate periodic stringencies in the money market,[40] though wide publicity was first given to the actions of Secretary Shaw in the early 1900's. Along with his two predecessors, Shaw viewed the Treasury as having great potentiality for such purposes. He employed various devices to preserve the legality of his actions, and Congress later specifically authorized such transfers in the act of March 4, 1907.

The effect on high-powered money of those operations was too short lived to be seen in the annual data of Chart 3. They are analyzed in detail later in terms of their effect on bank reserves (see Chapter 5, section 3).

[40] On that development, see Margaret G. Myers, *The New York Money Market*, New York, Columbia University Press, 1931, Vol. I, pp. 381–390; and Esther R. Taus, *Central Banking Functions of the United States Treasury, 1789–1941*, New York, Columbia, 1943, pp. 97–128; and Friedman and Schwartz, *A Monetary History*, Chap. 4.

4. Following the official devaluation of the dollar in 1934, the gold stock increased enormously and almost continuously until 1941. By 1936 the government became alarmed over the inflationary potentialities of the large rise in bank reserves and decided to prevent further inflows from expanding the monetary base. The only way, except by appreciation of the dollar, was to issue bonds to pay for the the gold acquired, referred to since as the sterilization of gold.

Beginning with December 24, 1936, all increases in the gold stock for the remainder of the fiscal year were sterilized—a little over $1 billion.[41] In the following fiscal year, upon recommendation of the Board of Governors of the Federal Reserve System, the Treasury helped to ease monetary conditions by paying out some of the gold previously sterilized and using the proceeds to retire an equal amount of bonds. Economic activity was on the downgrade at that time, and a stimulus to monetary expansion was desired. In April 1938, with business still depressed, all the remaining gold previously sterilized was desterilized and the program abandoned. For fiscal year 1938 as a whole, therefore, there was a net addition to high-powered money from that operation in an amount equal to the previous fiscal year's sterilization of gold.[42] The net effect of Treasury operations on high-powered money was negative in fiscal year 1937 and positive in fiscal 1938, but only by half the amount of the changes in the Treasury's inactive gold account (where the sterilized gold was recorded) because of offsetting changes in other Treasury operations.

The four instances described cover the main contributions to high-powered money of Treasury operations (excluding silver) that had a monetary purpose. In assessing the importance of Treasury operations, we should not overlook their effect on expectations, however intangible and elusive it may be. The first two of those incidents showed that Treasury operations could be decisive in making possible resumption and maintenance of convertibility. The Department usually displayed determination to act when necessary, which helped engender expectations of continued convertibility with the effect of smoothing out

---

[41] Through sale of bonds by the Treasury, not the Federal Reserve Banks, which it was felt did not hold sufficient bonds to undertake the operation. The Gold Reserve Act of 1934 gave the Treasury authority to finance gold purchases with bonds, should there persist any doubt whether it had that authority under prior legislation.

[42] In Table F-5, the issue and retirement of the sterilization bonds are included in the debt account.

minor fluctuations in the balance of payments. The importance of such expectations is illustrated by what happened in the first half of the 1890's, when doubts arose over the government's determination to stay on gold, and adverse expectations seem to have augmented the drain on the Treasury's gold reserve (though not as a result of flows to the public, as we found earlier). At other times in the pre-1914 period, the widespread assumption that convertibility could be relied upon may largely account for the smooth operation—mysteriously smooth, from a post-World War I perspective—of the gold-standard mechanism.

NATIONAL BANK NOTES

The stated chief purpose of the National Currency Act of 1863 and as amended in 1864 was to give nationally chartered banks authority to issue paper currency—national bank notes—and to set up arrangements for their backing and redemption, by which the government in effect guaranteed their full convertibility into Treasury currency. The act, as amended, limited note issues of individual national banks in two ways: first, to 90 per cent of their paid-in capital stock;[43] and second, to 90 per cent of the par or market value—whichever was lower—of certain U.S. bonds the banks were required to purchase on the open market and deposit with the Treasury as collateral for note issues. The act of 1900 changed those provisions to allow issues up to 100 per cent of the paid-in capital and of the par or market value of the bonds purchased.

The National Currency Act also restricted the aggregate amount of notes issued by national banks and apportioned the issue rights among individual banks according to state population, location, and certain characteristics of those banks. That provision was swept aside by the Resumption Act of 1875. The quantity of notes outstanding after 1875 therefore depended on their profitability under the capital limitations described in the preceding paragraph. Congress clearly intended the notes to provide a steadily growing quantity of currency for the nation's internal trade but, as Chart 3 shows, changes in the quantity outstanding fluctuated widely over the period, with significant effects at times on the growth of high-powered money. We may look to changes in profitability of the notes to explain the fluctuations.

[43] This limitation, 100 per cent in the act of 1864, was reduced by the act of March 3, 1865, to 90 per cent for banks with capital under $500,000 and to progressively lower percentages down to 60 per cent for banks with greater capital. The act of 1882 made it 90 per cent for all banks.

The profit in issuing the notes may be defined as the difference between the rate of return on capital used to issue notes and the rate on other investments. A bank obtained $90 (after 1900, $100) of notes for issue by purchasing a U.S. bond (of $100 par value) on the open market and depositing it with the Treasury (prices of the bonds were generally at par or above). The notes so obtained could best be spent, if obtaining and issuing them were profitable in the first place, by purchasing another U.S. bond and obtaining more notes for issue, and so on. To side-step the infinite progression implicit in the procedure, we may suppose the bank paid for its initial purchase of bonds with the notes obtained on the deposit of the bonds, plus enough of its own capital funds to make up the difference. (Since the bonds were purchased before the notes were obtained, the bank needed extra funds in the interim, producing a negligible cost in foregone interest earnings.) The capital tied up in acquiring one bond was simply the difference between the market price of the bond P, and the amount of notes issued on the basis of it which, before 1900, was $P - 90$; it would be $0.1 P$, if P were less than par. The return to the bank equaled the income on the bond the notes helped to purchase, which may be expressed as $Pi/100$, where i is the percentage yield on the bond to maturity. The annual expense for issuing $90 of notes may be designated by E and comprises an assessment levied by the Treasury to cover its cost of redeeming the notes (about 6 to 7 cents a year per $90 of notes) and a 1 per cent tax per year (reduced to one-half of 1 per cent by the act of 1900) paid by national banks to the government, as required by law.[44] The annual rate of return on capital invested in issuing notes up to 1900 may then be written:

$$\frac{Pi/100 - E}{P - 90},$$

assuming that the market price exceeds the par value of the bonds, as it generally did throughout the period.

Table 13 compares the rate of return on the notes with the average

[44] The issuing bank also had to hold a cash reserve at the Treasury (equal to 5 per cent of the notes authorized for issue), used to redeem notes received through public payments for taxes and other purposes (which the issuing bank could then re-issue). Until 1914, the redemption fund could be applied against the bank's statutory reserve requirements for deposits (sect. 3 of act of June 20, 1874) and so did not constitute a cost of issuing notes. The Federal Reserve Act discontinued inclusion of the redemption funds as part of reserves held, and thereafter the redemption fund constituted a cost of note issue.

rate on capital from all assets of national banks for the years 1879–97,
the period of large reductions in the quantity of notes outstanding.
The inclusion of notes themselves in all assets biases the figures in

TABLE 13

COMPARISON OF RETURN ON NATIONAL BANK NOTES WITH
CHANGE IN THEIR CIRCULATION, 1879–97

| Year | Rate of Return on Capital to National Banks from: (per cent per year) | | | Notes Issued (+) or Retired (−) in Fiscal Year (as per cent of amounts outstanding at beginning of fiscal year) (4) |
	Issuing Notes (in Jan.) (1)	All Assets (middle 6 months of fiscal year) (2)	Excess of Rate for Notes over that for All Assets (1)−(2) (3)	
1879	31.2	5.0	26.2	3.0
1880	21.5	7.4	14.1	3.2
1881	11.5	8.4	3.1	−1.9
1882	9.4	9.2	0.2	−1.0
1883	8.5	8.4	0.1	1.0
1884	7.1	8.6	−1.5	−5.5
1885	7.3	6.4	0.9	−8.5
1886	6.7	8.0	−1.3	−9.7
1887	7.5	9.0	−1.5	−29.7
1888	7.9	8.6	−0.7	−8.8
1889	4.8	9.0	−4.2	−16.7
1890	4.9	8.6	−3.7	−2.3
1891	6.2	9.2	−3.0	−1.6
1892	7.8	7.6	0.2	13.7
1893	9.3	7.8	1.5	9.2
1894	9.2	4.2	5.0	11.0
1895	9.3	5.2	4.1	3.5
1896	10.5	5.6	4.9	11.8
1897	9.3	5.4	3.9	−1.0

Source, by Column

(1): Computed by formula in text, where P is the price of the bond whose use
as security for national bank note circulation increased the most or decreased the least, arithmetically, over the fiscal years; i is the yield;
and E is the cost of issuing $90 of notes.

Data on use of bonds for national bank circulation, from Annual Report,
Comptroller of the Currency, 1897, Vol. I, p. 378. Calculations in the
table are for the bond whose use for securing notes increased the most or
decreased the least in the fiscal year, except in 1881. In that year, the
5 per cent and 6 per cent bonds, whose use increased the most, matured,
and so were dropped in favor of the 4 1/2 per cent bonds, whose use decreased the least. Due dates are from ibid. and Annual Report on the
Finances, Secretary of the Treasury, various years, particularly 1894,
table on outstanding principal of the public debt.

Price P: 1879–84, the average of the Jan. opening and closing prices;
for Jan. 1882, $1 was subtracted from the opening price which included
interest; 1885–86, from Annual Report, Comptroller of the Currency, 1896,
Vol. I, p. 551; 1887–97, from ibid., 1898, Vol. I, p. 402.

Yield i: Obtained from ibid., various years, when given; otherwise,
from semiannual yield tables, even though the bonds were quarterly--a
procedure that understates the yield by a negligible amount.

NOTES TO TABLE 13 (concluded)

Annual cost of note issue E per $90 of notes: 1883-97, 90 cents, plus
$90 times aggregate cost of note issue (<u>ibid</u>., 1896, Vol. I, p. 543; 1897,
Vol. I, p. 375), divided by an annual average, centered on Jan. 1, of
notes secured by U.S. bonds (<u>ibid</u>., 1897, Vol. I, p. 352). 1879-82, cost
per $90 of notes assumed to be same as in 1883 (96 cents).

(2): Ratio of net earnings to capital, including surplus (from <u>Annual Report</u>,
Comptroller of the Currency, various years, covering half-years ending
Mar. 1), doubled to give annual rate. This introduces a possible rounding
error of plus or minus 0.1. A tax on bank capital before 1883 should be
deducted from the figures, since the return on notes takes no account of
it. The tax affected the figures insignificantly, however, and was
ignored.

(3): Col. 1 minus col. 2.

(4): <u>Annual Report</u>, Comptroller of the Currency, 1918, Vol. II, pp. 254
ff., with interpolations of call-date figures to June 30, where needed.

column 3 downward, but the understatement is bound to be slight
since notes provided a small part of total bank revenue.

The preceding formula ignores the loss of income on notes in the
process of being re-issued after being returned to the Treasury or to
the issuing banks for redemption. The quantity of such notes must have
been a negligible fraction of the total outstanding, however, because
the public accepted them as a perfect substitute for greenbacks after
1874 and made no special effort to redeem them. Any national bank
could re-issue the notes of other banks; it did not have to send them
to the issuing bank for redemption and usually did not. Yet issuing
banks did on the average hold cash reserves at the Treasury in excess
of the 5 per cent of notes outstanding required for the redemption
fund (see footnote 44). The aggregate balance sheet for all national
banks shows an item "due from the Treasurer," which represented
the amount on deposit in excess of the 5 per cent redemption fund,
usually 10 to 20 per cent of the fund—that is, about one-half to 1 per
cent of the notes outstanding. It included balances kept at the Treasury
to replenish the 5 per cent fund (if depleted by note redemptions) and
money in transit between the banks and the Treasury to settle transactions involved in issuing notes. What part of the funds on deposit at
the Treasury represented a regular claim on banks' capital solely for
issuing notes is not clear; in any event, the whole part has been omitted
in the rate-of-return formula used for Table 13. If they had been
taken into account on the assumption that they constituted a regular
claim and hence produced an expected cost of issuing notes, the capital
tied up would be increased at most by 10 per cent—appropriate for a

bond selling at par, too high for a bond with a premium—and the rates in column 1 would be reduced at most by one-tenth, or less than one percentage point for a profit rate of 10 per cent.

Note Issues Before 1900. The cause of the decline in notes outstanding during the 1880's is readily apparent from the table. The handsome profit in issuing national bank notes (see column 3) available in the late 1870's[45] disappeared in the early 1880's until 1892, when once again the profit differential rose above zero. The fluctuations in profitability were due almost entirely to corresponding fluctuations in the premium on U.S. bonds. Since the law specified that notes could be issued only on the collateral of government bonds up to 90 per cent of their par value or market price, whichever was lower, any premium on the bonds above par value represented extra cost for which no notes could be issued. A rise in the premium thus raised the amount of capital tied up without a corresponding increase in income. A rise in the premium also lowered the yield on the bonds, but it was of much less importance for determining profitability than the amount of capital tied up was.[46]

There was a general decline in all long-term interest rates from about 1870 to 1899. The premium on U.S. bonds tended to rise, especially during the 1880's when the Treasury, after retiring all its callable bonds, bid for others on the open market in order to prevent a recurring budget surplus from devouring the money stock. The premium fell sharply twice: from 1876 to 1879, when the Treasury was

---

[45] In his 1873 *Annual Report* (p. xxxiii), the Comptroller of the Currency (John Jay Knox) computed the return on capital in issuing notes. His figure is too low, because he assumed the notes would be loaned to customers at the prevailing rate of interest, whereas their use in buying more bonds to secure more notes was much more profitable, as described in the text. In terms of banks' balance sheets, the operation was one in which banks obtained the income on U.S. bonds, held as assets, in exchange for issuing the notes as liabilities and tying up a small amount (after 1900, almost none) of their own capital. The Comptroller's computation, in effect, makes the capital tied up equal to the full price of the bonds, which is absurd. His method of computation and error appear in succeeding annual reports and in various histories of the notes. The purpose of his computations was to disprove a popular opinion—as a rule, a poor guide but in that case, correct—that the notes were at most times highly profitable. (See also Friedman and Schwartz, *A Monetary History*, Chap. 2.)

[46] Suppose, in the preceding formula, the bond was a perpetuity; then its yield could be expressed by its coupon rate, r (a constant), divided by the price. Hence, the formula becomes $(r - E)/(P - 90)$. In this form the return on notes clearly varies inversely and sharply with the price of the bond. For example, if P rose 10 per cent from par, the rate of return would be cut in half. If the bond has a finite maturity, the expression for $Pi/100$ is more complicated but, unless the maturity is very short, still tends to approximate r and so is largely unaffected by changes in P.

borrowing to accumulate a gold reserve and there was some question whether resumption would succeed; and from 1890 to November 1896, when the Treasury changed abruptly after 1893 from purchaser to heavy seller of its bonds, because of a succession of unplanned budget deficits and fear that the government might adopt the program of the silver supporters and be forced off the gold standard. To be sure, the yield on U.S. bonds rose by less than one-half a percentage point from its 1889–92 low, after which the notes became profitable again. Yet the rise in yield was enough to reduce the premium on the bonds by about $10 and was crucial to profitability of the notes. The 4's of 1907—the bonds that secured the largest fraction of the notes outstanding at the time—sold, on average, $28.25 above their par value of $100 in 1889. By the first of 1891 the premium had been cut by one-fourth and two years later was down to $13.

Note issues were widely criticized at the time for not being "elastic with the needs of trade." Among other things, that meant the notes were not quickly expanded in times of stringency or panic, when the desired currency ratio rises sharply. While elasticity of the money stock seems undesirable as a general rule, since during brisk trade it would fan the boom, there was a mechanism at work—albeit unintended by the authors of the National Currency Act—to accomplish just that kind of elasticity. When money tightened and interest rates rose, the price of U.S. bonds tended to decline, and the profitability of the notes thereby increased; even though yields on alternative investments also rose, the amount of the premium on U.S. bonds was crucial. When money eased, the opposite occurred. Nevertheless, changes in the quantity of notes outstanding in response to short-run financial conditions, including panics, were relatively small and so were, in the foregoing terms, unresponsive to the needs of trade. The reason was that the incentive for expansion of note issues apparently required a long time to produce an appreciable response; note issues appear to have been long-run investments for banks, and large short-run adjustments to changes in the rate of return were not attempted.[47]

[47] One restraining factor in effect since 1882 was the obligatory six months' wait, before issuing new notes, whenever banks deposited lawful money at the Treasury in order to reduce their notes outstanding; and even then the reduction was limited to $3 million a month for each bank. The Gold Standard Act of 1900 repealed the waiting period for new issues, and the act of March 4, 1907, raised the allowable rate of decrease in circulation to $9 million a month for each bank.

Apart from failing to provide for such elasticity—of doubtful desirability—the conditions for obtaining notes did indeed link their issue to the amount of the premium on U.S. bonds—again of doubtful desirability. In justice to the authors of the act, we should realize that the unprofitability of the notes in the 1880's and their consequent large-scale retirement were probably not foreseen or desired. If U.S. bonds had continued to sell near par, the notes would have been very profitable. When the bonds rose to a premium, permission to issue notes up to full par value instead of to only 90 per cent would have helped maintain their profitability—a change, as noted, made in 1900 when no longer necessary. No one proposed going further and allowing banks to issue notes up to the full *market* value of the bonds, because that was undesirable on other grounds: the premium on bonds should not serve as security for notes; the government could be expected to guarantee only notes issued against the par value of its bonds, which was all it stood ready to redeem. In retrospect, the mistake of proponents of national bank notes was to base their issue on government bonds. Various proposals—mainly to refund U.S. bonds at lower coupon rates which would have permitted selling at par—were in fact made at the time; but legislative attempts to enact them were blocked by the silver coalition, which preferred that increases in the money stock should favor silver dollars.

In consequence, nothing was done, with the unintended result that declines in the notes during the 1880's offset almost three-fourths of the concurrent purchases of silver, presumably made to inflate prices by expanding the money supply. After 1890, the notes became profitable again as a result of a rise in U.S. bond yields reflecting in part fears about maintenance of the gold standard after the silver supporters had enacted the Sherman Silver Purchase Act. Expansion of national bank notes together with the silver purchases may have seemed desirable to Congressional proponents of inflation, but the resulting additions to the money stock reinforced the drain on the Treasury's gold reserve and thereby threatened maintenance of the gold standard. On such alarming prospects, as we have seen, Congress mustered the votes to repeal the Sherman Act.

The relation between profitability and rate of note issue or retirement provides a means of estimating bias in our profitability figures, assuming banks expand circulation when the true profit is positive and contract when it is negative. If we regress changes in the notes outstanding on the computed profit rate (columns 3 and 4 in Table 13), the correlation coefficient is 0.48 excluding the first two years, which have extreme rates of return. According to the regression equation, no notes were issued when the computed profit rate was 1.7 per cent per year. That figure implies average costs, not included in our calculations for Table 13, of that amount in issuing the notes, reflecting possibly administrative and handling costs to the issuing bank over and above the assessment and tax levied by the Treasury.

Note Issues after 1900. Issuing notes became extremely profitable following the passage of the Gold Standard Act of 1900.[48] The quantity of notes in circulation expanded rapidly and did not level off until shortly before World War I. Notes outstanding, secured entirely by bonds (that is, not covered by lawful money deposited at the Treasury to redeem or retire notes), increased from $265 million in mid-1900 to just under $725 million in 1913, a rise of nearly 175 per cent. Acquisition of U.S. bonds by banks had no important effect on their prices and on the profitability of issuing notes. Since the capital stock of national banks after about 1905 exceeded the quantity of eligible bonds outstanding, the latter provided the only limit on the increase

[48] The return after 1900 was around 25 per cent per year. This may be illustrated by calculations for 1905 and 1913 based on the consols of 1930 as security, which paid 2 per cent and sold for less than $105 (yielding 1.76 per cent to maturity) in 1905, and after 1913, usually for less than $101. The act of 1900 made the tax on notes secured by the bonds one-half of 1 per cent per year, and other costs to the banks in issuing $90 of notes were reported by the Comptroller as $0.0625 per year. The capital tied up in 1905 was only the premium on the bond, about $5. After 1913, capital tied up included the premium, about $1, as well as the 5 per cent redemption fund (see footnote 44). By the preceding formula, the rate of return for 1905 was

$$\frac{105(0.0176) - 0.5625}{5} = 25.7 \text{ per cent per year;}$$

and after 1913, ignoring the slight effect on the 2 per cent yield of the $1 premium, was

$$\frac{101(0.02) - 0.5625}{6} = 24.3 \text{ per cent per year.}$$

Recomputing with a 5 per cent redemption fund raised by 20 per cent to take account of funds in transit gives rates lower by 1/6 and 1/7, respectively, a comparatively unimportant reduction.

In the foregoing computations, other costs in issuing the notes may, as suggested by the regression, have been overlooked, but that would not weaken the conclusion that the notes were profitable, given that banks issued them at all. If issuing some notes was profitable—as it obviously was—the same would be true of an unlimited quantity, because the profit was not in any apparent way affected by the volume of notes issued, so long as bond prices did not rise materially.

in national bank notes. On October 13, 1913, for example, national banks held as security for notes and government deposits (which also required such collateral) 84 per cent of the eligible bonds outstanding. That left little room for further expansion. By 1926, when the percentage had reached 98, further expansion was virtually impossible without an extension of the issue privilege to other bonds.

The number of eligible bonds actually fell after World War I. Their total value stood at about $900 million from 1901 to World War I, fell through debt retirement during the first half of the 1920's to about $675 million and remained at that level until 1932. In that year, Congress extended the circulation privilege to an additional $3 billion U.S. bonds then outstanding, but only for three years. Banks took advantage of that largesse to only a limited extent. Then in 1935, the Treasury decided to withdraw all such notes from circulation by retiring the last issue of bonds having the circulation privilege. The mechanics of the retirement were the transfer of liability for the notes from national banks to the Treasury, a transaction that canceled the Treasury's liability for an equal amount of the bonds previously used as security. The notes have been gradually retired and replaced by Federal Reserve notes. There was not, therefore, any sudden or long-run change in high-powered money outstanding as a result of national bank note retirement.[49]

These facts show how the shortage of bonds for collateral prevented national banks from increasing note issues very much after the mid-1920's, except for the temporary expansion allowed in 1932–35. It is nevertheless puzzling why, in view of the large profit in issuing the notes after the mid-1890's, their expansion occurred so slowly and never reached 100 per cent of the amount allowed. In 1905, more than five years after the profit had become extremely attractive, national banks had deposited, in order to secure notes and government deposits, less than 60 per cent of the eligible bonds outstanding; and by 1913, as noted, only 84 per cent. Why did banks not bid for the available bonds immediately? Furthermore, while no national bank could issue notes in excess of its paid-in capital, most of them kept under that limit. We might expect, therefore, that bidding for the available bonds would push their prices up high enough to wipe out most of the

---

[49] See J. D. Paris, *Monetary Policies of the United States 1932–1938*, New York, Columbia University Press, 1938, Chap. V, "The Passing of the National Bank Note."

profit in issuing notes. Yet quoted prices on the largest block of eligible bonds, the consols of 1930, never rose much above their par value. Immediately after their issue in 1900, they went to a premium, touching a high of $110.25 in October 1902 (at which price the return to capital tied up in issuing notes, by the preceding formula, was still an attractive 17.1 per cent per year); yet the premium had all but disappeared by 1909.

We may distinguish two separate puzzles here: First, why most banks did not expand their notes more rapidly; and second, why individual banks did not try to expand their circulation to the limit imposed by their paid-in capital and thus bid up bond prices. The slow expansion suggests that national banks waited until it seemed certain that no reason to withdraw the notes would arise in the near future. Why a withdrawal need be feared, however, is not clear. The bonds securing the notes could always be sold or, if called, redeemed to provide funds to retire the notes. No embarrassing drain on cash reserves of a bank retiring its notes need occur. There was, perhaps, one remote danger: should the market value of the bonds used for collateral fall below par, issuing banks would have to make up the difference immediately by a cash deposit at the Treasury. But that never occurred and never seemed likely to during the period.

Slow expansion aside, failure of prices of eligible bonds to rise much above par indicates that banks were not bidding aggressively for them on the open market. A possible explanation is that the bonds covered by those quotations could not for some reason be used as collateral; or that the quotations were irrelevant, possibly because trading at published prices involved mostly small lots, whereas large lots required much higher prices. This is only a conjecture, however.

Notwithstanding these puzzles, the factors underlying the major movements in notes outstanding are fairly clear and stem, as shown, from the conditions and limitations of their issue.

SUMMARY OF SECULAR MOVEMENTS

The foregoing pages present a historical commentary on the events connected with long-run changes in high-powered money. The discussion emphasizes the major role of the government: how in one way or another it has been involved in all the sources of change, even in the production of gold. Government monetary activities are of wider scope than those represented by statutory regulations.

The various sources of change are discussed separately and to some extent as though they were independent. As just concluded, however, all stood within the government's control. For this and other reasons, interrelations between them were likely. Consider the various sources of change: (1) Although Treasury operations (excluding silver) usually reflect the need to meet budget expenditures or financial requirements of various government agencies and so for the most part would be independent of the other sources, the four episodes examined were all connected with gold flows (the fourth, indirectly through market stringencies produced by gold outflows) and so represented attempts to affect movements in the gold stock; moreover, those episodes cover most of the largest contributions of Treasury operations to changes in high-powered money. (2) Silver purchases were intended to produce inflation and generally were made in times of deflation when the money stock had fallen below its long-run trend line. (3) Federal Reserve operations were obviously related to the other sources of change, because the Reserve Banks worked to offset undesired movements in high-powered money produced by the other sources. (4) The gold stock is related to the other sources indirectly through effects of changes in the money stock on the domestic price level and international trade. (5) When still permitted, issue of national bank notes, alone among the various sources, was unrelated to the others, although there was a possible connection through Congressional control over conditions of issue. On the whole, the profitability of the notes fluctuated (inversely) with the premium on U.S. bonds.

Such interrelations mean that changes in high-powered money cannot be explained simply as the sum of the sources of change, since these are partly determined by the behavior of the aggregate and of each other. Between 1879 and 1914, high-powered money was closely associated with the behavior of the gold stock, reflecting limits on changes in high-powered money set by the gold-standard mechanism. In mathematical terms, there was a constraint on the *long-run* trend of high-powered money expressed by a linear dependence between the sources of change. Short-run movements in the sources of change could be independent; reaction through the constraint was often delayed, sometimes considerably. After 1914 a more general kind of constraint prevailed—government policy on money and related matters. It operated even less rigidly than its counterpart in the earlier period; policy sometimes bent to the force of events and did not remain independent of past monetary developments. To the extent that high-powered money reflected government policies here and abroad in the later period, the relative contribution of the sources of change reflected the particular form in which those policies were implemented.

To stress government influences does not mean that the quantity of high-powered money was whatever government policy prescribed; far from it. The government often had no set policy and, when it did, was often hamstrung by political or economic limitations on its ability to achieve particular goals. It may help to summarize various parts of this chapter by listing briefly the economic factors that had important effects on the growth of high-powered money.

Commodity Prices. First, and most important in the long run, was the effect on the gold stock of changes in the commodity value of gold, chiefly changes in the dollar prices of commodities but also occasional alterations in the dollar price of gold. Domestic price movements affected the U.S. gold stock inversely, both through world gold production—insofar as U.S. prices followed world price levels—and through changes in the U.S. share of the existing world monetary gold stock— insofar as U.S. and world price movements diverged. Friedman and Schwartz found that purchasing-power parity between the dollar and the British pound mostly varied within a fairly narrow range,[50] suggesting that the balance of trade and gold flows may have been sensitive to differences in relative prices even in the short run, except for certain periods in which international trade was disrupted. The effect of price movements on gold production was also strong but, as we saw, occurred with long and varying lags. Consequently, effects of only the very largest movements in prices can be readily detected in the data on gold production and the U.S. stock. Emphasis on those effects does not of course deny important autonomous influences on world gold production owing to the depletion of mines or to the fortuitous discovery of gold-bearing ores. Nevertheless, the largest deviations from trend since 1875 have been related to price movements or devaluation.

[50] *A Monetary History*, Chap. 13, sect. 2.

Movements in commodity prices apparently did not greatly affect any of the other sources of change in high-powered money, except possibly silver purchases, which have been increased in periods of deflation.

Interest Rates. The only effect of other specific economic variables was that of interest rates on issues of national bank notes. The conditions of issue were so arranged (not intentionally) that a rise in interest rates depressed U.S. bond prices and increased the profitability of issuing the notes—and conversely. Hence, there was a positive relation between their issue and interest rates, though it was by no means close and only shows up in the large movements during the 1880's and 1890's. Thereafter, the quantity of U.S. bonds eligible as security for the notes limited further note issues, though the actual circulation approached the limit very slowly.

General Business Conditions. Federal Reserve operations and, before them, Treasury operations are primarily instruments of government monetary policies and, for that very reason, reflect developments in business activity, but not in a uniform or consistent way. If there was any consistent pattern, it was mitigation of the impact of gold-stock movements on high-powered money, at least temporarily, and of other sharp reductions in the money stock due to other sources of change. On the other hand, Federal Reserve operations have at critical times reinforced such reductions, as in 1921 and 1931, and have also been an independent source of large increases, as during the two world wars.

On the whole, however, the contribution of those operations to secular movements in high-powered money has been minor; they are of more interest in short-run movements, discussed in the next section. Indeed, if we confine our attention to major long-run movements and omit war periods, the principal source of change in high-powered money, by far, has been growth of the gold stock.

2. Cyclical Movements in the Sources of Change in High-Powered Money

The effects of different institutional developments and economic variables on the determinants can be partly disentangled, when the relevant movements are large and the number of important factors in any period is small—largely true for secular movements. Cyclical movements, however, are a kaleidoscope of many effects, commingling in a constantly changing pattern. Identifying even one effect is difficult. We can still find clues to the major effects from cyclical patterns of the principal sources of change in high-powered money. The series are plotted according to the National Bureau's chronology of expansions and contractions in reference cycles (Table 1). The period of expansion is divided into thirds, and standings for stages II, III, and IV are averages of the series for these three periods, respectively, centered at the midpoints. Standings for stages VI, VII, and VIII are averages for a similar division into thirds of the contraction period. For monthly data, stage I is an average of the three months surrounding the initial trough, stage V the peak, and stage IX the terminal trough.

Chart 6 presents the reference cycle patterns of change in high-powered money, in the gold stock, and in the residual, found by subtracting the second from the first. The residual is the sum of the sources listed in Table 10, columns 3–6, reflecting chiefly Treasury and Federal Reserve operations but also all other nongold sources of change. The patterns show the change in each series as a percentage of the average level of high-powered money over the cycle, which is convenient for tracing the sources of change in high-powered money. Some stages cover a short time span and may reflect sharp changes in the series that did not last long. Hence, we should not attach too much significance to sharp movements formed by just one stage of a pattern.

Chart 6 shows little uniformity from cycle to cycle for either of the sources of change. For the nongold sources before 1914, many of the cycles have large dissimilar movements. The only recurring pattern of any consequence is a rise in stage VII of the 1894–97, 1897–1900, and 1904–08 cycles, partly attributable to the Treasury's relief of banks, mentioned earlier,[51] and in stage VIII of the 1911–14 cycle, due to the emergency issues of national bank notes in the 1914 panic.[52] After 1914, in the two world war cycles, the Reserve Banks first expanded and then sharply cut the rate of growth of high-powered money. Aside from the war cycles, there is still no uniform pattern after 1914, though the fluctuations display a larger amplitude on the average and seem more responsive to major changes in economic

---

[51] Under Treasury Operations, item 3; see also Chapter 5, sect. 3.

[52] See Chap. 4, sect. 2; and O. M. W. Sprague, "The Crisis of 1914 in the United States, *American Economic Review*, Sept. 1915, pp. 522–23.

CHART 6

Reference Cycle Patterns of Sources of Change in High-Powered Money, 1879–1954
(change per year as percentage of average reference cycle level of high-powered money)

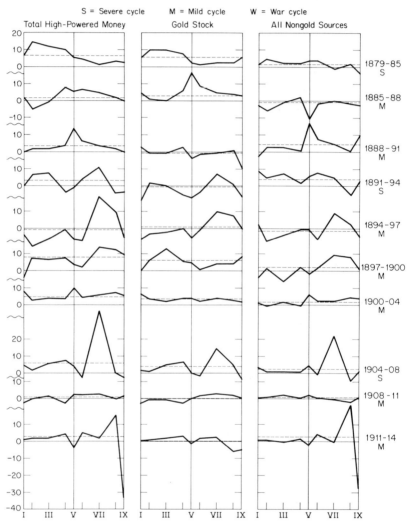

Source: Severe cycles comprise the six most severe reference contractions in business activity by the ranking in Table 1. All other nonwar cycles are mild. Stage standings were computed from changes in quarterly averages of seasonally adjusted end-of-month data, divided by the average level of total high-powered money over each cycle. Total high-powered money, the same as for Table F-1 (a monthly seasonally-adjusted version of the annual series described in the notes to col. 1 of Table F-5). The gold stock (valued at $20.67 per fine ounce through the 1927–33

CHART 6 (*concluded*)

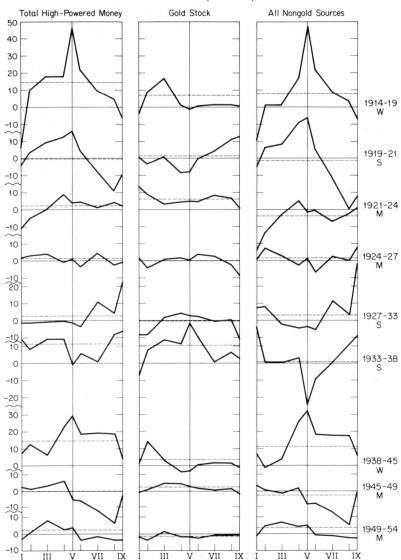

cycle and at \$35 in cycles thereafter) is a National Bureau series based on *Banking and Monetary Statistics*, pp. 373–377, for 1914–41 and *Federal Reserve Bulletin*, thereafter, and on monthly Treasury estimates 1879–1913 adjusted before 1907 to the level of annual bench marks given in *Annual Report*, Director of the Mint, 1907, p. 87. All nongold sources is the difference for each stage of the standing of total high-powered money and the standing of the gold stock; hence, the sum of the two patterns on the right equal the pattern on the left for the stages of each cycle.

Note: Horizontal broken lines show average values of the series over each cycle.

CHART 7

Average Reference Cycle Patterns of Sources of Change in High-Powered Money
(change per year as percentage of average reference cycle level of high-powered money)

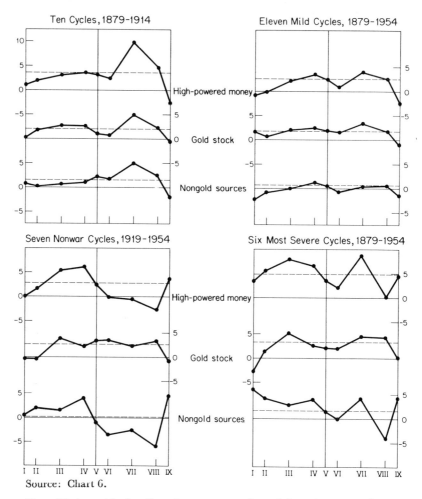

Source: Chart 6.

Note: Horizontal broken lines show average values of the series over each group of cycles.

activity, as shown by the comparatively sharp peaks or troughs formed in stage IV, V, or VI. The latter configurations are due largely to Federal Reserve credit outstanding, which is the main item in the nongold sources. The Reserve Banks responded to changes in the business climate, but not in any uniform way from cycle to cycle. Federal Reserve credit outstanding is largely responsible for the increased amplitude of fluctuations in the nongold sources after 1914.

For the gold stock, as well, no recurring movements run through a majority of the patterns. Changes in the gold stock result from domestic production and the balance of foreign payments. The former probably does not display much cyclical variation, except when there are unusually sharp changes in the commodity value of gold. The balance of foreign payments, on the other hand, is the focal point of myriad developments in international trade and finance and in both domestic and foreign economic activity. For most cycles after 1914, the structural disruptions of international trade may well have swamped any uniform cyclical responses that occurred. The absence of a uniform pattern is not unexpected, therefore, for the later period. Before 1914, one might expect to find clearer evidence of international influences but, whatever their role, they did not leave a consistent imprint on the gold stock.

A few tendencies running through some of the patterns may be brought out by two comparisons: one between the average pattern of nonwar cycles before and after 1914, and the other between cycles with severe and mild contractions in business activity. The comparisons are presented in Chart 7. Since the patterns for each cycle are expressed as percentages of the average level of high-powered money, the averages do not overemphasize movements in the later cycles, even though in dollar terms the original data have an upward trend.

In the earlier of the two periods, there was a tendency in contractions of the gold and nongold sources of change to reinforce each other. This might be expected of a monetary system committed to the gold-standard mechanism and with Treasury currency outstanding—generally true of the U.S. monetary system at that time. If the gold and nongold sources were uncorrelated, the gold flows would have a less than proportional effect on high-powered money and so on the money stock; whereas a high positive correlation tends to make the effect nearly proportional. In the later period, the correlation is slightly negative, indicating an offset, though cyclical variations in gold, moderate in the individual patterns, are nearly nonexistent in the average pattern. High-powered money acquired a new pattern produced by the nongold sources, chiefly as a result of Federal Reserve actions. The new pattern—expanded growth during reference expansions and reduced growth (often even decline) during reference contractions—undoubtedly did not represent a deliberate Federal Reserve policy. As can be seen in Chart 6, that pattern occurred mainly in mild cycles and is probably explained as the response of an agency willing to satisfy market demands for credit, which vary more or less with business activity. Yet this is not the whole story, since there was a tightening of credit just before peaks when the demand usually continues strong.

The mild and severe cycles differed in the tendency of the nongold sources to decline before peaks. Those sources declined throughout severe reference expansions but expanded until stage IV of mild expansions. The great diversity among severe cycles, however, indicates that such behavior falls far short of being an invariant pattern for such cycles. As Chart 6 shows, the four most recent severe cycles display a variety of patterns. The only safe generalization is that high-powered money has a greater amplitude in severe cycles, which is largely true of both the gold and nongold sources of change.

The diversity among cycles in Chart 6 accounts for the small amplitude of the average patterns in Chart 7. The averaging flattens out not only the most atypical movements but also many other fluctuations. Since there are few regularities to start with, what remains are muted reflections of the largest movements, and little else. In view of the diversity, it is advisable to avoid averages and to confine the analysis to groups of individual cycles. For that purpose, the establishment of the Federal Reserve Banks in 1914 seems a meaningful dividing line between earlier and later cycles. In the earlier period, gold was the dominant source of change in high-powered money, and international factors probably had much more influence then than later. In the later period, the Reserve Banks—a new source of change in high-powered money—introduced a new set of influences, of which the interdependence among the determinants analyzed in Chapter 2 is a partial reflection.

PRE-WORLD WAR I CYCLES

Changes in the gold stock result chiefly from imbalances between foreign payments and receipts. These international influences on high-powered money are brought out by Chart 8, which presents pre-1914 reference cycle patterns of the balance of commodity trade. The balance is given as a percentage of the average level of high-powered money during each reference cycle and so is comparable with the series in the two preceding charts. Data on services are unobtainable and cannot be added to make up the total trade balance. Although relatively large in average amount, the services balance probably displays a much smaller amplitude of cyclical variation than does the commodity balance.[53] The patterns to the right show all other sources of change in the gold stock, found by subtracting the stage standings for the commodity balance from the corresponding standings for the gold stock in Chart 6. Both patterns have the intra-cyclical trend removed and are displayed as deviations from the zero line, because the average levels of the patterns for the two series are not related.

Although there is not much uniformity among the patterns for the gold stock in Chart 6, one similarity is their tendency to dip sharply around reference peaks. The dip is most prominent in the 1891–94, 1894–97, and 1904–08 cycles, though many of the others before 1914, as well as some after, display traces of it. The dip largely accounts for the greater amplitude of the gold-stock patterns before 1914 than after. It shows up clearly in the patterns for the balance of commodity trade in Chart 8 and can be attributed to them. The behavior of the trade balance can be traced, in turn, to imports and exports. Partway through reference expansions, the rising volume of exports tapered off and declined, while the volume of imports continued to rise; during reference contractions imports declined, while exports recovered rapidly at first and then slowly.[54] The imports pattern reflects domestic business activity, which typically had the same effect on imports as on domestic expenditures. The causes of the pattern for exports are not so transparent. One explanation is that rising prices during reference

[53] See Ilse Mintz, *Trade Balances During Business Cycles: U.S. and Britain since 1880,* NBER, Occasional Paper 67, 1959, pp. 6–7.

[54] *Ibid.,* p. 15. This pattern for exports is less characteristic of post-World War I cycles.

CHART 8

Reference Cycle Patterns of Balance of Commodity Trade, and Residual Changes in the Gold Stock, 1879–1914
(amount per year as percentage of average reference cycle level of high-powered money)

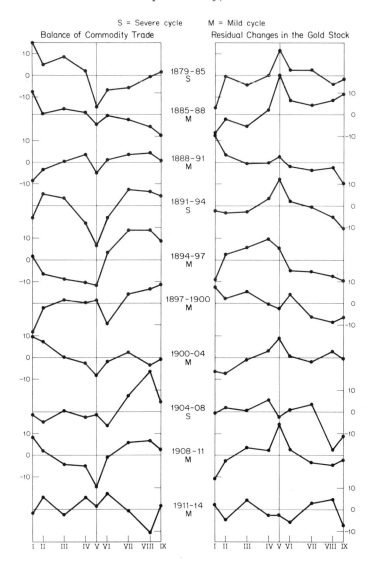

Source

Severe and mild cycles, same as for Chart 6. Stage standings were computed from seasonally adjusted quarterly data, divided by the average level of total high-powered money over each cycle. Intracyclical trend was removed by adjusting the standing of all nine stages to average zero for each cycle. Balance of commodity trade is from Mintz, *Trade Balances During Business Cycles*, Table A-1.

Residual changes in the gold stock are the difference for each stage between the standing of the gold stock in Chart 6 (after removing intracyclical trend as above) and the standing of the balance of commodity trade.

expansions eventually curtailed the amount demanded abroad and produced the pre-peak decline in the volume of exports. Yet by far the most important factors affecting exports were changes in foreign demand that seem unrelated to domestic prices.[55] Domestic price changes were secondary.

The dips in the trade balance around reference peaks were the most prominent part of what was often an inverse cyclical pattern. Although imports usually had a positive pattern, contributing to an inverse pattern in the trade balance, exports were usually out of step with domestic cycles, expanding or contracting in conformity with world trade. In that way, foreign business conditions had an irregular influence on domestic business cycles.[56]

Fluctuations in the trade balance have two related but distinct influences on domestic activity: a direct influence through current spending of the excess of foreign expenditures on U.S. exports over U.S. expenditures on imports from abroad; and an indirect influence through the accumulated effect of gold flows on the money stock. The two influences work in the same direction but with different timing. Insofar as fluctuations in the trade balance have an immediate influence—largely true of the direct impact on spending—the inverse pattern moderates domestic cycles, reducing aggregate expenditures during business expansions and augmenting them during contractions. Insofar as the fluctuations have a delayed influence—largely true of the accumulated effect of gold flows on the money stock—the inverse pattern might also reinforce domestic cycles, at least in part, and perhaps even help to initiate them. The declines during the latter

---

[55] See Mintz, *American Exports During Business Cycles, 1879–1958*, New York, NBER, Occasional Paper 76, 1961, especially Chaps. 3 and 6; and NBER, "Staff Progress Reports," Jan.–May 15, 1963 (mimeographed), p. 43.

[56] See Mintz, *Trade Balances*.

part of each business expansion might act with a lag to depress the economy during the first part of the subsequent contraction and, conversely, for contractions and subsequent expansions. When a variable moves counter to business cycles, as the pre-1914 trade balance did, it may help to moderate or to generate cycles or, at different times, both. Whether it has predominantly one effect or the other, allowing for lags, is difficult to determine.

Although the contribution of the trade balance and gold flows to business cycles is not clear, the monetary effects of the trade balance transmitted through gold flows may be further analyzed. Charts 6 and 8 indicate that the trade-balance and gold-stock patterns do not correspond closely, particularly in amplitude. A comparison of the right and left panels of Chart 8 shows why. The residual sources of change in the gold stock largely offset the monetary effects of the trade balance. Stage by stage of each cycle, the two patterns usually lie on opposite sides of the zero line. Only in one-tenth of the stages shown do the two lie on the same side. The negative association applies also to amplitudes of the patterns. The correlation coefficient between the two patterns, giving each stage equal weight, is -0.83, indicating that the trade balance is highly correlated with the residual sources and only faintly correlated with changes in the gold stock. This is doubtless an overstatement of the "true" association, since the residual patterns were derived by subtracting the trade-balance patterns from the gold-stock patterns, thus producing a spurious negative correlation between measurement errors in the trade balance and the residual. That might account for much of the observed correlation. However, if we assume the measurement errors are not unusually large, the correlation is highly significant.

The pre-1914 residual sources consist of domestic gold production, the services balance, and capital movements (both short and long term). Short-term capital movements are probably responsible for most of the offset; the other two items would not ordinarily be very sensitive to short-run developments. Chart 8 therefore provides important evidence that pre-1914 capital movements dampened cyclical variations in the gold stock. This is consistent with the observation of many commentators that gold movements in that period were small and infrequent relative to the large cyclical fluctuations in international trade patterns.[57] International lending apparently took care of most cyclical and other temporary imbalances of payments, and gold stocks were largely unaffected, except when there was a basic disequilibrium persisting for more than one or two cycles. How the offsetting capital movements came about is not clear. Were they induced by speculative arbitrage of exchange rate movements or by interest rate differentials? Whatever the answer, capital movements in that period acted to stabilize exchange rates, understandable in a milieu with no threat—except briefly in the 1890's—of government tampering with foreign exchange markets.

The capital flows offset movements in the trade balance incompletely, however. Many of the gold-stock patterns resemble movements in the trade balance. In addition, while capital offsets postponed the need for gold flows, they could not by their nature last long and may have engendered expectations which transmitted changes in the trade balance to the money market in other ways. Commercial banks may have managed their reserves partly with an eye on short-term capital movements, keeping more plentiful reserves than they otherwise would have when short-term capital flowed in, and keeping less reserves when it flowed out, in readiness for a reversal of capital movements later on. Such behavior by banks would produce part of the effects on the money stock that offsetting capital movements prevent the trade balance from producing directly. To determine whether banks behaved in that way requires a careful examination of banking data, so far not undertaken. Aside from expectations, the effect of the trade balance on the money stock appears to have been weak, blunted by capital movements and buffeted by the nongold sources of change in high-powered money. Nevertheless, it was real, since high-powered money owed much of its double-hump pattern before 1914 to the trade balance.

If business cycles are transmitted internationally through the balance of trade, one of the intriguing implications is that the balance has just the opposite effect in each direction. A favorable U.S. balance, for example, stimulates the domestic economy and at the same time

[57] See, for example, Arthur I. Bloomfield, *Short-Term Capital Movements Under the Pre-1914 Gold Standard*, Princeton Studies in International Finance No. 11, 1963, esp. pp. 43–44.

depresses the economies of other countries. Consequently, there has long been a tendency to attribute synchronous world cycles[58] to disturbances originating in one country and unilaterally transmitted abroad. For example, the United States is often thought to be the source of many worldwide cycles.[59] The generally inverse pattern of the U.S. trade balance in the pre-1914 period supports this view. If we ignore lags, an inverse trade balance sends gold abroad and stimulates foreign economies, while U.S. activity expands, and depresses them by bringing gold back, while U.S. activity contracts. In the other direction, the effect of the pattern is to moderate U.S. cycles.

Yet one might argue—about the pre-1914 period at least—that U.S. cycles frequently stemmed from foreign influences and were not usually transmitted abroad. This country's economy during the nineteenth century could not have counted heavily with most foreign economies, while world trade clearly affected U.S. exports. Their irregular cyclical pattern, as noted, reflected the ups and downs of foreign business activity, which often moved counter to domestic business. To be sure, since cyclical fluctuations in the U.S. trade balance were generally moderate, the direct effects on domestic expenditures may have been of minor importance, while the indirect effects on the money stock were partly offset by capital movements and were usually overshadowed by domestic factors. At certain times, however, fluctuations in the trade balance were large and—even when of short duration—may have triggered cyclical movements in other variables. The gold outflow in 1931 was brief but, as mentioned, had far-reaching repercussions.

The evidence is not clear-cut and does not allow firm conclusions. The inverse pattern of the U.S. balance may be misleading because of lags. Even if the direct expenditure effects occur more or less immediately, many of the indirect monetary effects may have appreciable lags. In addition, feedback cannot be assumed to be unimportant. A disturbance from one country travels out around the world, collides with those from other countries, and is sent back, modified and delayed,

[58] Business cycle peaks in Great Britain, France, and Germany matched U.S. reference peaks from 1882 to 1913, except 1887, 1893, 1895, and 1910. See Oskar Morgenstern, *International Financial Transactions and Business Cycles*, Princeton for NBER, 1959, Chap. II.

[59] For a discussion of the literature and the evidence, see Mintz, *Trade Balances*, especially pp. 1–5 and 83–90.

as a series of disturbances over time. Because of the difficulty of dis-entangling foreign and domestic influences, the extent to which business cycles are transmitted internationally remains obscure, except perhaps in countries closely tied, like the United States and Canada. Studies to clarify the international transmission of cycles have so far merely scratched the surface of a vast subject.

In view of its complexity, we might hope to illuminate the problem with evidence from later cycles. Unfortunately, foreign influences are hidden even more thoroughly in the later period, despite their ob-viously great importance. Gold flows became larger after 1914 but relatively less decisive in domestic monetary affairs owing to the increased role of central banks. The following discussion of the later period therefore largely ignores the cyclical role of gold, in acknowledg-ment of our ignorance of its role rather than because of any evidence of its unimportance after 1914.

POST-WORLD WAR I CYCLES

In Chapter 2 we estimated that high-powered money offset about one-quarter of the pre-1914 fluctuations in the currency and reserve ratios. Since it seemed to reflect parallel responses to business cycles rather than a direct relation, offsetting movements among the three determinants were disregarded in the preceding section. The estimate of the offset for the post-1918 period was much greater in certain stages, and most of the increase was tentatively attributed to steps taken by the Federal Reserve Banks to counteract the effects on the money stock of changes in the two ratios. Insofar as high-powered money reflects the behavior of the two ratios in part but not in full, the con-tribution of government monetary policies is difficult to interpret.

To clarify the behavior of Federal Reserve Banks, it may help to separate their discounts and advances to commercial banks from the other nongold sources of change in high-powered money. Loans to banks are sometimes viewed as a "passive" element in Federal Reserve actions compared with "active" steps like open market operations, since loans are made at the initiative of member banks and are con-trolled by the authorities only indirectly through the discount rate and persuasion. In Chart 9, reference cycle patterns of changes in loans outstanding to member banks are shown as a percentage of the average level of high-powered money during each reference cycle

CHART 9

Nonwar Reference Cycle Patterns of Change in Federal Reserve Loans to Member Banks and of Residual Nongold Sources of Change in High-Powered Money, 1919–54 (change per year as percentage of average reference cycle level of high-powered money)

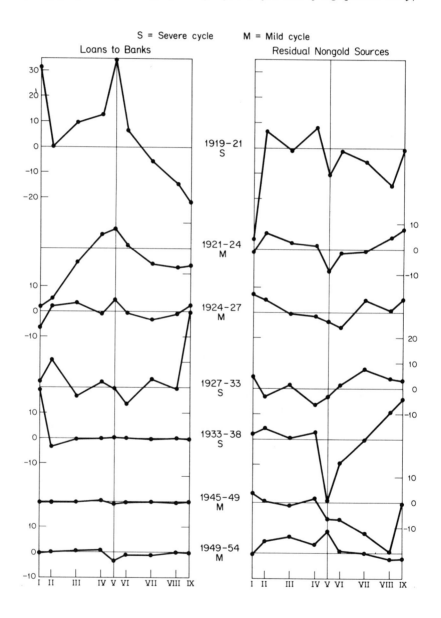

Source
For severe and mild cycles, the same as for Charts 6 and 8. The stage standings of loans to banks were computed from quarterly changes in seasonally adjusted monthly averages of daily figures (from *Annual Report*, Federal Reserve Board, 1928, pp. 47–49; *Banking and Monetary Statistics*, pp. 369 ff.; and *Federal Reserve Bulletin*). The standings were then divided by the average level of total high-powered money over each cycle. No adjustment was made for trend.
Residual nongold sources are the difference for each stage between the standing of all nongold sources in Chart 6 and the standing of loans to banks.

and so may be directly compared with patterns in the preceding charts. Also shown are the patterns of the residual nongold sources of change in high-powered money, found by subtracting the standings of the left-hand patterns in Chart 9 from those for total nongold sources in the right-hand strip of Chart 6. The residual comprises Federal Reserve open market operations, Treasury operations (including silver purchases), and issues of national bank notes. The latter two were minor except during the 1930's, when the Treasury for a while offset gold inflows, and national bank notes were retired (see Chart 3).

During the Federal Reserve Banks' first two decades, their loans to banks were an important source of changes in high-powered money. During the 1930's, however, those loans were hardly used at all, as commercial banks found it more advantageous to hold excess reserves than to borrow. Since the 1930's, the volume of loans to banks has grown but, relative to the quantity of high-powered money outstanding, they have remained insignificant, although they receive wide attention as an indicator (together with the quantity of excess reserves) of banks' ability and willingness to expand credit.

Changes in loans to banks conformed positively to the three reference cycles from 1919–1927. The patterns for the reference cycles since 1945 (including the 1954–58 and 1958–61 cycles, not shown), though of small amplitude, also conform positively and, in addition, lead at peaks both in amount of change and in absolute level. The positive conformity seems readily explained by cyclical fluctuations in the market demand for funds. Commercial loans fluctuate with economic activity and are a major source of cyclical variation in bank reserves. To help ease pressure during expansions, banks borrow from Federal Reserve Banks even for temporary relief, if the discount rate is not too high. Why loans to banks have declined before reference peaks in the post-1945 cycles is not clear, since bank loans to business typically continue to rise until or past the peak in economic activity. Perhaps the Federal Reserve System, through persuasion and increases in the discount rate, was responsible for the early decline, or banks might have been wary of raising their indebtedness beyond certain limits, despite the high demand by customers for more credit.

The pattern for the 1927–33 cycle, though erratic, conforms on the whole inversely, apparently for special reasons. Increases in the discount rate in 1928–29—which Federal Reserve officials hoped would dampen stock market speculation—discouraged banks from borrowing as much as might otherwise have been expected. In 1930–33, the deepening distress of banks forced them to borrow.

Given that loans to banks generally conform positively, one might, in search of countercyclical monetary policies, expect that the residual nongold sources of change in high-powered money would display inverse conformity with at least enough amplitude to offset the fluctuations in loans to banks. Or one might expect inverse conformity because, turning the direction of influence around, Reserve Banks allow member banks to borrow temporarily to cushion the impact of open market operations. If we put aside the post-1933 cycles, when loans to banks were negligible, the only earlier pattern to fulfill the expectation even approximately is that for 1924–27—in all respects a very mild cycle. The 1921–24 pattern has inverse conformity but lacks sufficient amplitude to offset the sharp recovery in loans to banks during the expansion stages. Possibly, though, the insufficient amplitude should be overlooked as allowing a welcome correction of the 1921 contraction in which credit liquidation had gone too far. The 1919–21 and 1927–33 patterns fail to meet the expectation because they reinforce the fluctuations in loans to banks, though under quite different circumstances. In the 1919–21 cycle, residual nongold sources offset some of the more extreme movements in loans to banks but had a positive conformity over all. Here, monetary policy and market forces worked in the same directions. Following the end of hostilities in 1918, the Federal Reserve Banks at first allowed the wartime expansion of credit to continue for fear of rocking the government bond market. Later, in 1920, the discount rate was raised to encourage a liquidation of credit, which proceeded to run out of control. In the expansion phase of the 1927–33 cycle, though the residual nongold sources offset some of the stage-to-stage movements in loans to banks, both patterns reflect the policy mentioned earlier of tightening credit to starve the bull market in stocks. During the subsequent reference contraction in 1929–33 both patterns rose, but with amazing restraint considering the magnitude of the disaster then overtaking the economy.

In Chart 7, the average pattern for total nongold sources in the post-1919 period displays positive conformity. Chart 9 helps to show why. The positive patterns of loans to banks are not offset by inverse patterns of the residual nongold sources. Only the 1924–27 cycle had even an approximate offset. In the 1921–24 cycle, the offset was partial, and in the 1919–21, 1945–49, and 1949–54 cycles the residual nongold sources had positive conformity. The special reasons for the positive pattern in the 1919–21 cycle have been mentioned. Special reasons partly explain the last two also. Countercyclical policies yielded to the bond-support program during World War II and until the early 1950's and exposed Federal Reserve credit outstanding to cyclical swings in interest rates and market demands for credit. That leaves the two cycles from 1927 to 1938 as the only ones in the post-1919 period in which the total nongold sources had inverse conformity (see Chart 6). Even then, the 1927–33 pattern, though inverse, can hardly be called countercyclical, when the money stock fell by one-third from 1929 to 1933. The 1933–39 pattern mainly reflects Treasury operations in sterilizing gold, since the Federal Reserve virtually ceased open-market operations during the second half of the 1930's.

If we exclude all these special influences, the remaining cycles are too few to support generalizations about Federal Reserve policies. Interpretation of the patterns is also obscured by their dependence on the currency and reserve ratios. High-powered money offset about nine-tenths of the contributions of the two ratios to the rate of change of the money stock in specific-cycle stages III through VI (Chapter 2). The offset accounted for about one-half the cyclical variation in the contribution of high-powered money in those stages and seemed to reflect in large part countercyclical measures taken by the authorities. In the other stages the offset was much lower and seemed to reflect simply parallel responses of the three determinants to business cycles. According to the average timing relations shown in Table 1, the specific-cycle stages with the high interdependence correspond roughly to stages I through IV of the post-1919 cycles. As can be inferred from

Chart 2 and is shown later, these stages correspond to a falling contribution of the currency ratio and rising contribution of the reserve ratio, with that of the currency ratio predominating. Offsetting behavior by high-powered money would be a slightly rising rate of change during reference expansions. This may explain why the average pattern for the nongold source in Chart 7 for the latter period rises from stage I to stage IV.

In general, however, the over-all positive conformity of changes in high-powered money to reference cycles cannot be explained by a dependence on the two ratios. One reason is that the dependence was estimated among cycles separately for each stage and so does not necessarily imply anything about stage-to-stage movements in high-powered money. It implies only that the contribution of this determinant was high when the combined contribution of the two ratios was low, and vice versa. Average patterns may well conceal such a relationship. Another reason already suggested is that the dependence accounts for only one-half the cyclical variation in high-powered money; the total variation is obscured by the other half, which has no uniform pattern.

SUMMARY OF CYCLICAL MOVEMENTS

Although their objectives and reactions to cyclical developments varied appreciably, therefore, credit policies of the Reserve Banks had a major impact on monetary conditions from the beginning. The average patterns for high-powered money shown in Chart 7 are substantially different before and after World War I. In the earlier period, the change in high-powered money fluctuates most during reference contractions, having a high peak in stage VII. This pattern can be attributed to corresponding movements in the gold and nongold sources of change and largely reflects the inverse cyclical pattern of the trade balance. In the later period, a high peak occurs instead during reference expansions, and the ensuing decline continues past the reference peak to stage VIII. This behavior reflects almost entirely the pattern of nongold sources, the gold stock showing no consistent pattern except a fall at reference troughs.

Chapter 2 describes cyclical fluctuations in high-powered money as erratic, at least compared with those in the currency and reserve ratios. In the post-World War I period, most of the erratic behavior resulted from special actions taken by the Reserve Banks and Treasury, as the economy passed through war, severe depression, and other difficult times. Although the second half of the 1950's has brought new problems for the monetary authorities, nothing so far compares with the preceding four hectic decades.

4

THE CURRENCY RATIO

IF BANKS maintain fractional reserve ratios and convert deposits into currency upon request, as in the U.S. monetary system, the currency ratio affects the distribution of high-powered money between banks and the public and thereby helps to determine the quantity of deposits created. Except when banks suspend payments, free convertibility allows the public to maintain any ratio desired up to unity, and desired changes can be and usually are made quickly. In the United States, for the period of this study, all high-powered money held by the *nonbanking* public has been in the form of currency and vice versa; the two concepts pertain to the same quantity. Under those circumstances the currency ratio indicates the distribution of money balances between deposits and currency and also of high-powered money between banks and the public, a dual role which greatly simplifies the analysis. Until 1866, state commercial banks also issued notes,[1] clearly not high-powered money by our definition of it as money banks can use for reserves. In that period, therefore, the fraction of its money balances the public wanted at any time to hold in the form of gold coin was also an important determinant of the money stock. In general, the amounts of gold and of currency held by the public behave differently. After the retirement of state bank notes, however, the public's gold ratio was ordinarily not of great importance. Since 1934 it has been zero. The public's demand for gold was discussed briefly in Chapter 3 (under Silver Purchases). The present chapter is concerned solely with the currency ratio.

A variety of factors appears to influence the demand for currency. It is not held just to facilitate current transactions. Currency outside banks per person in the United States averaged $164 in 1955 and $30 in 1929. Multiplying these figures by three or four to put them on a per-household basis gives an amount that seems far above the average transactions needs of a typical family. Retail businesses probably

---

[1] In 1866, a prohibitive federal tax was placed on their issue. By the early 1870's nearly all had been retired.

hold but a minor part of the total. Apparently a large amount of currency is held as a store of wealth, though the nature of such holdings may have changed over the years. In the mid-1800's, currency was for many people the sole financial means of holding wealth. Since then the alternatives have greatly expanded with the growth of time and savings accounts, deposit insurance, U.S. savings bonds, pension plans, and so on. Such alternatives may have reduced currency holdings. To some wealthy individuals, however, currency stored in a safe deposit box provides secrecy—a special advantage that may have become more appealing in recent decades as estate and income tax rates have risen substantially.

The main substitute for currency as a means of payment is a checking account; and as a store of wealth, probably a savings deposit. Assuming that individuals account for most currency demand (businesses temporarily holding only what they take in through retail trade), we may express the demand in terms of the public's preferences for currency as a medium of exchange and as a store of wealth. To explain changes in the amount demanded, two sets of variables are involved, one for the transactions demand and one for the store-of-wealth demand. Two important variables in the first set might be the volume of consumer expenditures and the cost of a checking account; in the second set they might be total private wealth and the return on a savings deposit.

Since we are concerned with currency holdings relative to total money balances, the preceding variables are relevant only to the extent that they affect the demand for currency and deposits differently. Changes in the net rate of return on deposits do have differential effects on currency and deposits by inducing substitutions between them. Growth in expenditures and wealth may also help explain the differing growth rates in currency and deposit holdings. The following section on secular movements discusses these developments. Cyclical movements, taken up in the second section, appear quite different in nature.

1. Secular Movements in the Demand for Currency

SHIFTS IN THE DEMAND RELATIVE TO OTHER ASSETS

The ratio of currency to the total money stock is affected by shifts between currency and deposits as well as shifts between either of these

CHART 10

The Currency-Money Ratio, the Currency-Expenditures Ratio, and Velocity of Money, Annually, 1874–1960

(per cent)

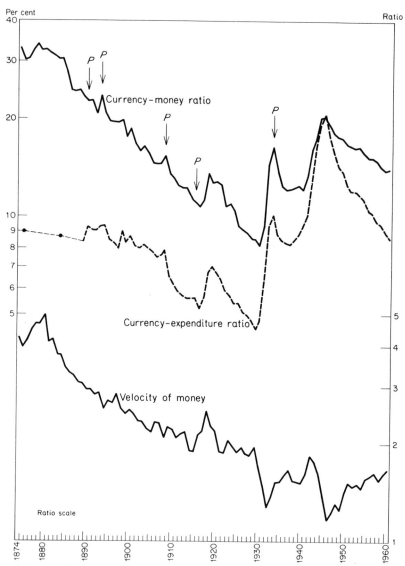

Source: Currency-money ratio, same as for Chart 1, June. Currency-expenditures ratio, Table F-18. Figure for 1874 is an average for 1869–78 and figure for 1884, an average for 1879–88.

Velocity of money, ratio of net national product to money stock, from Friedman and Schwartz, *A Monetary History of the United States, 1869–1960.*

Note: *P* denotes years in which panics occurred.

two and other assets. To help identify the factors affecting currency demand, Chart 10 presents annual data on the currency-money ratio, currency-expenditures ratio, and income-money ratio (the familiar velocity of money, income approximated here by net national product). The middle ratio uses the annual volume of consumer expenditures as a scale factor to deflate currency held outside banks. This deflator serves as a first approximation to all factors associated with long-run growth in the economy affecting currency, through the transactions as well as the wealth demand. We cannot distinguish empirically the effects on currency demand of expenditures and of wealth, since their long-run movements are so similar.

The currency-money ratio had a downward trend from the 1870's until 1930. It rose appreciably during the early 1930's and World War II. The trend after 1930 appears slightly upward, but in view of the earlier decline the later period may be interpreted as two sharp short-run increases superimposed upon a slackening or termination of the earlier downtrend. The currency-expenditures ratio parallels these movements, though with a smaller percentage decline during the pre-1930 period and larger movements in the 1930's and 1940's. The income-money ratio also parallels the pre-1930 decline, but moves generally opposite to the other two ratios in the latter period.

Some changes in demand affect either the currency-expenditures ratio or the income-money ratio but not both, producing independent movements. Thus substitutions between currency and commercial bank deposits do not involve the total amount of money demanded, and the effect on the currency-money ratio is entirely reflected in the currency-expenditures ratio. Substitutions between commercial bank deposits and other earning assets do not involve currency demand, and the income-money ratio shows the entire effect on the currency-money ratio. Certain demand shifts, however, affect both. If both currency and deposits are substituted for nonmonetary assets, other things the same, the currency-expenditures ratio rises and the income-money ratio falls, both reflecting the same shift.[2] It is not always clear to

[2] As a formal expression, the currency-money ratio equals the product of three other ratios:

$$\frac{C}{M} \equiv \frac{C}{E} \cdot \frac{E}{Y} \cdot \frac{Y}{M},$$

where the first on the right side is currency C to consumer expenditures E; the second, consumer expenditures to national income Y; and the third, the income velocity what extent currency demand takes part in such shifts, but the foregoing ratios suggest the direction of the net changes occurring, assuming that consumer expenditures and national income are appropriate scale factors. Declines in both the currency-expenditures and the money-income ratio point to substitutions of commercial bank deposits for currency and other assets—deposits are expanding and currency contracting relative to the scale factors; and conversely for increases in both ratios. A rise in the currency-expenditures ratio and decline in the income-money ratio point to gains in currency holdings at the expense of assets other than commercial bank deposits; the converse movements point to a shift from currency and perhaps deposits to other assets.

Chart 10 may thus be interpreted as follows: The decline in all three ratios up to 1930 suggests a shift in relative demand from currency and nonmonetary assets to commerical bank deposits. As indicated by the currency-expenditures ratio, the decline in currency demand accelerated after about 1904 (disregarding the 1907 panic). Currency demand rose thereafter, most sharply in response to the banking crisis of the early 1930's and wartime developments in the 1940's. The accompanying movements of the income-money ratio in those decades suggest that the increased demand for currency did not have neutral effects on the total amount of money demanded, but that the public shifted from nonmonetary assets to both currency and

---

of money. Even though the middle ratio on the right may be independent of the others in the long run, the other two will, as suggested, sometimes be related. Only when all three on the right move independently can changes in the left side be broken down into the three separate effects.

An argument that the currency-money ratio depends upon the velocity of money has been made by Frank Brechling (see "The Public's Preference for Cash," *Banca Nazionale del Lavoro Quarterly Review* 46, Sept. 1958). Brechling assumes that the demand for currency may be separated into demands for idle and active currency, and that these are each fractions of the demand for idle (M_1) and active (M_2) money balances, respectively. That is, $C = \alpha M_1 + \beta M_2$, whence $C/M = (\alpha M_1 + \beta M_2)/M$, where presumably $\beta > \alpha$. The currency ratio therefore depends on the distribution of money between active and idle balances, which may be measured by the velocity of total money balances.

The empirical implications of this formulation are brought out by assuming that α is virtually zero and that the ratio of active to total money balances is some function of velocity, $f(Y/M)$. Then we have $C/M = \beta f(Y/M)$. If we further assume that β is a function of the ratio of currency to consumer expenditures, we obtain a relationship similar to the preceding identity.

It is doubtful, however, that α is either small or constant, though it might be reasonably constant in the short run.

commercial bank deposits. The rise in the income-money ratio during the 1950's points to the opposite shift.

These secular movements in the relative demand for currency may be attributed to numerous developments. We may assess the contributions of three factors often cited—the net rate of return on deposits, growth in real income and wealth, and urbanization—and other special factors contributing to the wartime increases.

NET RATE OF RETURN ON DEPOSITS

The rate of interest paid on deposits net of service charges represents the attractiveness—if the rate is positive—or the cost—if negative—of holding deposits instead of currency. Do these rates behave in a way that could explain major movements in currency demand? The rates on demand and time or savings deposits have behaved differently and require separate discussion.

Demand Deposits. Although the average rate paid on all demand deposits was not inconsiderable before such payments were prohibited for member banks in 1934 and for insured banks in 1935, small accounts, which are the main substitutes for currency, have never earned interest. Before 1934, banks commonly paid interest on amounts due to other banks and the U.S. Treasury and on some large holdings of businesses and individuals. In 1927, for example, when interest payments on demand deposits were first reported separately, the average rate paid by member banks was $1\frac{1}{4}$ per cent (see Appendix E for data on rates). When paid, the typical rate was probably around 2 per cent, which implies over one-third of member bank demand deposits earned no interest. Also, in a special survey of all national banks made by the Comptroller of the Currency in 1870, one-third of the banks paid no interest on any deposits.

Service charges were not common in the 1920's and earlier, a reason large city banks and perhaps others typically did not encourage small checking accounts. When data on charges were first reported in 1933, those of member banks averaged 15 cents a year per $100 of demand deposits. Although only small depositors paid such charges, the typical rate, when charged, was probably well below one-half of 1 per cent. Services charges have spread since the 1930's, and by 1960 the average charge, based on all publicly held demand deposits with insured banks, had risen to nearly one-half of 1 per cent. Federal deposit insurance, introduced in 1934, has lowered losses on small accounts virtually to zero, but it does not fully compensate for the charges.[3]

The rise in service charges after 1933, while moderate, was of some consequence. The currency-expenditures ratio, as Chart 10 shows, reached an all-time low in 1929. It declined moderately from its high point after the 1933 panic[4] but then started to rise again. The rise during World War II reflects special factors and is discussed later. The decline during the 1950's has erased the wartime rise but, so far, no more; by 1960 the ratio stood at about the 1939 level and seemed to be leveling off. The high level in 1939 and 1960 compared with 1929 seems partly to reflect the increase in service charges.

Whatever its effect later, the rate of return on demand deposits probably had negligible effect on currency use in the pre-1930 period, simply because the rate paid on small accounts was constant at zero and losses were generally low and not alarming, even in panic years.

Savings Deposits. These deposits[5] have always paid interest, though the rate has varied from 5 or 6 per cent in the early 1870's to less than 1 per cent in the 1930's and 1940's. The data for commercial and mutual savings banks, discussed in Appendix E, indicate that most rates on these deposits move together. The rates generally fell after the 1870's until the turn of the century, and rose during the 1920's. Fragmentary evidence places a long-run trough in these rates in 1904. After 1930 they fell to the unusually low levels noted, reaching a trough in the second half of the 1940's. Thereafter there was a sharp rise continuing through the 1950's (see Chart 18, p. 168).

Insofar as savings deposits substitute for currency as a store of wealth, fluctuations in these rates produce opposite movements in the

[3] The average annual rate of loss from 1920 to 1929 ran from 9 to 19 cents per $100 of deposits (based on *Annual Report*, Federal Deposit Insurance Corporation, 1940, p. 66).

[4] The increase in demand for currency from 1929 to 1933 is readily explained by a sharp rise in actual and expected losses on deposits. The demand shot up much higher than in previous panics, because the 1933 episode was the culmination of two years of ruinous bank failures. In earlier panics, suspension of payments usually came quickly, removing the obligation to pay out currency until the panic passed and allowing even most weak banks to survive.

[5] The majority of time deposits at commercial banks are small savings accounts of individuals (see Chap. 5, "Shifts Between Time and Demand Deposits"), similar to deposits at savings banks. All such substitutes for currency are referred to here as savings deposits.

currency-expenditures ratio. This effect therefore helps explain the accelerated decline in the ratio from 1904 to 1930, the rise during the 1930's and 1940's, and the decline thereafter. The secular decline in the ratio from the 1870's to 1930, however, must reflect other factors, inasmuch as savings deposit rates fell until the turn of the century and apparently were higher in the early 1870's than at any time since. The wartime rise in currency demand seems much too steep to attribute more than a small part to the decline in these rates. However, they no doubt contributed, along with the rise in check charges, to the higher level of the currency-expenditures ratio in 1939 than in 1930.

The effect of deposit rates on the currency-*money* ratio is less certain because of parallel movements in general interest rates. A rise in deposit rates, for example, induces shifts from currency to deposits; but when interest rates at large also rise, the public may at the same time shift from demand deposits and perhaps time deposits to other assets, depending upon yield differentials. Parallel movements in the spectrum of interest rates are the rule. Although savings deposit rates move sluggishly, the differential yield on other assets generally widens less than the rise in the level of the rates, and narrows less than the decline. Therefore, shifts between deposits and other assets from this source, though they tend to moderate the effects of currency shifts on the currency-money ratio, probably do not reverse them. For demand deposits, however, which offered a zero return to small accounts before the 1930's and since then have imposed charges largely unrelated to general interest-rate movements, a rise in interest rates induces a shift from demand deposits to other assets but not from currency to demand deposits. With a rise in interest rates, therefore, the over-all demand for commercial bank deposits might decrease proportionately more than that for currency, producing a rise in the currency-money ratio, and conversely with declines in interest rates. Such opposite movements in the currency-money and currency-expenditures ratios have generally not occurred, however, suggesting that the demand for currency has a larger response to changes in deposit rates than the demand for commercial bank deposits has to interest-rate movements at large.

In any event, deposit rates partly explain the post-1930 movements in the currency-money ratio, but not the earlier secular decline.

INCOME GROWTH AND URBANIZATION

Although many factors might account for the secular decline in currency demand, only two seem capable of a sufficiently persistent and pervasive influence to be important—growth in income and wealth, and urbanization. Both could affect institutional arrangements for making payments and holding wealth, and most changes in such arrangements can be related to one or both of those two developments.

The rise in real income per capita would reduce the relative demand for currency if it enhanced the appeal of making payments by check and having a bank account, or, in technical terms, if the income elasticity of currency were less than unity. This may at first seem strange, because we customarily associate such a phenomenon with "necessities." With higher incomes people switch from them to more expensive items; similarly, in their portfolios they might forego income to acquire lower-yielding securities that offer nonpecuniary advantages, such as liquidity. From this point of view, we should not be surprised to find a shift to money balances from higher-yielding assets when real income rises. But why a shift from currency to deposits? Before the 1930's, a small checking account cost nothing, and a large account or a savings deposit paid interest. A shift from currency to deposits cannot be described as providing an asset with greater convenience at the expense of a lower yield. To be sure, some devices for avoiding currency may cost something (as with credit cards and checking accounts today), but this qualification is not applicable to most of the pre-1930 period except to the extent (apparently rare) that banks required a minimum balance to open a checking account.

The way out is not to argue that the income elasticity of currency cannot be less than unity but to recognize that income growth is a proxy for a host of other developments which, on balance, may work to increase the demand for deposits relative to currency. Rising real income changes our mode of life and somewhere along the way may convert practices of holding wealth and making payments from currency to deposits. Interrelated as these developments are, it may still be possible (and if possible, certainly revealing) to separate the effects on currency demand of some of them, such as urbanization, from the others, which may then be combined into an all-inclusive "income effect."

Urbanization is a favorite explanation of the spread of banking, and it is tempting to assume that it must also have produced a substantial reduction in the use of currency. It must be remembered, however, that this factor works in two directions. First, the impersonal nature of urban trade discourages the use of checks and credit. Historical commentaries suggest that it was once much more common for laborers to buy on credit between pay periods, at least in small communities, and to settle their accumulated debts on payday. Payment of retail purchases in this way would decrease the use of currency. The growth of cities may have reduced this practice and so have increased the use of currency. To be sure, charge accounts are still widely used even in large cities, but their importance may be less than it was fifty or seventy-five years ago—the recent proliferation of credit cards to the contrary notwithstanding.

A second, quite different effect of urbanization on the demand for currency is sometimes deduced from various facts suggesting that larger bank deposits are held by individuals in cities than in country districts. The inference drawn is that urban life provides familiarity with the advantages of checking accounts and encourages the banking habit. For example, payment of wages by check is (or once was) more common in urban than in rural business. Inconveniences of banking by mail and possible inefficiencies of small banks may also have limited the spread of banking in rural communities, though only the most sparsely settled areas would seem to be unable to support one bank, or at least a branch of a nearby bank. Branch banking is illegal in many states, but it is questionable whether the prohibition would have endured if rural communities had demanded banking facilities that could be supplied economically only by branch banks.

Yet the same can be said of the use of currency. All the preceding argument says is that rural areas have less demand for all kinds of money than cities do, or at least until quite recently, because barter was prevalent in frontier areas and wages were paid partly in kind. This implies nothing about shifts in demand between currency and deposits. The question is whether migrants from rural areas to cities become familiar with banking practices and expand their use of checking facilities in place of currency. Without evidence, there is little basis on which to judge.

Combining the second effect of urbanization with the first throws the over-all effect of this variable into doubt. These two supposed effects of urbanization on currency demand work in opposite directions, and there is no a priori basis for expecting their net effect to work one way or the other.

In an earlier study of mine on currency demand,[6] a comparison of U.S. and British data indicated that urbanization alone might explain part but not all of the early decline in the currency-money ratio. Estimates of the British ratio of currency to consumer expenditures support the same conclusion. The British ratio had a downward trend from 1883 to 1914. While the urbanization movement in Britain declined sharply after 1900, the ratio fell 1 percentage point from 1903 to 1914 (from 7.8 to 6.8 per cent).[7] The American ratio fell 2.6 points in that period (from 8.2 to 5.6 per cent, see Table F-18), suggesting that the larger decline here reflected a combination of continued urbanization and rising deposit rates.

Whether income growth or urbanization had the greater influence is relevant to the interpretation of later movements in the ratio. The urbanization movement declined sharply after the 1920's in the United States, while the income effect—unless it was merely a proxy for developments like urbanization or geographical expansion—has continued and therefore has influenced the ratio after 1930 as well. Later movements in the ratio are too volatile to resolve the question.

Although definite conclusions are not possible, we can narrow the possibilities. If urbanization, or some combination of like factors all of which diminished after 1930, accounts for the earlier downtrend in the currency-expenditures ratio, the future trend in the ratio will be horizontal, once the wartime rise has been fully erased and assuming no large changes in deposit rates. There is a slight indication that the ratio was leveling off in 1960 at about the 1938–39 level. On the other hand, if the ratio continues to decline, a leading explanation would be the continuing influence of income growth. In either event, we should explain the higher level in 1939 relative to 1929 by an increase

---

[6] *The Demand for Currency Relative to the Total Money Supply*, Occasional Paper 62, New York, NBER, 1958 (originally published without appendix in *Journal of Political Economy*, Aug. 1958). The first part of this chapter summarizes and reinterprets the results of that study.

[7] Currency figures are based on the sources cited for Table 2, *ibid.* Consumer expenditures are from J. B. Jefferys and D. Walters, "National Income and Expenditure of the United Kingdom 1870–1952," in *Income and Wealth*, London, International Association for Research in Income and Wealth, 1955, Table I, pp. 8–9.

in service charges on checking accounts and a decline in rates paid on savings deposits. By 1960 the factors associated solely with the war had largely disappeared, and the continued high level of the ratio relative to 1929 may be attributed to service charges, somewhat lower savings deposit rates despite their rise in the 1950's, and, since the 1940's, to evasion of income taxes, discussed further below.

FACTORS RESPONSIBLE FOR THE WARTIME RISE IN CURRENCY DEMAND

From 1939 to 1945 the currency-expenditures ratio rose 12.0 points. On the basis of the 1945 volume of consumer expenditures, $14.6 billion of currency was hoarded in that year.[8] By comparison, the rise from 1917 to 1919 was 1.4 points, or about $600 million. (The British ratio also rose during both world wars.) This section discusses the rise in U.S. currency holdings during the second war.

Although the 1945 peak in the currency-expenditures ratio may be somewhat overstated because wartime controls led to illegal consumer expenditures of various kinds, which our data may in part omit, the error on this account cannot be large and indeed is probably negligible. Other factors mentioned for secular movements seem unimportant. Check charges were almost constant during World War II and rose slowly from 1946 to 1960, contributing to a currency-expenditures ratio only slightly higher after the war than earlier. The rate of return on savings deposits fell during the war and rose thereafter, which possibly explains part of the movement in currency demand. But the decline in the rate during the war was less than 1 percentage point, and it took more than a decade after the war to rise by that amount; its earlier movements were far greater (see Appendix E). The wartime peak in the currency-expenditures ratio therefore far exceeds effects attributable to deposit rates. Since the ratio declined

[8] Calculations of that hoarding according to the currency-money ratio, which incorporates the offsetting effect of a fall in the velocity of money, put the "excess" at $10 billion.

That "hoarding" is the right word to describe the excess currency in circulation is confirmed by the reduced rate of deterioration of large bills. Before the war, $20 bills "normally circulated at a rate several times faster than $100 bills judging by the rates of return of unfit currency to this bank. Currently, because such a large proportion of $20's apparently are being hoarded, the turnover of the total amount outstanding is approximately the same as that for the $100's" (*Monthly Review*, Federal Reserve Bank of New York, July 1948, p. 74). See also *Federal Reserve Bulletin*, Apr. 1942, pp. 312–316.

rapidly after 1945, and large increases in deposit rates came only after 1956, the wartime rise in currency demand appears to involve special factors which partly disappeared after the war.

The income-money ratio fell during, and rose after, the war. This no doubt reflected some of the same shifts in asset demand affecting currency holdings. The currency-money ratio nevertheless followed the movements in the currency expenditures ratio, but with less amplitude.

My earlier study reviewed all the factors that seem of possible importance: black-marketing, travel, changes of residence, foreign demand, and tax evasion. The first two were dismissed. Black-marketing did not lead to a rise in the amount outstanding of large-denomination bills ($20 and up) over what the wartime inflation induced, as it would have if it had created an important demand for currency. Total miles traveled per person did not rise during the war; increased train travel was offset by limitation of automobile use by gasoline rationing and by restrictions on civilian flights.

The second two factors merit attention. Changes of residence under the impact of war were unprecedented, and all industries attracted workers of every type to new plants in southern towns and cities and to converted plants in the North and West. Many of the migrants may have been unfamiliar with money substitutes and may have found currency preferable to checking accounts in strange cities. Intending to return home at the end of hostilities they may have accumulated savings in the form of currency from their high wartime earnings.[9] If they did, they might have gradually dishoarded their currency after the war wherever they lived, which would explain the sharp fall in the ratio after 1946. If so, the increased demand for currency in the 1940's was not at the expense of deposits, and the increase produced both the rise in the currency-expenditures ratio and part of the concurrent decline in the velocity of money.

Another factor was foreign hoarding of U.S. currency. In such times of inconvertibility and worldwide upheaval, many foreigners may have picked U.S. currency as the safest refuge for their funds. One estimate of foreign demand is $4 billion.[10] This would then

[9] There were of course many attractive alternatives available, in particular, U.S. savings bonds, their purchase in payroll savings plans being actively encouraged. Those plans likely siphoned off much of the currency hoarded by migrants.

[10] *Monthly Review*, Federal Reserve Bank of N.Y., July 1948, p. 75.

explain part of the wartime rise in the ratio and also part of its subsequent decline during the 1950's with the return of convertibility
and political stability.[11]

While it seems impossible to say definitely whether changes of residence and foreign demand alone accounted for the extra currency
outstanding in 1945, by almost any reckoning they seem inadequate.
Even an assumed $4 billion due to foreign demand leaves over
$10 billion of the total $14.6 billion to be explained by changes of
residence—an unreasonably large figure. A rough estimate of migration between 1940 and 1945 is 5 million people, or at most 2.5 million
families. Savings of $10 billion during the war would mean $4,000 for
the average family, an inordinate amount for even a five-year period,
when the annual gross earnings of manufacturing workers averaged
less than $2,500 even in 1945.[12] And surely not all savings were held
as currency.

By implication, the fifth factor listed—tax evasion—appears to be
important. Some people evade income taxes by making as many
transactions as possible with currency, not reporting currency receipts.
Obviously, evasion will occur on a large scale only if tax rates are high
enough to create an incentive. The only widely levied tax on transactions with high rates is the income tax, though the rates have become
exceptionally high only since the late 1930's. For practical reasons
the possibility of evasion by use of currency is limited to professional
and unincorporated business income. An estimate of the unreported
amount of income from this combined source for 1945 is $10 billion.[13]
If unreported income required a stock of currency equal to one-half
of annual transactions—approximately true of total money balances
in relation to national income—currency demand for this purpose
(not counting currency hoards for storing wealth secretly) would be
$5 billion. Whether this estimate is too high or too low is difficult
to determine.

[11] Another wartime factor worth a glancing reference was the deterioration of
bank services due to employee shortages. Long queues at tellers' windows during
peak hours led some government agencies and perhaps other employers to pay wages
in currency instead of by check, for the duration.

[12] See my The Demand for Currency, p. 16, for discussion of the figures on migration
and earnings.

[13] C. Harry Kahn, Business and Professional Income Under the Personal Income Tax,
Princeton for NBER, 1964, Table 6. This estimate has been revised downward from
the one cited in The Demand for Currency.

Hoarding due to income-tax evasion might therefore account for what remains unexplained of the wartime rise in the currency-expenditures ratio. Since income taxes have not declined much from wartime levels, evasion probably accounts for little if any of the subsequent fall in the ratio—assuming that improved enforcement of taxes or new methods of evading payment have not materially reduced the use of currency for evasion. Most of the decline in the ratio immediately after the war may therefore be attributed to the disappearance of demand from foreigners and migrants, and most of the decline thereafter to the rise in deposit rates.

SUMMARY OF SECULAR MOVEMENTS

The secular decline in currency demand in the period preceding 1930 may be explained by myriad developments in pay practices. No technological revolution occurred in the cost or convenience of banking services, and presumably at any time in the nation's development the public could have had whatever banking facilities it was willing to pay for. Demand factors seem paramount, among them geographical expansion; growth of public education; shift to payment of wages by check; increasing expenditures on consumer durables requiring large payments and often credit financing; expansion of use of charge accounts of many types, including credit cards; growth of various financial means of storing wealth. All these factors might reduce currency demand. Merely enumerating the possibilities does not supply a satisfactory explanation, however, since many of them reflected declining use of currency but did not cause it. Most of them, moreover, are not independent developments. They reflect or are related to growth in real income, and this variable serves conveniently to represent all related factors that on balance reduce currency demand. Similarly, urbanization represents all such factors that became less important after 1930. It is plausible to attribute the pre-1930 decline in the currency-expenditures ratio to the steady growth in real income and of urban centers.

Rates of return on savings deposits apparently fell from 1873 to around the turn of the century, then generally rose until 1930. They were lower at the end of that period than at the beginning and so cannot account for the decline in currency demand. They may explain the accelerated decline in the currency-expenditures ratio after 1904, however.

The rise in the ratio during the first half of the 1930's can be attributed to bank failures and panic; during the second half, to the introduction of service charges on checking accounts and decline in savings deposit rates. The continued high level of the ratio in 1939, compared with 1929, despite the slackening of urbanization and spread of deposit insurance, is not readily explained in any other way. That the long-run developments reducing the use of currency until 1929 suddenly reversed direction during the 1930's is possible but doubtful.

Hoarding of currency and deposits during World War II absorbed unprecedented quantities of money and then, after the war, subsided. People laid away their high wartime earnings, and businesses their profits, in anticipation of plentiful consumer and producer goods after the war. Two reasons usually given for hoarding bank deposits were, first, that many people were not familiar with or distrusted savings institutions and bonds and, second, that low rates of return on assets invested in those ways were extremely unattractive. Whatever the reason for hoarding demand and time deposits, there was no parallel reason for hoarding currency. Judged by the subsequent decline in the currency-expenditures ratio, currency hoarding gradually disappeared after the war. The wartime rise evidently reflected temporary factors, of which changes of residence by workers and foreign hoarding of U.S. currency seem the most important. These alone were probably inadequate to explain fully the wartime increase and subsequent decline in currency, and it was suggested that a combination of tax evasion and changes in deposit rates might account for what remains unexplained. The smaller magnitude of changes in these factors in World War I would explain why the rise in currency demand was so much smaller in the first than in the second war.

The wartime rise is fascinating but is important only because its explanation holds the key to interpreting the postwar decline in the currency-expenditures ratio. The relative importance of the various factors in the postwar decline is, likewise, relevant to an interpretation of the pre-1930 downtrend and the future trend of the ratio. The ratio in 1960, after receding from its wartime peak, had the same level as in 1939, because the effect of tax evasion and rising check charges had offset the effect of rising savings deposit rates. The ratio was higher in 1960 and 1939 than in 1929 apparently because of continuing tax evasion and higher check charges, even though rates on savings deposits were still somewhat lower in 1960 than in the 1920's.

The relatively high levels of the ratio since the 1920's suggest that the pre-1930 institutional developments reducing currency demand associated with income growth have not continued. On the other hand, they may have continued but were offset since 1930 by the other factors discussed. In that event the downtrend will reappear in the future unless there are large reductions in savings deposit rates or increases in check charges.

The post-1930 behavior of the currency-expenditures ratio has produced similar but smaller movements in the currency-money ratio because of the income-money ratio. The demands for commercial bank deposits and for currency shifted in the same directions over this period, no doubt partly for related reasons, and thus partly canceled their effects on the currency-money ratio.

2. Cyclical Movements in the Demand for Currency

THE GENERAL PATTERN

Besides strong secular movements, the currency-money ratio also displays short-run fluctuations. Although not prominent or easy to identify in the graph of the series in Chart 1, those fluctuations were the proximate source of half the cyclical variation in the rate of change in the money stock (disregarding the offsetting movements of high-powered money in part of the post-1918 cycles). The fluctuations show up clearly in Chart 2 and, as Table 6 indicates, the contribution of this ratio to cycles in the money series is the most regular found for the three determinants. Another way to describe its behavior is by reference cycle patterns. In view of their regularity, cyclical movements in the ratio are adequately summarized by the average reference cycle patterns plotted in Chart 11. It should be emphasized that these patterns show the level of the ratio, not its contribution to the rate of change in the money stock, as in Chart 2. The solid line is an average for fifteen reference cycles. Atypical reference patterns for four cycles are excluded: the two war cycles, in which the currency-money ratio rose for special reasons examined earlier; and the 1927–33 and 1933–38 reference cycles, in which the banking panic of 1933 produced an unusually large rise in the ratio.

CHART 11

Average Pattern and Deviations from Trend of the Currency-Money Ratio for Two Sets of Reference Cycles, 1879–1954

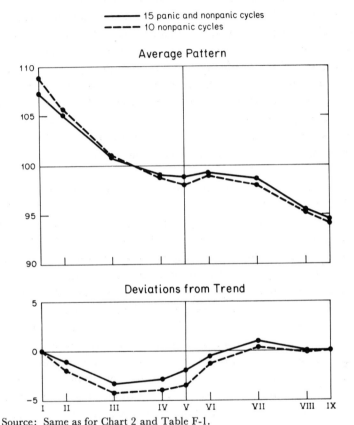

——— 15 panic and nonpanic cycles
– – – – 10 nonpanic cycles

Source: Same as for Chart 2 and Table F-1.

Note: The fifteen panic and nonpanic cycles exclude the two war cycles and the 1927–33 and 1933–38 cycles. The ten nonpanic cycles exclude four cycles omitted from the other pattern and all other panic cycles (see Table 14 for identification of panic cycles). Stages II, IV, VI, and VIII are based on the post-1908 cycles only. Trend determined by a straight line connecting stages I and IX.

The average pattern for fifteen cycles levels off relative to its trend from stage III to stage VII, more clearly shown by the deviations from trend in the lower panel of the chart. Nearly all the individual reference cycle patterns have that break in the rate of decline, though there are differences in amplitude and timing. The typical cycle in the currency-money ratio is inverted and, adjusted for trend, has an expansion phase starting about stage III or IV and ending about stage VII. Without adjustment for trend, the expansion phase is often only a sidewise movement starting with stage IV or V. (Stages II, IV, VI, and VIII are not computed for annual data; their standings in Chart 11 are based on monthly data for the post-1908 cycles only.) Of the nine nonwar reference cycles covered by our monthly data, only four have higher levels in stage VII than in stage IV or V, and all four rise from IV to V. Of the others, most have a monthly rate of decline lower from IV to V than from I to IV. The tendency of the currency-money ratio to decline at a diminishing rate during reference expansions means that the peak in its contribution to the rate of change of the money stock occurred long before reference cycle peaks.

Banking panics, which sharply increase the demand for currency, do not account for these cyclical fluctuations in the ratio. The dash lines in Chart 11 show the average pattern and deviations from trend after excluding all panic cycles (identified later in Table 14). The two patterns are virtually the same in timing and amplitude. An average pattern excluding cycles that followed panic cycles (not shown in the chart) is also the same, indicating that the diminishing rate of decline in the ratio during reference expansions does not reflect recoveries from preceding panics. Such episodes usually had little effect on the patterns, therefore, in part because panics generally did not last long and the ratio fell rapidly afterward to a normal level, and in part for other reasons discussed below. By contrast, the 1933 panic, which forms the dividing trough for the two cycles of the 1930's and affected the behavior of the ratio to an unusual extent, was the culmination of an extended period of banking difficulties and, unlike most other panics, came at the end of the business contraction. It was therefore excluded.

Since the series in the bottom panel of Chart 11 remove the trend imperfectly, we should not be overly precise in describing the cyclical pattern. We may simply say that, even after excluding panics and their after effects, cycles in the currency ratio have an expansion phase beginning in the latter part of reference expansions and ending midway through contractions. Whether the ratio is a leading or lagging series in terms of reference dates is not clear; its behavior may be

described as roughly 90 degrees out of phase.[14]   It has positive or
inverted conformity depending on whether one views the phasing
as 90 degrees behind or ahead of reference cycles. As suggested in
Chapter 6, there may in fact be a mutual relationship reflecting effects
of business on the money stock together with the effects of money on
business. Since the largest increases in the ratio have usually occurred
from stage V to stage VII, I shall speak of the pattern as inverted.

Important differences between individual cycles can be inferred
from Table 14.   It gives the change per month in reference cycle
relatives of each cycle from stage IV or V to stage VII—the typical
period for which the downward trend is suspended and the currency-
money ratio remains level or rises—and compares it with the change
per month during the preceding and succeeding stages of the reference
cycle. As shown in column 1, the change for that period of suspended
trend was upward in only about half the cycles. Even in cycles without
a rise, however, the decline was usually less than that in the other
stages of the cycle, as shown by the preponderance of positive values
in columns 2 and 3. Moreover, the few negative values in these two
columns are fairly small, indicating that the exceptions to the typical
pattern were moderate in amplitude. Indeed, the largest of the negative values, that in column 2 for the 1891–94 cycle, is spurious; it
would probably be positive and not an exception if we had monthly
data for that period. That cycle contains the 1893 panic, which produced the usual sharp rise in the currency-money ratio in June, well

[14] To check the nature of the relation, first differences in the currency ratio were
plotted on an inverted basis (to show its contribution to rates of change in the money
stock positively) and compared with reference cycles. Cyclical turning points in the
contribution series were selected that match reference turns, first on a negative basis
(that is, peaks in the former with reference troughs, and troughs with peaks) and then
on a positive basis (peaks with peaks, etc.). The period was 1877–1957 excluding
wars, covering 18 reference cycles. In the first comparison, turning points in the first
differences lag reference turns on the average by 2.8 months at reference peaks and
5.6 months at troughs. This comparison views the currency ratio as having positive
lagging conformity to reference cycles. In the second comparison, turning points in
the first differences lead reference turns on the average by 10.5 months at reference
peaks and 11.1 months at troughs. This comparison views the currency ratio as having
inverted leading conformity to reference cycles.
  To help identify the dominant relation, standard deviations of the leads and lags
were computed according to each relation. On the first comparison of reference
cycles with first differences inverted, the standard deviation of lags was five months
at reference peaks and thirteen months at troughs. On the second comparison, the
standard deviation of leads was eleven months at both reference peaks and troughs.
This evidence is therefore mixed: for reference peaks, the first basis of comparison
has the more stable timing relation; for reference troughs, the second has.

TABLE 14

CHANGE IN THE CURRENCY-MONEY RATIO DURING REFERENCE CYCLES, 1879-1954

Reference Cycle Dates[a]			Special Cycles[b]	CHANGE PER MONTH OF REFERENCE CYCLE RELATIVES		
					Stages IV or V to VII, Minus the Change for:	
Trough	Peak	Trough		Stages IV or V to VII (1)	Stages I to IV or V (2)	Stages VII to IX (3)
				A N N U A L D A T A[c]		
Mar. '79	Mar. '82	May '85	pf	-0.1	+0.1	+0.4
May '85	Mar. '87	Apr. '88		0.0	+0.6	-0.1
Apr. '88	July '90	May '91	p	+0.1	+0.4	0.0
May '91	Jan. '93	June '94	pf	-0.5	-0.6	+0.4
June '94	Dec. '95	June '97	f	-0.1	+0.3	-0.1
June '97	June '99	Dec. '00		+0.4	+0.8	+0.8
Dec. '00	Sept. '02	Aug. '04		+0.1	+0.6	+0.4
Aug. '04	May '07	June '08	p	+0.8	+1.0	+1.4
				M O N T H L Y D A T A		
June '08	Jan. '10	Jan. '12		-0.3	+1.0	+0.5
Jan. '12	Jan. '13	Dec. '14	p	-0.2	-0.4	+0.1
Dec. '14	Aug. '18	Apr. '19	w	+1.5	+1.2	+3.6
Apr. '19	Jan. '20	Sept. '21	f	+0.4	+1.3	+1.2
Sept. '21	May '23	July '24	f	+0.1	+1.0	+0.8
July '24	Oct. '26	Dec. '27	f	-0.2	+0.3	+0.6
Dec. '27	June '29	Mar. '33	pf	+0.4	+0.5	+4.2
Mar. '33	May '37	May '38		+0.3	+1.2	+0.6
May '38	Feb. '45	Oct. '45	w	+0.4	-0.2	+0.9
Oct. '45	Nov. '48	Oct. '49		-0.1	+0.3	+0.1
Oct. '49	July '53	Aug. '54		-0.1	+0.1	+0.4

Average of nonwar cycles:

6 panic cycles				+0.08	+0.02	+1.08(0.46)[d]
10 panic cycles and high-failure-rate cycles				+0.07	+0.30	+0.90(0.53)[d]
7 other cycles				+0.04	+0.66	+0.39

Source: Currency ratio figures same as for Chart 2 and Table F-1.

[a] Some of the dates have been revised since this table was computed, but the revisions would not affect the measures significantly. (Revised reference dates are used in Table 1.)

[b] Meaning of symbols:

p = panic cycles, so designated because payments were suspended or Clearing House loan certificates were issued in New York City.

f = high failure rate among commercial banks; defined as ratio of bank failures (Historical Statistics of the United States, 1789-1945, Bureau of the Census, 1949, Series N-135) to total commercial banks at midyear (ibid., Series N-27, N-45, and N-47) above 1.5 per cent for any full year of the reference contraction. Before 1892, the ratio pertains to fiscal years and excludes private banks; thereafter, to calendar years and includes all commercial banks.

w = war cycles.

[c] Semiannual data 1879-81; monthly data beginning May 1907.

[d] Figures in parentheses: excluding the 1927-33 cycle.

after the date of the reference peak in January 1893. The computed currency ratio does not show this timing because the data are annual. The figure for the reference cycle peak is an interpolation of adjacent June figures. The figure for June 1893, which is high because of the panic, makes the computed level for stage V higher than the computed level for stage VII. As a result, the computed change from I to V is positive and from V to VII, negative. Such distortions were probably unimportant in the other cycles.

All sudden large increases in the currency-money ratio during peacetime have reflected banking panics, stemming from expectations that banks might suspend payments. The attempt by the public to convert deposits into currency at such times produced sharp increases in the currency ratio. All panics since the Civil War occurred during reference contractions. Four of them—in 1873, 1893, 1907, and 1933—involved suspension of payments by the banking system, though in the first three, banks remained open to handle checks that circulated through local clearing houses. Further conversions of deposits into currency were then cut off, except for partial accommodation of important and needy depositors, and the computed currency-money ratio understates the desired ratio. Hence, the figures in Table 14 for the four cycles with suspensions do not fully reflect desired changes in the currency ratio. For this table and Chart 11, a panic is interpreted broadly to include periods of financial stringency which, for our purposes, can be identified by the issue of loan certificates by the New York Clearing House to settle interbank payments.[15] The certificates helped avert suspension by facilitating transfer of deposits between member banks of the Clearing House. Although the certificates were issued at the first signs of trouble in the 1873, 1893, and 1907 panics (none were issued in 1933), they did not in those panics prevent a subsequent suspension of payments.

Panics in which unauthorized note issues circulated to alleviate the "shortage" of currency had greater increases in the currency-money ratio than our figures show. There are no official estimates of those issues, and their amounts have not been included in the time series.

---

[15] Loan certificates were backed by assets pledged by member banks of the Clearing House. Except in 1884, clearing houses in other cities also issued certificates when the New York Clearing House did. In a few unimportant instances certificates were issued in some cities but not in New York. See J. G. Cannon, *Clearing Houses* (S. Doc. 491, 61st Cong., 2d sess.), National Monetary Commission, 1910, Chap. X.

In 1893 and 1907, clearing house certificates were printed in small denominations and paid out to the public. In those two panics as well as that in 1933, scrip currencies were also issued by manufacturers and various kinds of "town councils" to facilitate payroll disbursements and retail trade. All such issues, no less than the suspension of payments by banks except during legally established state banking holidays, were illegal, but their legality was not seriously questioned by the

TABLE 15

CORRECTION OF CURRENCY-MONEY RATIO FOR UNAUTHORIZED NOTE
ISSUES IN PANICS OF 1893, 1907, AND 1933

Date of High Point in Uncorrected Currency Ratio	Currency Outside Banks ($ millions)		Currency-Money Ratio with Unauthorized Issues (per cent)	
	Excluding Unauthorized Issues	Estimated Maximum Issue of Unauthorized Currency	Excluded	Included
June 1893	985	80[a]	23.5	25.0
Jan. 1908	1,857	270[b]	17.1	19.1
Mar. 1933	5,223	1,000[c]	17.3	19.9

[a] John D. Warner, "The Currency Famine of 1893," Sound Currency, Feb. 15, 1895, p. 8.

[b] A. Piatt Andrew, "Substitutes for Cash in the Panic of 1907," Quarterly Journal of Economics, Aug. 1908, p. 515.

[c] A rough guess from H.P. Willis and J.M. Chapman, The Banking Situation, New York, 1934, p. 35.

public or government authorities. At least no lawsuits appear to have been initiated against the offending parties. Yet their amounts were not insignificant. Table 15 cites rough estimates of the quantity of unauthorized notes circulated in 1893, 1907, and 1933, and the implied correction in the currency-money ratio. In terms of the usual cyclical fluctuations in the ratio, increases of 1.5 to 2.6 percentage points, as estimated for those three panics, are extremely large.

On the other hand, the currency-money ratio is overstated by the treatment of banks that closed rather than just suspended payments temporarily. The ratio excludes deposits at such banks and includes their vault cash in currency outside banks. A closed bank may open again, and even a bankrupt bank eventually makes good on a large fraction of its deposits. Temporarily, these funds are not available and, technically speaking, pass out of the money stock. From the holder's point of view, however, they are not all lost, and he no doubt counts some fraction of them as still part of his money balances in the expectation of receiving them some day, even though in the meantime they cannot be spent. Most such inaccessible deposits were eventually paid off. Their total quantity was relatively minor in the pre-World War I panics, simply because failures were not extensive, but it was certainly not minor in 1933, when a large number of banks remained closed after the banking holiday until licensed to reopen by federal authorities, and some never reopened. The deposits of unlicensed banks in 1933–34 are excluded from the money stock, but not all such funds should be excluded from what individuals considered to be their money balances and from the money stock as herein defined, to which part of those funds were eventually restored. Consequently, our series for the stock shows a sharp dip in the spring of 1933 and then rises sharply whereas, if properly adjusted, most of the dip would disappear. While no attempt to adjust for closed banks in any of the panic periods has been made, we may guess that the adjustment would lower the difference between the last two columns in Table 15, though probably not reverse it or eliminate it entirely.

The only authorized issue of emergency currency occurred in the 1914 panic. The Aldrich-Vreeland Act allowed banks to form national currency associations and to obtain, for issue with collateral other than U.S. bonds, notes from the Treasury. The amounts issued in 1914 under that act are recorded in Treasury figures on national bank notes outstanding and are included in our data. The bulk of them circulated for but a few months[16] and had little effect on the pattern of the currency-money ratio in the 1912–14 reference cycle. That panic, the only one in which emergency currencies were issued early and freely, was the mildest and shortest of the lot—no doubt not entirely a coincidence.

The computed ratios used for Table 14 therefore greatly understate the panic-induced increases in currency demand. In part for this reason, the panic cycles are not responsible for the expansion phase of the ratio, as indicated in Chart 11 and confirmed by the averages at the bottom of Table 14. The ratio increased on the average very little more from stage IV or V to stage VII in the six panic cycles than it did in the other cycles (as shown by column 2) and rose considerably less in the panic cycles than in the others relative to the decline in the

---

[16] See O. M. W. Sprague, "The Crisis of 1914 in the United States," *American Economic Review*, Sept. 1915, pp. 522–523.

preceding stages (as shown by column 3). To be sure, the rise from stage IV or V to stage VII relative to the decline in the *succeeding* stages was greater on the average for the panic cycles, but the difference is cut down considerably when the exceptional rise of the 1927–33 cycle is excluded (as shown by the figures in parentheses). If we could measure the large increase in the *desired* ratio during bank suspensions, we should no doubt find a larger difference between panic cycles and all others, though perhaps not by much, since currency hoarding usually started to decline as soon as banks reopened. In any event, the expansion phase of the cyclical pattern depicted in Chart 11 is not due to panics.

Nor can that expansion phase be attributed to fear of suspensions that never occurred or to expectations of increased losses on deposits through bank failures. If we add to panic cycles those cycles in which the annual rate of bank failures was especially high, the resulting averages (second line from the bottom of Table 14) differ little from the averages for panic cycles alone. There is little relation between the amplitude of cyclical movements in the ratio and the ability of the banking system to avoid suspension of payments or large losses on deposits through default.[17]

These results, at first sight surprising, can be explained by the sudden and largely unexpected occurrence of most panics. The widespread bank failures and panic that characterized some reference contractions were generally short-lived affairs; they could not immediately lead to large increases in currency hoarding, because with suspension of payments the public could not obtain currency. Moreover, expectations of future loss probably depend on past experience, for which the "past" includes considerably more than just the very recent scene. The total response to a sudden high rate of loss on deposits appears to be small if the upheaval does not last long.

All financial panics in the past have come after the downturn in business activity, and financial institutions usually do not show the strains of a business contraction until it has progressed for some time.

---

[17] The same conclusion is suggested by the behavior of the total amount of change in the reference cycle relatives, which disregards the duration of individual cycles and is not shown in Table 14. For the six panic cycles alone and the ten cycles grouped together in the next line, the average change in the currency-money ratio from stage IV or V to stage VII is +0.26 and +0.25, respectively. For the seven other nonwar cycles, it is even higher, +0.39.

The resulting increase in the currency-money ratio may come even later in the reference contraction if the response to a rise in the rate of bank failures is delayed. This sequence, however, does not explain the typical behavior of the currency-money ratio. The ratio displays a diminishing rate of decline, or even a rise, before the peak in business activity. It therefore seems most unlikely that public apprehension about the solvency of banks or increased losses on deposits can account for the expansion phase in the ratio, though such fears might subsequently reinforce the rise in the ratio.

The timing of the rise makes service charges on checking accounts or rates paid on savings deposits unlikely causes. These fluctuate little over the typical cycle. Any alterations banks do make in charges and rates in competing for funds tend to reflect variations in the interest rates they receive on earning assets (or changes in legal ceilings). Interest rates have generally risen during reference expansions and usually have not turned down until after the reference peak. Hence the turning points in charges and rates probably occur much later than those displayed by the currency-money ratio.

EXPLANATIONS OF CYCLES IN CURRENCY DEMAND EXAMINED

The Mitchell-Hawtrey Theory. The most famous theory of currency demand comes from the work of Wesley Mitchell and R. G. Hawtrey.[18] Their arguments are quite similar and can be summarized together as follows: Two relationships allegedly work to raise and lower the use of currency with ups and downs in business activity. First, retail transactions, which use more currency per dollar of payment than other transactions do, rise relative to total transactions during expansions

[18] See W. C. Mitchell, *Business Cycles and Their Causes,* Berkeley, 1950, pp. 47–48 and 137–138 (originally published as Part III of his *Business Cycles,* 1913); and R. G. Hawtrey, "The Trade Cycle," *Readings in Business Cycle Theory,* American Economic Association, pp. 343–344 (originally published in 1926), and *Currency and Credit,* 4th ed., London, 1950, pp. 20–25 (1st ed., 1919). The importance to Mitchell and Hawtrey of a rising use of currency in expansions was that it drains banks of reserves and thereby eventually contributes to a contraction of bank credit. In their writings, that contraction has an important role in downturns of business activity. The original works were published before central banks began as a normal procedure to offset such drains.

See also F. Lavington, *The English Capital Market,* London, 1921, pp. 174–175; and a more recent reference, J. Polak and W. White, "The Effect of Income Expansion on the Quantity of Money," *Staff Papers,* Vol. IV, International Monetary Fund, 1954–55, pp. 398–433.

CHART 12

Nonwar Reference Cycle Patterns of Currency-Expenditures Ratio, Annual Data,
1891–1958

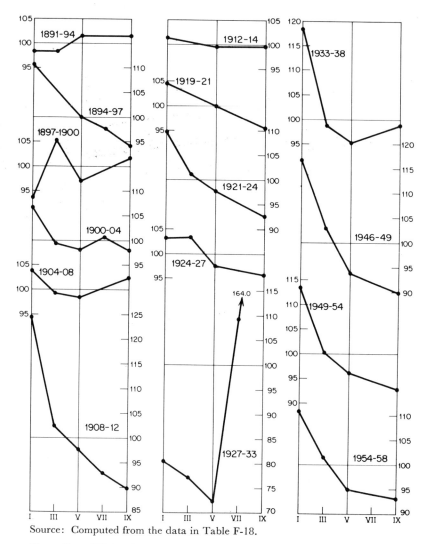

Source: Computed from the data in Table F-18.

Note: Stage III has been omitted from 1894–97 and 1919–21 cycles, and stage
VII from all cycles except 1894–97, 1900–04, 1908–12, and 1927–33.

in business activity and fall during contractions. Second, the relative income of wage earners (who, it is assumed, spend most of their income in retail outlets and are the largest users of currency) conforms positively to business activity and helps to explain the cyclical behavior of retail trade.

So far as it goes, this theory is consistent with the facts. The evidence is clear that retail trade prospers more or less directly with the level of employment, which in turn is a close barometer of business conditions. While neither Mitchell nor Hawtrey had direct evidence on cycles in the relative income of wage earners, recent research confirms their hypothesis: wage income tends to rise relative to total income during reference expansions and to fall during reference contractions, though the amplitude of variation is quite small and the behavior is not the same in all cycles.[19] This implies that the *quantity* of currency rises and falls with business activity. Mitchell observed such behavior with annual data for the period 1890–1911 in his early study of business cycles.[20]

This argument seems to assume that the ratio of currency to *consumer* expenditures is fairly constant over cycles. In fact, however, it is not. Charts 12 and 13 show nonwar reference cycle patterns of the currency-expenditures ratio since 1891 and include the 1954–58 cycle not covered by Chart 11. Chart 12 is based on ratios of annual data. Where stage III or VII is too short to be computed from annual data, it is omitted and the line connects adjacent stages. To show the pattern in more detail, Chart 13 presents nine stages and is based on the monthly ratio of currency to personal income, which is not available for a full cycle earlier than 1933–38. This approximates the behavior of the product of the currency-expenditures ratio and the average propensity to consume. We might expect this propensity to exhibit an inverted conformity to reference cycles, in which case the patterns in Chart 13 would show less tendency to rise before reference peaks and to fall before troughs than corresponding patterns for the currency-expenditures ratio show—to some extent apparently true.

In broad outline, the patterns in the two charts have the same shape as those for the currency-money ratio summarized in Chart 11. The

[19] Daniel Creamer, *Personal Income During Business Cycles*, Princeton for NBER, 1956, pp. xvii-xviii.
[20] Mitchell, *Business Cycles* (1913), pp. 295–300.

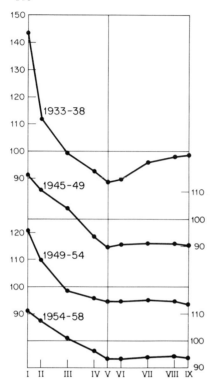

CHART 13

Nonwar Reference Cycle Patterns of Currency–Personal Income Ratio, Monthly Data, 1933–58

Source: Currency outside banks, same as for Chart 12 and Table F-18; personal income, Department of Commerce seasonally adjusted monthly data.

patterns in Charts 12 and 13 generally fall during reference expansions, and most of them fall at a slower rate during contractions, or even rise. This is also true for changes on a per-year basis (not shown), and so is not a statistical artifact resulting from the combination of a downward trend and the shorter duration of reference contractions than of expansions. There is also a tendency for the rate of decline during expansions to slow down after stage III, though it is far from uniform and less clear (particularly in Chart 13, as we might expect) than for the currency-money ratio.

These generalizations are of course rough. The currency-expenditures ratio displays several large noncyclical movements which make its cyclical fluctuations difficult to isolate. In addition, measurement errors in the year-to-year changes of consumer expenditures further handicap analysis, particularly for the cycles before 1900, which might otherwise be revealing because they seem less distorted by irregular secular movements. Granted the qualifications, this ratio nevertheless seems to account for a substantial part of the cycles in the currency-money ratio.[21]

Sectoral Shifts in Money Holdings and Currency Demand. Since the currency-expenditures ratio is not constant over cycles but indeed accounts for much of the variation in the currency-money ratio, Mitchell's and Hawtrey's theory seems unsatisfactory. Yet both authors discussed the *quantity* of currency outstanding rather than the currency-money *ratio*,[22] which makes the full implication of their theory unclear. Perhaps a better interpretation, which avoids some of the drawbacks of the preceding one, is that their theory assumes a redistribution of money holdings between consumers and businesses over the cycle. If the currency-money ratios maintained by these sectors differ, as is most likely, the aggregate ratio will vary, even though the ratio of each sector does not change. Specifically, if the sector ratios differ by a constant, changes in the aggregate ratio are proportional to changes in the distribution of money holdings.[23]

[21] The positive conformity of the income-money ratio to business cycles partly offsets the cyclical effect of the currency-expenditures ratio on the currency-money ratio.

[22] To look at the quantity of currency alone can be misleading. Although the public can maintain any ratio of currency to deposits it wants, since it can exchange the two freely, it cannot unilaterally hold any quantity of currency it may want. From the basic identity presented in Chap. 1, we have the following:

$$C = H \left(1 - \frac{1}{\frac{C}{D} + \frac{R}{D}} \right) \quad \text{where} \quad \frac{C}{D} = \frac{\frac{C}{M}}{1 - \frac{C}{M}} .$$

The division of a given quantity of high-powered money between banks and the public is jointly determined by the two. In the face of a currency drain, of course, it may take time for banks to contract credit, and for short periods they may find themselves with a reserve ratio lower than desired. But large differences between actual and desired reserves are not likely to exist for long.

Cyclical variations in the reserve ratio have an amplitude 30 per cent larger on the average than variations in the currency ratio have (based on Table 16, Chap. 5, and Table 14). Over half the cyclical fluctuation in the quantity of currency outside banks, therefore, reflects the behavior of the reserve ratio.

[23] The aggregate currency-money ratio may be expressed as follows:

$$\left(\frac{C}{M} \right)_a \equiv \left(\frac{C}{M} \right)_c \frac{M_c}{M_a} + \left(\frac{C}{M} \right)_b \frac{M_b}{M_a}$$

$$\equiv \left(\left[\frac{C}{M} \right]_c - \left[\frac{C}{M} \right]_b \right) \frac{M_c}{M_a} + \left(\frac{C}{M} \right)_b ,$$

where the subscript c stands for the consumer sector, b for business, and a for the aggregate. Hence, if the sector currency ratios remain constant,

$$\frac{d \left(\frac{C}{M} \right)_a}{dt} = \left[\left(\frac{C}{M} \right)_c - \left(\frac{C}{M} \right)_b \right] \frac{d \left(\frac{M_c}{M_a} \right)}{dt} .$$

There are various reasons money holdings might shift among sectors. Changes in the money stock, from whatever source, are largely channeled through banks and, in the first instance, affect the balances of borrowers, mainly businesses. Later on, the changes work into the spending stream and affect consumer balances. With this sequence, changes in the money stock may cause temporary variations in the distribution of money holdings (which, of course, have repercussions on the money stock). Or, alternatively, a redistribution of money holdings between consumers and businesses may reflect different responses of the two sectors to business cycles. Business firms may be more alert than consumers are to profitable uses for funds during periods of high activity and may act more quickly to take advantage of them. During periods of slack activity, when opportunities for investment are poor, firms may have few inducements to keep money balances low and may allow them to accumulate. Consumers may be less affected by economic conditions in these matters. To make these explanations fit the particular timing of the currency-money ratio over cycles requires introducing some lags at certain points, but such lags do not seem implausible.

The attempt to determine whether the distribution of money holdings does in fact fluctuate in a way to explain cycles in the aggregate currency-money and currency-expenditures ratios is impeded by limited data. The flow-of-funds accounts provide quarterly estimates on the distribution of money holdings back only to 1952 and annual estimates back only to 1945. Similar (though not entirely comparable) estimates are available for the 1930's. That is all, and even these are far from reliable. The nature of these estimates raises the suspicion that they may tend to understate cyclical variations. The estimates— for what they are worth—are presented in Chart 14, which shows the nonwar reference cycle patterns from 1933 to 1961 of the fraction of the money stock (including time deposits) held by consumers.

The timing of some of the patterns is similar to that for the currency-expenditures ratio; however, their amplitude is much too small to have an important effect on that ratio. To see this, we may apply the formula of footnote 23. Most of the cyclical movements in Chart 14, abstracting from trend, have an amplitude of at most 2 per cent. Since the fraction of the money stock held by consumers over the period covered has been about 60 per cent, the cyclical change in the fraction has been 2 per cent of 60 or about 1 percentage point. The

CHART 14

Nonwar Reference Cycle Patterns of the Fraction of the Money Stock Held by the Consumer Sector, Annual and Quarterly Data, 1933–61

Source: *Flow of Funds/Savings Accounts 1946–60,* Suppl. 5, Board of Governors of the Federal Reserve System, 1961, Table 8; and S. Shapiro, "The Distribution of Deposits and Currency in the United States, 1929–39," *Journal of the American Statistical Association,* December 1943, Table II, p. 441. Annual data to 1951; thereafter, quarterly data seasonally adjusted by NBER.

Note: Stage VII has been omitted from 1933–38 and 1946–49 cycles.

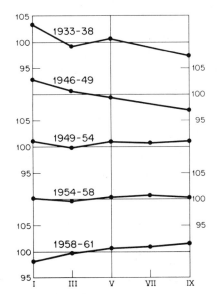

maximum difference between the fraction of money held by consumers and by all other sectors may be estimated by assuming that the former holds all currency outstanding. The estimate of the difference for 1960 is 23 percentage points, and it is roughly the same for the other periods covered. Hence, by the formula, the cyclical movements produced by changes in distribution have been around one-fourth to one-half a percentage point. Charts 12 and 13 show that the actual movements were much larger. The redistribution of money holdings does not appear, therefore, to account for cycles in the currency-expenditures ratio.

Permanent Expenditures and Currency Demand. If the fraction of the money stock held by consumers does in fact fluctuate no more than the patterns indicate, the currency-expenditures ratio of this sector, which holds most of the currency outstanding, must account for cycles in the aggregate ratio. Since none of the usual explanations appears satisfactory, we may discuss one other possibility.

Since the currency-expenditures ratio might be described as conforming more or less inversely to reference cycles, its reciprocal—the velocity of currency—conforms positively, just as the velocity of money does. Though similar, the patterns are obviously not identical for, if they were, the ratio of the two would not vary cyclically and would have no effect on the currency-money ratio. The main difference in timing is that the velocity of currency seems to level off its rate of rise from stage III to stage V and to rise gently in the final stages of reference contractions. The velocity of money often levels off in a similar fashion but not always or typically. The similarity of patterns for the two velocities suggests the influence of common factors.

What factors affecting the velocity of money might also explain the velocity of currency? A popular explanation of the velocity of money is based on movements in interest rates over the cycle. As already suggested, however, this cannot be applied to the velocity of currency, because the relevant interest rates—check charges and savings deposit rates—move too slowly during most cycles.

One interpretation of cycles in the velocity of money proposes that the demand for money depends on permanent income.[24] Conceivably, the demand for currency depends on "permanent" expenditures. The meaning of such a dependence would be that the demand for currency adjusts slowly to changes in expenditures and wealth. Then cyclical fluctuations in the ratio of measured expenditures to currency would be dominated—though not determined—by the fluctuations in the numerator. This could occur if changes in the volume of expenditures between cyclical peaks and troughs (in large part for durables) were mostly handled by checks, so that transactions made with currency varied much less than total consumer expenditures did over the cycle, and if adjustments in currency holdings as a store of wealth were made slowly.

A direct test of this explanation is whether currency outstanding can be satisfactorily related to permanent consumer expenditures or wealth, estimated perhaps by a weighted average of past expenditures. It does seem that a ratio of currency to such a weighted average would approximate the patterns in Chart 13 after adjustment for trends, though not perhaps in all details. A definite answer is not at present possible, however. Much depends on the particular weighting scheme used, and that cannot be properly estimated because there have been so few cycles undistorted by steep secular trends or other influences like panics and wars. With luck, the future will be more sparing with special influences and give us undistorted cycles in greater abundance, allowing a better test of this explanation.

[24] Milton Friedman, *The Demand for Money: Some Theoretical and Empirical Results*, Occasional Paper 68, New York, NBER, 1959.

5

THE RESERVE RATIO

THE RESERVE RATIO of commercial banks has varied considerably and with important effects on the rate of growth of the money stock. The aggregate reserve ratio is a weighted average of the ratios for individual banks, and fluctuations in the aggregate may reflect either shifts in the distribution of deposits—a change in weights—or changes in the reserve ratios of individual banks. The latter in turn may reflect either changes in reserve requirements or decisions of individual banks to alter their reserve positions. Such decisions can be viewed as one part of the broader decisions banks regularly make concerning the composition of their portfolios. The advantages of certain assets offering a high degree of liquidity and little risk of loss—such as call loans with securities as collateral in an earlier day or Treasury bills today—are balanced against the advantages of less liquid assets providing substantially higher return—such as mortgages or term loans. The desired fraction of cash in the portfolio to provide a margin of safety against future withdrawal of deposits is not the same for every situation and is constantly reappraised in the light of new alternatives and changing circumstances.

Such appraisals are not different in principle from those of individual investors, but there are important practical differences. Banks are subject to legal restrictions on the composition of their portfolios and follow certain well-established practices of commercial banking. In particular, because most of their liabilities are subject to withdrawal on demand or short notice, they need large cash reserves. Nevertheless, changing conditions constantly offer choices between acceptable assets with different qualities and rates of return. Selection depends upon price and quality of alternatives as well as the aforementioned needs for liquidity and safety.

The broad subject of portfolio selection is only touched upon here, but its omission does not appear to hamper the analysis of major fluctuations in the cash reserve ratio. Many of the factors affecting reserve ratios differ in their influence only as between cash and all other assets and are unrelated to the composition of noncash assets. Two such factors are the distribution of deposits among banks and statutory reserve requirements, both largely unrelated to the response of individual banks to the profitability or liquidity of the noncash portions of portfolios. The first, discussed in section 1, involves shifts in the distribution of deposits between banks with different ratios or between time and demand deposits, which can alter the aggregate ratio even though the ratio for deposits of each kind remains unchanged. In fact, however, those shifts have usually not had important effects.[1] The second factor, requirements imposed by law on reserves, discussed in section 2, has had an important influence on banks' cash holdings.

In addition to the effects of changes in legal reserve requirements, there are other sizable movements in the reserve ratio over both long and short periods. These are discussed in sections 3 and 4. The important factors for long-run movements are various institutional changes in the monetary system that improved stability and lessened the need of banks for cash reserves. The short-run movements are related to the business cycle. In part they may reflect changes in interest rates and in the demand for bank loans, and to that extent involve the noncash assets of banks. On the whole, however, an analysis of these assets is not necessary for interpretation of the major fluctuations in the cash reserve ratio.

1. Shifts in the Distribution of Deposits

Any redistribution of deposits may affect the aggregate reserve ratio. Banks vary in their needs and preferences for high-powered reserves per dollar of deposits, and deposits transferred from one bank to another are not likely to have exactly the same backing as before. Yet random shifts among banks of deposits held by the public probably affect the aggregate ratio very little, except perhaps temporarily while banks adjust. Large sections of the banking system operate under the same legal restrictions, face similar circumstances, and tend as a consequence to maintain roughly the same ratios. Moreover, the effects of many random shifts occurring at the same time tend to cancel out. Large

[1] The reader who wishes to skip the detailed analysis may turn to the summary at the end of sect. 1.

changes in the aggregate ratio are usually produced either by shifts of deposits between sectors of the banking system having appreciably different reserve practices, or by a change in the legal reserve requirements governing a bank because of a change in its legal status, which is equivalent to a shift in deposits between two banks subject to different requirements.

Although not the only source of different reserve ratios, legal requirements are an important one and so provide a convenient basis for classifying the banking system for study of the quantitative importance of shifts in deposits among banks. Reserve requirements differ among types of banks and also, for particular banks, among types of deposits. (1) The required reserve ratio of national or member banks (that is, national banks before the Federal Reserve System and member banks thereafter) has always been considerably higher than that of other commercial banks as a group, which are regulated by widely varying state laws. Banks under state jurisdiction generally have less stringent regulations on high-powered reserves than national or member banks do. (2) Among national or member banks, there is a further difference according to location: Banks in central reserve cities, in other reserve cities, and in country districts are subject to successively lower requirements. Though some state regulations make similar distinctions, the data on state banks do not; consequently, analysis of the redistribution of deposits among banks classified according to their reserve location must be confined to national or member banks. (3) The major difference by type of deposits is the lower requirements imposed on time deposits than on demand deposits by the Federal Reserve System. Prior national banking legislation did not make such a distinction. Many states had modified their laws to impose separate requirements for time and demand deposits even before 1914; most others have since then. In view of this diversity and of the inadequacy of the data, the analysis of the effect of shifts between time and demand deposits is confined to national or member banks. Each of the three kinds of shift is considered in a subsection to follow.

SHIFTS IN DEPOSITS BETWEEN NATIONAL OR MEMBER
BANKS AND OTHER COMMERCIAL BANKS

The magnitude and time pattern of such shifts for the period 1875–1955 are shown in Chart 15, by a graph of deposits at national or

CHART 15

Percentage of Commercial Bank Deposits Created by National or Member Banks,
Annually and Semiannually, 1875–1955

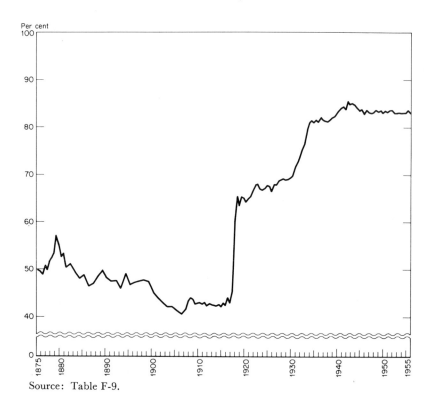

Source: Table F-9.

member banks as a percentage of total deposits (except U.S. and interbank deposits) at commercial banks.[2] The distribution of deposits
between the two classes of commercial banks changed appreciably in
only five periods: 1877–79, 1879–86, 1898–1906, 1916–22, and 1929–
34. In the first[3] and the last, there was a tendency for national or

---

[2] The level of this series is slightly too high because lacunae in the data enforced
an inexact treatment of balances of mutual savings banks held at commercial banks—
the assumption that they are all held at national or member banks. The overstatement
in the series on this account is bound to be fairly small, however.

[3] The sharp peak in the series in 1879 apparently reflects the exceptionally large
inflows of gold in that year, which were initially deposited in New York City national
banks before spreading throughout the banking system, and perhaps also the massive
refunding of government debt undertaken in the last years of that decade.

member banks to gain deposits relative to all commercial banks, possibly as a result of severe depressions. A similar movement of more moderate size occurred also during 1887–89, 1893–94, 1907–08, and 1921–22, periods of depressed business, all but the first, severely so. Consistent with this, the relative importance of national banks declined during 1898–1906, a period of general prosperity; that was the time of the spectacular development of loan and trust companies, especially in New York City. The percentage also declined throughout 1879–86, however—a period encompassing both expansion and contraction. There was little variation during most of the mild business cycles or those after 1934.

The shifts in deposits during severe cycles and before the institution of deposit insurance in 1934 seem at first sight to have a simple explanation. Would not the more easily established and less restricted state and private banks multiply in a favorable climate and go under more readily in hard times? Though not all federally supervised banks have weathered such storms without mishaps, they have had to meet certain minimum standards which probably made them stronger than most state and private banks. Evidence for such a difference can be found in figures on bank suspensions.[4] The rate of suspensions was much greater among nonmember than member banks during the early 1930's, and among state and private than among national banks in the panic periods of 1907–08, 1893, and 1873–74.

Yet it seems doubtful that suspensions are the main explanation. Except in 1930–33, they were not sufficiently widespread to account for more than a small part of the redistribution of deposits. Moreover, in two of the periods previously listed in which national banks gained deposits, 1877–79 and 1887–89, all classes of banks were increasing in number. The shift in deposits away from other commercial banks in those two periods, therefore, could not have resulted from suspensions. This phenomenon will receive further examination in the next subsection, which covers the distribution of national or member bank deposits by reserve classification. It is suggested there that the shifts in deposits may reflect a more general shift between large city banks and all others, which could produce the behavior just discussed

[4] For the annual number of suspensions, see *Historical Statistics of the United States, 1789–1945*, Bureau of the Census, 1949, Ser. N135–138; for the total number of banks in each class, see *Banking Studies*, Board of Governors of the Federal Reserve System, 1941, p. 418.

because city banks are heavily represented in the national banking system.

The exceptional rise in the proportion of deposits at national or member banks from 1916 to 1922 reflects a change in federal law. When the act of June 20, 1917, removed certain objectionable features of membership in the Federal Reserve System, a sizable number of state banks joined, most of them immediately, as indicated by the ensuing movement in the series. Although that movement represents a shift in the legal status of banks rather than in the location of depositors' accounts, the effect on the aggregate reserve ratio is the same.

The importance of the shifts can be measured by comparing with the actual ratio a hypothetical reserve ratio, computed as a weighted average of the ratios for the two classes of banks and having constant weights and so assuming no shifts occurred. For the present purpose, the distribution of deposits at the beginning of each period can serve as the constant set of weights. Comparison of the periods having the largest shifts shows the largest effects and so gives a measure of their maximum importance. The results are summarized in Table 16 for the five periods previously identified.

Column 4, which shows changes in the aggregate ratio due to shifts in distribution, is the difference between two weighted averages of the separate reserve ratios for the two classes of banks, the weights in each case being the proportion of total deposits at each class of banks. For one weighted average (column 2) the weights are the actual proportions, and the average equals the actual aggregate reserve ratio. For the other average (column 3) the weights are the proportions at the beginning of the period and are kept constant to its end, so that the average equals the ratio that would have prevailed had no redistribution of deposits occurred between the two classes of banks.

The reserve ratio for each class of banks is defined as the aggregate ratio is for all commercial banks—high-powered reserves to deposits. This is not entirely satisfactory here because such a ratio takes no account of the balances other commercial banks hold at national or member banks: while these balances are not high-powered reserves, they nevertheless affect the amount of such reserves held by both classes of banks. Other commercial banks, being mostly small-town banks, have as a group a larger sum due from than to national or member banks. Part of the high-powered reserves of national or member banks can therefore be regarded as held by them for other commercial banks. If deposits are shifted from a nonmember to a member bank, for example, part of the otherwise required transfer of high-powered reserves is handled by a reduction in the balances held by the nonmember bank at member banks. In consequence,

TABLE 16

EFFECT ON RESERVE RATIO OF FIVE LARGEST SHIFTS IN DEPOSITS BETWEEN
NATIONAL OR MEMBER BANKS AND OTHER COMMERCIAL BANKS, 1875 TO 1955

Period[a]	Percentage of Commercial Bank Deposits Gained (+) or Lost (−) by National or Member Banks[b] (1)	Numerical Change in Percentage Reserve Ratio of All Commercial Banks		
		Actual[c] (2)	Assuming No Shift in Distribution of Deposits[d] (3)	Due to Shifts in Deposits (2) − (3) (4)
Aug. 1877–Aug. 1879	+8.1	−0.8	−1.4	+0.6
Aug. 1879–June 1886	−11.5	−0.9	+0.3	−1.2
June 1898–June 1906	−7.0	−5.4	−4.6	−0.8
Dec. 1916–June 1922	+24.7	−3.2	−4.9	+1.7
Dec. 1929–June 1934	+12.1	+7.8	+6.3	+1.5

[a]Selected from Chart 15.

[b]Based on Table F-9. This is equivalent to the actual change in deposits at national or member banks minus the expected change on the basis of the actual change in deposits of all commercial banks, expressed as a percentage of deposits at all commercial banks at the end of the period.

[c]From Table F-10, col. 4.

[d]The change in a weighted average of the reserve ratios for national or member banks (Table F-10, col. 2) and for other commercial banks (Table F-10, col. 3), where the weights (given by Table F-9) are those for the beginning of the period. By ignoring net deposits of other commercial banks at national or member banks, the change in col. 4 is slightly understated (see text).

such a shift in deposits will not require so large a reduction in high-powered reserves and hence in deposits of nonmember banks, nor allow so large an increase for member banks, as might be inferred solely from the ratio of high-powered reserves to deposits. That ratio is lower for other commercial banks and higher for national or member banks than the corresponding ratio of all cash reserves, including balances at other banks, to total deposit liabilities, including balances owed to other banks. Hence, use of the ratio of high-powered reserves to deposits held by the public exaggerates the effects of deposit shifts, because it overstates the difference between the reserve positions of the two classes of banks. In computing the appropriate reserve ratio for each class of banks, for strict accuracy we should reduce the high-powered reserves of national or member banks and increase those of other commercial banks by that amount.

Unfortunately, an accurate adjustment for these interbank balances can not be made, because the net amount due by national or member banks to other commercial banks is not separated from the net amount due to mutual savings banks and foreign commercial banks. Some rough calculations using the data available suggest that this adjustment would enlarge the bottom three figures in column 4 by at most one-half a percentage point in absolute value and leave the top two figures largely unchanged.[5]

Even so, the estimated effect is still relatively small, which indicates that the actual effects account for only a small part of the major movements in the aggregate reserve ratio. In the final three periods represented in the table, during which sizable movements in the reserve ratio accompanied the deposit shifts, the shifts accounted for less than one-fifth of those movements in two periods (beginning in 1898 and 1929) and worked against the prevailing movement in the third (1916–22). In the latter, enlargement of membership in the Federal Reserve System reduced by almost one-third the decline in the aggregate ratio which would otherwise have occurred. In the two earliest periods, the estimated effect of redistribution is almost the same in absolute magnitude as in the other periods. It is, however, large relative to the actual change, which happened to be small. As noted, Chart 15 reveals no other shifts of comparable size, and it seems clear that the effects of shifts other than those listed in Table 16 must have been negligible.

---

[5] One way to estimate the high-powered reserves (call them T) that national or member banks hold behind the net amounts they owe to other commercial banks (I) is to assume the ratio is the same as for other deposits. If H denotes total high-powered reserves and D deposits held by the nonbanking public, the assumption is that $T/I = (H - T)/D$, which implies that the corrected reserve ratio for national or member banks is $(H - T)/D = H/(D + I)$. The reserves $T(=IH/[D + I])$ are assumed to belong to other commercial banks, and so their high-powered reserves are to be increased by T. An estimate of T requires a figure for I, which we can only approximate. The correction suggested in the text for col. 4 is based on this method.

Since interbank deposits can be highly volatile, banks may hold larger reserves behind them than behind regular deposits. If so, the preceding estimate of T is too small; and, since the reserve ratio for national or member banks is greater than the other, the corrected ratios are further apart than they should be. Hence the correction suggested in the text is likely to be too large in absolute value.

SHIFTS IN DEPOSITS AMONG NATIONAL OR MEMBER
BANKS IN DIFFERENT RESERVE CLASSIFICATIONS

Since a shift in deposits between national or member banks and other commercial banks explains little of the movements in the aggregate reserve ratio, the movements must reflect the behavior of the component ratios (national and nonnational, member and nonmember banks). So far as this finding goes, each component could exhibit movements that do not appear in the aggregate ratio because the other component offsets them. In fact, however, movements in the two have a high degree of correspondence. The correlation coefficient for the period 1875–1955 is 0.67, and omitting the turbulent years 1935–45, the coefficient is 0.84.[6]

The question then arises: Might some of the movements in the reserve ratios for the two classes of banks reflect shifts in deposits among banks according to their location by city size or reserve requirements?[7] The two breakdowns can be examined together for national or member banks, since reserve requirements happen to be imposed on these banks roughly according to the population density of their localities. Central and other reserve cities, in which banks have higher requirements than elsewhere, generally encompass the nation's largest cities. State reserve requirements also vary with the location of banks; for reasons given, however, further examination of shifts in deposits will be confined to those among national or member banks. Because of the high correlation between the ratios for these and other commercial banks, the results for one class probably apply to the other.

To gauge the importance of the shifts, we may compare the actual reserve ratio with one corrected for shifts. The latter may be computed as a weighted average of the ratios for the three classes of national or member banks (central reserve city, reserve city, and country) with weights equal to the proportion of their aggregate deposits at each of the three classes of banks. If the weights are kept constant over a given period, the average is a hypothetical aggregate ratio for these classes assuming no shifts in the relative size of their deposit liabilities. If the true weights are used throughout, the average is the actual

[6] The series correlated were cols. 1 and 3, Table F-10.

[7] Asset size of banks is probably also important, but data for that breakdown are unavailable; the breakdown by class of bank approximates one by asset size, though imperfectly.

CHART 16

Actual and Hypothetical Reserve Ratios and the Difference Between Them, National or Member Banks, Annually, 1875–1955

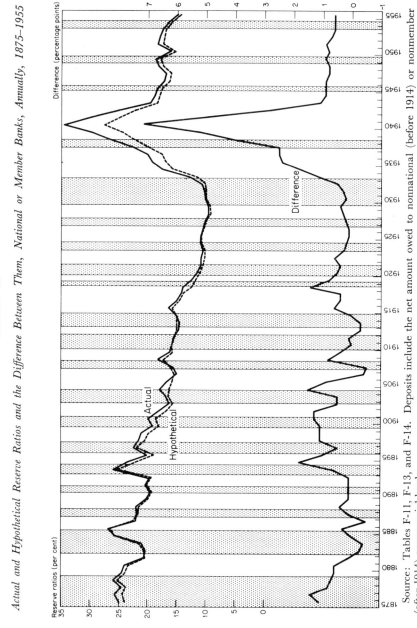

Source: Tables F-11, F-13, and F-14. Deposits include the net amount owed to nonnational (before 1914) or nonmember (after 1914) commercial banks.

Note: Shaded areas represent reference cycle contractions; unshaded areas, expansions. Hypothetical ratio constructed aggregate ratio. The two ratios are plotted in Chart 16. The constant weights for the hypothetical ratio are the distribution of deposits in 1914, the approximate mid-point of the time scale. Differences between the two ratios represent departures from the 1914 distribution of deposits. Between any two dates the approximate effects of redistribution are shown by changes in the gap between the two series, displayed at the bottom of the chart on an enlarged scale.

The reserve ratio in this comparison is defined as the ratio of high-powered reserves to deposits, including in deposits the net amount owed to nonnational (before 1914) or nonmember (after 1914) commercial banks. The inclusion assumes that these interbank deposits have the same fraction of high-powered reserves behind them as regular deposits do (see footnote 5). To have also adjusted each of the three ratios in the hypothetical average ratio for the amount of high-powered reserves held by each class of banks behind their deposits at other national-member banks would be desirable, for reasons given for the components (national and nonnational or member and nonmember) of the commercial bank ratio. Country banks hold balances at central reserve city and reserve city banks, and the latter hold balances at central reserve city banks, which prevent the full adjustment to deposit shifts between classes of these banks from falling on high-powered reserves. Such balances satisfied part of the legal reserve requirements for national or member banks before June 1917. Even since then, such balances have been held voluntarily to facilitate interbank transfer of funds. The adjustment of the three ratios is not feasible, however, in the absence of published figures on the net amounts owed each of the three classes of member banks. The data for member banks, used for the ratios in the chart after 1917, give total interbank deposits due from and to all other banks, including nonmember banks. The data permit estimates of the net amount due to nonmember banks by each class of member banks. That estimate, as noted, is included in the denominator of the reserve ratios. Amounts due to and from other *member* banks by each class, however, cannot be segregated. Though the necessary data were reported before 1917, the adjustment was omitted for the earlier period, as well, to preserve comparability. The size of total interbank deposits indicates that the maximum possible effect of the adjustment would not alter the results significantly, so this omission can be safely ignored in interpreting

Chart 16. If the adjustment could be made, it would reduce the spread between the three ratios slightly and also the estimated effects of redistribution.

The first and more important impression to be gained from Chart 16 is how close together the two series remain over the entire period. Use of the 1914 distribution of deposits throughout for the weights results in an only slight divergence between the two series, even at the beginning and end when the 1914 weights are least likely to apply so well. Since the reserve ratios for the three classes of banks differ considerably in level, the result indicates that shifts in deposits among those classes have been fairly small.

The main divergence between the two series is in 1933–40, when the actual ratio rose 17 percentage points and the hypothetical ratio only 12, a reduction of almost one-third of the increase in the actual ratio. The divergence implies a shift of deposits to the classes of banks with higher reserve ratios, namely, central reserve city and other reserve city banks. Surprisingly enough, most of the divergence came well after the period 1930–34 when, as Table 16 and Chart 15 show, most of the shift in deposits in favor of member banks at the expense of nonmember banks occurred. Part of that shift was tentatively attributed to a high rate of suspensions among small banks. The shift in 1933–40, shown in Chart 16, in favor of reserve city member banks at the expense of country member banks was clearly not due to a wave of suspensions among country banks. Indeed, the number of licensed country member banks increased sharply from 1933 to 1934 and then remained roughly constant through 1940. Obviously, country banks gained less than their usual share of the increase in total deposits. Country banks, of course, deposited most of their excess funds, which typically pile up during business depressions, with correspondent city banks; that transfer shifted the distribution of interbank deposits in that direction. But the figures underlying Chart 16 exclude interbank deposits between member banks, and such transfers from nonmember banks were too small to make much difference.

The major factor accounting for the redistribution was a shift of deposits held by the public to reserve city member banks, the largest shift being to central reserve city banks in New York City. The importance of those banks is shown by the increase in deposits held by the public from 1933 to 1940 for the various classes of member banks: for country banks the increase was 78 per cent; for noncentral reserve city banks, 84 per cent; for Chicago banks, 88 per cent; and for New York City banks, 114 per cent. The figures indicate that a large share of the cash balances accumulated by the nonbanking public during the 1930's gravitated to New York City. The shift, to be sure, encompassed a small part of the total balances accumulated. The increase in deposits of noncountry member banks in excess of the 78 per cent increase in country member bank deposits—which serves as a basis for comparison—accounted for but 12 per cent of the total increase in member bank deposits, 1933–40. Nevertheless, the effect of that shift on the member bank reserve ratio and thence on the stock of money was striking (see Chart 16).

The difference between the two series in other periods is less pronounced but still revealing in the enlarged scale at the bottom of the chart, which also shows the conformity of the difference series to reference cycles. The difference series typically rises during contractions and falls during expansions, indicating a shift of deposits to city banks when business lags and to country banks when business prospers. Two of the strongest exceptions to that pattern can perhaps be explained by other factors. The rise in the difference series during the 1933–37 reference expansion, just discussed, may have been due to the depressed conditions of the economy throughout that period leading to the usual behavior for contractionary periods. The rise during the 1917–18 inflation reflected the character of the early growth of the Federal Reserve System. Spread of membership to state banks occurred only after 1917. The rise in the difference series after 1917 and its subsequent decline suggest that the first state banks to become member banks swelled the ranks of reserve city banks rather than of country banks and that subsequently the numerical preponderance of new entrants swung the other way.

Despite the exceptions, the cyclical behavior of the difference series exhibits high inverse conformity to cycles. A simple test confirms this. When the items in the series nearest to monthly peaks and troughs of reference cycles are selected and the successive directions of change in the items listed, there are two expansions and two contractions in which there was no change, thirteen out of the remaining sixteen expansions in which the change was downward, and eleven out of the remaining sixteen contractions in which the change was upward. This count omits the incomplete reference contraction at the beginning of the series but includes every phase thereafter from 1879 to 1954, eighteen reference cycles in all. These results are statistically significant: the 24 "correct" moves in 32 cyclical phases (omitting the four cases of no change) would occur by chance less than 5 per cent of the time. Deposits tended to shift in favor of city banks during contractions and in favor of country banks during expansions with considerable regularity. Such a shift probably accounts for the relative decline of other commercial banks in severe contractions, a phenomenon commented on in the preceding subsection, since those banks are chiefly located in country districts.[8]

An explanation might be that one group of money holders whose cash balances undergo greater cyclical fluctuation than the aggregate does keeps most of its holdings at reserve city banks. Such a group might be large business corporations and financial intermediaries most of which have their main banking connections in large cities.

The largest movements in the difference between the actual and the hypothetical ratio, except during 1933–40 and the subsequent period of return to normal levels, amounted at most to 2 percentage points and even then did not coincide with the major movements in the reserve ratio. In the analysis of the reserve ratio, we can ignore the effects of shifts in deposits among national-member banks in different reserve classifications.

SHIFTS BETWEEN TIME AND DEMAND DEPOSITS

A third change in the distribution of deposits which affects the reserve ratio is shifts between time and demand deposits. The Federal Reserve Act imposed substantially lower reserve requirements on the former than the latter. While the National Bank Act had made no distinction between different kinds of deposits, many state banking statutes did even before 1914. Aside from statutory requirements, banks no doubt view time deposits as needing only small cash reserves.

---

[8] The effect of these shifts is to make New York City banks tighter than the rest of the banking system during business expansions, and easier during contractions. Insofar as Federal Reserve countercyclical policy is based on the condition of New York City banks, the policy will, because of the deposit shifts, be too easy for the economy at large during expansions and too tight during contractions.

CHART 17

Ratio of Time to Total Deposits at Commercial Banks, Annually, 1914–60

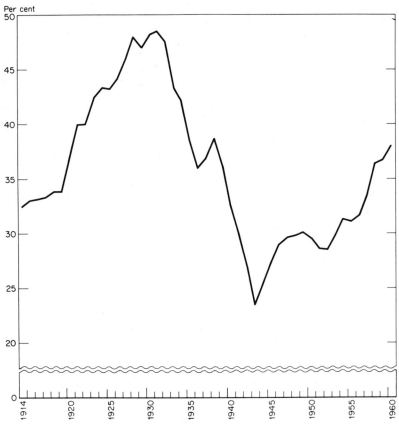

Source: Same as for Chart 2 and Table F-1.

The direction and magnitude of such shifts from 1914 to 1960 is shown by the ratio of time to total deposits at all commercial banks in Chart 17. The ratio rose sharply from 1919 until 1931, then fell with comparable rapidity until 1943, and rose again but more slowly thereafter. After 1956 it rose rapidly. The wide fluctuations in the ratio over those forty-six years has elicited considerable comment. The rise during the 1920's has been attributed to transfers of demand deposits to the time classification. The rise during the 1950's has been attributed to the growing competition of other financial assets with demand deposits as a form of wealth holding. Side by side these two explanations of different periods point up the main difficulty of interpreting this ratio: movements may reflect a shift between time and demand deposits or between one of them and other financial assets, either of which could be primarily responsible.

A broader perspective on the behavior of time deposits may be obtained by a comparison, not only with demand deposits, but also with a larger group of liquid assets that seem to be especially close substitutes. As a first approximation, we may treat time deposits, at least for recent decades, as almost entirely a repository of long-term savings, in contrast to the use of most checking accounts for current transactions. This is the way banking laws view time deposits. It is the rationale for low reserve requirements and delayed withdrawal privileges. Some evidence that time deposits are in fact mostly long-term savings is that, since at least 1940 and very likely much earlier, virtually all have been classified as savings accounts (restricted by law to individuals and nonprofit institutions) rather than time certificates of deposit. Savings accounts are relatively small in average amount (presumably mostly held by people of moderate means), and they have low turnover compared with demand deposits.[9] Indeed, their turnover is not much above that of savings accounts in other financial institutions. Accordingly, the main substitutes for time deposits, in addition to demand deposits, appear to be U.S. savings bonds and savings accounts at mutual savings banks, savings and loan associations, credit unions, and the Postal Savings System. The cash value of life insurance is sometimes also included, but it seems an altogether different and more distant substitute.

For Chart 18 total liquid assets are defined as the deposit liabilities of the above institutions (excluding insurance companies), plus com-

---

[9] See "Time and Savings Deposits at Member Banks," *Monthly Review*, Federal Reserve Bank of New York, July 1960, pp. 118–23; *Federal Reserve Bulletin*, April 1958, pp. 422–426; G. Garvy, "The Velocity of Time Deposits," *Journal of American Statistical Association*, June 1953, pp. 176–191; W. R. Burgess, *The Reserve Banks and the Money Market*, New York, 1946, p. 38; and S. Shapiro, "The Distribution of Deposits and Currency in the United States, 1929–1939," *Journal of the American Statistical Association*, Dec. 1943, pp. 438–444. See also W. Welfling, "Some Characteristics of Savings Deposits," *American Economic Review*, Dec. 1940, pp. 748–758.

mercial banks. The chart shows the ratios of time and of demand deposits to that total from 1896 to 1960, as well as to that total plus U.S. savings bonds, separately, introduced in 1935. The figures for time and demand deposits at national banks before 1914 are estimated from reports made to the Comptroller of the Currency;[10] the official call reports of those banks did not require such data. The breakdown between nonnational bank time and demand deposits was reported for only a few states, and the estimates are particularly unreliable before 1909. There was no standard definition of time and savings deposits before 1914, when the Federal Reserve Act defined time deposits at member banks as payable after thirty days. The earlier data apparently include all deposits not payable immediately, and the new definition excluded some previously classified as time deposits. The resulting changes are minor, as the small drop in the ratio in 1914 attests.

A conceptual problem remains, however. Time certificates of deposit, which have fixed maturities and are generally held by businesses or wealthy individuals, were a much larger fraction of total time deposits in the earlier years than they have been since the 1930's. Also, in the 1920's and perhaps earlier, some commercial banks permitted checking against time deposits by the simple device of keeping an extra passbook on hand at the bank and honoring a depositor's written order for payment as a check. The practice was effectively prohibited by the banking acts of 1933 and 1935 by stipulating that savings deposits can be paid only to the depositor or upon presentation of his passbook.[11] Consequently, a sharp distinction between demand and time deposits based on their present characteristics encounters conceptual problems in earlier periods and loses significance. What the closest substitutes for time deposits have been, therefore, may well have changed over the years.

The ratios in the top panel of Chart 18 may be divided into four periods: 1896 to World War I, when the share of time deposits in total liquid assets rose and the share of demand deposit stayed the

[10] See *All-Bank Statistics, United States, 1896–1955*, Board of Governors of the Federal Reserve System, 1959, pp. 18 and 40. It presents a breakdown of time and demand deposits separately for every year back to 1896. Years for which the breakdown is based solely on interpolations have been omitted in Chart 18. Estimates for years before 1907 were based on a survey made by the Comptroller in 1907 and are therefore subject to considerable error.

[11] See *Federal Reserve Bulletin*, Nov. 1938, pp. 969–970; and Mar. 1961, p. 288.

CHART 18

Share of Time Deposits and Demand Deposits in Total Liquid Assets, and Rates of Return, 1896–1960

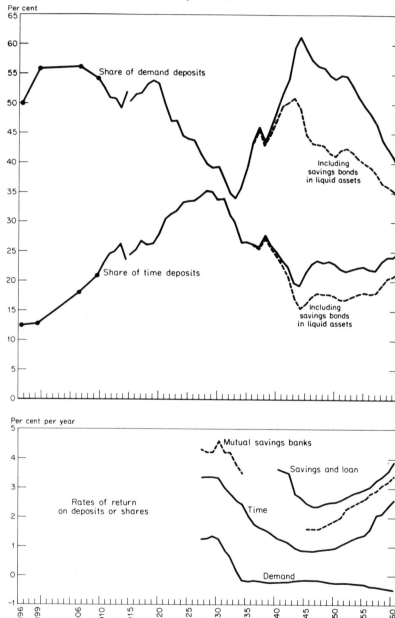

Source

UPPER PANEL
Demand and time deposits at commercial banks and mutual savings bank deposits:
June figures, 1896–1914, from *All Bank Statistics*; Dec. figures, 1914–60, from Friedman
and Schwartz, *A Monetary History*, Table A-1.
Postal savings: June figures, 1911–14, and Dec. figures, 1914–60, from *A Monetary
History*.
Savings and loan shares: Raymond Goldsmith, *A Study of Saving in the United States*,
Vol. I, Princeton, 1955, p. 441, Table J-5, col. 2; and *Federal Reserve Bulletin*.
Credit union shares and deposits: Goldsmith, *Study of Saving*, p. 427, Table L-40,
cols. 2 and 4; and Federal Home Loan Bank Board.
U.S. savings bonds: Dec. figures from *Banking and Monetary Statistics*, Board of
Governors of the Federal Reserve System, 1943, and *FRB*.
LOWER PANEL
Savings and loan association rate: Goldsmith, *Study of Saving*, p. 447, Table J-11,
col. 2, and *FHLBB* (data not available before 1940).
Mutual savings bank rate: Table E-2 (data not available 1935–44).
Time deposit rate: Table E-1.
Demand deposit rate: Interest paid, if any, minus service charges, divided by the
average level of deposits for the year (no deduction for losses due to defaults). Rate
paid or charged in Table E-1 (for 1933 only, difference between rate paid and
charged).

Note: The breaks in series of upper panel indicate the new definition of time
deposits for member banks beginning December 1914. Total liquid assets are demand
and time deposits at commercial banks, deposits at mutual savings banks, postal
savings, savings and loan shares, credit union shares and deposits, and (in dotted line
only) U.S. savings bonds.

same overall; World War I to 1929, when the share of time deposits
gained and that of demand deposits declined; 1929 to 1943, when
the movements of the preceding period were reversed; and 1943
to 1960, when time deposits rose and demand deposits fell in relative
position during the first part and again during the latter part of the
period. These movements swamp the small cyclical ripples in the
series, which suggests that cyclical shifts among these assets were of
minor significance. Let us examine each period in turn.

1896 to World War I. The rise in the share of time deposits occurred
mainly at the expense of mutual savings banks, which were then the
chief competitor of commercial banks for savings deposits. Since
banking spread rapidly through the West, it is tempting to conclude
that commercial banks took over much of the savings business in the
expanding areas simply because mutual savings banks were not
chartered there. Table 17 shows, however, that this explanation is
inadequate. The ratio of time to total deposits in commercial banks
increased as much from 1896 to 1914 in states with mutual savings
banks as in states without them or as in western states as a group,

with no mutual savings banks. Indeed, nonnational banks in western states had virtually no increase in time deposits relative to total deposits over the period.

Why nonnational banks had proportionately so much larger time deposits than national banks had, as the table shows, is understandable. As noted, some state reserve requirements were lower for time than for demand deposits even before 1914, giving nonnational banks an

TABLE 17

RATIO OF TIME DEPOSITS TO TOTAL DEPOSITS AT COMMERCIAL
BANKS, SELECTED AREAS, 1896 AND 1914
(per cent)

	1896	1914
States with mutual savings banks		
National banks	3.1	16.9
State and private banks	24.1	31.1
States without mutual savings banks[a]		
National banks	6.6	22.4
State and private banks	45.4	50.1
States west of the Mississippi[b]		
National banks	7.8	22.1
State and private banks	52.0	52.3

Source: Compiled from data in <u>All-Bank Statistics</u>.

[a]Includes District of Columbia.

[b]Excludes Minnesota.

incentive to expand them. Even by 1896, time deposits comprised a third of the total deposits at those banks. What is strange (assuming the data are correct) is that national banks pursued the savings business when they apparently derived no comparable advantage from lower reserve requirements. Perhaps the business became especially profitable and inviting when interest rates on bank assets started to rise around 1904 following a long decline (see Appendix E). National banks could expect to attract—and did—a fair share of that business with the advantage of offering all banking facilities at one place. While the rate of interest paid by commercial banks on deposits appears to have risen after about 1904 (Appendix E), it rose also on mutual savings bank deposits; there is no indication that the differential rate changed appreciably. Apparently there was a ready market for time deposits in the period, and a higher differential rate was not necessary.

In any event, demand deposits held their share over the period as a whole and so, on this evidence, do not appear to have been affected by the growth of time deposits.

World War I to 1929. The rising share of time deposits during the 1920's was attributed by an official committee of the Federal Reserve Board to transfer of deposits from the demand to the time classification.[12] Banks had an incentive to encourage such transfers because of the previously mentioned lower reserve requirements for time deposits. Allegedly, national banks were the chief culprits, since some state member banks operated under such differences in reserve requirements earlier. Banks supposedly induced depositors with large checking accounts to hold part of their funds in time accounts at higher rates of interest.[13] Although the differential rate on time over demand deposits appears not to have risen, depositors may still have been willing to make such transfers on assurance that the funds were safe and readily accessible when needed. The advent of the Federal Reserve System seemed to enhance the ability of banks to avoid those stringencies which previously had delayed the payment of time (and demand) deposits.

The view is plausible that some growth of time deposits was at the expense of demand deposits because of the above-mentioned legal changes. Time deposits in national banks grew from a much lower level and more rapidly relative to demand deposits during the 1920's than they grew in nonnational banks. According to Chart 18, the share of total demand deposits fell from 1914 to 1929 (ignoring the temporary rise during World War I) just over 10 percentage points, almost exactly the amount the share of total time deposits rose. Yet, the 10 per cent shift amounts to 25 per cent of demand deposits and over 30 per cent of time deposits held by the public in 1929—a very large amount all to be explained by transfers induced by banks. There is also some direct evidence weakening this explanation. The growth of time deposits did not lodge predominantly in large city banks, where large time deposits were concentrated and most of the alleged transfers might be expected to occur. The number of time depositors in national banks grew commensurately with the growth of such deposits,

---

[12] *FRB*, Nov. 1938, pp. 969–970; and Mar. 1961, p. 288 and *Report of Committee on Bank Reserves of the Federal Reserve System*, 1931, pp. 14–15.

[13] Allegedly there were also some illegal misclassifications of deposits, especially in New York City. See the remarks of Irving Fisher in *Econometrica*, Apr. 1946, p. 179.

and their average increase was not more than the increase in other
commercial banks, contrary to expectations if depositors with large
accounts were responsible. Interviews with bankers suggest that large
transfers were minor. Small transfers were undoubtedly important
in total, but they appear unable to explain the entire movement
shown in Chart 18. Commercial banks, and particularly national
banks, succeeded in capturing, one way or another, an increasing
share of the savings business during the 1920's, as in the preceding
two decades, and not entirely at the expense of demand deposits.[14]

Time deposits rose relative to demand deposits during the period
also in many Western European countries including Great Britain,[15]
where differences in reserve requirements were not involved. Since
there is no evidence of widening interest rate differentials, the explanation might be that prosperity and financial stability, characteristic of that decade in the United States, lessened the demand for
checking accounts relative to all other assets. That is to say, the list
of liquid assets used for Chart 18 needs to be broadened to include other
kinds of assets for judging movements in demand deposits. (Whether
the movement in the British ratio occurred for the same reason may
be questioned, however, since her economy was depressed during
much of the 1920's.) The post-World War II period is similar, but
U.S. rate differentials clearly widened then (see below), which makes
a direct comparison of the two periods for this country of little
value. The full explanation of these data for the 1920's remains
uncertain.

1929 to 1943. For this and the next period, changes in interest rate
differentials were large and seem to have played a major role (see
the bottom panel of Chart 18). In the early 1930's the share of both
time and demand deposits fell mainly because of the worsening financial situation, which damaged commercial banks more than other

[14] For the evidence cited in the second half of this paragraph, see D. R. French,
"The Significance of Time Deposits in the Expansion of Bank Credit 1922–28,"
Journal of Political Economy, Dec. 1931, pp. 759–782.
An additional factor of uncertain importance is that the Comptroller of the Currency ruled in 1919 that national banks could actively promote savings deposits.
Previously, doubt existed whether national banks could legally use the term "savings
deposits," though they could pay interest on deposits; see *Instructions and Suggestions
of the Comptroller of the Currency Relative to the Organization, Etc. of National Banks*, 1907
(Treasury Doc. 2476), p. 41, and subsequent editions.
[15] See Elmer Hartzel, "Time Deposits," *Harvard Business Review*, Oct. 1934, pp.
33ff.; and J. M. Keynes, *A Treatise on Money*, Vol. II, 1930, Chap. 23.

financial institutions. The continued fall in the share of time deposits in the later 1930's and early 1940's may be attributed partly to a reversal of the transfers induced during the 1920's and now prohibited by the Banking Acts of 1933 and 1935, but no doubt largely to the growing rate differential between time and other savings deposits.[16] During the war, U.S. savings bonds also became a strong competitor for all deposits.

The relative position of demand deposits, on the other hand, recovered after 1933 and grew appreciably until 1942 (or 1943, excluding savings bonds). The rise would appear smaller if we were to include currency among liquid assets. Nevertheless, the contrasting behavior of time and demand deposits is striking. No doubt some of the difference reflects a shift from time to demand deposits; although the rate paid on demand deposits was negative, the differential between the two actually declined after 1934 until 1944. Earnings on bank assets fell and could no longer justify a high rate on any deposits. The same was also partly true of assets of other financial institutions, however, and demand deposits probably gained at the expense of all assets in the economy (except for currency and probably U.S. savings bonds). Undoubtedly, too, special wartime factors were also involved in the large accumulation of demand deposits.

1943 to 1960. The rate differential between time and other savings deposits widened from 1947 to 1955, then narrowed, and the share of time deposits seems to have followed these movements, though their over-all share did not change much. The rapid growth of savings and loan associations in the postwar period, which seems to reflect the improvement in 1950 of the federal insurance for their shares,[17] has encroached to no apparent extent on time deposits (except perhaps

[16] Confirming evidence of interest-rate effects by regression analysis is given by C. F. Christ, "Interest Rates and 'Portfolio Selections' among Liquid Assets in the U.S.," *Measurement in Economics: Studies in Mathematical Economics and Econometrics in Memory of Yehuda Grunfeld*, Stanford University Press, 1963. The results of his careful study should be viewed as tentative, because the data limited the analysis to the short period 1934–59, during which rates first fell until after World War II and then rose, providing only two fully independent observations of the effects of rate movements.

[17] Congress set up the Federal Savings and Loan Insurance Corporation in 1934, along with the Federal Deposit Insurance Corporation for commercial banks. The FSLIC expanded slowly at first and did not insure a majority of savings and loan shares until World War II. A factor initially limiting the appeal of savings and loan shares was that the terms of federal insurance, until changed in 1950, were less liberal than those of the FDIC.

briefly in the early 1940's) but mainly on other assets, particularly mutual savings bank deposits.[18]

Confusion is avoided by distinguishing between effects of changes in interest-rate differentials—a movement *along* a demand curve for an asset—and effects of changes in preference for an asset, given the differential rate—a shift in the demand curve. The widely noted long-run growth of nonbank financial intermediaries probably reflects primarily shifts in the demand curve due to gradual revisions of the public's estimate of their safety. Two important contributing factors in recent decades have been extension of federal insurance to private financial assets and the improved stability of the economy (absence of severe contractions). Compared with adjustments to such shifts in the curve, which may span many years, changes in interest-rate differentials are likely to be minor and short lived unless, of course, they are maintained by legal ceilings. In the latter case, the regulated assets acquire a permanently unfavorable return relative to all other assets.

The declining share of demand deposits very likely reflects the substitution of a wide range of assets, no one of which can be identified as particularly important. No doubt the decline to 1949 represents simply a dispersal of large holdings accumulated during the first part of the war. It is the decline since 1951 reflected in the postwar rise in the velocity of money which has received so much attention. The decline in share (or rise in velocity) more or less coincided with generally increasing rates of return on time and savings deposits; since World War II and until about 1951 those rates had drifted upward, but slowly. It was in March 1951 that the Treasury–Federal Reserve Accord began a gradual rejuvenation of the conventional monetary measures for restraining credit. By September 1953, the Reserve System's policy of supporting the prices of U.S. bonds was explicitly abandoned, and market interest rates thereafter moved upward more sharply. Inasmuch as demand deposits have continued to bear a negative rate because of service charges, the decline in their share is widely attributed to the more attractive yields on alternative

[18] See the discussion in Milton Friedman and Anna Jacobson Schwartz, *A Monetary History of the United States, 1867–1960*, Princeton University Press for National Bureau of Economic Research, 1963, Chap. 12. See also "Time and Savings Deposits in the Cycle," *Monthly Review*, Federal Reserve Bank of New York, June 1962, pp. 87–88, and W. C. Freund, "Financial Intermediaries and Federal Reserve Controls Over the Business Cycle," *Quarterly Review of Economics and Business*, Feb. 1962, pp. 21–29.

assets. Whether changes in the rate differential are a major or a minor part of the explanation, however, is not clear.

The foregoing discussion of Chart 18 reviewing the interpretations usually proposed for those periods rests upon the appropriateness of the list of assets selected as close substitutes for time and demand deposits. That list, with minor variations, is now so commonly used in such discussions that its tentative nature needs to be stressed. Although these assets are all likely to be close substitutes among themselves, they may well differ in degree of substitutability for other nonliquid assets (like bonds or tangible assets). As a result, a shift may occur from mutual savings deposits to time deposits and from demand deposits to bonds, which appears to be a shift from demand to time deposits. The shifts are not distinguishable in the Chart 18 series. Such difficulties weaken the analysis, particularly of the liabilities of financial intermediaries such as savings and loan associations, which may experience rapid growth, perhaps, because in portfolios of individuals they substitute as much for stocks and bonds as for time or demand deposits. The analysis implicitly assumes that the liquid assets listed are much closer substitutes among themselves than with other assets. While the assumption may have some validity for savings deposits held by individuals, it seems insupportable for most demand deposits, for which many other assets may be important substitutes. Without more evidence, an analysis of relative movements in time and demand deposits is highly tentative.

The causes aside, the effects of the large shifts between time and demand deposits on the member bank reserve ratio are given in Table 18. The proportion of time deposits to total deposits at member banks has had a greater amplitude of variation than the proportion at other commercial banks has, and the difference between the required reserve ratio for demand and for time deposits is smaller for other commercial banks than for member banks (demonstrated in Table 20, below). Consequently, the effects of those shifts on the ratio for all commercial banks, if computed, would be smaller than the effects found for member banks alone.

The estimates in Table 18 were found by adjusting the reserve ratio for each of the three reserve classes of member banks for the effect on required reserves of shifts between demand and time deposits. Required reserves were increased by the amount legally released by a

TABLE 18

CHANGES IN THE MEMBER BANK RESERVE RATIO, SELECTED PERIODS, 1914-55

		NUMERICAL CHANGE IN PERCENTAGE RESERVE RATIO	
			Due to Shifts:
Period[a]	Actual (1)	Between Time and Demand Deposits[b] (2)	Between Time and Demand Deposits, and in Total Deposits Among the Three Reserve Classes of Banks[c] (3)
1. 1914-31	-4.5	-1.7	n.c.
2. 1931-43	+9.3	+2.7	n.c.
3. 1943-55	-4.6	-0.8	n.c.
4. 1917-29	-4.6	-1.5	-1.4
5. 1929-40	+24.9	+1.5	+6.6

Source: Data underlying Tables F-11 and F-13. Data for 1914 and 1917 cover national banks only. Data for the small number of state member banks before 1918 are not available.

Note: n.c. = not computed.

[a]End of June except 1914, which is Dec. 31. For selection of periods, see text.

[b]Col. 2 is a weighted average of changes in the reserve ratio for each class of member banks, assuming the ratio of time deposits to total deposits had remained the same as at the beginning of the period. The weights are the proportion of total member bank deposits at each class at the beginning of the period. (Using the end-of-period proportions would give almost the same results.) An algebraic formula for the changes in any one class of banks follows: Let the reserve ratio for demand deposits D be R^D and that for time deposits T be R^T. Then the ratio R for total deposits is

$$R = \frac{R^D D + R^T T}{D + T}.$$

Any shift in the proportion of time deposits to total deposits between years o and t would produce the following change in the total ratio:

$$R_t - R_o = \frac{R^D D_t + R^T T_t}{D_t + T_t} - \frac{R^D D_o + R^T T_o}{D_o + T_o}$$
$$+ (R^D - R^T) \left(\frac{T_o}{D_o + T_o} - \frac{T_t}{D_t + T_t}\right).$$

The change in the ratio for all member banks is then a weighted average of the change for each class of banks. The quantity $R^D - R^T$ is measured as of the end of the period, removing effects on the calculations of changes in requirements over the period. Its value for central reserve city banks, other reserve city banks, and country banks, respectively, was: .10, .07, and .04 for 1929 and 1931; .1775, .125, and .07 for 1940; .14, .14, and .08 for 1943; and .15, .13, and .07 for 1955.

[c]Computed as follows: changes resulting from shifts in the proportion of time deposits to total deposits were eliminated from the reserve ratio for each class of banks at the end of the period; the corrected ratios were then averaged by the distribution of total deposits among the three classes at the beginning of the period; finally, the resulting adjusted aggregate ratio was subtracted from the actual aggregate ratio at the end of the period.

shift to time deposits and were decreased by the amount legally added by a shift away from time deposits. A formula for their derivation is presented in a note to the table.

Lines 1 to 3 of the table for member banks cover the main shifts between time and demand deposits in all commercial banks (Chart 17). The first period, December 1914 to June 1931, covers the full duration of relative growth in member bank time deposits. The next two periods cover the years of maximum rise or fall in the proportion of time deposits at member banks (and all commercial banks; major turns in the proportions for both classes of banks approximately coincided). Column 2 shows the change in the ratio calculated as resulting solely from shifts between time and demand deposits to be compared with the actual change in the ratio in column 1. The changes in column 2, ranging from less than 1 to less than 3 percentage points, explain relatively little of the actual changes, except for the first period when the actual change was small.

The shifts contributed even less to the two major movements in the member bank reserve ratio since 1917 (see Chart 16), as shown by lines 4 and 5 in Table 18. The relative growth of time deposits from 1917 to 1929 subtracted 1.5 points from the member bank ratio, and their relative decline in the 1930's restored it. In the last period, the addition accounted for less than one-tenth of the rise in the ratio. The effect in the 1917–29 period was relatively larger but was offset in the early part of the period by the shift in all deposits, previously discussed, in favor of member banks (see Table 16). The entire decline of the ratio in that period and most of its rise during the 1930's, therefore, must be attributed to other factors.

Since Table 18 gives the effects produced on the required reserve ratio, it does not necessarily show the effects produced on the actual reserve ratio. Banks usually hold more reserves than required, and presumably the excess depends on, among other things, the relative amount of time and demand deposits, that is, there is one ratio for demand deposits and another for time deposits. The difference between the two ratios could be larger or smaller than that prescribed by legal requirements, so long as aggregate reserves satisfy total requirements. If the actual difference between the ratios for time and for demand deposits is larger than the required difference, the effects of shifts between time and demand deposits on the actual aggregate ratio would be magnified as compared with the effects on the required aggregate ratio; and, if smaller, the effects would be reduced. The foregoing evidence alone does not show how the actual ratio was affected by the shifts examined; we need to know how the desired reserve ratios for the two kinds of deposits compared with the required ratios.

Nevertheless, reserves above required amounts do not create a serious problem in interpreting the results for most of the periods covered in Table 18. Such reserves were quite low in all but one of the terminal years. If reserves are not appreciably above requirements, banks must follow changes in required ratios closely. In the 1920's, for example, banks could not have expanded as they did without the benefit of reduced requirements provided by the shift to time deposits. The one exception is the second half of the 1929–40 period, when reserves were far above requirements. Banks may have used part of the excess reserves to satisfy the increased requirements arising from the shift in favor of demand deposits. Had no such shift occurred, they might still have had the same aggregate reserve ratio. On the other hand, they might have accumulated more reserves than required against demand deposits rather than time deposits; the shift to demand deposits would then have induced banks to augment their reserves.

If we assume all reserves in excess of requirements in 1940 were held against demand deposits, we attribute the maximum possible effect to the shift during that period, for this assumption gives the maximum spread between the ratios for the two kinds of deposits and so the maximum effect of the shift to demand deposits. An estimate of the effect based on this assumption is +4.5, three times the estimate given in the table. While probably an exaggeration, the larger estimate is still a small fraction of the actual change in the ratio.

In conclusion, the effects of shifts between time and demand deposits were not large relative to the major fluctuations in the reserve ratio. The effects appear relatively large only when changes in the ratio due to other factors were small. This finding may appear strange in view of the large fluctuations displayed by the proportion of time deposits to total deposits and in view of the close attention paid to rises in that proportion during the 1920's. The effects were small because the largest shifts between time and demand deposits occurred in country member banks. The difference between requirements for the two kinds of deposits at country banks has been about one-half the difference at reserve city banks and even less than that at central reserve city banks. Consequently, a large part of the shifts had little effect on reserves. The importance of this point is brought out by a comparison of the effects of those shifts with the effects of deposit redistribution among the three classes of member banks. Col. 3 of Table 18 shows the combined effect on the reserve ratio of the two kinds of shift. In the 1920's their combination had slightly less effect than the shift between time and demand deposits alone. There was almost no redistribution of deposits among member banks during the 1920's (Chart 16). In the 1930's, however, the combined effect was considerably larger than the effect of shifts between time and demand deposits alone.[19] Shifts of deposits among banks, when they occur, are potentially important, because of the diversity between the reserve ratios for different classes of banks. Those differences are wider than those between the required ratios for time deposits and demand deposits of country member banks, where most of the shifts between the two types of deposits have occurred.

SUMMARY OF SHIFTS IN DEPOSITS

Shifts in deposits in the period 1875–1955 were not in general important. Shifts between demand and time deposits were large but did not appreciably affect reserves. A radical geographical re-distribution of deposits could produce sizable effects if it involved banks having quite different reserve requirements, but only during the 1930's did that occur on a scale sufficient to have an important effect. The combined effect of the two kinds of shift, shown in column 3 of Table 18 for two major movements in the member bank reserve ratio since 1914, probably had even less effect on the reserve ratios of other commercial banks. Deposit redistribution probably had less effect on nonmember than on member banks, because most of the former fall in the lowest reserve classification. In addition, the pro-portion of time deposits to total deposits fluctuated less in nonmember than in member banks.

[19] This statement needs qualification for the possible influence of excess reserves, previously noted. The maximum possible effect of shifts between time and demand deposits for the 1929–40 period, taking excess reserves into account, was estimated to be +4.5, and the combined effect incorporating this estimate is +9.6. The shift between time and demand deposits, therefore, may possibly have been almost as important as the shift of deposits among banks.

On the presumption that the magnitude of those effects on other commercial banks was less than on national or member banks, we can compute a range that brackets the combined effect of the three types of shift on the reserve ratio for all commercial banks. Such a range is

TABLE 19

SUMMARY OF EFFECTS ON COMMERCIAL BANK RESERVE RATIO OF SHIFTS IN
DEPOSITS, THREE SELECTED PERIODS, 1898-1940

| Period (midyear dates) | NUMERICAL CHANGE IN PERCENTAGE RESERVE RATIO | | | | |
| | | | Due to Shifts: | | |
	Actual[a] (1)	Total[b] (2)	Between Time Deposits and Demand Deposits[c] (3)	Among Reserve Classes of Banks[d] (4)	Between National or Member and Other Commercial Banks[e] (5)
1898–1906	−5.4	−1.5 to −2.3		−1.4	−0.8
1917–29	−3.7	1.0 to −0.2	−1.5	0.1	1.5
1929–40	23.1	8.6 to 10.6	1.5	5.1	4.1

[a]Table F-10.

[b]Change in actual ratio minus change in hypothetical ratio, assuming no shifts. The latter ratio is a weighted average of ratios for national or member banks and other commercial banks (from Table F-10, cols. 2 and 3), adjusted for the effect of shifts recorded in cols. 3 and 4, above, where the weights are the distribution of deposits between the two classes of banks at the beginning of the period (Table F-9).
  The change in the ratio for other commercial banks was assumed to be the same as for national or member banks in deriving the right-hand figure and was assumed to be zero in deriving the left-hand figure. Consequently, the right-hand figure equals the sum of cols. 3 to 5, except for rounding errors, and the left-hand figure is a weighted average of assumed changes in the ratios for the two classes of banks.

[c]For national or member banks only (same as col. 2, Table 18). Whatever the size of such shifts 1898-1906, in all likelihood they had small effects, because the difference in reserve requirements between time deposits and demand deposits was zero for national banks and probably not large for other commercial banks, as a group.

[d]Difference between a weighted average of ratios for three classes of member banks at the beginning and at the end of the period, where the weights are the proportionate share of deposits in each class. This average equals col. 3, minus col. 2, in Table 18.

[e]Computed as for Table 16, col. 4, and therefore too large in absolute value (see note d to that table).

shown in column 2 of Table 19 for three of the largest movements in this ratio. The combined effect accounted for about 40 per cent, more or less, of the actual rise in the ratio during the 1930's and was due in part to all the distributional shifts. The same can be said about the fall in the ratio from 1898 to 1906, with the qualification that whatever shifts occurred between time deposits and demand deposits can not be measured. In 1917–29 and other periods, the effects of those shifts were much smaller in absolute terms, even though sometimes large

relative to actual changes in the ratio. There was no inherent reason
the shifts should work in the same direction, and they did not always.
In the 1917–29 period, the effect of the shift in favor of time deposits
was almost completely offset by the other two types of shift, and the
combined effect of all three on the ratio was negligible.

Cyclical shifts of deposits occurred between reserve city national or
member banks and other banks. A possible explanation is that deposits shift to large cities in recessions and away from them in prosperity, and that a majority of the banks in large cities are central and
other reserve city national or member banks. The phenomenon has
interesting implications for the relative demand to hold money of
different groups over the cycle and merits further study, even though
its effects on the reserve ratio were relatively small.

The largest differences in the ratios for individual banks are mainly
between those subject to different reserve requirements. For that
reason, shifts in deposits between such banks, on which the preceding
analysis was based, are likely to be the most important.

2. Legal Reserve Requirements

Legal reserve requirements give monetary authorities immediate
control over the capability of banks to extend loans. A substantial
increase in requirements with no compensating increase in high-
powered money or decline in the currency ratio may make the amount
of reserves above requirements—usable reserves[20]—temporarily negative and thereby force banks to contract earning assets in order to
accumulate funds. A reduction in requirements may present banks
with such large usable reserves that terms and interest charges on loans
are quickly lowered to take advantage of the new opportunities for
expanding earning assets. Historically, most new requirements have
been intended to influence the disposition of banks to expand credit,
but usually the size of the changes were small and the effects un-
dramatic. Sometimes they resulted merely from technical changes

[20] The more attractive words "excess" and "free" have been usurped by common
usage to mean something else than usable in this context, so usable reserves is the
closest synonym. "Excess" reserves stand for actual balances with Federal Reserve
Banks *less* required balances. "Free" reserves stand for excess reserves *less* member
bank borrowings from Reserve Banks. Usable reserves, as defined here, equal excess
reserves *plus* vault cash. (From June 1917 to December 1959, no part of vault cash
satisfied member bank reserve requirements; since November 1960, all does.)

in the definition of the deposit base on which required reserves were computed. Reasons for the major changes in national or member bank requirements are briefly reviewed below, after which the effect of changes in requirements on the reserve ratio are examined. The requirements for other commercial banks, also discussed below, varied among states and are best summarized on an average basis for selected dates.

MAJOR CHANGES IN NATIONAL OR MEMBER
BANK RESERVE REQUIREMENTS

From 1864, when the National Currency Act of the year before was amended, until 1914, the legal reserve requirements for national banks were changed only three times. First, the act of June 20, 1874, repealed the reserve requirements for notes and provided that a redemption fund equal to 5 per cent of the notes outstanding be deposited with the Treasury, though the full amount of the fund could be counted toward the reserve requirement for deposits. Second, in 1902, U.S. deposits were exempted from reserve requirements.[21] Third, the Federal Reserve Act disallowed the inclusion of the 5 per cent redemption fund for notes in legal reserves for deposits.

Since passage of the Federal Reserve Act, requirements have been changed many times. The first occurred late in 1914 when national banks, as members of the newly established Federal Reserve System, had their reserve requirements reduced. While part of the reduction helped member banks finance the compulsory purchase of capital stock in Federal Reserve Banks without contracting other earning assets, required reserves were intentionally reduced more than the amount of those purchases to attract state banks into the System. The act also stipulated that required reserves deposited at correspondent banks, authorized under the national banking system, be transferred gradually to Federal Reserve Banks over a period of three years, after which only vault cash and deposits at Federal Reserve Banks were to qualify as legal reserves.[22] The effect of this provision

---

[21] For an engaging recital of the circumstances surrounding that ruling, see A. Piatt Andrew, "The Treasury and the Banks Under Secretary Shaw," *Quarterly Journal of Economics*, Aug. 1907, pp. 519–568. By later extensions that exemption lasted until June 30, 1914, and was subsequently reinstated for the period Apr. 24, 1917, to Aug. 23, 1935. Nearly all U.S. deposits were again exempted during World War II.

[22] The first instalment was payable entirely in gold or lawful money and the rest, half in eligible paper. Also, in figuring requirements, deposits due from banks were still deductible from deposits due to other banks, so that a fraction of interbank deposits in effect counted as legal reserves.

was gradual reduction of the amount of deposits member banks could create per dollar of high-powered reserves. Six months before the transitional period was scheduled to end, the 1917 amendment to the act was passed specifying that all required reserves be deposited immediately with Federal Reserve Banks. That provision would have raised reserve requirements, but a further stipulation of the amendment, designed to make it acceptable to member banks, lowered the total amount of required reserves. Transfer of all reserves to Reserve Banks aided the campaign of the Federal Reserve Board to acquire as much of the domestic gold stock as possible, a step thought necessary to meet the demands for credit expected to arise out of the nation's entry into World War I.[23]

The requirements instituted at that time remained in force until August 1936, when the Federal Reserve took steps to eliminate member banks' large holdings of excess reserves. Accumulated from gold inflows in the preceding years of business recovery, they were viewed as a potential source of inflation. The Banking Act of 1935 had endowed the Board of Governors with new authority to set reserve ratios at any level between specified minimums and maximums. The August increase was the first of three which, together, raised the required ratio by May 1937 to the legal maximum for all member banks.

Since then, the Board of Governors has changed requirements many times, though never by so much in so short a period. It reduced them moderately during the severe business contraction in 1938 and then in 1941 reinstated maximum requirements. During 1942, requirements for central reserve city banks were reduced to facilitate the continued active participation of those banks in Treasury financial operations. Requirements for the other banks remained unchanged until 1948, when temporary legislation was enacted raising the maximum required level of reserves in an effort to stem the inflationary consequences of wartime financial policies. The Board immediately utilized the authority granted and put higher requirements into effect. When the 1949 contractionary tendencies of business were recognized, the Board rescinded over one-half the previous increase and, in June when the special authority expired, the rest. Further reductions followed in August and September of that year. Since 1949, requirements have been changed frequently but in small steps: from 1950

---

[23] See W. P. G. Harding, *The Formative Period of the Federal Reserve System*, Boston, 1925, pp. 70 ff.

through 1955 the highest required ratio imposed exceeded the lowest by only 4 percentage points for central reserve city banks and by only 2 for other banks.

Of the five largest changes since 1914, two worked to counter the prevailing movement in the money stock: one raised requirements during World War II; another lowered them during the 1949 contraction, though somewhat late. The other three were ill timed so far as monetary stability was concerned. One, which was the largest reduction in requirements ever granted at one time, was made during World War I and enabled banks to aid in the inflationary financing of Treasury deficits. The other two in 1936–37 and 1948, each a series of increases imposed over a relatively short period, reversed policies of credit ease which threatened to produce inflation but, as it turned out, coincided with or slightly preceded downturns in the economy.

CHANGES IN REQUIREMENTS OF OTHER
COMMERCIAL BANKS

Reserve requirements for other commercial banks vary from state to state and cannot be so handily summarized. Considerations of short-run monetary stability have not played much part, as they do to a large extent in changes of member bank requirements. For one thing, requirements in many states can be altered only by their state legislatures,[24] rather than, as in others, by authority delegated to state banking commissions. Consequently, state requirements as a whole have been changed much less frequently than member bank requirements have and primarily for purposes related to long-run goals of banking regulation.

Federal regulations have provided a standard toward which state requirements have slowly gravitated.[25] Before the Civil War, only Louisiana, in 1842, and Massachusetts, in 1858, passed laws specifically requiring reserves against deposits. After passage of the National Currency Act, the first state to impose reserve requirements was Michigan, in 1871. New York State, often a leader in such matters,

[24] Twenty-five states as of 1951. See *Monetary Policy and the Management of the Public Debt*, Joint Committee on the Economic Report, 82d Cong., 2d sess., 1952, Part 1, p. 471.
[25] The rest of this paragraph is based on R. G. Rodkey, *Legal Reserves in American Banking*, Michigan Business Studies, Vol. VI, 1934, Chaps. 3 and 5.

did not act until 1882, though most members of the New York City Clearing House agreed among themselves in 1858 to maintain a minimum reserve of 20 per cent. As late as 1900, only seventeen states had enacted such provisions. Thereafter, interest in the regulation of banking quickened, and all but six states imposed some kind of restriction on deposit reserves before passage of the Federal Reserve Act, and the six fell in line soon after.

Because of the great variety in state reserve requirements, the best way to summarize them is to treat other commercial banks as a group and compute total required reserves as a percentage of total deposits by taking an average of state reserve requirements weighted by the deposits of the commercial banks subject to them in each state. Construction of an average for frequent intervals would be tedious, and has not been attempted. A summary of requirements for all states has been published for ten different dates from 1909 to 1950, from which a good indication of the trend in the aggregate reserve ratio for those banks can be derived.

Averages for the ten dates are given in Table 20. Because of the assumption that all state regulations apply to private banks—though some may not—these figures may overstate the true average requirement including those private banks. The overstatement is negligible, however, since deposits of private banks have accounted for a very small part of the total covered by the table. A more important difficulty is that many states impose higher requirements on banks in designated reserve cities than elsewhere. Since deposits in such banks are not usually listed separately in state banking reports, their requirements could not receive separate weighting—New York excepted. In that state, the wide variety of requirements for different classes of banks and the large amount of deposits warranted special treatment. For other states, two averages were made, one treating all banks as though subject to the highest requirement in the relevant state, and the other, as though subject to the lowest. The range so obtained and recorded in Table 20 is, on the whole, fairly narrow and does not obscure the main trends in the aggregate ratio. The bulk of banks and deposits probably fall in the low reserve classifications, despite the inclusion of most larger banks in the high classifications, and a correctly weighted average would probably fall close to the lower end of the range.

TABLE 20

REQUIRED RESERVE RATIO OF OTHER COMMERCIAL BANKS, SELECTED YEARS, 1909-50

	High-Powered Reserves Required[a] per $100 of:			Total Cash Reserves Required[b] per $100 of:		
Year	Demand Deposits (1)	Time Deposits (2)	Total Deposits (3)	Demand Deposits (4)	Time Deposits (5)	Total Deposits (6)
1909	5.5-7.6	2.1-3.2	4.2-6.0	12.9-14.4	6.9- 9.1	10.7-12.5
1913	5.2-7.1	2.8-4.4	4.2-6.0	14.1-17.1	9.3-13.2	12.1-15.4
1915	5.0-7.0	2.6-4.2	4.7-5.9	13.4-16.2	8.4-11.9	11.4-14.5
1917	5.0-6.9	2.5-3.9	4.0-5.7	13.1-16.5	8.1-11.1	11.1-14.4
1924	5.1-5.9	1.3-2.9	3.4-4.6	12.6-14.7	7.7- 9.3	10.5-12.3
1928	3.9-5.6	1.1-2.1	2.6-4.0	12.4-14.5	7.0- 8.4	9.9-11.6
1930	4.1-5.6	1.1-1.4	2.7-3.7	12.2-14.1	6.3- 8.0	9.5-11.3
1937	4.8-6.3	1.2-2.1	3.5-4.8	12.4-14.4	5.9- 7.6	10.1-12.0
1944	2.7-4.1	1.0-1.7	2.2-3.5	10.8-12.8	6.0- 7.4	9.5-11.4
1950	0.4-1.3	0-8.1.1	0.6-1.2	13.8-16.2	7.0- 8.0	11.8-13.8

Source, by Year

1909: Samuel A. Welldon, Digest of State Banking Statutes, National Monetary
Commission, 61st Cong., 2d sess., S. Doc. 353, 1910, Charts A and C (there are
a couple of negligible disagreements between this source and Rodkey, Legal
Reserves).
1913 and 1915: Annual Report of the Federal Reserve Board for 1915, pp. 104-113.
1917: Federal Reserve Bulletin, Oct. 1917, pp. 768-796.
1924: FRB, Mar. 1924, pp. 154-181.
1928: FRB, Nov. 1928, pp. 778-804.
1930: FRB, Sept. 1930, pp. 570-597.
1937: FRB, Mar. 1937, pp. 188-219.
1944: Provisions of State Laws Relating to Bank Reserves as of December 31, 1944,
Board of Governors of the Federal Reserve System (no date).
1950: Reserve Requirements for Non-member Banks, American Bankers Association,
Sept. 1950. (For 1951, not shown, see source in text footnote 24.)
    Note: These ratios are averages of state reserve requirements weighted for
the quantity of demand, time, or total deposits held by the public at other
commercial banks in each state (from All-Bank Statistics). The lower end of the
range is an estimate using the lowest requirements in each state, and the upper
end, using the highest requirements. Both sets of requirements were averaged
by the same weights, except for New York State, for which a weighted average
was computed for the different classes of banks.
    The exact date within each of three years to which the requirements apply is
Dec. 31 for 1944, Jan. 1 for 1937, and May 31 for 1930. For the other years no
exact date was specified, and the requirements for different states may have
been compiled as of different dates within the year given. Most state requirements change infrequently, however, and the averages generally apply to the
entire year for which they were computed.
    [a]Cash in vault only.
    [b]Cash in vault plus balances with approved banks.

Table 20 helps to explain the difference between the total reserve
ratios for member banks and other commercial banks over the years.
The difference reflects a tendency of state regulations to permit banks
under state control to rely heavily for reserve purposes on total cash
reserves, that is, on balances at other approved banks as well as on
vault cash. The main reason for disallowing unlimited use of interbank
balances for reserves is, of course, that the practice permits banks to
create a pyramid of credit which can be very unstable. The Federal

Reserve System was founded to correct such weaknesses of the national banking system and, accordingly, has authorized only high-powered money for legal reserves of banks under its jurisdiction. Deposits at nonmember banks have dwindled to a small share of the total, and the resources of Federal Reserve Banks help to strengthen the financial security of all banks. These considerations perhaps explain the growing tendency of states to allow interbank balances to satisfy reserve requirements and so to produce a gradual reduction in high-powered reserve requirements without a corresponding decline in total cash reserve requirements of other commercial banks.

The smaller difference between required high-powered reserves for time deposits and demand deposits in 1944 and 1950 stems from the gradual elimination of vault cash as a required component of total reserves, making required high-powered reserves zero; it may also stem from a redistribution of deposits toward states with lower demand requirements. (In 1950, the latter tendency actually reversed the usual relation between requirements for the two kinds of deposits and made the average high-powered requirement for time deposits greater, even though in every state except Missouri required reserves were at least as large for demand deposits as for time deposits.) The difference between requirements for time and demand deposits in the early years helps to explain why, during the 1920's, the increase in the proportion of time deposits in member banks exceeded the increase in that proportion in other commercial banks. Some nonmember commercial banks had lower requirements on time deposits than on demand deposits well before the Federal Reserve Act introduced that distinction into the regulations for national banks; and the relative advantage to other commercial banks in the lower requirement for time deposits changed little during the 1920's.

As for the general movement of state reserve requirements over time, Table 20 shows little change between successive dates, at least in comparison with the sharp variations in member bank requirements. As noted, changes made by individual states have been infrequent, though often quite drastic and all at once. Since the actions of most states were taken at infrequent intervals, no one group of actions had much effect. Consequently, the average tends to smooth variations in the individual components.

One of the largest changes in high-powered reserve requirements

CHART 19

High-Powered Reserve Ratio of Other Commercial Banks,
Annually and Semiannually, 1875–1955

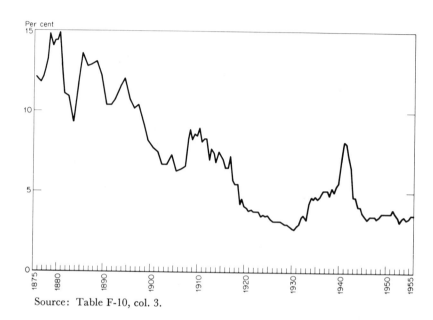

Source: Table F-10, col. 3.

for total deposits of other commercial banks was a reduction of 1.3
percentage points from 1915 to 1924. It corresponds with a decline
of 3 points or more in the total reserve ratio for those banks from
1916 to 1924, as shown by Chart 19. The decline in requirements,
therefore, can explain less than half the decline in the total reserve
ratio. The chart shows considerably more variation than could be
accounted for by changes in requirements. Moreover, most of the
changes in requirements were too small for their effects to show up, and
the data offer little evidence on reactions of banks to different levels of
requirements. For present purposes, we must rely on national-member
banks, whose reserve requirements have undergone wide variation.

EFFECTS OF CHANGES IN NATIONAL AND MEMBER BANK RESERVE REQUIREMENTS

Table 21 shows the effects of all changes in national-member bank
reserve requirements greater than 1 per cent of total high-powered

reserves (required plus usable reserves). All changes in the same direction and in steps within a year of each other have been grouped together and listed as a single change, except in lines 13 and 14. The latter include some changes dated slightly less than a year apart but nevertheless listed separately, because more than a year separates the largest change in each group. Columns 1 and 2 give two measures of the amount of reserves released or tied up by the change in requirements. The second in column 2, expressed as a percentage of deposits, gives the change in the required reserve ratio. These measures are calculated for the call date immediately preceding the date of the change in requirements, in order to exclude immediate increases or decreases in deposits that may have resulted from banks' reactions to the changes. This procedure, of course, ignores any alteration in reserves made before the preceding call date, in anticipation of the change in requirements; changes were not announced long in advance, however, and anticipatory actions were probably minor.

Whether a change in the required reserve ratio affects the total ratio depends on the reactions of banks. At first, the entire effect falls on the usable reserve ratio, since there is no time to adjust total reserves. If banks allow their usable reserves permanently to absorb the full change in requirements, no subsequent adjustment in total reserves will occur, and the changes would have no effect on the total reserve ratio. The total ratio would be affected if usable reserves do not fully absorb changes in requirements, after time for adjustments. As one possibility, banks might maintain their usable ratios at predetermined levels wholly unrelated to their required ratio, by contracting non-monetary assets to meet all increases in requirements and using additions to reserves produced by decreases in requirements to acquire such assets. Changes in the required reserve ratio would then have no effect on usable ratios, except during a short-run adjustment period, and would eventually produce an equal change in total ratios.

Columns 3–5 in Table 21 indicate whether, within a given time span, the total or the usable ratio tended to absorb most of the historical changes in requirements. These columns give changes in semiannual series of the total, required, and usable ratios, from the nearest June or December preceding the initial date of a new set of requirements to the first June or December at least three months after

TABLE 21

EFFECTS OF ALL MAJOR CHANGES IN RESERVE REQUIREMENTS ON NATIONAL OR
MEMBER BANK RESERVES, 1875-1955

Dates of Impositon of New Reserve Requirements	Reserves Released (−) or Tied Up (+) by Changes in Requirements as Percentage of:[a]		Numerical Change in Percentage Reserve Ratios Between Dates Before and After New Requirements[b]		
	High-Powered Reserves (1)	Deposits (2)	Total Ratio (3)	Required Ratio (4)	Usable Ratio (5)
1. Oct. 4, 1902	−3	−0.6	n.c.	n.c.	n.c.
2. Jan. 14, 1914	3	0.5	−0.1	0.8	−0.9
3. Nov. 16, 1914	−13	−1.9	0.7	−3.0	3.7
4. Nov. 16, 1915-16	14	2.1	0.4	3.1	−2.7
5. June 21, 1917	−21	−3.1	−2.8	−4.5	1.7
6. Aug. 16, 1936 to May 1, 1937	47	8.8	4.7	8.2	−3.5
7. Apr. 16, 1938	−10	−2.2	3.3	−2.0	5.3
8. Nov. 1, 1941	8	2.4	−4.4	2.5	−6.9
9. Aug. 20 to Oct. 3, 1942	−9	−2.3	−5.7	−2.8	−2.9
10. Feb. 27 to Sept. 24, 1948	16	2.9	2.7	2.9	−0.2
11. May 1 to Sept. 1, 1949	−18	−3.7	−3.8	−3.7	−0.1
12. Jan. 11 to Feb. 1, 1951	11	1.8	1.6	1.9	−0.3
13. July 1 to 9, 1953	−5	−1.0	−0.4	−0.4	0.0
14. June 16 to Aug. 1, 1954	−7	−1.3	−1.3	−1.3	0.0

Source, by Column

(1): Beginning Nov. 16, 1914, comprises seasonally unadjusted data for vault cash and amounts due from Federal Reserve Banks; before that date, comprises vault cash of national banks (National and Member Bank Call Reports).

(2): Comprises seasonally unadjusted data on individual and postal savings deposits and net amounts due to nonnational banks (before 1914) or nonmember banks. Since the percentages are essentially a weighted average of changes in reserve requirements for different classes of deposits, the weights are unlikely to contain much seasonal variation (National and Member Bank Call Reports).

(3-5): Based on Table F-11 and the seasonally adjusted series in Table F-12, derived according to the same definition of deposits and reserves used for cols. 1 and 2. The series are annual (call dates nearest Oct. 1) until June 1914, semiannual (call dates nearest June and Dec.) thereafter.

Note: The decrease on Oct. 4, 1902, and the increase on Jan. 14, 1914, were the only changes in national bank required reserves from 1875 through Oct. 1914, with one exception: the redefinition of net demand deposits on June 30, 1914, to include U.S. deposits, which amounted to a change in requirements on that date equal to only 0.8 per cent of reserves held and 0.1 per cent of deposits.

The table includes all changes for member banks through 1955 except a few involving a redefinition of net demand deposits (see Banking and Monetary Statistics, p. 66, n. 13). The date of the redefinition with the largest effects was Aug. 23, 1935, when U.S. deposits were included, and demand deposits due from other banks could be deducted from total demand deposits instead of from demand deposits of other banks only, as before. The data are not available to make exact calculations of the effects of such changes, but all were negligible. The effect on reserves of the 1935 change was only about 0.6 per cent of reserves held and 0.1 per cent of deposits on June 29, 1935 (as derived from estimates given in "History of Reserve Requirements for Banks in the United States," Federal Reserve Bulletin, Nov. 1938, p. 961). Exemption of U.S. deposits from net demand deposits, beginning Apr. 24, 1917, freed less than 0.2 per cent of reserves held. The effect of the wartime exemption of U.S. deposits in War Loan Accounts after Apr. 1943 cannot be computed, because there were no such accounts previously.

NOTES TO TABLE 21 (concluded)

n.c. = not computed, because data for the nearest available date after the change were for a year later, hence not comparable with the 3-to 9-month period used in later entries in the table.

Changes Covered, by Line

1-5: Cover national banks only; the required figures for state member banks before 1918 are not available. This restriction of coverage results in little error, since there were few state member banks before passage of the act of June 21, 1917.

2: Represents the $35 million increase in required reserves owing to the Federal Reserve Act's discontinuance of the inclusion in lawful reserves of the 5 per cent redemption fund for national bank notes (sect. 20), enforcement delayed by Comptroller until after call date on Jan. 13, 1914.

3-4: Cover changes in high-powered reserves required by the Federal Reserve Act. Reserves held at central city or other reserve city banks, as previously allowed for national banks, had to be gradually transferred to Federal Reserve Banks. As to requirements for vault cash and amounts held at Federal Reserve Banks, the act provided for an immediate reduction when the System was established, shown in line 3. (Calculations were made on the basis of deposits classified as demand and time on Oct. 31, 1914; no allowance was made for possible transfers of demand deposits to time deposits when the lower requirement for the latter was instituted.) This line also covers the $54 million reserves tied up when national banks purchased Federal Reserve Bank stock equal to 3 per cent of their paid-in capital and surplus, as required upon becoming member banks.

The 1917 act required high-powered reserves to be increased through transfer of balances at national bank reserve agents to Federal Reserve Banks, in three semiannual instalments to begin 12 months after the Reserve Banks opened for business. The transfers came between Nov. 16, 1915, and a year later, and their effects have been grouped together in line 4.

5: Covers the change in requirements specified by the act of June 21, 1917, partly amending the preceding provisions of the 1913 Federal Reserve Act. The comparison is with the requirements in effect from Nov. 16, 1916, to June 20, 1917.

[a]Computed for the nearest call date preceding date of change in requirements on the basis of reserves required against time deposits and net demand deposits.

[b]Dates are just before, and three to nine months after, imposition of new requirements.

the final date of the set. By this method of selection, the end of the period could be as little as three months or as long as nine after the final date of the set. The derived period was selected because it never overlaps a subsequent change in requirements. The varying length of the period covered appears to be less serious for present purposes than the presence of sizable cyclical and random fluctuations in the required and usable reserve ratios, which may conceal tiny adjustments to small changes in requirements. Such fluctuations account for the discrepancy between columns 2 and 4. Only fairly large statutory changes in requirements are likely to provide reliable evidence on responses of banks to them.

A sharp difference in responses to the statutory changes in requirements before 1948 and after is suggested by columns 3–5. In the later changes the usable reserve ratio returned almost exactly to its previous level; in the earlier changes, the usable reserve ratio absorbed a sizable part of the new reserve requirements. This might suggest that,

CHART 20

Reserve Ratios of National or Member Banks, Annually and Semiannually, 1875–1955

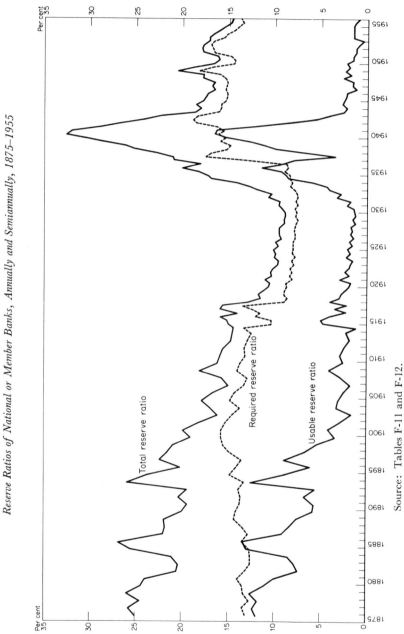

Source: Tables F-11 and F-12.

only since World War II, has the usable ratio been unaffected by changes in requirements, an interpretation consistent with the three changes from 1914 to 1916, when the usable ratio offset most of the required change and the total ratio hardly varied. (The lack of semi-annual figures before 1914 precluded an entry for the 1902 change.) For the others before 1948, however, the evidence is mixed. The usable ratio absorbed over one-third of the 1917 and 1936–37 changes, two of the largest ever imposed. For the remaining three changes in 1938, 1941, and 1942, other factors were obviously at work. The usable ratio changed considerably more than necessary to offset the new requirements in 1938 and 1941 and changed in the same direction the new requirements did in 1942. Usable reserves might offset either part or none of a change in required reserves but would not—unless for some other reason—offset more than the required change or reinforce it. These three cases offer little evidence, therefore, on responses of banks to changes in requirements.

One important factor in the postwar changes is the low level of the average usable reserve ratio consistently maintained by banks since World War II. This is evident in Chart 20, which shows the national or member bank total, required, and usable reserve ratios from 1875 to 1955. Before the end of World War II, the usable ratio fell below 2.5 per cent and remained below that level through 1955. With low usable reserves banks could meet increases in required reserves only by increasing total reserves or reducing earning assets; there were insufficient usable reserves to absorb higher requirements. The low usable ratio also indicates that banks had invested all but a minimum amount of their usable funds intentionally and did not wish to hold any more, for they quickly turned the reserves freed by the two postwar reductions in requirements into earning assets and so kept the usable ratio at the same level. In earlier periods, the usable ratio was at higher levels and could absorb at least part of the new increases in requirements, without the need for immediate increases in total reserves. This may explain why banks were slow to replace usable reserves absorbed by the earlier increases in requirements, and why they were slow to take advantage of the earlier reductions in requirements.

One interpretation of this evidence is that banks are quick to offset the effect of changes in requirements on the usable reserve ratio when it is very low; moderate variations when it is fairly high do not cause concern, and usable reserves are allowed to absorb all or most of increases in requirements. By this reasoning, failure of the decline in total reserves to match the large 1917 reduction in requirements and failure of their rise to match the large 1936–37 increase could be ascribed to the high level of the usable ratio at those times. This interpretation is implicit in the reasons given by the authorities for most of the large increases: they were specifically designed to remove the inflationary potential of large usable reserves rather than to induce a rise in total reserves.[26] The actions assumed that accumulation of usable reserves results from the temporary unavailability of earning assets banks are willing to purchase. It follows that an increase in requirements then has no effect on the amount of total reserves banks desire.

This interpretation is open to question. That the usable reserve ratio can no doubt undergo larger variations when high than when low does not necessarily mean that banks are indifferent to the level of those reserves, even when large. An alternative interpretation is that banks want to keep their usable reserves at desired levels and will offset all but small variations in them—an explanation consistent with the postwar and also the earlier changes in requirements, when they are examined more closely. We may ask whether, at the time of the earlier changes, the usable ratio was strongly affected by other factors and, if they are taken into account, whether the total or the usable ratio did absorb most of the new requirements in the long run. Chart 20 will facilitate such an examination, because it shows movements in the usable ratio over the whole period and avoids the arbitrary limits of periods used in Table 21. The large abrupt changes in the required ratio which stand out in the chart reflect the imposition of new requirements. The other variations in this series, occasionally fairly large especially before 1910, reflect redistribution of deposits.[27]

The 1914 Increase in Requirements. The usable ratio had still absorbed most of the increase six months later. After that, the usable ratio series is swamped by the effects of the much larger reduction in

[26] For statements of policy on four of the increases when usable reserves were unusually large, see the *Annual Report*, Board of Governors of the Federal Reserve System, 1937, pp. 2–5; 1941, p. 7; 1948, p. 10; and 1951, p. 1.

[27] There are also minor changes of another kind in the required ratio: the deposit base for computing required reserves differs slightly from deposits as defined for the series in Chart 20, and the two need not maintain a constant proportion, though on the whole they did.

requirements in 1914, so the effect of the earlier reduction cannot be followed beyond six months in this series. That seems long enough, however, for banks to adjust to such a small increase. Apparently at that time banks were willing to see their usable reserves decline.

The 1914 Reduction and 1915–16 Increases in Requirements. Usable reserves rose to absorb the reduction in 1914 and later fell to absorb the increases in 1915–16. Banks kept their total reserve ratios roughly constant and allowed the usable ratios to fluctuate. There seems to be a special reason for the response to those changes: The Federal Reserve Act not only provided for the 1914 reduction in requirements but also scheduled increases somewhat greater in total amount to take effect at six-month intervals beginning one year later. Member banks made no noticeable short-run adjustment to the 1914 reduction probably in anticipation of the increases for which they prepared by saving reserves released by the reduction. The after effects of the panic of August 1914 were short lived and cannot explain the failure of the reserve ratio to decline. Beginning in 1915, there were large additions to high-powered money due principally to gold inflows. Such large and sudden increases in bank reserves cannot be quickly invested and may partly account for the rise in total and usable ratios in the year following the 1914 reduction in requirements.

The 1917 Reduction in Requirements. The total reserve ratio had absorbed about two-thirds of that reduction in the first six months and in the next twelve months had absorbed all of it, as Chart 20 shows. All the usable reserves freed by the reduction were therefore converted into earning assets, though the investment took a year and a half to complete. Such a slow adjustment might suggest that banks were not initially interested in investing all the freed reserves and only changed their minds because of the high wartime demand for loans or perhaps for other reasons. The slow adjustment can also be explained in another way: Not only was the 1917 reduction in requirements large, but it also removed vault cash from the category of legal reserves for the first time. Banks probably relinquished this traditional first line of defense cautiously and experimentally—a more plausible explanation, since the usable ratio remained low during the business recessions of 1919 and 1921 and the ensuing decade.

The 1936–37 Increases in Requirements. The total reserve ratio had absorbed only about half that series of changes in the six months following the last of them, but that was probably too little time to allow a full adjustment. Those changes were by far the largest ever imposed within a year's time. Chart 20 shows that the level of the usable reserve ratio in mid-1936, just before the changes began, was fully restored by the end of 1938, two and a half years later, a recovery suggesting that banks increased total reserves in order to replace the usable reserves lost by the increase in requirements. This is not conclusive evidence, however. Unlike the other episodes considered so far, the total reserve ratio had been rising sharply before the 1936 increase in requirements and might have continued to rise even if requirements had not changed. In 1936, business activity, though rising, was still depressed, and interest rates were low. The state of the economy, therefore, might explain the further rise in total reserves. One interpretation consistent with the latter explanation is that large usable reserves reflect the unavailability of suitable investment outlets; under such circumstances, banks hold the funds idle, and an increase in requirements has no effect on desired levels of total reserves. The increase, by immediately wiping out part of the usable reserves, will actually prevent an expansion of credit if in the near future suitable investment opportunities arise. The official explanation of the series of increases in 1936–37 is explicit on this point:

Notwithstanding the fact that recovery [in 1936] was far from complete and that there was still a large amount of unemployment, boom conditions were developing in particular industries and boom psychology began to be manifested . . . . In August 1936 the Board of Governors had raised reserve requirements for member banks by 50 per cent in order to absorb a part of the $3,000,000,000 of reserves in excess of requirements held by member banks . . . . The Board's action was in the nature of a precautionary measure to prevent an uncontrollable expansion of credit in the future . . . . The increase in requirements had no perceptible effect on the credit situation, and money rates continued low . . . .

It was estimated that . . . , if requirements were increased by an additional $33\frac{1}{3}$ per cent, the banking system would still have the basis of a potential expansion of more than $5,000,000,000 without recourse to the Federal Reserve banks . . . . An increase in reserve requirements would not diminish the large volume of deposits of bank customers seeking investment which were ample to assure the continuance of favorable money rates for capital purposes.[28]

[28] *Annual Report*, Board of Governors of the Federal Reserve System, 1937, pp. 2–5.

TABLE 22

RESERVE RATIOS OF SELECTED FINANCIAL INSTITUTIONS, ANNUALLY, 1929-40

(per cent)

Year (end of June)	MEMBER BANKS						OTHER FINANCIAL INSTITUTIONS		
	Usable High-Powered Reserve Ratio			Total High-Powered Reserve Ratio			Total High-Powered Reserve Ratio for Other Commercial Banks	Total Cash Reserve Ratio	
	Central Reserve City Banks	Other Reserve City Banks	Country Banks	Central Reserve City Banks	Other Reserve City Banks	Country Banks		Mutual Savings Banks	Savings and Loan Associations
	(1)	(2)	(3)	(4)	(5)	(6)	(7)	(8)	(9)
1929	1.5	1.4	2.1	15.4	9.0	7.1	2.9	2.4	n.a.
1930	1.3	1.5	2.5	18.2	8.9	7.5	2.7	3.2	n.a.
1931	1.6	1.9	3.0	17.0	9.0	7.7	3.0	3.9	n.a.
1932	3.5	2.0	3.2	17.6	8.9	8.0	3.6	4.4	n.a.
1933	4.0	3.9	4.3	18.9	11.1	9.1	4.3	4.4	n.a.
1934	12.5	7.9	6.7	26.9	15.5	11.6	4.6	5.3	n.a.
1935	15.8	8.2	7.2	30.3	16.1	12.2	4.6	5.3	5.4
1936	14.6	10.3	8.0	30.7	18.3	12.3	5.1	5.4	5.3
1937	4.4	4.1	5.5	34.9	20.5	14.4	5.1	5.3	5.7
1938	19.0	8.2	6.7	46.5	22.0	13.9	5.2	5.6	5.7
1939	24.0	9.9	7.0	52.1	24.0	14.3	5.4	6.6	7.1
1940	29.1	14.6	8.9	55.7	28.8	16.0	7.1	9.1	7.5

Source, by Column

(1)-(6): Total reserve ratio (Table F-13) minus required reserve ratio (required reserves from Banking and Monetary Statistics, Board of Governors of the Federal Reserve System, 1943, divided by deposits (used for computations in Table F-13).

(7): High-powered reserve ratio (see Table F-10, col. 3).

(8): Total cash reserve ratio, including balances held at commercial banks (see Table F-17, col. 3).

(9): Ratio of total cash assets, including balances at commercial banks, to private share capital of all operating associations (see Federal Home Loan Bank Review, Statistical Suppl., 1947, p. 7, Table 7).

If banks raise their total reserve ratios in the face of stiffer requirements that merely reduce usable reserves, we can not know for certain whether their decision to bolster reserves was related to the new requirements. There are, however, other aspects of the behavior of member banks and other financial institutions, particularly in that period, which can shed light on the motives behind the increase in member bank reserves.

Evidence on the effect of the 1936–37 increase is afforded by the diversity of behavior of the usable ratios for the three classes of member banks. In columns 1–3 of Table 22, there is a pronounced variability in the usable ratio of central reserve city banks, much less in that of reserve city banks, and relatively little in that of country banks. One interpretation of this pattern is that, following the 1933 panic, central reserve city banks, and to a lesser extent other reserve city banks, fearful of further withdrawals, especially of deposits held by other banks, built up their usable reserves in defense. Since country banks held few deposits of other banks and could rely in emergencies on their balances at reserve city banks, they looked upon large usable reserves as less imperative. By this interpretation, the 1936–37 increase in requirements accentuated the differences between reserve city and country banks by striking deepest into the usable reserves of those

TABLE 23

EFFECT OF 1936–37 INCREASES IN RESERVE REQUIREMENTS ON USABLE
RESERVE RATIOS, THREE CLASSES OF MEMBER BANKS
(per cent)

Class of Member Banks	USABLE RESERVE RATIO[a]			Increase in Total Reserve Ratio as Percentage of Increase in Required Reserve Ratio
	June 30, 1936			
	Actual (1)	According to Requirements in Effect a Year Later (2)	Actual, June 30, 1938 (3)	$\frac{(3) - (2)}{(1) - (2)}$ x 100 (4)
Central reserve city	14.6	−1.6	19.0	127
Other reserve cities	10.3	−2.2	8.2	83
Country	8.0	+3.6	6.7	70

[a]Same as in Table 22.

banks in greatest need of them. Table 23 indicates that the required increases wiped out more than all the usable reserves held by central and other reserve city banks in June 1936, the first call date preceding the increases. It is significant that by the middle of 1938 central reserve city banks replaced somewhat more than their losses, other reserve city banks somewhat less, while country banks, which lost less than half their usable reserves, the smallest fraction of their losses. Since the first and second classes of banks outpaced the third in accumulating reserves before 1936, the repetition of the pattern after 1936 is not readily explained without taking account of required increases. Member banks appear, therefore, to have augmented their reserve position from 1936 to 1938 mainly to replace the reduction in usable reserves produced by the 1936–37 increases in requirements.[29]

This interpretation is strongly supported by the behavior of other financial institutions. Table 22 also shows that reserve ratios for other commercial banks, mutual savings banks, and savings and loan associations, none of which experienced important changes in reserve requirements during the period 1929–40, behaved similarly to the total and usable ratios of all classes of member banks, except in 1936–38. The ratios for all institutions rose moderately during the contraction in business of 1929–33 and then climbed markedly following the 1933 panic. In 1936–38, however, the member bank ratio is the only one not remaining relatively constant. Then, after 1938, all rose again, presumably in consequence of the continued low level of business activity and, perhaps, further decline in interest rates. This evidence indicates that only some factor specific to member banks—like increased requirements—can explain the 1936–38 rise in their reserve ratio.

---

[29] Clark Warburton reached a similar conclusion; see his "The Turning Points in Business Cycles," *Quarterly Journal of Economics*, Nov. 1950, pp. 547–548. See also Friedman and Schwartz, *A Monetary History*, Chap. 9; and Karl Brunner, "A Case Study of U.S., Monetary Policy: Reserve Requirements and Inflationary Gold Flows in the Middle 30's," *Schweizerische Zeitschrift für Volkswirtschaft und Statistik*, 94, 1958, pp. 160–201. For alternative explanations, see M. D. Brockie, "Theories of the 1937–38 Crisis and Depression," *Economic Journal*, June 1950, pp. 292–296, and G. Horwich, "Effective Reserves, Credit, and Causality in the Banking System of the Thirties," in *Banking and Monetary Studies*, D. Carson, ed., Homestead, Ill., Irwin, 1963.

A factor of some importance not mentioned in the text was the extremely large inflow of gold from abroad during that period. The inflow probably made the actual reserve ratio greater for a time than the desired ratio. This might account for the actual ratio's being somewhat higher than usual, but could not explain the continual rise in the ratio unless the size of the gold inflow continually became larger over the period—which was not the case.

Further evidence is provided by Canadian banks, which had no change in requirements and maintained roughly the same total reserve ratio through the second half of the 1930's[30], even though Canada experienced the same sharp decline in output during 1938, and in interest rates during the 1930's, as the United States did.

Increased requirements are not the only possible explanation of the rise in the member bank usable reserve ratio, to be sure, since the evidence does not rule out the possibility that it may have resulted from continuing apprehension instilled by the 1933 panic and by the business contraction from May 1937 to June 1938. Although central and other reserve city banks unloaded an appreciable part of their bond holdings beginning in early 1937—well before the downturn in business and hence caused by the increase in required reserves[31]—they were faced with a moderate reserve deficiency and had to contract earning assets to meet it. The original intention might not have been restoration of the usable ratio to its former level; the subsequent rise in the ratio might have reflected the sharp contraction in business during 1937–38. The behavior of the other financial institutions covered in Table 22 seems inconsistent with this explanation, but possibly not. Banks that owe large amounts to other banks may adopt special rules for safe operation, especially in a period like the five years following 1933, and cannot be compared with other financial institutions. On these grounds, the evidence in columns 7–9 of the table does not provide a norm for the behavior of central and other reserve city member banks, which are particularly vulnerable at a time of financial stringency and behave with prudent regard for their central position in the banking structure.

Such an argument, whatever its validity, cannot be applied to country member banks, however. The character of their liabilities is much the same as that of nonmember banks. While the total ratio for country banks did not rise so dramatically as that for all member banks and did not differ so markedly from that for other financial institutions, it did rise considerably from 1936 to 1938 when the ratio for other commercial banks was virtually constant. This suggests that the 1936–37 series of increases in requirements was the chief

[30] See George R. Morrison, "Liquidity Preference of Commercial Banks," unpublished Ph.D. dissertation, University of Chicago, June 1962, Chap. IV and Table 4.1.

[31] See Kenneth D. Roose, *The Economics of Recession and Revival*, New Haven, Yale University Press, 1954, pp. 104–117.

factor behind the concurrent rise in member bank total reserves.

The 1938 Reduction in Requirements. If the foregoing interpretation of the 1936–37 increases is correct, and if banks took more than a year to adjust to them, then the 1938 reduction of just a year later only served to speed the adjustment. The large rise in the usable reserve ratio immediately following the 1938 reduction, therefore, primarily reflects a continued adjustment to the preceding increases. The further rise in the next two years, however, was much too large to be ascribed to the preceding changes in requirements. Other factors seem to have been present.

The 1941 Increase and 1942 Reduction in Requirements. The 1941 increase wiped out usable reserves which member banks were already working down. The downward sweep of the usable reserve ratio hides whatever small effects the required increase in reserves may have produced. It is not possible to say whether, had there been no increase in requirements, the usable reserve ratio would have gone so far down as it did in the following year. In any event, the increase was nullified by the decrease less than a year later, in 1942, too soon to judge at what level the usable ratio would have come to rest. Nothing can be concluded about these two changes.

The effects on the usable ratio of changes in member bank reserve requirements up to 1942 are therefore mixed. The 1914 reduction was known not to be permanent; it was more than offset by the 1915–16 increases, which the Federal Reserve Act authorized along with the earlier reduction. The 1938–42 changes partly offset each other and also occurred during violent swings in the usable ratio, large enough to obscure small adjustments in the ratio.

The other three changes before World War II in 1917 and 1936–37 appear from the evidence presented to have been followed by off-setting changes in the total reserve ratio with the return of the usable reserve ratio to its former levels. The complete adjustments took well over a year, perhaps because of the magnitude of the changes. Those two were the largest ever imposed except the reduction in 1949, which slightly exceeds the 1917 one as measured in column 3 of Table 21. The remaining change, the fairly small increase in early 1914, was absorbed by usable reserves with no apparent attempt by banks to adjust total reserves. It offers the only clear-cut exception to the proposition that banks in due course largely offset the effects on usable reserves of changes in requirements.

The post-World War II changes provide the clearest evidence, as previously noted, in favor of this proposition. None of them were accompanied by violent swings in the usable ratio which obscured the reactions of banks to earlier changes. In 1948 and 1951, the required increases appear to have reversed movements of steady decline in the total reserve ratio. In 1948 the total ratio rose sharply after requirements were increased and before the recession beginning in the last months of that year could have initiated a large addition to reserves. Moreover, the ratio fell back just as fast when requirements were reduced in early 1949, well before the revival in business activity beginning in October. The usable reserve ratio fluctuated very little about a slightly falling trend, indicating that the rise in the total ratio fully reflected the required increase in reserves. In the first half of 1951, the increase immediately appeared in the total reserve ratio, while the usable reserve ratio continued a slow unbroken descent. The 1953 and 1954 changes, as well, though fairly small, show up immediately in the total ratio.

For all the changes considered together, therefore, the evidence suggests that the desired level of usable reserves—though not constant— is usually independent of required reserves, no matter how large the usable reserve ratio may be. When that ratio is fairly low, however, the adjustment of the usable ratio to its former level is perhaps quicker. While we might also expect a faster adjustment to reductions in requirements than to increases of the same size—on the ground that to spend excess funds is easier than to recall loans and sell securities— there is no indication of that difference. The 1948 increase and 1949 reduction provide a useful comparison for this purpose: they were about the same size and occurred during the middle of successive years; the total ratio offset both changes in about the same length of time.

The apparent independence of the required and the usable ratios might, of course, be coincidence: each change in requirements might have coincided with a change in usable reserves in the same amount and direction, undertaken for other reasons. If the change in requirements offset the predetermined change in usable reserves, the latter would remain at the same level—but such an offset would be rare. Most of the larger changes in requirements were made for special reasons unrelated to the predetermined level of usable reserves likely to be desired by banks. Other changes were ostensibly made to counteract business cycles, to be sure, but they have usually tended to correlate negatively with desired changes in usable reserves. When requirements have been raised to dampen a business boom, the desired level of usable reserves was likely to be falling, and conversely. Hence, while the effect of business cycles, as well as failure of banks to offset effects of changes in requirements on usable reserves, would have produced a negative relation between the required and the usable reserve ratios, on the whole the data show no relation.

From a bank's point of view, required reserves apparently are not reserves at all. They can be used only when a reduction in deposits releases them. It is not required reserves but unrestricted holdings of high-powered money and—except when all banks are under pressure—balances at correspondent banks that provide the first line of defense against heavy withdrawals. Under the national banking system, the Comptroller of the Currency had authority to close a bank that did not maintain its reserves above required levels except for temporary lapses. There was nothing to prevent the suspension of payments in time of heavy withdrawals except usable reserves and, perhaps, crude expedients like issue of clearing house loan certificates. Under the Federal Reserve System, an immediate penalty charge must be imposed for reserve deficiencies, and the Board has always limited borrowing to meet expected reserve deficiencies.[32] Banks have therefore held reserves above requirements to meet unexpected needs, and the existence of usable reserves has not meant that they maintain their desired level of total reserves regardless of the part tied up by requirements. By this interpretation, reductions in required reserves provide banks with extra funds, which gradually become invested in earning assets. Similarly, when required reserves are increased, usable reserves are maintained at previous levels mostly by contracting earning assets.

3. The Long-Run Decline in the Usable Reserve Ratio

Apart from changes in reserve requirements, the total reserve ratio reflects large variations in the usable ratio. Although we cannot

[32] See Robert V. Roosa, *Federal Reserve Operations in the Money and Government Securities Markets*, Federal Reserve Bank of New York, 1956, p. 24.

compute the usable ratio of other commercial banks, it undoubtedly has a high correlation with the total ratio of those banks, because their reserve requirements have changed only gradually. As indicated in Table 20, the required reserve ratio declined slowly after about 1917 and, before that, probably rose gradually as more and more states passed legislation dealing with reserves of state banks. Consequently, the total ratio of other commercial banks shown in Chart 19 probably fell slightly slower than their usable ratio did up to World War I and fell slightly faster thereafter. In general outline, its behavior appears to be similar to that of the usable ratio of national or member banks shown in Chart 20.

TIMING OF THE DECLINE

In addition to the pronounced cyclical variations in the usable ratios, both had a long-run trend, generally downward up to 1930, upward to about 1940, and then downward again to 1955. If we interpret the rise in the 1930's as a violent but essentially short-run cyclical movement, the trend appears at first sight to have been steadily downward since at least 1875. Yet, cyclical fluctuations obscure the movements before World War I; as a preliminary to discussing the possible factors behind that trend, we should determine the periods when the reserve ratio—omitting the effects of cycles—was declining and when it was relatively stable.

The fairly steady declines in the ratios from 1875 until 1930 could be illusory if the initial years were high for special reasons. The period 1875–79, for example, was one of severe depression and followed the panic of 1873, both of which undoubtedly caused banks to hold larger than usual reserves. To judge the trend properly, it is desirable to look at the behavior of the series in earlier years, for which the reserve ratios for national banks have been extended back to 1865 in Table 24. The data for 1863 and 1864 do not appear comparable and are omitted.

A change in requirements accounts for the decline in the required reserve ratio from 1873 to 1874 and seems to have affected the usable ratio in the way such changes worked in later years: the usable ratio first absorbed the full amount of the reduction in requirements and then later began to work down to its previous level. The movement in 1873–74 is obscured, however, by the panic of September 1873 just after the date of the entry for that year in Table 24. The ensuing

TABLE 24

NATIONAL BANK RESERVE RATIOS, ANNUALLY, 1865-75
(per cent)

Call Date Nearest Oct. 1	Total[a] (1)	Required[b] (2)	Usable (1)-(2) (3)
1865	45.3	20.8	24.5
1866	48.2	24.4	23.8
1867	43.3	24.7	18.6
1868	40.2	23.1	17.1
1869	39.4	23.5	15.9
1870	35.8	22.9	12.9
1871	31.6	22.4	9.2
1872	28.6	21.2	7.4
1873[c]	27.4	21.1	6.3
1874	27.3	13.2	14.1
1875	25.0	13.1	11.9

[a]Ratio of specie and currency holdings (including small amounts of state bank notes) to individual deposits, state bank notes outstanding, and net amount due to nonnational banks. National bank notes were excluded from the denominator to maintain comparability with the series for later years in Table F-11.
There are reports on national banks back to 1863, but reserve ratios for 1863-64 are not comparable with later years because of the rapidly changing structure of the national banking system in the first years of its organization.

[b]For 1868 and after, ratio of all required reserves (Annual Report, Comptroller of the Currency) to denominator used for col. 1. For 1865-67, required reserves are not published and had to be estimated from statements of national banks for the three reserve classifications. These earlier estimates are approximations only, because there are no exact figures on permissible deductions from aggregate liabilities to derive the base on which legal requirements were computed. It was assumed that "cash items in process of collection" were deducted with the tacit approval of the Comptroller (see Annual Report, 1868, p. XXIII), but that permission to deduct "due from banks" from "due to banks" was not granted until after 1867.

[c]Dated Sept. 12 just before the panic of that year broke out.

depression caused banks to hold for a time most of the subsequent increase in their usable reserves provided by the change in requirements. Hence, the level of the usable ratio in 1875–78 was undoubtedly above normal, and its level in the preceding years of prosperity will be a more reliable indication of what it would have been in subsequent years if business conditions had not taken a turn for the worse in 1873.

From 1865 to 1873, the usable ratio had fallen rapidly—seeming to reflect a steep secular decline. Yet such a conclusion is questionable because there are good reasons the usable ratio may have been abnormally high in 1865. During the Civil War, specie payments were suspended and the currency depreciated; yet it was widely expected that convertibility would be resumed soon after the end of hostilities. Convertibility, when resumed, would produce a contraction in money and prices to reverse the wartime inflation and to restore the currency's prewar parity with gold. In anticipation of the storm, banks probably bolstered their defenses by augmenting reserves. When, after 1865, convertibility appeared not imminent and the country had weathered the initial readjustments to peacetime conditions with little difficulty, they no longer needed large reserves and proceeded to run them down. Incomplete data on state banks for the period lend some support to this interpretation. The total reserve ratio of reporting state banks[33] rose at the outbreak of the Civil War and then fell after the suspension of convertibility. This series is not entirely comparable with the later series on national banks, however, and the two series do not overlap (the Treasury temporarily stopped collecting reports on state banks in 1863).

Though we cannot be certain, therefore, it is likely that the decline in the usable ratio for national banks from 1865 to 1873 at least partly reversed an earlier increase and so does not point to a long-run downward trend. It seems best to ignore the evidence of the immediate post-Civil War years and to judge the trend of the ratio from its course after the 1860's. To abstract from cyclical movements, we may look at its average levels during consecutive business cycles. The averages shown in Table 25 cover periods between successive business cycle peaks. The table shows a marked secular decline. The usable ratio for all national banks shows a drop of about three-quarters from 1869 to 1907, reflecting a decline for all three classes. The total ratio for other commercial banks also shows a decline, though not by so much. Since reserve requirements for state banks were being extended in the 1870's and 1880's, however, their usable ratios probably declined about as much as that for national banks.

The decline in the ratios progressed in spurts. For all national

[33] Total specie holdings of reporting state banks, as a percentage of deposits and bank notes outstanding on Jan. 1, was 18.9 in 1860, 20.4 in 1861, 22.6 in 1862, and 17.3 in 1863 (see *Annual Report* of the Secretary of the Treasury, 1863, p. 233). The usable reserve ratio, of course, was somewhat lower. Quarterly data for New York and Pennsylvania banks also show the same general pattern. The earlier data need adjustment, not done here, for the premium on gold in valuing specie holdings and gold deposits.

banks, there was little change up to 1887, then a sharp drop to a lower level was completed by 1890 and was not extended further until after 1899. Country national banks, however, made substantial reductions in their ratio earlier than city banks did. Central reserve city banks had about the same ratio in the late 1890's as in the 1870's and did not make

TABLE 25

AVERAGE LEVELS OF RESERVE RATIOS DURING REFERENCE
CYCLES, 1869-1907
(per cent)

Reference Cycles[a] (peak to peak)	Usable Ratio of National Banks				Total Ratio of Other Commercial Banks[b] (5)
	Central Reserve City (1)	Other Reserve Cities (2)	Country (3)	All (4)	
1869-73	n.c.	n.c.	n.c.	10.2	n.a.
1873-82	4.9	11.4	13.3	10.9	n.a.
1882-87	8.9	10.7	10.7	10.4	11.8
1887-90	4.5	5.8	8.2	6.9	12.3
1890-92	4.0	5.4	7.4	6.2	10.5
1892-95	11.4	6.4	9.3	9.1	11.4
1895-99	4.3	5.3	7.9	6.4	9.8
1899-1902	1.9	1.5	4.5	3.1	7.6
1902-07	1.5	1.3	3.4	2.5	6.7

n.c. = not computed.
n.a. = not available.

Note: Average levels computed from annual data (Tables 24 and F-11). Beginning and terminal years were given one-half weight.

[a]Year for which Oct. 1 was nearest the peak month of National Bureau reference cycles.

[b]Table F-10, col. 3. Undoubtedly declines less rapidly than the unavailable usable ratio for those banks.

most of their reductions until after 1899. (Since their ratios seem abnormally high in the mid-1880's and early 1890's, probably as a result of panics, it is safer to ignore the exceptional levels.) For other commercial banks, as well, most of the decline since the 1880's came after 1899. These observations of timing are based on average standings over business cycles. Some turns read from the annual series differ; in particular, Charts 19 and 20 show that the large decline in the averages after the 1899 reference peak actually began in 1897–98 in the annual series.

Some further declines in the average level of the ratios occurred in the 1920's and 1950's (Charts 19 and 20). Since by the early 1900's usable reserves had fallen about as low as they could reasonably go without danger of becoming negative at the slightest jump upward in the currency ratio, the possibility of further declines was severely limited.

POSSIBLE EXPLANATIONS OF THE DECLINE

The decline is not the result of a quirk in the definition of the reserve ratio used. If we include in reserves balances due from other banks, and, in deposits, gross (rather than net) balances due to other banks, the ratios for national and for other commercial banks still show secular declines of roughly the same total amount though a few years later, around the turn of the century (see Tables F-15 and F-16), not before. This suggests that the decline in the high-powered reserve ratio of national banks from 1887 to 1899, before the all-inclusive ratios show much decline, reflected a shift to interbank reserves. The decline in the all-inclusive ratios after 1899 was greater for country banks than for the other two classes of national banks, suggesting that country banks, having relatively less high-powered reserves to begin with, went further than other national banks in replacing interbank balances with other earning assets. The ratio for reserve city banks, on the other hand, rose slightly during the 1890's and early 1900's, in contrast with the decline in their high-powered reserve ratio, in-dicating that they substituted interbank balances for high-powered reserves.

The all-inclusive ratios for all classes of banks fell again and more sharply after the Federal Reserve Act was passed; since the act reduced reserve requirements and ended use of interbank balances as legal reserves, the reduction in total reserves fell mostly on those balances. The all-inclusive ratio for other commercial banks also fell during the 1920's, but not much more than their high-powered reserve ratio did, since state requirements showed no tendency to remove interbank deposits from the list of legal reserves. The ratio for mutual savings banks exhibits no decline until after 1915 (see Table F-17). Hence the decline around 1900 apparently applied to commercial banks only. All our ratios exclude U.S. deposits, but they were usually too small to make any difference. At times, such as during World War II, U.S. deposits were large, but they were conveniently exempted from reserve requirements and not withdrawn except with advance notice; consequently, they probably had little effect on the reserve ratio.

Interest Rates. A possible explanation lies in the movements of interest rates. Banks hold usable reserves as an alternative to earning assets and will tend to balance the security provided by $1 of cash against the income derived from $1 invested. The higher interest rates are, the greater the incentive is to get along with less cash; conversely, when interest rates are low, the advantage of holding large cash reserves appears high compared with its cost. Presumably, short-term rates approximate bank charges on call money and on commercial loans, and long-term rates reflect the prices of most bonds that banks invest in. Hence banks are likely to be sensitive to the entire range of rates.

For practical purposes one long and one short rate should suffice to represent the spectrum. Take long-term rates first. Macaulay's work[34] indicates that long-term rates around 1900 were at the lowest levels ever recorded before the late 1930's; yet the usable reserve ratio was then reaching new all-time lows, not the highs to be expected from an inverse relation between the two variables. It is true that long-term rates turned up moderately in 1899 on the first leg of a twenty-year rise, and it might be argued that the reduction of usable reserves beginning in 1897–98 anticipated that improvement in bond earnings. By buying when rates were low (and bond prices high), however, banks would suffer capital losses as rates rose. If they had anticipated the rise in rates, they would not have committed all their usable funds at the lowest rates, as in fact they largely did, though mostly in loans rather than bonds. Indeed, whether banks wanted a high yield or large capital gains, their funds should have been heavily invested in the late 1860's and early 1870's before the secular decline started and when rates were still high. Yet we saw that the usable reserve ratio was highest at that time. The yields on bonds with long maturities clearly do not explain the downward trend in the reserve ratio. No obvious transformation of those yields in an attempt to approximate banks' expectations of future movements in interest rates would alter this conclusion.

A long-run relation between the usable reserve ratio and interest

[34] F. R. Macaulay, *Some Theoretical Problems Suggested by the Movements of Interest Rates, Bond Yields and Stock Prices in the United States since 1856*, New York, NBER, 1938.

rates fares no better with short-term rates. True, those rates were rising after about 1897, when the usable ratio was falling; but they had been higher in earlier years, when the ratio was high, and touched levels at least as low in later years, when the ratio remained low. This evidence does not rule out some effect of interest rates on bank reserves, particularly for short-run cycles or for extreme movements like the 1930's, discussed further later, but it seems clear that any such effect is of secondary importance at best for secular movements and certainly cannot explain the downward trend in the reserve ratio.

Since interest rates are no help, we may look to developments in the economic and institutional environment to explain the downward trend in the ratio. Such developments are hard to quantify, and we must rely largely on qualitative evidence.

Establishment of the Federal Reserve System. One possibility is that the stability of the monetary system tended to improve over time. The most publicized contribution to that development was passage of the Federal Reserve Act. Previously, the banking system had to handle emergencies itself. After 1914, banks could look to Federal Reserve Banks to supply unforeseen demands for currency and could put all but required and working balances into earning assets. The creation of the Federal Reserve System probably accounted for part of the small but gradual reduction in the usable reserve ratio during the prosperous first decade and a half of its operation. In addition, member banks satisfy reserve requirements by their average holdings over a week or two, whereas national banks before 1914 had to meet requirements on a day-to-day basis. The founders of the System did not foresee these expansionary effects on the money supply.[35]

Although banks raised the usable reserve ratio in the 1930's to levels not seen in over fifty years, it does not seem necessary to treat the 1930's as a special chapter in banking history to be explained by economic stagnation and an unusual decline in the demand for loans. Confidence in the Federal Reserve System built up during the 1920's must have been shattered in 1933 when the System failed to prevent a disastrous deflation of bank credit and the highest rate of suspensions among federally supervised banks in history. In that year the number of suspended member banks was a catastrophic 18.7 per cent of all

[35]See Seymour Harris, *Twenty Years of Federal Reserve Policy*, Harvard University Press, 1933, Vol. 1, p. 261.

member banks operating at the first of the year. In the preceding three years suspensions had been much higher than normal but nothing like the contagion of bankruptcies in 1933.[36] The usable reserve ratio in the 1929–33 contraction did not rise to unusually high levels, and from 1933 to 1936 it went no higher than after panics or in depressions before 1914—1875–78, 1884–85, and 1894 (see Chart 20). Indeed, because usable reserves were so low in the early 1930's, partly in response to the supposed security provided by Federal Reserve Banks, member banks were hard hit by the 1933 panic. This, we may conjecture, goes a long way toward explaining why it wrought such havoc within the banking system when, by comparison, recuperation from previous panics had been remarkably fast. In the historical perspective of Chart 20, the large ascent of usable reserves from 1929 to 1935 does not seem extraordinary for such a period.[37] Part might also reflect a delayed adjustment to large gold inflows, though that would explain a temporarily higher level of the ratio, not a continued rise. After 1938, the usable reserve ratio reached unprecedented levels perhaps attributable in some degree to the extreme duration of depressed business conditions and extremely low interest rates, especially on short-term securities.

Since World War II, banks have apparently regained confidence in the Federal Reserve's ability and willingness to lend ample funds in a crisis. The large influx of gold during the 1930's and 1940's provided the Reserve Banks with a new margin of excess lending power over their statutory reserve requirements, which, in addition, were reduced in 1945. Hence, their ability to avert a liquidity crisis was not questioned in the prosperous climate of the 1945–55 decade.

[36] The percentage rate for 1930 was 2.3; 1931, 6.4; and 1932, 4.6. The highest previous rate for member banks was 1.7 per cent in 1926; the highest corresponding percentage for national banks prior to the Federal Reserve System was 1.8 in 1893. The highest rate for all commercial banks before the 1930's was 5.8 per cent in 1893 (see *Banking and Monetary Statistics*, p. 283; *Historical Statistics*, 1949, series N135; and *Banking Studies*, p. 418). Suspensions are closing of banks by civil authorities, other than during special holidays, and include suspensions subsequently lifted after reorganization or mergers. The 1933 figure does not include banks closed after the banking holiday but licensed to reopen by June 30 of that year, following the nationwide bank examinations during the holiday. There was, of course, a higher than usual rate of bank failures during the 1920's, but that reflected the agricultural distress and not lack of liquidity in the banking system as a whole like that during the early 1930's.

[37] Warburton (*Turning Points*) lists many possible reasons for the high level of the ratio in addition to the panic itself.

Federal Deposit Insurance. Deposit insurance has probably been a more important factor accounting for the low levels of the usable reserve ratio since the mid-1940's. Instituted in 1934, the Federal Deposit Insurance Corporation grew rapidly and soon insured nearly all commercial bank deposits up to a specified amount. The insurance strikes at the root of banking panics—fear of loss through suspension of payments—and thereby removes the main reason for holding large usable reserves. Since participating banks pay the estimated cost, its principal value is not so much as insurance to spread the risk of loss as a remedy to reduce the risk; its very existence reduces the incidence of losses by removing the likelihood of runs on banks. With wide participation in the FDIC achieved by the mid-1940's, banks returned the usable reserve ratio to low levels. In the prosperous year 1955, for example, this ratio for all member banks hovered around 1 per cent, barely enough to fill day-to-day needs for working balances.

The exact timing of the decline in the usable ratio in the early 1940's from the high levels of the late 1930's can be attributed to an improved business outlook and also to a change in government policy. In 1942, the Federal Reserve Banks promised to keep U.S. bonds at fixed prices, and banks soon converted their huge usable reserves into those near-moneys that paid interest. The purchases were made despite the historically low rate paid, which suggests that fear of capital losses—allayed now by the support program—was an important factor holding back such investments by banks in the late 1930's. The price-support program ended in 1951, and the low usable reserve ratio since then must be attributed to factors previously discussed and to the active market for federal funds, which developed during the 1950's.

Establishment of the National Banking System. Since creation of the Federal Reserve System and later of federal deposit insurance can explain the decline and continued low levels of the usable reserve ratio in most of the period since 1914, what explains its much more pronounced decline before that? The answer seems the same: improvement in the stability of the monetary system, even without the dramatic remedies instituted since 1914. There is no question that the national banking system set up in 1863 appreciably toned down monetary disturbances. The operation of national banks was a model of prudence compared with pre-Civil War banking practices and, although periodic panics still occurred, they did not match the financial upheavals of former years. One important factor was the issue of clearing house loan certificates during panics, which helped alleviate the extreme distress of currency shortages. We may conjecture that banks gradually decided that usable ratios could safely be reduced in view of the improved financial climate.

Treasury Operations. A clue to an important factor in that decision is the timing of the largest noncyclical reduction in the 1897–1902 period. At that time, the Treasury began to use its cash holdings regularly for easing stringencies in the money market. The Treasury increased its deposits at national banks in the last quarter of each year to offset the seasonal drain of currency from bank reserves and, in business downturns, to offset the cyclical drain. It will be recalled (Chapter 4) that the currency-money ratio often rose moderately in reference stages IV through VII and by large amounts in panics, though the reference cycle patterns did not reveal the full amount of the rise. Those periodic pressures on bank reserves necessitated ample cash reserves. Before the late 1890's, as Chart 20 shows, banks kept large usable reserves, presumably for that reason. Afterward, 1897–1902, when Treasury intervention in the market in times of stress could be relied upon, banks were quick to find alternative uses for their large usable reserves.

That the Treasury might assume the functions of a central bank and alleviate monetary conditions had been recognized much earlier, but various difficulties stood in the way.[38] The main difficulty centered around the restrictions imposed by the Independent Treasury Act (1846), a relic of the pre-Civil War banking era which Congress could not be persuaded to repeal for a long time afterward. As originally passed, the act forbade the Treasury to make or receive payments with bank checks and notes or to hold its own funds on deposit at banks. Regional subtreasuries were set up to make and receive all payments in gold (or, as amended in 1862, in greenbacks, except government interest payments and customs duties). Since Treasury receipts and disbursements did not exactly coincide, the arrangement produced variations in high-powered money outstanding which upset the money market. To avoid a continual transfer of high-powered money to Treasury coffers throughout the 1880's, when the government budget was running a surplus, the Treasury had to retire its outstanding interest-bearing debt (mentioned in Chapter 3). To avoid variations

[38] This paragraph draws upon Margaret G. Myers, *The New York Money Market*, New York, 1931, Vol. I, Chap. XVII.

in high-powered money outside the Treasury in the short run, owing to discrepancies between receipts for tax revenues and disbursements for budget expenditures or bond purchases, the Treasury might have wanted to buy and sell short-term certificates of indebtedness or to deposit its cash holdings at banks. But the Treasury had no short-term debt outstanding or authority to purchase private debt, and the deposit of funds at banks was restricted by the Independent Treasury Act (as later amended) to revenues other than customs at the time of their collection; funds deposited in the Treasury could not be transferred to banks. In consequence, while the maximum level of the Treasury's cash holdings was kept down during the 1880's by bond purchases, it fluctuated erratically in the short run and generally to the detriment of monetary stability, as we shall see shortly. Treasury officials were so hard pressed just to hold down the government's cash surplus that they made various "interpretations" of the Independent Treasury Act and breached the restrictions on funds to be deposited at banks. The act's definition of proper collateral was successively relaxed, and various excuses for holding certain specified funds at banks were found. Congress finally authorized those actions after they had become precedents. By the early 1890's, however, when the Treasury had succeeded to some degree in learning how to live with the act, the budget condition turned from surplus to deficit, and for five years the Treasury concerned itself with little else than preserving its solvency. Until 1896, it repeatedly had to borrow and was in no position to come to the aid of the banks as a disburser of money in stringencies.

This brief review of the period helps to explain why the Treasury suddenly assumed the functions of a central bank in the late 1890's. After 1895, business improved, the government's finances again showed a surplus, and Secretaries of the Treasury turned their interest to wider horizons. A remarkable series of controversial pronouncements—for that era—emanated from that normally sedate post. It was proclaimed that the stability of the money market was the proper interest of the Treasury, and even that it had the power and obligation to eradicate monetary crises from the western world.[39] While the

[39] I refer to Secretary Shaw's famous 1906 report (see *Treasury Report*, 1906, p. 49); see also Friedman and Schwartz, *A Monetary History*, Chap. 4, sect. 1; and R. H. Timberlake, "Mr. Shaw and his Critics: Monetary Policy in the Golden Era Reviewed," *Quarterly Journal of Economics*, Feb. 1963, pp. 40–54.

Treasury may have been ready and willing to adapt its cash holdings to the needs of the market, how "able" was it?

In his study of seasonal movements in Treasury funds deposited at national banks, Kemmerer[40] found a marked contrast between the period before and after 1897. Before then, those deposits were usually low in the last three months of the year relative to the beginning months; the main exception was a slight increase in 1893, apparently because of Treasury bond sales. Otherwise, the Treasury tended to depress bank reserves in the autumn when they most needed bolstering. To check Kemmerer's results, which are based on absolute amounts, I computed the ratio of U.S. to individual deposits at national banks. It was usually around 1 per cent from 1880 to 1896 and, while more often lower than higher in the last months of the year, changes over the year were relatively unimportant. In comparison, the period from 1897 to 1908 was just the reverse: in seven of the eleven years, the ratio was higher in the last quarter of the year. (Kemmerer also had found that U.S. deposits in the last three months at that time were generally higher than those in the first nine months.) The amount of change in the ratio over the year was also considerably higher than it was before 1897. From 1909 to 1914 it renewed its earlier erratic behavior, though its variations again became fairly small. Notwithstanding that lapse, the year 1897 marked a clear change in the seasonal movement of U.S. deposits at banks, small and irregular before that year and, thereafter, larger and usually upward during each calendar year.

As for the importance of Treasury policy to the long-run level of the reserve ratio, perhaps a better indication than seasonal movements is cyclical movements in U.S. deposits. Banks might have been able to eliminate part of the seasonal increase in their usable reserve ratios during the spring and summer months because of stabilizing variations in U.S. deposits, but they would still have needed sizable reserves during cyclical expansions to prepare for the stringencies which often develop midway through cyclical contractions. Only if the Treasury supplied funds in contractions and withdrew them in expansions might banks dispense with much of their usable reserves. The correspondence

[40] Edwin W. Kemmerer, *Seasonal Variations in the Relative Demand for Money and Capital in the United States* (61st Cong., 2d Sess., S. Doc. 588), National Monetary Commission, 1910, p. 159. Treasury deposits were not placed at nonnational banks until 1917.

of Treasury actions to such a policy is shown in Table 26. In the late 1890's, cyclical movements in U.S. deposits began systematically to alleviate the normal pattern of stringencies by providing more funds in contractions than in expansions.

As column 3 demonstrates, by comparing the level during contractions with the average level during the preceding and succeeding expansions, the contribution of U.S. deposits to monetary stability changed

TABLE 26

RATIO OF U.S. TO INDIVIDUAL DEPOSITS AT NATIONAL BANKS: AVERAGE
DURING REFERENCE EXPANSIONS AND CONTRACTIONS, 1873–1918
(per cent)

Peaks of Reference Cycles	Contractions (1)	Expansions (2)	Contractions Minus Average of Preced- ing and Succeeding Expansions (3)
Oct. 1873–Mar. 1882		0.9[a]	
Mar. 1882–Mar. 1887	1.0	1.1	0.0
Mar. 1887–July 1890	2.7	2.9	0.7
July 1890–Jan. 1893	1.6	0.8	−0.3
Jan. 1893–Dec. 1895	0.6	0.8	−0.2
Dec. 1895–June 1899	0.9	2.3	−0.7
June 1899–Sept.1902	3.6	3.5	0.7
Sept.1902–May 1907	4.4	2.4	1.4
May 1907–Jan. 1910	4.5	1.6	2.5
Jan. 1910–Jan. 1913	0.7	0.7	−0.4
Jan. 1913–Aug. 1918	1.0		

Note: Ratios shown are unweighted averages of ratios for call dates falling within reference expansions and contractions (Annual Report of the Comptroller of the Currency).

[a] Excludes first two call dates of the expansion phase for which the ratio was abnormally high, because of Treasury refunding operations.

dramatically in the late 1890's. That behavior shows up in Chart 6 in a rise from reference expansions to contractions in the nongold source of changes in high-powered money, greater from 1897 to 1908 than the corresponding rise in the contribution of the gold stock; that is, the ratio of high-powered money to the gold stock rose.[41] (We may also note that Treasury operations shown in Chart 6 were considerably less erratic after 1897 than before.) The actual contribution of Treasury operations to banks' usable reserves was even greater than it was to high-powered

[41] The nongold source also rose during the contractionary phase of the 1894–97 reference cycle, but the significance of the rise is obscured by the upsurge in gold inflows which started at the same time.

money, because the funds were deposited directly in banks. When such funds are used to buy bonds from the public, instead (as in open market operations of Federal Reserve Banks), the operation also increases the public's cash balances, but only part of the increase is deposited at banks and is subject to reserve requirements. The currency-money ratio indicates the fraction eventually held as currency. When the Treasury deposits funds directly in banks, the whole supplements usable reserves except what is deducted for required reserves. After October 1902, when reserves behind U.S. deposits were no longer required, all deposits supplemented usable reserves.[42]

The percentages in Table 26 are approximately equal to the changes in the total reserve ratio produced by Treasury operations. The changes of 1 to 3 percentage points may not seem very important, but their effect may have been greater than these figures indicate, for two reasons. First, most of the changes applied only to New York City banks, which held about one-fifth of individual deposits in all national banks. Hence the effect on the reserve ratio of New York City banks could have been as much as 5 times greater than the amount shown. Table 25 shows that most of the long-run decline in the level of the usable reserve ratio of central reserve city national banks occurred simultaneously with that change in Treasury policy. Second, the change in policy superseded former actions that were a source of cyclical instability in bank reserves. Column 3 of Table 26 shows that the Treasury reduced the reserve ratio by 0.7 percentage points in the contraction following the 1895 peak and increased it by 2.5 points in the contraction a decade later following the 1907 peak. The difference of over 3 points provides a crude measure of the net gain to usable reserve ratios, though the gain was less in other contractions. National banks actually reduced their usable reserve ratios almost 4 points, on the average, from the late 1890's to 1907. While the pattern of U.S. deposits in the 1910–13 period was moderately procyclical, financial conditions never degenerated to the point where banks needed much

---

[42] Around 1900, the required reserve ratio for all national banks was roughly 15 per cent and the currency ratio roughly 17 per cent. A dollar of high-powered money added to the public's cash balances therefore increased usable reserves by $\$(1 - 0.17) \$(1 - 0.15)$, or \$0.71. A dollar deposited directly in national banks by the Treasury increased usable reserves by $\$(1 - 0.15)$, which exceeds the increase of the other method by $[(1 - 0.15)/(1 - 0.17)(1 - 0.15)] - 1$, or 20 per cent. After reserve requirements against U.S. deposits were removed in 1902, the second method exceeded the other by $[1/(1 - 0.17)(1 - 0.15)] - 1$, or 41 per cent.

outside help, and there was no reason to believe the Treasury did not remain ready to provide substantial help if needed. We may conclude, therefore, that the Treasury's new policy after 1897 contributed reserves up to about three-fourths of the subsequent reduction in the usable reserve ratio. The actual contribution may have been larger or smaller, depending on the confidence of banks in the Treasury's ability and willingness to pursue its self-appointed role as central banker. The related timing of the events just rehearsed suggests that confidence was strong or, at any rate, strong enough to sweep away the prior reluctance of banks to sacrifice the safety of large usable reserves for increased earnings from their investment. From the banks' point of view, the Federal Reserve Act confirmed a policy the Treasury had already inaugurated more than a decade before.

Although the change in Treasury policy probably explains most of the long-run decline in the reserve ratio after 1897, it seems unlikely to explain much of the decline in the national bank reserve ratio from 1887 to 1890 (Table 25). The improvement in the Treasury's handling of its funds in the eighties was short lived (Table 26); yet the reserve ratio for all national banks declined (except in the difficult 1892–95 period).[43] It is not possible, therefore, to attribute the early decline to Treasury actions. That decline can be attributed to the over-all improvement in the stability of the monetary system.

It might be argued that the long-run decline in the usable reserve ratio after 1897 coincided with increases in the rate of growth of high-powered money, not accounted for by Treasury operations, and that the prospect of rising future reserves led banks to reduce present usable reserves. They might also have relied on the continued expansion of the credit base to take care of possible temporary stringencies. The year 1897 marked the end of the protracted deflation which had gripped the country since the end of the Civil War. Huge gold inflows in 1896 and subsequent years heralded a major reversal of trend, as we saw in Chapter 3. From the depression years of 1893–97,

[43] The *Commercial and Financial Chronicle*, however, did attribute most of the early decline to Treasury operations. In 1890 it deplored the following alleged practice: "The time was when our banks provided beforehand for the fall trade, and so trimmed their sails, if we may be permitted to use the expression, through the summer months as to avert a storm, by preparing themselves for the crop demand. Of late years they have looked to the Treasury wholly, and have gone through the summer trenching on their reserves regardless of any increased drain sure to come later." (Dec. 6, 1890, p. 764; quotation also in Kemmerer, *Seasonal Variations*.)

money and prices started to rise sharply, and a wave of prosperity spread across the country in vivid contrast to the preceding years. That turn in the business and financial outlook surely made a big difference to banks and might have led them to work down their usable reserves. It allowed the Treasury to engage in long-desired operations, previously impossible.

The latter part of the 1890's is an example of those decisive—and, for the historian, exasperating—periods when so many things happened all at once. Yet other relationships that might be proposed to explain the decline in the reserve ratio then do not hold consistently at other times. There is little relation over the long run between changes in the usable reserve ratio and the rate of growth of high-powered money; the ratio fell a few times when the rate rose but in general did not rise when the rate fell. Other financial developments due to improved business conditions after 1897 might have affected the speed with which banks adjusted the level of the reserve ratio, but much less the long-run desired level.

In conclusion: The explanation for the downward trend in the usable reserve ratio which seems most consistent with the data, therefore, is the greater stability of the monetary system produced during and after the Civil War by increased state and federal regulation of banking, after 1897 by the assumption of central banking functions by the Treasury, after 1914 by the Federal Reserve Banks, and after 1934 by federal deposit insurance.

4. Cyclical Movements

In addition to a secular decline, the reserve ratio displays short-run cyclical fluctuations, not explained by shifts in deposits and changes in reserve requirements. Since the total ratio is affected by changes in requirements and shifts in deposits, over which individual banks have no control, the usable reserve ratio would be preferable for cyclical analysis, but a series on usable reserves is not available for all commercial banks. The preceding examination of changes in reserve requirements helps us to allow for their major effects. The reference cycle patterns of the total reserve ratio, plotted in Chart 21, show the level of the series, not its contribution to the rate of change in the money stock as in Chart 2.

CHART 21

Reference Cycle Patterns of the Reserve Ratio of All Commercial Banks,
1879–1954

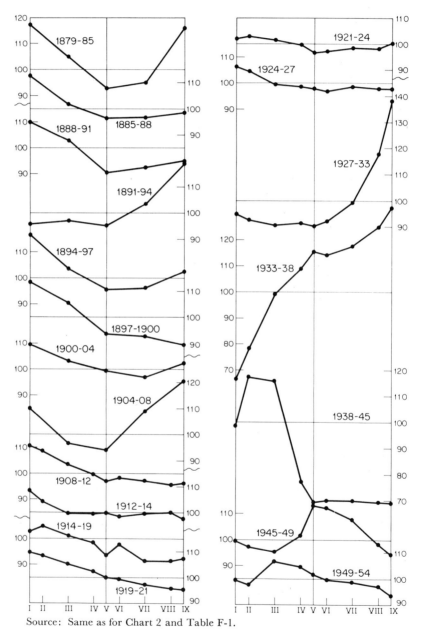

Source: Same as for Chart 2 and Table F-1.

Note: For annual data before 1908, stages II, IV, VI, and VIII are omitted, and some of the standings for stages III and VII are based on interpolations.

The reference cycle patterns show a high inverse conformity of the reserve ratio to business cycles. The ratio generally declined during business expansions (stages I to V) and either leveled off or rose during business contractions (stages V to IX). The major turning or inflection point in the patterns usually coincided with the peaks and troughs of reference cycles. That the amount of decline during expansions usually exceeded the amount of rise during contractions reflects the downward trend of the ratio.

The chart shows movements during similar stages of different cycles. Because the actual time covered by the different cycles varies, the impact on the economy of a given change in the reserve ratio, and thereby in the money stock, depends on how fast the change occurs. It is appropriate to look also at changes in the ratio per time period. The average change per month in the relative reference cycle standing of the ratio during reference expansions and contractions is presented in Table 27. The average change per month for contractions minus that for the preceding expansion, shown in the last column, is uniformly positive except for the two post-World War II cycles—that is, the rate of change in the ratio generally rises more or falls less in contractions than in the preceding expansions. This supports the visual impression from Chart 21 that movements in the ratio conform closely to reference cycles. Moreover, the two cases of nonconformity can be attributed to the effects of changes in reserve requirements. Member bank requirements were raised during the expansionary phases of the 1945–49 and 1949–54 cycles and lowered during the contractionary phases (Table 21). These changes in requirements largely account for the concurrent variations in the total ratio. The usable ratio for member banks shows little change from stage I to stage V and from V to IX in these cycles (Chart 20). The other major changes in member bank requirements either worked to enhance the inverse conformity of the patterns to reference cycles or to reduce but not eliminate it. If adjusted for changes in reserve requirements, therefore, the reserve ratio would uniformly display inverse conformity to business cycles.

Although conforming closely to cycles, the short-run fluctuations have varied greatly in amplitude. The large increases during reference contractions appear to be associated with financial disturbances and deep depressions. To confirm such an association, averages of the

TABLE 27

CHANGES IN THE RESERVE RATIO DURING REFERENCE CYCLES, 1879-1954

Reference Cycle Dates[a] Trough, Peak, Trough	Special Cycles[b]	Average Change per Month of Reference Cycle Relatives During:		Difference Between Average Change per Month of Relatives for Reference Contraction and Preceding Expansion (2) − (1) (3)
		Reference Expansion (1)	Reference Contraction (2)	
		ANNUAL DATA[c]		
Mar.'79 Mar.'82 May '85	ps	−0.67	0.61	1.28
May '85 Mar.'87 Apr.'88		−0.75	0.18	0.93
Apr.'88 July'90 May '91	p	−0.73	0.46	1.19
May '91 Jan.'93 June'94	ps	−0.02	1.40	1.42
June'94 Dec.'95 June'97		−1.17	0.39	1.56
June'97 June'99 Dec.'00		−0.82	−0.22	0.60
Dec.'00 Sept.'02 Aug.'04		−0.49	0.14	0.63
Aug.'04 May '07 June'08	ps	−0.48	2.03	2.51
		MONTHLY DATA		
June'08 Jan.'10 Jan.'12		−0.71	−0.03	0.68
Jan.'12 Jan.'13 Dec.'14	p	−0.71	−0.10	0.61
Dec.'14 Aug.'18 Apr.'19		−0.21	−0.15	0.06
Apr.'19 Jan.'20 Sept.'21	s	−1.07	−0.24	0.83
Sept.'21 May '23 July'24		−0.26	0.24	0.50
July'24 Oct.'26 Dec.'27		−0.30	0.01	0.31
Dec.'27 June'29 Mar.'33	ps	−0.25	1.07	1.32
Mar.'33 May '37 May '38	s	0.98	1.40	0.42
May '38 Feb.'45 Oct.'45		−0.36	−0.02	0.34
Oct.'45 Nov.'48 Oct.'49		0.37	−1.71	−2.08
Oct.'49 July'53 Aug.'54		0.05	−0.60	−0.65
Averages				
6 panic cycles			0.91	1.39
6 severe cycles			1.04	1.30
11 nonpanic and nonsevere cycles			−0.16	0.26
9 nonpanic and nonsevere cycles, excluding 1945-54 cycles			0.05	0.62

Note: The ratio here is the ratio of high-powered reserves to deposits of the public at all commercial banks, as in Chart 21.

[a]Some slight revisions in these dates, made since this table was computed, would not change the figures significantly.

[b]p = Panic cycles, so designated because payments were suspended or Clearing House loan certificates were issued by New York City banks, as in Table 14.

s = six most severe nonwar contractions, as judged by the percentage decline in aggregate output (see Table 1).

While there is no sharp dividing line between severe and moderate contractions, slight changes in the designations do not greatly affect the averages at the bottom of the table. For example, if the severest of the moderate contractions from 1879 to 1954, that of 1895-97, is shifted to the severe-cycle group. the three affected averages for cols. 2 and 3 are:

Averages	(2)	(3)
7 most severe cycles	0.95	1.33
10 nonpanic and nonsevere cycles	−0.22	0.13
8 nonpanic and nonsevere cycles, excluding 1945-54 cycles	0.22	0.51

The war cycles are not separated here unlike the analysis of high-powered money and the currency ratio, where there is strong reason to exclude them as atypical.

[c]Semiannual data 1879-81; monthly data beginning May 1907.

measures in columns 2 and 3 of Table 27 are shown for three groups: six most severe cycles, as judged by the percentage decline during reference contractions in aggregate output; panic cycles in which payments were suspended or New York City banks resorted to Clearing House loan certificates to ease a currency shortage; and all other cycles.

The averages for panic and severe cycles are much higher than the average for all other cycles,[44] even when we exclude from the mild cycles the two post-World War II contractions, in which the usual pattern was reversed by the effects of changes in reserve requirements. The ratio appears to react sharply to financial panics and severe contractions. Whether both are of equal importance cannot be readily judged from these figures, since the averages for the two groups contain practically the same cycles.

We may assess their separate effects by looking at cycles in which only one occurred. There are four: 1888–91 and 1912–14, which had panics but were not severe; and 1919–21 and 1933–38, which were severe but did not have panics. Unfortunately, two of these cycles, 1912–14 and 1933–38, provide little evidence on the separate effects of panics and severe contractions and must be discarded. The panic of 1914, as noted in Chapter 4, was a rather mild affair, thanks to the ability of national banks to make emergency issues of national bank notes under the Aldrich-Vreeland Act of 1908. Before that, issue of scrip currency was really illegal, and clearing houses undoubtedly resorted to its issue at a later point in panics and in smaller quantities than desirable. When the outbreak of war in 1914 touched off a financial panic, the special notes were issued quickly and freely. (The Federal Reserve Banks were not yet organized and so could not make loans.) With that new source of currency on hand, it was to be expected that banks would face the panic with unaccustomed calmness. As evident in the reference cycle pattern of the reserve ratio for the cycle ending in 1914, banks did not contract appreciably, a suspension of payments did not occur, and the panic subsided quickly. The cycle never developed the repercussions that would be expected from large unsatisfied increases in the demand for currency. It offers

[44] Amplitude measures like those in Table 27 are smaller for annual than for monthly data. The table therefore tends to understate the average for the panic cycles more than for the other groups, since four of the six panic cycles occurred before 1908 and are measured with annual data.

no proof, therefore, that ordinary panics do not affect the ratio. During the 1933–38 cycle the ratio was affected by changes in requirements. The behavior of other financial institutions, discussed earlier, suggests that the reserve ratio for commercial banks would have remained more or less constant had requirements not increased, and therefore that the severity of the business decline itself had no effect. Be that as it may, that cycle cannot be cited as reliable evidence for the importance of severe contractions.

When those two cycles are omitted, there remain only two, 1888–91 and 1919–21, to show the separate effects of panics and severe contractions on the reserve ratio. They will have to serve as the basis for a tentative hypothesis. They indicate that panics produce a sharp rise in the reserve ratio but severe contractions in business do not. In the 1890–91 contraction, not severe but with a panic, there was a sizable rate of rise in the ratio. According to column 2 of Table 27, the rate of rise was larger than in any of the mild cycles and was exceeded only by rises in the other panic cycles except 1912–14 and 1937–38, which should be omitted. In the 1920–21 contraction— severe but without a panic—the ratio actually declined, though at a slightly slower rate than in the preceding expansion, a pattern characteristic of its behavior in mild contractions. The measure of over-all cyclical variation in column 3 for that cycle is only a little above the average for the mild cycles. The clear implication is that panics have an important effect on the ratio and that severe business contractions, per se, do not.

Why panics are important is not hard to understand. Such a disturbance threatens the solvency of banks, and they respond by curtailing operations sharply. Every effort is made to bolster cash reserves, not only to meet heavy withdrawals but also to attain sufficient liquidity to allay depositors' suspicions of financial weakness. The banking system can honor only a small fraction of its demand liabilities at one time, and the more deposits it is asked to redeem, the weaker its position becomes. The first rule of banking practice is to instill confidence and avoid a thorough test of the basis for that confidence. Great efforts to obtain ample cash reserves are therefore to be expected when financial markets become disturbed.

Appraised by hindsight, those efforts do not produce substantial results until the panic is over and large reserves are no longer needed.

Panics are a harrowing experience which apparently leave a residue of caution for some time even with bankers who survive it. The post-panic increases in the reserve ratio may have gone higher, however, than most banks desired, owing to a heavy inflow of currency (and in the earlier period, gold from abroad) just when the demand for loans became quite low.

There are two reasons why a severe contraction alone might be expected to produce a sizable rise in the reserve ratio: A sharp down-turn in economic activity, while it does not of itself threaten the solvency of banks, does produce a sharp fall in the demand for loans and so in the rate of interest. Banks might also hesitate to commit a large fraction of their portfolios to bonds at low rates of return and might prefer to hold some of their funds idle. The evidence as a whole suggests that effects of these factors on the reserve ratio are far less important than effects of panics are.

If the foregoing interpretation is correct, it is to be expected that a panic would usually be followed by a severe contraction. Financial panics cause large increases in the reserve and currency ratios. The result is a substantial reduction in the money stock unless the increases are offset by increases in high-powered money. As the analysis of Chapter 2 shows, such changes in high-powered money have usually not occurred. Panics produce a sharp contraction in the money stock, therefore, and this wrenches the credit structure of the whole economy and disrupts commerce. The two nonsevere panic cycles, 1888–91 and 1912–14, did not have such effects on the money stock and so are not exceptions to the importance of those effects. In the 1890–91 contraction the increase in the reserve ratio was not accompanied by a sharp rise in the currency ratio (the panic was largely confined to New York City, and a general suspension of payments did not occur) and was partly offset by increases in high-powered money. The 1914 panic did not initiate the customary rise in the reserve ratio. All other panics since 1873 have been accompanied by severe business depressions. Of these, only the 1884 crisis did not involve a suspension of payments, but the rise in the reserve ratio was nonetheless still appreciable. The paucity of evidence—few severe contractions and panics not occurring together—indirectly supports the foregoing interpretation.

The argument cannot be turned around to plead the importance of severe contractions as a cause of panics and hence of the reduction in the money stock, because the panics were not caused by a low level of business activity. This much can be said even though we cannot specify the actual causes. Panics are a strange phenomenon, not readily explained in any satisfactory way except by reciting the particular series of events setting off each one. They are often described as chain reactions going from worsening expectations to mass hysteria. But there is nothing irrational about the behavior of each individual in a panic; if a bank is subject to a run, there is no point in being the last person in line. The difficulty is in specifying the precise conditions in which a run starts and keeps going. Certain contributory factors can be identified. Panics were more frequent before 1914 owing to the pre-World War I banking system with its inverted pyramid of credit resting on New York City banks and absence of emergency reserves provided by a central bank—though the worst panic came under the Federal Reserve System. Panics have usually developed in the early stages of cyclical downturns (1933 is the most dramatic exception), when the usable reserve ratio was comparatively low. No doubt the accompanying downturn in business activity set the stage but was not alone the cause. Banks were typically vulnerable to a rise in the currency ratio or a gold outflow at such times, yet only because of some series of shocks to confidence did the public panic. Banks were not much tighter before panics than at many other reference peaks. In their time sequence, panics have not been spontaneous but have been sparked by failure of a few large financial companies, often involving fraud or mismanagement frequently brought to light but hardly caused by the business downturn. In any event, it is impossible to associate most panics with the severity of a business contraction since they typically arose early in the downturn.

There is no reason a severe contraction could not occur without a large increase in the reserve ratio and so without a panic. Large increases in the reserve and currency ratios, which are characteristic of panics, are not always responsible for the relation (Table 1) between the amplitude of decline in the rate of change of the money stock and the amplitude of the subsequent decline in economic activity. A large decline in the growth of high-powered money could account and sometimes has accounted for the relation. To be sure, a sufficiently drastic decline might endanger the liquidity of the banking system and so precipitate a panic. This could explain why so many more panics occurred before 1914 than after: before 1914, sharp outflows of gold sometimes forced banks to contract credit too fast; after 1914, Federal Reserve Banks could offset such outflows, at least temporarily, by an expansion of their credit. A decline in the growth of high-powered money need not have this effect, however, and the 1921 contraction is a notable example. Federal Reserve Banks contracted credit in 1921 to liquidate their "overextended" position following the wartime expansion. The reduction did not proceed faster than member banks were able to contract loans, and the solvency of the banking system was not endangered. Such a large reduction in high-powered money, though it has rarely occurred without producing a liquidity crisis, nevertheless suggests that a panic, not the resulting collapse of economic activity, leads banks to scramble for cash.

The reference contractions containing the panics of 1884 and 1933 might seem to support the importance of severe business declines for large increases in the reserve ratio, since those panics came late in the contractions. Yet, these contractions support the opposite conclusion, if anything. Chart 21 shows that the steep rise in the reserve ratio during the two cycles came, not immediately after the reference peak, but later. In the 1882–85 contraction the ratio rose most rapidly in the second half and, so far as the annual data show, after the panic. In the 1929–33 contraction it rose most rapidly in stages VIII and IX, after the breakdown of the banking system had started, though the panic did not come until stage IX. That disaster was imminent for some time before the authorities declared a banking holiday, as indicated by the rise in the currency ratio and the high incidence of bank failures before the suspension of payments in March 1933.

In summary: A financial panic reflects a deterioration of public confidence in banks, owing principally perhaps to their precarious reserve position. It is caused by a variety of factors, of which a severe decline in economic activity by no means appears to be the only or even an important one. A panic impairs the solvency of banks, which contract credit drastically in an effort to raise the reserve ratio. The contraction of credit in turn has deflationary effects on the economy which aggravate the decline in output. Panics have not precipitated cyclical downturns; all of them cited here have followed peaks in economic activity. Many panics have also come during the first half of contractions, too early to be the result solely of a severe decline in economic activity, and so were, to a large extent, independent factors aggravating the decline.

Apart from panic cycles, fluctuations in the reserve ratio conform also to mild reference cycles, though the amplitude of fluctuation in such cycles is fairly small. The ratio rose slightly or had a lower rate of decline in all mild reference contractions except those in which new reserve requirements were imposed. Chart 21 shows that the rate of decline in the ratio usually falls midway through reference expansions as well. Consequently, in mild cycles the ratio plays a role in forming the specific cycle peak in the rate of change of the money stock (Chart 2), which precedes the peak in business activity. That the decline in the reserve ratio during reference expansions is arrested well before the peak in business activity suggests that banks try to prevent the usable reserve ratio from falling below some minimum level, although the minimum is subject to secular changes. The existence of such a minimum would explain why the fall of the ratio is not continuous throughout reference expansions but stops before the peak, even though business prospects remain bright. What is not clear, however, is why the usable reserve ratio rises above the minimum during business recessions.

One might expect the rise to reflect a decline in interest rates. If a panic occurs in the early stages of a recession, of course, interest rates first rise sharply. As the recession deepens, however, a decline in the demand for capital tends to outweigh public preferences for liquidity, and rates on borrowed funds fall. The fall, making cash reserves more attractive to banks, might explain the rise or reduced rate of decline in the reserve ratio during contractions. The a priori plausibility of such a relationship tells us nothing about its actual importance, however.

Secular movements in the ratio are inconsistent with that relationship (Section 3). The usable reserve ratio of national or member banks fluctuated about the same level, or possibly a slightly declining one, from 1875 to around the turn of the century; bond yields declined during that period, whereas the postulated relationship requires inverse movements. Although short-term rates rose after 1896 and the ratio fell, the rise in rates was no more than the decline during the 1890's. Bond yields fell until 1902 and then rose until 1920, while the ratio fluctuated about the same level from 1902 until 1914. After a moderate rise during World War I, the usable ratio slowly fell during the 1920's to a lower level than ever reached before, while bond yields were declining. For the whole period from 1875 to 1930, the only evidence of inverse movements is the short period 1896–1902—for short-term rates only; otherwise the correlation either is nonexistent or has the wrong sign. Unlike bond yields, short-term interest rates, such as commercial paper rates, did not have a clear-cut secular trend up to 1930 except possibly a sharp fall during the 1870's and so cannot explain secular movements in the reserve ratio before 1930.

During World War II, the usable reserve ratio fell sharply, well before interest rates reached a long-run trough in 1946. The ratio then fluctuated about the same level until 1950 and declined only slightly thereafter, while interest rates registered one of the sharpest increases on record. The 1950's may be disregarded, however, since usable reserves were too low to permit a large decline.

Evidence in favor of an inverse relation between interest rates and the usable reserve ratio may be cited for only the 1930's (though our earlier interpretation of this period was entirely different) and possibly for 1896–1902. But there are other factors that can explain those movements, factors of sufficient importance to make the interest-rate relationship relatively minor.

Cyclical movements in the ratio may still reflect interest-rate effects even though secular movements do not. To assess the evidence, let us look at changes in the ratio over reference expansions and contractions. The changes shown in Chart 21 for the total ratio of commercial banks will be adequate for this purpose, though we should allow for important changes in requirements. Chart 22 plots, as a scatter diagram, changes over reference expansions and contractions in the relative standings of the reserve ratio shown in Chart 21 against the corresponding changes for short-term interest rates. The dated phases since the 1929 reference peak include all the extreme points on the diagram.

If the two expansions and two contractions of the 1930's on the edges of the second and third quadrants are deleted, very little negative correlation in the remaining points can be detected, though it is improved if we also delete the other three dated points in the post-World

CHART 22

Scatter Diagram of the Reserve Ratio and Short-Term Interest Rates: Changes in Reference Cycle Relatives over Expansions and Contractions, 1879–1954

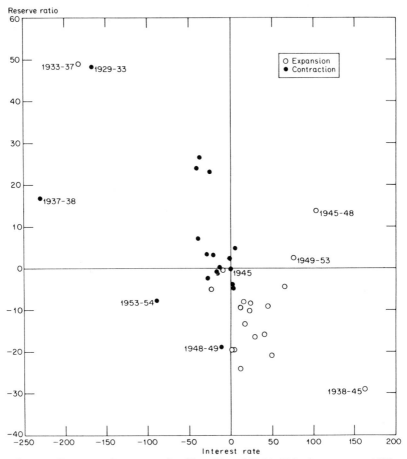

Source: Reserve ratio, same as for Chart 21 and Table F-1; interest rate, 1879–1927, commercial paper rates, and, 1927–54, short-term U.S. securities.

Note: Cyclical phases since 1929 are dated.

War II period. The slight negative correlation in the undated points disappears almost entirely if we treat the expansions and contractions separately. In other words, the undated points are correlated only because the ratio declined and interest rates rose over reference expansions and vice versa over contractions. This is hardly evidence of dependence, since many series have corresponding movements over reference cycles with no implication that they are directly related to each other. There would have to be a correlation of changes among expansions and also among contractions to support an implication of negative correlation. There is virtually none, except when the 1929–45 phases are included—a special period for which movements in the ratio can be readily explained without interest rates. In a similar diagram of the reserve ratio and bond yields (not shown), deleting just the point for the 1933–37 expansion removes all trace of correlation.

These findings seem out of step with many studies in recent years which allege a close relation between cash holdings and interest rates. Surely bankers would be as sensitive to the costs of holding money as any one, and so their portfolios should exhibit the alleged relation. Supporting evidence can indeed be forced out of the period since 1929; a rough negative correlation does exist if we ignore the timing of movements (a big "if"). As we have seen, the reserve ratio rose during the 1930's and fell thereafter, whereas interest rates fell drastically during the 1930's and then rose after World War II. Laid out on a scatter diagram, annual data for those years provide an attractive negative correlation, but the evidence involves essentially two observations: one movement from 1929 to 1940, and another in the reverse directions in the subsequent period to 1955. All our other evidence suggests that this apparent correlation is fortuitous. The correlation is absent from earlier periods, and the rise in the ratio after 1930 can be interpreted as a response to the 1929–33 financial disaster and to the 1936–37 increases in reserve requirements.

One might argue, of course, that banks became more sensitive to interest rates after the 1920's than they had been previously, though it is hard to see why. The trouble with this argument is the failure of more recent experience to support it. Interest rates rose sharply in the 1949–53 reference expansion and fell just as sharply in the 1953–54 contraction, yet the points for these two phases are far out of line with the others in Chart 22. Although the reserve ratio moved counter to its usual pattern because of changes in member bank requirements, the usable reserve ratio of member banks (after adjusting to the new requirements) and the total ratio of other commercial banks responded hardly at all to those sharp movements in interest rates.

The only short-run movement that interest rates might explain is the 1938–40 rise in the usable reserve ratio. By 1938, as was indicated earlier, member bank usable reserves had regained their level of 1936 before the 1936–37 increases in requirements. From 1938 to 1940 that ratio, as well as that for other financial institutions presented in Table 22, rose steadily; short-term interest rates dropped to practically zero, and long-term rates fell to historically low levels. With business still depressed, banks and other financial institutions may have considered cash to be as attractive as any alternative asset even though they felt no need to bolster their liquidity position further. On the other hand, banks continued to expand loans and investments, though less rapidly than gold flowed in from abroad. Such high levels of usable reserves have no precedent, not even in the immediately preceding years 1930–37, which do not appear unusual by pre-1900 standards. An effect of exceptionally low short-term rates on the desired reserve ratio cannot be ruled out, though the effect at higher levels appears negligible.

An effect even at such low rates is still questionable, however, since the usable reserve ratio fell rapidly during the early 1940's, while interest rates, as noted, remained at low levels until after 1946. The change in the economic climate with the outbreak of war clearly had a much greater effect on the ratio than the rate of return available on loans and investments had.

The cost of borrowing money may, of course, affect banks' borrowing from Federal Reserve Banks. The preceding evidence concerns the distribution of banks' funds between high-powered reserves and other assets; nothing is implied about the distribution of funds among these other assets—which the rates available no doubt influence—or about changes in total assets through borrowing. There is no reason interest rates cannot be important in one set of decisions and unimportant in another.

Indeed, some studies point to a fairly close relation between Federal Reserve loans to member banks and interest rates (or, more appropriately, the differential rate on Treasury bills over the discount rate). The relation allegedly accounts for part of the variation in the free reserve ratio—that is, the ratio of excess reserves minus borrowings to deposits.[45] Borrowings produce most of the interest sensitivity of the free reserve ratio; they fluctuate much more over business cycles than total reserves do.[46] These studies are not relevant, therefore, to the relation between interest rates and the total or usable reserve ratio.

We may conclude that cyclical fluctuations in the reserve ratio mainly reflect business conditions, not the cost of holding reserves, insofar as the two differ, as they often do. Apparently banks find their reserves reduced below a comfortable minimum near reference cycle peaks, possibly because they have been loath to deny loan applications by valued customers enjoying prosperity, and take the first opportunity in a business downturn to replenish reserves. The build-up is moderate and does not go far, if currency drains in the absence of a panic are light. The increase exceeds original plans during the ensuing low points of business activity, presumably because loan demands become unexpectedly small.

For these and perhaps other reasons, banks contribute to variations in the rate of growth of the money stock. The reserve ratio displays considerable irregularity, shown in the patterns for individual cycles in Chart 21. There is nevertheless a typical pattern. When business recovers, the reserve ratio begins to decline and apparently continues until the banks' desired minimum level is reached. In the vicinity of that minimum, the rate of decline in the reserve ratio decreases and so contributes to a reduced rate of growth of the money stock. Whether the ratio rises or remains more or less constant until the onset of a reference contraction, it generally rises thereafter and so contributes to a decline in the rate of growth of the money stock. Its average pattern in Chart 2 shows that the reserve ratio played a major part in forming peaks in specific cycles of the money series but a minor one, if any, in forming troughs except in panic cycles.

[45] See, for example, J. J. Polak and W. H. White, "The Effect of Income Expansion on the Quantity of Money," *Staff Papers*, IV., International Monetary Fund, 1954–55, pp. 398–433, Chart 8; and A. J. Meigs, *Free Reserves and the Money Supply*, Chicago University Press, 1962.

There is also a close relation between call money rates and the reserve ratio of New York Clearing House Banks during the pre-1914 period, though the relation is poor for all national banks (See W. M. Persons, "Cyclical Fluctuations of the Ratio of Bank Loans to Deposits, 1867–1924," *Review of Economic Statistics*, Oct. 1924, pp. 260–283).

No studies have separated the effect of interest rates on bank reserves and the effect of reserves and bank credit on interest rates. The observed relation undoubtedly reflects both.

[46] See article in *Monthly Review*, Federal Reserve Bank of New York, Nov. 1958, pp. 162–167.

6

THE CAUSE-AND-EFFECT RELATION BETWEEN MONEY, PRICES, AND OUTPUT

ASSEMBLING EVIDENCE on the behavior of the three determinants of the money stock has taken us far afield—into details of financial history for high-powered money, into various aspects of consumer behavior for the currency ratio, and into many of the developments in banking and other financial institutions for the reserve ratio. Even though frequently tentative, the findings help to show how far changes in the money stock can be regarded as resulting from concurrent variations in prices and output and how far they occurred independently of such variations. In this respect, the findings bear upon the causal connection between the money stock, on the one hand, and prices and output, on the other.

Chapter 1 summarizes the evidence on the covariation of cyclical movements in money and economic activity; the first section of this chapter documents an equally close covariation over longer periods between changes in the money stock and in prices. The covariation was either accidental, which is hardly plausible, or reflected a one-way or mutual dependence between the variables. This chapter is concerned with the direction of influence: whether the dependence is mutual or runs primarily from money to prices and output or primarily from prices and output to money.

The method of inquiry will be to examine the effects of price and output movements on the three determinants of the money stock to see whether such effects are sufficient to explain the observed covariation. Insofar as these effects are not sufficient, the implication is that the covariation reflects in large part the reverse effect of changes in the money stock on prices and output. Directions of influence can thus be determined, at least to some degree, by extending the evidence of previous chapters on the factors affecting the determinants of the money stock.

The radical difference between short- and long-run sources of change in the money stock advises a separate treatment, as in the preceding chapters, of secular and cyclical movements. In the discussion of secular movements, taken up first, changes in the rate of growth of real income and output are largely ignored and attention is confined to price changes, though a concluding section adds some remarks on variations in the secular growth of output.

1. Secular Movements in Money and Prices

THE EVIDENCE

If long-run price changes produced the variations in growth of the money stock, they must have done so through one or more of the three determinants. Accordingly, to determine whether the money stock or the price level is the independent variable in their long-run association, we may start by examining the possible effects of price changes on secular movements in the three determinants.

Identifying the source of secular movements in the money stock is greatly simplified by the dominant contribution of one determinant. Chapter 2 shows that changes in high-powered money accounted for nine-tenths of the over-all growth in the money stock from 1875 to 1955. In the first half of the period, from 1875 to 1917, this fraction was only 68 per cent, mainly because of a steady decline in the currency-money ratio, which accounted for most of the remaining growth of the money stock. From 1919 to 1955 and excluding World War II, the fraction attributable to high-powered money was more than 100 per cent. The currency ratio was slightly lower in 1955 than in 1919, the reserve ratio slightly higher; together, the changes in the two ratios alone would have produced a small decline in the money stock during that period. The expansion of high-powered money contributed over 100 per cent because it more than offset the negative contribution of the two ratios.

Table 28 indicates that the two ratios played a minor role in most subperiods as well. The table gives eighteen average rates of change in the variables between successive reference cycle bases from 1877 to 1954. The corresponding rates for wholesale prices are also shown

TABLE 28

SECULAR MOVEMENTS IN PRICES AND IN THE MONEY STOCK, AND SOURCES OF MOVEMENTS IN THE MONEY STOCK,
1877-1954: AVERAGE RATES OF CHANGE BETWEEN REFERENCE CYCLE BASES CENTERED AT PEAKS
(per cent per year)

Period Between Reference Cycle Bases, Centered at Peaks	Prices[b] (1)	Money Stock[c] (2)	AVERAGE RATE OF CHANGE IN MONEY STOCK ATTRIBUTED TO:[a]			
			High-Powered Money		Currency Ratio (5)	Reserve Ratio (6)
			Total (3)	Gold Stock (4)		
Mar. 1882 – Mar. 1887	-3.3	5.0	2.8	6.2	2.4	-0.2
Mar. 1887 – July 1890	-0.3	4.9	2.6	2.8	1.1	1.2
July 1890 – Jan. 1893	-3.0	5.7	4.6	-3.6	1.1	0.1
Jan. 1893 – Dec. 1895	-3.5	0.9	-0.7	-2.7	1.9	-0.3
Dec. 1895 – June 1899	2.3	7.4	5.3	11.5	0.7	1.2
June 1899 – Sept. 1902	3.7	11.2	6.5	9.4	2.3	2.5
Sept. 1902 – May 1907	1.4	5.8	4.2	4.9	1.0	0.6
May 1907 – Jan. 1910	2.8	7.0	4.7	7.5	3.5	-1.4
Jan. 1910 – Jan. 1913	1.0	5.8	1.8	3.4	2.2	1.9
Jan. 1913 – Aug. 1918	7.1	6.7	6.4	4.7	0.0	0.4
Aug. 1918 – Jan. 1920	19.1	27.4	25.5	8.5	-4.1	5.3
Jan. 1920 – May 1923	-9.5	1.8	-1.7	8.9	2.7	0.8
May 1923 – Oct. 1926	0.5	5.7	2.5	3.7	2.4	0.7
Oct. 1926 – June 1929	-7.0	-0.2	1.2	-0.7	-1.6	-0.6
June 1929 – May 1937	-0.6	-1.1	5.7	10.1	-1.9	-4.8
May 1937 – Feb. 1945	2.0	8.6	11.3	10.2	-0.8	-2.1
Feb. 1945 – Nov. 1948	12.4	16.9	14.1	2.6	-1.7	4.7
Nov. 1948 – July 1953	3.5	2.4	1.0	0.7	1.1	0.5

	(1)	(2)
June 1869 – Oct. 1873	-5.24	5.35
Oct. 1873 – Mar. 1882	-2.13	5.01

Note: Rates of change between successive cycle bases. A cycle base is the average value of the series from
the initial to the terminal trough of each reference cycle and centered at the reference peak.
Data for two earlier reference cycles which became available too late to be used in the analysis allow the
following additions:

[a]Computed by formula 2 in Chap. 2. Source of data except gold stock, same as for Chart 2. Gold stock
same source as for Chart 6.

[b]Wholesale prices, Historical Statistics, 1949, App. 23-24, p. 344.

[c]May not equal the sum of cols. 3, 5, and 6 because of rounding and approximation errors. Rankings
(used later in Table 29) of the values for July 1890-Jan. 1893, Sept. 1902-May 1907, Jan. 1910-Jan. 1913,
and May 1923-Oct. 1926 were based on three significant figures: 5.73, 5.79, 5.83, and 5.70, respectively.

TABLE 29

CORRELATION BETWEEN SECULAR MOVEMENTS IN PRICES AND
IN THE MONEY STOCK AND ITS SOURCES, 1877-1954

	RANK CORRELATION COEFFICIENT[a] BETWEEN AVERAGE RATES OF CHANGE IN PRICES AND IN:				
				Money Stock, Attributed to:	
					Ratio of High-Powered Money to Gold Stock and to:
Reference Cycle Bases Covered[b]	Money Stock (1)	Gold Stock (2)	Ratio of High-Powered Money to Gold Stock[c] (3)	Reserve Ratio (4)	Reserve and Currency Ratios (5)
All	$.81^{ss}$	$.24^{n}$	$.28^{n}$	$.31^{n}$	.34
Nonwar	$.82^{ss}$	$.25^{n}$	$.26^{n}$	$.24^{n}$	.37
Pre-1914	$.92^{ss}$	$.75^{s}$	-.52	-.62	$-.45^{n}$
Post-1919	$.79^{s}$	$-.14^{n}$	$.79^{s}$	$.79^{s}$	$.86^{s}$

[a] Significance levels are based, for top two lines, on the $\underline{t}$ test; for bottom two lines, on E. G. Olds, "Distributions of Sums of Squares of Rank Differences for Small Numbers of Individuals," *Annals of Mathematical Statistics*, June 1938, pp. 133-148, Table IV. Use of figures for two earlier reference cycles (see note to Table 28) in the rank correlations gives:

	(1)
All cycles	$.78^{ss}$
Nonwar cycles	$.75^{ss}$

[b] Same as in Table 28.

[c] That is, the average rate of change of high-powered money, minus the average rate for the gold stock.

s   = significantly different from zero at .025 level or less.
ss = significantly different from zero at .001 level or less.
n   = not significantly different from zero at .10 level.

No citation means significantly different from zero at a level between .05 and .10.

for comparison. The rates were computed from the average levels of the variables, trough-to-trough of each reference cycle, in order to eliminate cyclical variations. While no measure eliminates them entirely, this particular one is likely to be as effective as any. The importance of high-powered money is evident from the high fraction of the growth of the money stock attributable to it in most of the subperiods. When the fraction attributable to it was low, moreover, the growth of the money stock usually was comparatively small or negative. Put differently, variations in the growth of high-powered money and of the money stock were nearly proportional: the regression coefficient of column 3 on column 2 of the table is 0.88, and the square of the correlation coefficient is 0.84. Variations in the secular growth of the money stock have a much lower correlation with the contributions of the other two determinants.

Table 29 summarizes the evidence by means of some correlation coefficients derived from Table 28. They show that, before 1914 and for the period as a whole, price changes correlated with variations in the growth of the money stock much more closely than with any of the sources of those variations separately. All the correlations except that with gold after 1919 are positive. This is to be expected if the major direction of influence is from money to prices, since each determinant is then associated with price movements through its effect on money. Any discrepancies between changes in the money stock and in one of its determinants will tend to make the correlation between prices and that determinant lower than between prices and money. The higher correlation between money and prices might be consistent with the opposite direction of influence, from prices to money, if prices affected most of the determinants in a positive direction. The higher correlation between money and prices might then reflect a combination of the price effects on each determinant.[1] But prices affect the gold stock negatively, and probably did not strongly affect the other sources of change in high-powered money in a positive direction, either.[2] Any effects of prices on the money stock in a positive

[1] When the intercorrelation among the determinants is fairly low, the correlation coefficient between prices and money will exceed an average of the coefficients between prices and each determinant.

[2] The positive correlations in Table 29 are no indication of such effects. If changes in the money stock affect prices, then prices will for this reason alone show a correlation with components of the money stock, which may explain a large part, possibly all, of the correlation shown in cols. 2 to 5 in Table 29.

direction must have occurred entirely through the currency and re-serve ratios or, at most, through all the nongold sources of change in the money stock. Yet, before 1914 and for the period as a whole, the correlation of prices with those nongold sources, singly or in com-bination, is substantially weaker than it is with the money stock itself, and is even negative for the pre-1914 period. An effect running primarily from prices to money would produce a higher (positive) correlation of prices with the nongold sources of change in the money stock than with the money stock itself; and it would produce a negative correlation of prices with changes in the gold stock. Neither is ob-served for the pre-1914 period.

The correlations for the post-1919 period, taken alone, are con-sistent with either or both directions of influence. The correlation of prices with the gold stock is moderately negative and yet strongly positive with the other determinants and with the total money stock—a result of the contribution of Federal Reserve credit. The correlation in column 5, higher than that in column 1, would point to an effect running primarily from prices to money if certain conditions prevailed: if the difference were large and significant—as it is not—and if the behavior of the determinants could be attributed to price effects. The preceding chapters provide no evidence, however, of such price effects. For that reason, the high correlation between prices and the money stock for the post-1919 period offers evidence for the im-portance of the opposite effect, running from money to prices, even though the observed correlations of prices with the determinants for that period offer no evidence either way. On this interpretation, the high correlations in columns 3 to 5 for the post-1919 period reflect primarily the effect of money on prices.

These comparisons are based on rank correlation coefficients. The differences between the coefficients are large and so appear significant, but unfortunately appropriate tests of significance do not exist. To conduct such tests, the product-moment correlation coefficients presented in the tabulation on p. 240 serve as an addendum to the table. They cover the period 1877–1954 for the three most relevant variables: prices, the money stock, and the nongold sources of change in the money stock. These coefficients are larger than the corresponding ones in Table 29, because the extreme values, which receive greater weight, lie near the same linear regression that fits the other values.

PRODUCT-MOMENT CORRELATION COEFFICIENT
BETWEEN AVERAGE RATES OF CHANGE
IN PRICES AND IN:

Reference Cycle Bases	Money Stock	Money Stock Attributed to Ratio of High-Powered Money to Gold Stock and to Reserve and Currency Ratios
	(1)	(5)
All	0.88	0.69
Nonwar	0.90	0.71

By Hotelling's test,[3] the difference between the coefficients in the two columns for both lines is significant at the 0.025 level, thereby confirming the impressions derived from Table 29 for the whole period that the major direction of influence is from money to prices.

The implication of this evidence, even for the pre-1914 period, is not that prices had no effects on the determinants but that those effects are insufficient to explain the long-run covariation between prices and the total money stock. Such effects probably did occur, though usually not in the direction required to explain the covariation. Treasury operations and silver purchases tended at times to expand high-powered money, when the growth of the gold stock was low and prices were falling, and conversely. For example, the ratio of high-powered money to the gold stock, as shown by Chart 4, was higher in the 1880's and 1890's when prices were falling, than in the following two decades when prices were rising. The ratio was at its lowest point during the 1930's when the growth rate of the gold stock was highest. Treasury operations as a whole have blunted the impact on the money stock of changes in the rate of gold production, which may in part be the reason for the negative correlations for the pre-1914 period (columns 3 to 5 of Table 29). For the later period, that effect was either not strong or was more effectively counteracted by positive covariations reflecting the effect of money on prices.

[3] See Harold Hotelling, "The Selection of Variates for Use in Prediction with Some Comments on the General Problem of Nuisance Parameters," *Annals of Mathematical Statistics*, Sept. 1940, pp. 271–283. This test takes account of the association between the money stock and its nongold components; the correlation coefficient between them is 0.79 for nonwar and 0.77 for all cycles. The test is designed to answer the question: Which predicts prices better, the money stock or its nongold components? It is not entirely appropriate for use in this study, which asks a different question: Does the money stock predict prices better than prices predict the nongold components? How the different use may affect the results of the test is not apparent.

Insofar as movements in interest rates and prices were correlated, there was a tendency toward expansion of issues of national bank notes when prices and interest rates rose, and conversely. But that was a minor factor in the growth of high-powered money.

As for the currency and reserve ratios, analysis of their long-run behavior did not reveal a dependence on prices. To be sure, some of the largest deviations of the ratios from their long-run trends reflected financial panics, which were accompanied by sharp price swings. While temporary, those price swings often left an imprint on the data covering a longer period than the business cycles in which the swings originated. Since the greater part of the price swings came after rather than before each panic, however, the jump in the ratios, which was immediate, reflected the panic rather than the ensuing behavior of prices.

Interest rates had some effects on the two ratios. A rise in rates paid on time and savings deposits appears to reduce the demand for currency, though if general interest rates also rise, the demand for commercial bank deposits may decline, moderating the reduction in the ratio of currency to the money stock. A rise in interest rates also induces a shift from demand to time deposits, which reduces the required reserve ratio of banks and hence the total reserve ratio. These effects produce a slight positive relation between interest rates and the money stock (defined to include time deposits). No effect was found, however, of an effect of interest rates on the usable reserve ratio.

Insofar as prices and interest rates move together, prices can affect the money stock through these channels. The effects operate mainly in the long run, however, and shifts between demand and time deposits had little effect before 1914, when reserve requirements only for some state banks distinguished between the two kinds of deposits.

The behavior of Treasury operations and the two ratios, however interpreted, is largely irrelevant to the present discussion, since together they account for only a small part of the secular variations in monetary growth. If the effects of prices on money are to explain the long-run covariation between them, they must have occurred largely through high-powered money. It happens that two important components of high-powered money—the gold stock and Federal Reserve credit outstanding—are or might be thought to be dependent upon price movements. The evidence pertaining to these two components should be reviewed, therefore, with a discussion also of some of the possible objections to the conclusions derived from Table 29.

The Gold Stock. The growth of the domestic gold stock (Chapter 3) was broken down into two parts: one, from growth of the world stock through production in excess of current consumption in industry and arts; and the other, from changes in the U.S. share of the world stock through international trade. Both made substantial contributions. How were they affected by price movements?

The growth of the world gold stock is closely affected by changes in commodity prices. So long as some governments commit themselves to the gold standard and exchange their currency for gold at a fixed rate, the production and nonmonetary uses of gold depend on the general level of prices in gold-standard countries. When that level falls, the real value of gold in terms of commodities rises. The rise enhances the incentive to find new mines and new means of refining gold-bearing ores and to substitute other metals for gold in industry and arts, leaving more of current world production to be added to the monetary stock. When prices rise, the reverse occurs: profits from mining gold fall, and output is curtailed, inducements to increase the sources of supply fade, and nonmonetary uses expand. That price changes affect world gold production and with varying lags is confirmed by the evidence examined in Chapter 3.

A given country's share of the world gold stock is affected by its balance of payments, which incorporates the trade and the capital balance and includes effects of changes in monetary standards and of foreign central bank actions. So long as its internal prices change in rough proportion to world prices and there are no drastic changes in either the pattern of international trade and capital flows or the quantity of domestic currency and deposits created per unit of gold by monetary institutions, its share will vary more or less in proportion to the size of its national output relative to world output. Changes in the purchasing-power parity of each country's currency also have an important effect on its share. A fall in the level of internal prices relative to world prices will ordinarily increase the gold inflow and the total stock—and conversely, if internal prices rise. In this respect, internal price movements affect domestic gold stocks in the same direction that world price movements affect the world gold stock.

Such effects on the secular growth of the U.S. gold stock and their

varying lags are discussed in Chapter 3.[4] A good example is provided
by the well-defined turn during the mid-1890's in the long-run trend
of prices. The cumulative effect of falling world prices from 1873 to
the 1890's increased world gold production and eventually also the
growth of the world and the U.S. gold stock—but not until the mid-
1890's. A similar reaction occurred during the 1930's but much more
rapidly. That is probably why concurrent changes in prices and the
gold stock have even a slightly negative correlation in Table 29 for
the post-1919 period, in contrast to the strongly positive correlation
for the pre-1914 period.

It is important to note the lags in these effects, because the positive
relation between concurrent changes in prices and the gold stock
before 1914 is opposite to that produced by the lagged effects just
described. To extend the foregoing example: when the growth of the
gold stock finally responded in the mid-1890's to the long decline in
world prices which had started in 1873, prices began a long-run rise.
The coincidence of turns cannot be attributed to the effect of price
movements on the gold stock; that effect is a lagged inverse relation
between prices and the gold stock. Furthermore, if price movements
had an entirely nonmonetary origin, they would not except by accident coincide with movements of the gold stock in the same direction.
Yet, generally, the gold stock grew slowly during the latter 1800's,
just so long as prices fell, and subsequently grew rapidly, just so long
as prices rose. It seems far more plausible to attribute this positive
correlation, not to chance, but to the effect of changes in the gold
stock on the money stock and hence on prices.

If prices affected the gold stock with little or no lag, there would
have been little long-run variation in prices before 1914 except as a
result of autonomous changes in gold production, since changes in the
gold stock accounted for most of the long-run changes in the money
stock. Changes in the price level would have been limited by a tight
feedback-control mechanism. The lagged reaction of the gold stock
to changes in commodity prices, therefore, is what makes the gold
standard a poor means of stabilizing the price level, rather than
failure of gold-stock changes to affect prices—as often contended.

---

[4] That discussion is couched in terms of the commodity value of gold instead of
commodity prices; the former moves inversely to prices and also takes account of
changes in the gold content of the dollar.

After 1914, the long-run effect of prices on the gold stock appears to have had a much shorter lag. Yet, long-run variations in prices could and did still occur, because long-run changes in the gold stock were no longer the sole major determinant of secular growth of the money stock.

The preceding explanation of the lagged covariation between prices and the gold stock might be combined with one of two separate explanations for the concurrent covariation. (1) Whenever domestic prices rose (say), the rise was less rapid than the rise in prices abroad, and so domestic prices actually fell in relation to world prices. Then, gold would have flowed in and produced the observed rise in the U.S. stock; and conversely, for a decline in domestic prices. This explanation posits a relation between domestic and world price movements that would hold for no particular reason other than chance and so would be unlikely to prevail, except occasionally. Moreover, the available data for other countries, mainly Great Britain, do not show such behavior of relative price levels; and, contrary to this explanation, they do not show a concurrent covariation between the British gold stock and prices opposite to that for the United States.

(2) Another explanation of the concurrent covariation, intellectually more interesting but also unsatisfactory, starts with the assumption that long-run domestic price changes were accompanied, for various reasons, by movements of domestic interest rates in the same direction. If these movements were sufficient to produce corresponding movements in domestic rates relative to world levels, and if the resulting international rate differentials led to capital movements, gold would flow in a direction to produce the observed positive covariation between gold and prices. Bond yields, at least in this country and Great Britain, have moved in the same direction as prices have— the so-called "Gibson Paradox," discussed in detail later. The first part of this explanation, therefore, appears consistent with the facts. Beyond that, it encounters difficulties. To begin with, there is no indication that interest rate differentials here and abroad moved in the suggested manner.[5] Furthermore, what data we have on long-run capital movements, unreliable as they may be, indicate that capital

[5] See Oskar Morgenstern, *International Financial Transactions and Business Cycles*, Princeton University Press for National Bureau of Economic Research, 1959, Charts 18, 19, 20, 58, 60, and 61. Compare the periods before and after the upsurge of the U.S. gold stock in 1896.

was imported on a large scale into this country during the latter part of the nineteenth century, when domestic prices were falling and the growth of the gold stock was slower than its secular trend. They also indicate that the capital inflow fell off abruptly after the turn of the century, when prices were rising and the growth of the gold stock exceeded its long-run trend.[6] This explanation, however, would require the opposite relation in both cases.

Both these explanations pertain to movements in the U.S. share of the world gold stock and so imply opposite movements in the share of the rest of the world. Both overlook entirely, therefore, the general uniformity of long-run price movements for all gold-standard countries and the tendency of these movements to coincide with the growth rates of the world gold stock. Capital movements, in general, and those responding to international interest-rate differentials, in particular, have no doubt affected the distribution of the world gold stock. Nevertheless, interest rates cannot explain the *long-run* movements in the gold stock of the United States or of all countries together. We are therefore led to interpret secular movements in the traditional way: The growth of the U.S. gold stock was much slower in the first half than in the second half of the pre-World War I period for two reasons. Primarily, it was because the rate of world production was slower and, secondarily, because the required reduction in the growth rate of the U.S. stock was delayed for various reasons, the chief one being the preparations for resumption of convertibility in 1879. The domestic monetary disturbances over silver in the 1890's then carried the reduction, once begun, too far which, together with the rapid growth of the U.S. economy, led to a rise in the U.S. share in the second part of the pre-1914 period. By this interpretation, therefore, the effect of prices on gold flows and production cannot explain the positive correlation for the pre-1914 period, shown in column 2 of Table 29. Even if it could, such an effect certainly cannot explain the much higher correlation between prices and the money stock for that period, shown in column 1.[7]

[6] See Milton Friedman and Anna Jacobson Schwartz, *A Monetary History of the United States, 1869–1960*, Princeton for NBER, 1963, pp. 102 and 140 ff.

[7] Since capital movements can be expected to reflect opportunities for profitable investment, it is plausible that high growth of output which presses against capacity attracts capital from abroad. Hence, during a period of rapid growth (like the 1880's), induced capital movements may offset part of a trade deficit arising from high

Federal Reserve Credit Outstanding. Federal Reserve powers have sometimes been used to offset or reinforce the other determinants in order to achieve desired changes in the money stock. If price movements were relevant to the purposes for which these powers were used, such movements might have influenced the behavior of high-powered money. It is conceivable, therefore, that this influence has worked since the founding of the Federal Reserve Banks in the direction required to produce the observed correlation between long-run movements in prices and in the money stock. For example, Federal Reserve Banks might have extended credit in response to the market demand for loans. If so, they might have produced movements in high-powered money corresponding to those in prices and real output, which could account for the long-run correlation observed between money and prices. In that event, little of the correlation need necessarily be attributed to the effect of money on prices.

This or any similar explanation of the correlation nevertheless seems highly unreal. A central bank's freedom from the profit-and-loss restraints facing commercial enterprises and its dedication to the general welfare are expected to lead to just the opposite result. A central bank's credit policy is normally designed to counteract price movements, not to reinforce them. During the Reserve System's first three decades, of course, its officials did not fully accept that goal. At first, official explanations of its policy were tinged with the "real bills" doctrine, which required that credit be increased when

_____

merchandise imports; and, conversely, for slow growth (as during most of the 1890's). (See J. G. Williamson, "Real Growth, Monetary Disturbances and the Transfer Process: The United States, 1879–1900," *Southern Economic Journal,* Jan. 1963, pp. 167–180.)

It is conceivable also that the capital movements may dominate, thus causing the balance of payments to improve and gold to flow in when domestic output expands; and conversely. This might then explain an association between the money stock and prices.

It cannot explain the major movements over the pre-1914 period, however, although it might account for some of the shorter-run variations within those movements. In general, capital movements, whether or not influenced by the growth rate of output, did not completely offset the trade balance and, over the long run, gold flows reflected largely the movements in the trade balance. (Williamson's interesting and suggestive discussion cited above is handicapped by understating the importance of gold flows, which he found not closely related to changes in the money stock on a year-to-year basis. He overlooks the cumulative effect of gold flows.) That gold flows were sometimes offset temporarily by nongold sources of change in high-powered money does not mean that long-run changes in the money stock were determined by capital movements or the growth rate of domestic output. The offsets were not that important and, moreover, can be largely explained by other factors.

business, and so the "needs of trade," expanded—and conversely. In wartime it devoted itself to the Treasury's budgetary needs. Nevertheless, the historical record does not indicate that extensions of Federal Reserve credit were intended to conform positively to price movements. The record indicates the reverse, if anything. Federal Reserve policies seem to have reflected other, chiefly short-run considerations (see Chapter 3).

In part, of course, Federal Reserve policies took account of the level of employment, and it might be argued that dedication to the maintenance of "full" employment could link the money stock to prices and so account for the observed correlation between them. Post-World War II events have been widely interpreted along these lines, as follows: Because downward movements in prices and wages are impeded by rigidities which have become more entrenched in the last two decades or so, business recessions no longer produce as much deflation of prices as in the past, but mainly lead to reductions in output and employment. To maintain full employment, the Federal Reserve increases high-powered money and thereby the money stock until a revival in business activity promises to restore full employment, possible only if the money stock is increased enough to support the prevailing level of prices and wages. In the absence of decline during recession, the level reached by prices and wages in each boom is thereby sustained. Transitory upward impulses in the price level are made permanent, which puts it in a meta-stable equilibrium. Under such circumstances we have a modern equivalent of the old real bills doctrine, in which the needs of trade are replaced by the "inviolability of full employment."

The foregoing argument assumes that increases in the money stock are necessary to maintain each upward step of prices and so takes for granted that such increases affect prices. The argument could be modified, however, to contend that this Federal Reserve policy accounts for the long-run correlation between money and prices, but that the System's belief that it must increase the stock of money to promote recovery is mistaken. Even if the System did not respond as it is alleged to do, the long-run rise in prices would be the same, because it results from various pressures wholly unrelated to changes in the money stock. This reasoning is implicit in much literature and, for that reason at least, deserves consideration.

Although high-powered money and the money stock could at times be determined in the foregoing manner, it seems clear that they have not been for most of the period since the founding of the Federal Reserve Banks. Whatever the merits of the wage-price spiral as an explanation of changes in the money stock for some part of the period since World War II, it can hardly explain the experience of either the pre-World War II period (except perhaps 1933–37) or the major part of the period since. In the first place, prices and wages were not very rigid in previous periods; before World War II declines were frequent and sometimes of considerable size. More important, the largest historical changes in Federal Reserve credit outstanding were unrelated to insistence on full employment; they were the increases during wartime and the decreases in 1921 and 1931. The increase in Federal Reserve credit outstanding in 1950, when the outbreak of the Korean War created fear of shortages and produced scare buying, might be interpreted as a "passive response" to an upsurge in demand. The increase came, however, from sale of bonds by member banks to Federal Reserve Banks and was permitted, not to stimulate full employment, but to perpetuate the support of U.S. bond prices.

Although the evidence for the post-1919 period summarized in Table 29 neither proves nor disproves that changes in the money stock affected prices, it is hardly credible that the effect of money-stock changes was unimportant. First, the data before 1914 can be fully explained, as was shown, only by an effect of money on prices; if a 1 per cent change in the money stock had certain effects then, a 1 per cent change must have had largely the same effects after 1914. It is most unlikely that the economy underwent structural changes of a kind to alter those effects. One can imagine—though reasons are hard to find—that developments since 1914 in financial markets and emergence of assorted substitutes for money might have altered the speed with which those effects occurred, but not the ultimate result. Second, it is far-fetched to explain the over-all behavior of Federal Reserve credit outstanding in the interwar years or in the post-World War II period as rigidly tied to a full employment policy—and to argue that the Reserve Banks pursued such a policy without the means to implement it. In fact, their actions had varied purposes and results, none of which closely paralleled a full-employment policy. On the whole, price effects on Federal Reserve credit outstanding seem unable to account for the very high correlations for this period, shown in Table 29. Though covering only seven cycle-to-cycle changes, the rank correlation coefficient of 0.79 is highly significant. The most plausible explanation is that changes in the growth of the money stock produced most of the associated movements in prices.

SOME LONG-STANDING OBJECTIONS RECONSIDERED

The above interpretation of the U.S. data since the Civil War is the same, aside from details, as that adopted for England and Europe by many classical economists of the last century, though their data were inadequate to support a detailed analysis. Jevons' discussion was unusually explicit and may serve as one of the best examples:

Between 1809 and 1849 we notice a vast decline of prices .... Since [1849] the course of prices seems to have been entirely altered, and a permanent rise has been established .... Even if it were [individual] commodities which were altered in their conditions of supply and demand, the result would not the less be an alteration in the purchasing power or value of gold. But considering that . . . a most extraordinary change has taken place in the conditions of supply, the probability is excessively great that we find the true cause in the gold discoveries.

To complete the argument, I have only to ask those who think that the growth of population, the increase of demand, or the progress of trade is the cause of the rise of prices, whether population, demand, trade, etc., were not expanding before 1849, not so rapidly perhaps as since, but still expanding; and how it is that causes of the same kind have produced falling prices before 1849 and rising prices since? . . . I think that the growth of population and trade tend to lower prices by increasing the use of gold, and to this cause we may reasonably attribute the fall of prices before 1849. But to attribute to the same cause, as some do, the diametrically opposite change which has occurred since 1849, is illogical in the extreme. The normal course of prices in the present progressive state of things is, I think, downwards; but for twenty years at least this normal course has been checked or even reversed, and why should we hesitate to attribute this abnormal effect to the contemporary and extraordinary discoveries of gold?[8]

[8] W. Stanley Jevons, letter to *The Economist*, May 8, 1869, reprinted in his *Investigations in Currency and Finance*, London, 1894, pp. 155–158. Similar statements of other writers are too numerous to cite, though the very astute observations of John E. Cairnes should at least be mentioned: "Essay Toward a Solution of the Gold Question" in *Essays in Political Economy*, London, 1873. On the development of these ideas, see F. Hayek, *Prices and Production*, London, 1931, pp. 8–25.

Criticism of this view, widespread from the beginning, has intensified since the 1930's. An early and continuing objection has been that the data fail to show a very close association between movements in money and prices. Analysis of the U.S. data invalidates this objection. Although the association is not perfect, it is closer than is typically required in economics to confirm a relationship between variables. If one concludes from the evidence that price movements in the United States reflect primarily changes in the money stock, the same explanation must apply to all countries, including England, that were on the gold standard and had close commercial ties with the United States. There cannot be one explanation of major long-run price movements for this country and another for England, at least while both countries adhere to the gold standard. The objection that arose to Jevons' view is understandable, however. Early critics of the classical interpretation did not have good data. Until recently the U.S. data lacked complete coverage, with the relative importance of the missing parts unknown; and the accuracy of the data for other countries was even less. Worse still, their inaccuracy was not fully appreciated. The inadequate data for England then available were used to justify the contention of a poor association. New estimates of English bank deposits for the nineteenth century, though still far from satisfactory, suggest that the association was just as close during that period as it was in the United States.[9] In any event, the proponents and critics of classical monetary doctrines intended their arguments to apply to all gold-standard countries, including the United States, and for this country the critics were in error.

[9] See René P. Higonnet, "Bank Deposits in the United Kingdom 1870–1914," *Quarterly Journal of Economics*, Aug. 1957, pp. 329–367.

An article by J. T. Phinney in the early 1930's ("Gold Production and the Price Level: The Cassel Three Per Cent Estimate," *Quarterly Journal of Economics*, Aug. 1933, pp. 647–679, especially sect. IV) argued that the ratio of the money stock to the gold stock for each of several Western countries was not constant over the last half of the 19th century. The evidence refuted the views of Cassel and others that an appropriate constant rate of growth in the gold stock would produce "monetary equilibrium." Though Phinney drew no further conclusions, his results left the implication that the gold stock did not account for most of the growth of the money stock during that period. Such a belief could have reinforced the widespread view that gold production had little relation to money-stock changes and even less to price movements. It seems to have been implicitly assumed that nongold contributions to changes in the money stock, alleged by Phinney to be important, made the association between money and prices more tenuous than that between prices and the gold stock. Actually, the facts for the U.S. are just the reverse.

Aside from long-run movements, the monetary data for most countries were sufficient, at least for certain periods, to show short-run swings. Studying this evidence, many observers have denied that the money stock is closely associated with prices and output in the short run; on these grounds they have rejected the classical monetary theory, even though it pertained for the most part to long-run movements. Many concluded that periods of business stagnation and low prices often coincide with a money stock that is rising, sometimes faster than its long-run trend. Since the 1930's, the evidence on that decade has become Exhibit A of this argument. Aside from such extreme episodes, which usually followed banking panics and so may be interpreted as reflecting instead the aftereffects of severe monetary disturbances, the evidence as a whole does reveal a short-run association—not perfect but still fairly close—between output and the rate of change in the money stock (see Chapter 1 and the discussion below).

The important point, however, is that the short-run evidence, no matter how interpreted, is largely irrelevant to the long run. We are often told that the long run is composed of a succession of short runs, in supposed proof of the analytical equivalence of the two time spans. The proof is false, because what is true of the short run is not also necessarily true of the long run. Effects that are important in the short run may be relatively unimportant in the long run, and vice versa, for two reasons: First, nonmonetary factors may hide the effects of changes in the money stock over the duration of a business cycle. If such factors are entirely cyclical and are unrelated to the money-stock changes, they tend to cancel out in the long run. The long run should therefore be defined as a period long enough for any such shift in the relative importance of variables to show up. Second, changes in the money stock may induce offsetting variations in the demand to hold money. The effects of the money-stock changes are thereby halted, but only temporarily unless the variations in demand are permanent. When these offsets wear off, the monetary effects appear, though with a lag. The short-run effect of these changes is no evidence therefore of their long-run importance. The record of short-run movements, irrelevant as it is and misinterpreted as it has been in addition, has served in the past, probably more than any other consideration, to discredit the importance of changes in the money stock for the long run.

Another objection to the classical monetary theory for the long run was suggested by the Gibson Paradox—the observation that concurrent, secular movements in the price level and in long-term interest rates appear to be in the same direction.[10] This appeared to contradict the implications of the classical theory, because changes in the money stock might be expected to affect prices and interest rates in opposite directions. Under the institutional arrangements widely prevalent in commercial and industrial economies, changes in the money stock occur primarily through the banking system, and banks expand or contract credit by lowering or raising their interest rates on loans, which would induce similar movements in open-market rates. When prices are rising, therefore, interest rates should be low; and conversely. How explain the opposite behavior of interest rates? Since this behavior appears in the long run, it cannot be explained simply by the tendency of prices and interest to ride in the same direction up and down the business cycle.

An intriguing explanation of the paradox was offered by Wicksell and later by Keynes.[11] They advanced two propositions: (1) large and prolonged fluctuations in the demand schedule for loanable funds occur as a result of changes in the rate of return on producers' goods; and (2) bank rates on loans follow with a lag changes in the demand schedule for loans. In consequence, the supply of bank loans increases when the demand for loans rises and decreases when the demand falls. Such changes in the amount of loanable funds supplied reflect changes in the money stock, and, in terms of its three determinants, can be attributed to changes in the reserve ratio. When loan demand rises, banks raise their charges, but not sufficiently to prevent loans outstanding from increasing, thus allowing their reserve ratios to fall; and conversely, when loan demand falls. In Wicksell's terms, the bank rate lags behind the natural (i.e., equilibrating) rate of interest. The resulting changes in the money stock convert the fluctuations in demand for loanable funds into corresponding fluctuations in commodity prices. Thus is allegedly produced the association

---

[10] So named by John Maynard Keynes (see his *A Treatise on Money*, New York, Harcourt, Brace, Vol. II, 1930, p. 198) after A. H. Gibson, who wrote several articles on the phenomenon (see especially *Banker's Magazine*, London, Jan. 1923, pp. 15–34). It had been discussed by other economists earlier.

[11] See Keynes, *A Treatise on Money*, pp. 198–208; K. Wicksell, *Lectures on Political Economy*, London, Vol. II, 1935, pp. 190–208, and *Interest and Prices*, London, 1936.

between movements in money, prices, and interest, all following the independent, initiating fluctuations in the demand for loanable funds.

For Wicksell and Keynes, adaptation of the money stock to changes in loan demand is a necessary condition for the price movements, in the sense that, as both would have argued, prices could not, at least in the long run, fluctuate without supporting changes in the money stock.[12] Changes in the money stock and in prices both result from fluctuations in the demand for loanable funds or, more basically, from fluctuations in the rate of return on capital, reflecting nonmonetary ("real") developments in the economy. This interpretation is not simply the old classical theory in modern attire.[13] Although it recognizes that changes in the money stock are a necessary condition of price movements, this interpretation regards such changes as dependent on other factors that initiate the movements. The classical theory does not remain intact, but is undermined in two ways: First, since monetary institutions and the supply of gold do not produce independent changes in the money stock but respond to factors originating elsewhere in the economy, one does not look to these institutions and the gold supply for explanations of price movements but to the factors affecting the demand for loanable funds and the rate of return on capital. Second, if changes in the money stock are not independent of movements in prices and loan demand, how do we know such changes are in fact a necessary condition? After all, if the association between money and prices can be explained by a link running from loan demand to money to prices, there is no direct evidence that price movements depend on changes in the money stock. Perhaps if government measures broke the dependence, that is, kept the rate of growth of the money stock constant (say), prices and interest rates would continue their long-run fluctuations as before, without any important alteration. From this point, it is one short step to the assertion that changes in the money stock are not necessary for long-run price movements. All that needs to be proved is that historical price movements were produced by nonmonetary factors. The proof has never

[12] Both writers appear to have recognized that changes in the demand to hold money induced by interest-rate movements would not be large enough to account for long-run swings in prices.

[13] For the counter view, see Lauchlin Currie, *The Supply and Control of Money in the United States*, Harvard University Press, 1934, pp. 4–9.

been supplied, but candidates for such factors have abounded. In the reasoning of later writers, changes in the money stock, though not considered to be totally unimportant, receded into the background and were neglected; interpretation of the experience in the 1930's then cemented the position that major price movements often bear little relation to changes in the money stock.[14]

The Wicksell-Keynes theory implies particular routes whereby long-run changes in the money stock are brought about. Wicksell argued that variations in banks' reserve ratios would follow fluctuations in the natural rate of interest and so produce conforming movements in the money stock. Keynes argued that central banks and governments would perform the same function by allowing the ratio of their gold reserve to their monetary liabilities to contract when interest rates rose, and to expand when rates fell.[15] The facts for the United States before 1914, which provide the clearest evidence of the Gibson Paradox, correspond with neither of these patterns. Neither changes in banks' reserve ratios nor in the ratio of the domestic gold stock to high-powered money account for any sizable part of the long-run movements in the U.S. money stock before 1914. Moreover, the long-run movements that occurred in banks' reserve ratios can be better explained by changes in legal requirements and banking practices than by factors related to the long-run demand for loanable funds. Movements in the ratio of the gold stock to high-powered money can be better explained by the government's response to gold flows than to changes in interest rates. The U.S. monetary authorities cushioned the economy against variations in the growth of the gold stock. In the pre-1914 period, the cushioning was incomplete, and most of the variations in the gold stock were still transmitted to the money stock. Consequently, the gold ratio was lower before 1896 when prices were falling than from 1896 to World War I when prices were rising. That is the reverse of the relation implied by Keynes' argument.

---

[14] See, for example, E. H. Phelps Brown and S. A. Ozga, "Economic Growth and the Price Level," *The Economic Journal*, Mar. 1955, pp. 1–18, especially pp. 1–8. See also W. W. Rostow, "Explanations of the Great Depression" (of the 1890's), Chap. VII in his *British Economy of the Nineteenth Century*, Oxford, 1948; Wicksell, *Interest and Prices*, Appendix; and B. Ohlin, "On the Quantity Theory of Money" in *Money, Growth, and Methodology*, in Honor of Johan Åkerman, Sweden, 1961, especially pp. 113–120.

[15] Wicksell, *Interest and Prices*, Chap. 8; Keynes, *A Treatise on Money*, p. 205.

Wicksell and Keynes did not deny that changes in the rate of gold production have an independent effect on prices, but they did not believe that such changes account for much of the actual movements in prices.[16] Neither realized how fully the cumulative effect of changes in the U.S. gold stock accounted for the variations in growth of the money stock of the United States (and probably of all gold-standard countries) up to World War I, despite the sizable contributions of the other determinants. Slight modifications of their theory cannot render it consistent with the evidence. No theory of prices that ignores the importance of gold production can account for the behavior of the money stock in the early period, and there is no obvious way to link the rate of gold production to variations in the demand for loanable funds. Gold production itself was too small an operation to affect aggregate demand directly and could only do so indirectly through the monetary system. Even though one finds nothing seriously wrong with their theory on logical grounds, therefore, it is empirically irrelevant for long-run movements up to World War I.

In the later period, the contribution of the gold ratio to changes in the money stock correlated closely with price movements, as Table 29 indicates, because the cushioning of gold flows was carried to greater extremes. Federal Reserve credit outstanding and not the gold stock has accounted for most of the long-run changes in the money stock since World War I. Here Keynes' view is consistent with the sources of change in the money stock, but our interpretation above of the association between changes in Federal Reserve credit and price movements is different.

The Wicksell-Keynes theory may still be valid for short-run price movements. Since the theory is based on lags in the behavior of banks, it describes more appropriately short-run phenomena. Indeed, its extension to secular developments, where the time span is too long for most lags to be significant, was a bold step, taken partly to reconcile classical monetary theory with the Gibson Paradox. Yet, the long-run behavior of interest rates, while perhaps puzzling, does not alter the preceding interpretation of the evidence on the association between money and prices, for that interpretation does not rule out the influence of other factors on interest rates.

[16] Wicksell, *Interest and Prices*, p. 167, and *Lectures on Political Economy*, Vol. II, pp. 204–205; Keynes, *A Treatise on Money*, Vol. II, p. 206.

Since movements in interest rates do not explain the over-all behavior of the money stock—as they are supposed to do in the Wicksell-Keynes theory—what then underlies the Gibson Paradox?[17] Although no explanation can be firmly established here, one supplied by Irving Fisher merits attention: the effect of commodity price changes on the market value of assets, such as bonds, returns on which are fixed in money terms. A long-continued rise in commodity prices depreciates the real value of the principal and interest of bonds, and a long-continued fall appreciates them. Insofar as lenders and borrowers anticipate changes in the purchasing power of money, bond yields tend to move in the same direction as those changes, which helps preserve the real value of the principal and interest of bonds. Bond prices tend to be lower and nominal yields higher, therefore, when commodity prices are rising, and the reverse, when commodity prices are falling. In a perfect adjustment, bond yields in real terms would be the same as they would have been with expectations of no change in commodity prices. Because price movements are not anticipated, at least not always fully, the adjustment will, of course, usually not be perfect. When price movements have an almost unbroken trend for a long time, however, part of the adjustment seems likely to occur. Interest rates will tend to be higher when prices are rising and lower when prices are falling.

Such an effect still does not explain the Gibson Paradox, which is based on rising and falling interest rates accompanying like movements in prices. One further assumption, however, takes care of the discrepancy. Following Fisher, we may suppose that the adjustment of interest rates, just described, occurs with a lag. When prices are rising (say), interest rates eventually climb to and stay at a higher level, but get there slowly, so that for some time the rates rise together with prices. How fast and how long interest rates will rise depends on how quickly they react to a change in the trend of prices. The lag may be expressed mathematically by making the level of interest rates

---

[17] We may immediately dismiss one popular answer of long standing: that a rise in interest rates for whatever reason raises costs of production and so leads to a higher average level of product prices. This fallacy, prominently expounded by Thomas Tooke over a century ago, was laid to rest by Ricardo and Wicksell, among others (see Wicksell's *Lectures on Political Economy*, Vol. II, pp. 179–183). It nevertheless keeps reappearing, though now chiefly in the press and the *Congressional Record;* most economists have shunned it for some time.

a function of past rates of change of prices. Viewing this function as a weighting scheme, we may presume that it entails less emphasis on rates of change further back in time; if so, the function in many cases will more or less approximate the current level of prices. For this reason, movements in the level of prices and interest rates may appear to be related, though the true relation would still be described by the preceding function.[18]

There is no doubt this effect accounts in some measure for the Gibson Paradox. But to what extent? Fisher's explanation implies that turns in bond yields lag behind turns in an index of commodity prices, so far as long-run movements are concerned. It also implies that the yields should be more closely correlated with an average of past rates of change in prices (weighted in some way) than with the concurrent level of prices. Fisher computed such correlations, using British and U.S. data, and the results presented in his *The Theory of Interest* seem to substantiate his hypothesis. At the same time, his work raises some doubts. The lag implicit in the results of his correlations is distributed over decades; it is so long as to seem implausible. It seems too long when compared with the several years lag of major turns in bond yields behind those of prices. Fisher invariably displayed ingenuity in his empirical work but, to this reader's annoyance, he apparently did not consider the over-all plausibility of his results.

Misgivings about Fisher's empirical evidence have led me to try alternative tests of his hypothesis. One appealing direct test, now made possible by data on stock yields, not available when Fisher wrote, is a comparison of yields on common stocks and bonds. The return on common stocks is not fixed in money terms, and so their yield should not be affected by long-run price movements as that of bonds is presumed to be. According to the Wicksell-Keynes theory, on the other hand, all yields, including those on stocks and other assets, should

---

[18] Fisher did not explicitly introduce a lag into his analysis until he tried empirical verification, presented in his *The Theory of Interest*, New York, 1930, Chap. XIX. In his earlier work he seemed to realize the importance of a lag, however, and did refer to the imperfect adjustment of interest rates to price movements (see "Appreciation and Interest," *Publications of the American Economic Association*, Vol. XI, 1896, p. 76; and *The Rate of Interest*, New York, 1907, pp. 277–280).

Keynes did not distinguish between an equilibrium rate of interest and *movements toward* an equilibrium level. As a result, he overlooked the crucial part lags play in Fisher's explanation and concluded it could not account for the Gibson Paradox (see Keynes, *A Treatise on Money*, pp. 202–203).

follow movements in commodity prices. If we compare the money yield on bonds with that on common stocks, the expectation of Fisher's hypothesis is that the differential in favor of stocks should widen as prices fall, and by roughly the amount that bond yields decline; and the differential should narrow as prices rise by as much as it previously widened. Under the Wicksell-Keynes hypothesis, stock yields should behave as bond yields and prices do; what should happen to differential yields is not specified.

Such a test, using some U.S. data, is presented in Appendix B. The results are mixed. As I read the evidence, Fisher's hypothesis appears to explain the Gibson Paradox in part but may or may not in full. Whether this evidence shows, in addition, that real rates of interest were low when commodity prices declined and high when prices rose, as the classical monetary theory seems to imply, is uncertain. The question remains open.

One difficulty in judging classical monetary theory by this implication is that the required magnitude of interest-rate movements cannot be specified. Even granted the implication that real rates should ease when the money stock grows faster—and conversely— which is a far from certain proposition for our complex economy, the question of how much remains. The quantitative effect of changes in monetary growth depends on many factors, such as the long-run interest elasticity of demand for loanable funds, the repercussions on expectations, and so forth—not to mention the difficulty of translating the effect into specified changes in those interest rates that happen to be quoted and published. Conceivably, the effect on recorded bond and stock yields may usually be so slight that we should not expect to detect it.

Whatever the explanation of the Gibson Paradox, a theory based on the effect of changes in the demand for loanable funds on interest rates and prices is inadequate, because such an effect implies a behavior of the determinants of the money stock which conflicts with our data. Strictly speaking, therefore, the Paradox is irrelevant to a discussion of the long-run effects of the money stock on prices. While it neither proves nor disproves the importance of those effects, it has played an important part in the historical controversy over the relation between money and prices. If the past is any guide, the controversy over the relation between money and prices, even for long-run movements, will not subside until the Gibson Paradox is settled to everyone's satisfaction.[19]

CONCLUDING REMARKS ON SECULAR MOVEMENTS IN MONEY AND PRICES

The evidence points to a strong effect of money on prices in the long run. This does not deny other effects. Many nonmonetary factors, of course, affect prices. Such effects can be interpreted as changes in the demand to hold money and measured by changes in turnover or velocity rates. The high correlation between prices and the money stock shown in Table 29 demonstrates that changes in velocity, whatever their explanation, have been comparatively small in the periods covered. Nonmonetary factors have doubtless affected prices, but as yet none has been shown to correlate as closely with long-run price movements as does the money stock.

This result is not surprising. After all, the dollar prices of commodities reflect the value of a dollar. Just as the supply of a commodity is one of the most important determinants of its value, so it would be strange if the supply of money did not have important long-run effects on its value. Yet, this proposition, once widely accepted as obvious, has come full circle in the work of many writers, who explain the supply of money by its value and its value by factors unrelated to its supply. The foregoing discussion has described the main steps of this doctrinal about-face.[20] The behavior of the determinants of the money stock favors the original proposition.

Furthermore, most of the nonmonetary factors affecting the value of money are probably independent of its quantity in the long run (even if not, perhaps, of its concurrent rate of change) and so would have behaved as they did, whatever had happened to the supply. The stronger proposition may therefore be warranted: long-run changes in the money stock have led *eventually* to a proportional change

[19] The Gibson Paradox seems to be still with us. For ten years or so following World War II, prices and bond yields rose. For a different interpretation of this phenomenon treating the postwar period as a special case, see John G. Gurley, "Liquidity and Financial Institutions in the Post-war Period," *Study of Employment, Growth, and Price Levels*, Joint Economic Committee, 86th Cong., 1st sess., Jan. 25, 1960, Study Paper 14.

[20] See also Rostow, "Explanations of the Great Depression."

in prices relative to the level that would otherwise have prevailed.[21] To that extent, one could predict the eventual effect on prices of changes in the money stock though not the exact level of prices on a particular date, since there will also be independent and unforeseen changes in velocity. Even such restricted prediction has great value. It is near-sighted to belittle monetary effects because they may be slow to appear. Granted that "in the long run we are all dead," we should also remember that every day is a long run which brings the consequences of past events.

These findings carry implications for the connection between secular movements in prices and aggregate real output. Indexes measuring the rate of growth of output and productivity in different sectors of the economy show unmistakable long-run swings, with turning points that tend to cluster within a few years. Rates of change in prices show the same tendencies at about the same dates.[22] The conformity of price movements is not perfect and may, of course, be accidental; the available data cover only a few long swings. Nevertheless, it is not out of the question that more than coincidence is at work. If so, the preceding conclusion that long-run price movements are primarily due to changes in the money stock suggests that any causal connection must run from prices to the output variables. The only alternative is that changes in the growth of output or of related variables influence prices by way of the rate of growth of the money stock—which the present study indicates is very doubtful.[23]

---

[21] The regression coefficients for the correlations reported in the addendum to Table 29 (p. 240) support this proposition. The regression function has a slope of 0.87 for all cycles (0.88 including the two earlier cycles reported in note to Table 28), and does not differ from unity at the 0.05 level of significance.

The proposition in the text differs from the quantity theory of money, as conventionally stated, by relating changes in money and prices rather than the levels of the two variables. The difference is more of empirical than of theoretical importance.

[22] See Arthur F. Burns and Wesley C. Mitchell, *Measuring Business Cycles*, New York, NBER, 1946, pp. 431–440. See also the material presented by Moses Abramovitz in *Employment, Growth, and Price Levels*, Part 2, Joint Economic Committee, Hearings, 86th Cong., 1st sess., Apr. 1959, pp. 411–466.

On the other hand, Friedman and Schwartz (*A Monetary History*, Chap. 13) find a relationship between the degree of stability in the money stock and in output, but not between their secular rates of change.

[23] If price changes do affect output in the long run, the question arises how the effect occurs. Appendix C reviews some of the ways that have been suggested.

2. *Cyclical Movements in Money, Prices, and Output*

The effect of changes in the money stock on prices in the long run means that such effects must also play a role in short-run business cycles. The long-run evidence implies little, however, about the importance of these effects in short-run cycles. Although the money stock sometimes fluctuates widely in the short run, the effect of these fluctuations could be swamped by other factors. The short-run covariation between the rate of change in the money stock and cyclical fluctuations in economic activity[24] (Chapter 1) is close, but it might result largely from passive movements in the money stock induced by fluctuations in activity, and only slightly from the influence of money on prices and output. There need be no contradiction in denying such passivity for long-run movements and affirming it for short-run fluctuations, nor in concluding that changes in the money stock are of primary importance in the long run but of minor importance in the short run.

Is the money stock in fact largely passive in the short run? One test of short-run passivity is similar to that just applied to long-run movements: whether the cyclical behavior of the three determinants can be fully explained by cyclical fluctuations in prices and real output. If not, the observed conformity of the rate of change in the money stock to reference cycles must be either accidental—which is unreasonable—or at least in part the result of its effects on the economy. Although the cyclical behavior of the three determinants is not easy to interpret, it seems safe to conclude that most of their short-run variations are closely related to cyclical fluctuations in economic activity—the opposite of the conclusion reached for the long run. Such effects provide a plausible explanation of recurring cycles in the money stock whether or not the reverse effect occurred.

Granted that the money stock is dependent on economic activity in the short run, does the evidence imply a mutual dependence? Although much evidence has accumulated, a full answer does not seem possible at present. Further evidence is provided, however, by a largely

---

[24] It should be emphasized that, in contrast with the comparison in the preceding section between long-run movements in the rates of change of both prices and the money stock, the comparison here for short-run cycles is between the rate of change in the money stock and the level of economic activity (including both prices and real output).

neglected part of the subject, the behavior of the determinants of the money stock. Two aspects of their behavior are relevant: large fluctuations, and changes in response to alterations in monetary institutions and practices.

LARGE FLUCTUATIONS: WAR AND SEVERE CYCLES

These fluctuations are important, not only because they occur in periods of especial interest, but also because they bring out in bold relief the relations between the variables. Random disturbances ordinarily hide these relations but recede into the background in times of drastic change.

The two major wartime periods of this century in the United States—World Wars I and II—saw large increases in the money stock and roughly proportional increases in price levels, if the changes are measured from the beginning of hostilities to the postwar year in which prices stopped rising. Nearly all the increases in the money stock were due to issues of high-powered money, which in turn reflected the wartime exigencies of government finance. Attempts to raise taxes failed to cover the sudden expansion of military expenditures, and the Treasury had to borrow. It sold bonds in large volume but never enough at the interest rates offered. Since the government felt that higher rates were undesirable, easing the Treasury's predicament and easing the bond market went hand in hand. The central bank's purchases of bonds amounted to financing part of the Treasury's budget deficit by issuing high-powered money. In view of wartime experiences the world over, such increases in the money stock were inevitable. The particular amount issued, however, was far from inevitable; the fraction of government expenditures financed by issuing money is variable. The association between percentage increases in the money stock and prices over each wartime period as a whole makes it reasonable to attribute the inflation primarily to increases in money. Yet, the associated movements in prices and money are often explained as common effects of nonmonetary factors.[25] It is true that wartime controls on prices and nonmilitary spending

[25] The contention is, in effect, that the price increases were as likely to be matched by permanent increases in velocity as by increases in the money stock. In fact, however, wartime price increases throughout the world were invariably accompanied, during the period as a whole, by large increases in the money stock; the net change in velocity, while sometimes of comparable magnitude, was often a decrease.

sometimes temporarily hide the usual indications of monetary expansion, which may not appear openly for a year or two after wartime controls have ended. Moreover, many nonmonetary factors add to inflationary pressures during wartime, though they are usually temporary and gradually disappear after war's end. To make nonmonetary factors paramount, one must contend that in some way they also produce the increases in the money stock and do so in rough proportion to the over-all rise in prices. This implies that these factors closely determine the issue of high-powered money in wartime, which is doubtful in view of the almost universal government control over high-powered money and the varied (but easily identified) reasons for the particular amounts issued.

However major wartime inflations are interpreted, they are sufficiently unlike business cycles to warrant separate attention and so are mostly excluded from the tabulations here pertaining to cyclical fluctuations.

All severe contractions in U.S. business activity have been accompanied, during about the first half of their length, by an unusually sharp decline in the rate of change in the money stock; near its lowest point, the rate became negative, signifying an absolute decline in the stock. In mild business contractions the drop in the rate of change was not nearly so deep and seldom as prolonged. If we take the reference cycles containing the six largest business contractions as representing severe business declines, Table 1 shows that the matching specific-cycle contractions in the rate of change in the money stock were also the six largest. (That correspondence applied as well to the severe reference contraction of 1873–79, the amplitude of which was not included in Table 1, making seven since the Civil War.) The patterns of the six declines in monetary growth are shown in relation to reference cycles, along with the contributions of the three determinants, in Chart 23. The patterns are adjusted to have an average level of zero. The sign of changes in the currency and reserve ratios is reversed to show their contributions to the rate of monetary growth.

Most of the declines reached their lowest point in stage VII or VIII. The first two severe cycles appear to be exceptions, only because the annual data distort the true pattern. In 1878–85, the full force of the panic came mainly in fiscal 1884 with a sharp drop in the contribution

CHART 23

Reference Cycle Patterns of the Rate of Change in the Money Stock and the Contributions of the Three Determinants, Six Cycles with the Most Severe Business Contractions, 1878–1938

(*per cent per year*)

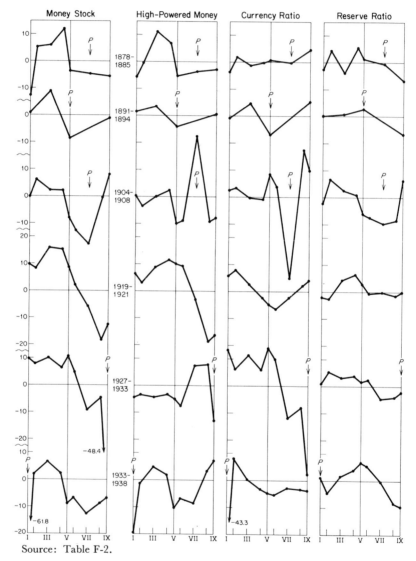

Source: Table F-2.

Note: *P* denotes stages in which panics occurred. Fiscal-year data from 1878 through stage IV of 1904–08 cycle; monthly data thereafter. Nine-stage patterns were computed throughout, except the 1878–85 contraction and 1891–94 expansion, for which there is one stage standing between the peak and trough; and the 1891–94 contraction, for which only the peak and terminal trough standings were computed.

(or rise in the level) of the currency ratio (see Chart 1). Stage VII
of this cycle, however, is an average of 1884 and the preceding fiscal
year, and so smoothes out the deep trough produced by the panic.
In 1891–94, the annual data put the panic in stage V, though it
actually occurred in May 1893, four months after the monthly reference
peak in January. The annual data do not permit an independent
computation of the mid-contraction stages. The 1927–33 severe
cycle, therefore, is the only one with a trough in the money series at the
end of the reference contraction; here the banking holiday reversed
the incipient recovery in monetary growth from stage VII to
VIII.

Most severe business contractions have involved financial panics, as
evidenced either by banks' suspension of payments or by issue of
Clearing House loan certificates in New York City. The panics
represented a scramble for currency, in which the public and the
banks attempted to increase the currency and reserve ratios and so
contributed to declines in the rate of change in the money stock. In
two severe business contractions without panics—1921 and 1937–38—
the rate of change also declined, not because of liquidity crises, but
mainly because of reduced contributions from high-powered money—
and, in 1937–38 only, also because of a large increase in reserve requirements. In the pre-World War I cycles, gold flows often contributed to
a fall in monetary growth in the early part of business contractions, as
Chart 23 shows.

How can this association between monetary growth and the severity
of business contractions be explained? The accompanying financial
panics seem to be a link, because they were responsible for the large
increases in the two ratios, frequently responsible for a sizable part of the
decline in monetary growth. The only exceptions, as already noted, were
1921 and 1937–38. The 1929–33 contraction was not an exception,
because the growing distress of banks in the three years preceding the
1933 holiday had the same effect of drastically increasing the demand
for currency. It is tempting to explain the panics as resulting from the
severity of the accompanying business contractions. Timing inconsistencies, however, plague this explanation. Some of the earlier
panics came during the first part of the business contractions (1873,
1890, 1893, 1907) and before the contractions became deep enough
to undermine the financial structure. A partial exception is the panic

of 1884, which occurred midway during the long contraction of 1882–85. (The two later panics of 1914 and 1933, of course, came at the end of business contractions.) It is extremely doubtful that severe contractions are, from the beginning, so special a breed that they can precipitate panics even before their full repercussions hit economic activity at large. Most panics appear to have reflected special circumstances, perhaps conditioned by declining business activity, but not dependent upon a severe contraction or low level of activity. One might still deny that deep depressions originate in money-stock changes by contending that they are initiated by panics, which also produce the ensuing decline in the money stock. This contention asks us to assign separate economic effects to a panic itself and to the resulting contraction in bank deposits, ignoring how closely connected they are.

Even if that could be done, the argument stumbles over severe business contractions in which no panics occurred or, if they did, occurred late but were not exceptions in terms of the behavior of the money stock. Two severe business contractions had no panic—1921 and 1937–38—and two had panics that came late—1882–85 and 1929–33. In all four the money stock declined, and in the last, before and during the panic. Exceptions on other grounds also occurred: the 1890 and 1914 panics accompanied mild business contractions and comparatively mild declines in the rate of change in the money stock, because both had mild repercussions on the banking system. To explain such inconsistencies, one might argue that a severe business contraction causes an increase in the reserve ratio because of a falling demand for loans (it is hard to conceive of other possibilities) and in this way reduces monetary growth; and that panics are epiphenomena with no important effects on either the money stock or business activity. That is an extreme position. It ignores all we know about how banking panics jolt the economy, especially when banks suspend payments. In addition, it conflicts with the evidence (see Chapter 5, section 4). Both the reserve and the currency ratios appear to respond mildly to declines in economic activity, no matter how deep, and sharply only to financial panics.[26] Although the currency ratio recovers quickly after panics, the reserve ratio has a delayed response and recovers slowly, so that their combined response covers an extended

---

[26] The reserve ratio also responds sharply, of course, to a large increase in reserve requirements.

period. Severe contractions are an important exception, therefore, to the above statement that fluctuations in business activity seem to produce the cycles in the money series. For severe contractions, this effect may explain the timing, but apparently a deep depression cannot account for the sharp decline in the rate of change in the money stock associated with it.

Since there have been so few cycles with severe contractions and banking panics for which there exists the documentation needed to draw inferences, the evidence is admittedly limited and any conclusion, necessarily tentative. Still, the evidence just reviewed makes no sense if monetary developments are assumed to have played a minor role. Without that assumption, each piece falls in place: panics made ordinary business contractions severe when they led to substantial decline in the rate of monetary growth, and not otherwise. Substantial decline in this rate, by itself with no panic, could and has produced severe business contractions. The variety of reasons for decline in monetary growth during severe depressions rules out any single cause and rules out, in particular, a sharp fall in business activity as the main reason for the associated decline in monetary growth. The evidence is therefore consistent with and, taken as a whole, impressively favors emphasis on the decline in the rate of monetary growth as the main reason some business contractions, regardless of what may have initiated them, became severe.

This proposition is hardly novel, though the supporting evidence is much stronger than is generally recognized. Yet, severe business contractions are often cited as a prime example of how unimportant monetary factors are. The period most often cited is the 1930's. Although it is widely conceded that the panic in 1933 made the business contraction worse, one event allegedly buries all monetary interpretations of that period and settles the issue—the several years' failure of monetary expansion to usher in full employment.

The failure does not, however, prove monetary effects to be unimportant. The events can be interpreted differently. A large part of the increases in the money stock after the spring of 1933 only restored what the preceding decline had destroyed. Those increases and the following ones were accompanied by the rise of prices and output from the depths of the depression. Indeed, the expansion of real income from 1933 to 1937 proceeded at a faster rate than that during any other four-year period since 1869 and roughly matched in magnitude the rate of decline from 1929 to 1933. That employment did not absorb the intervening growth in the labor force for many years proves only that full recovery from a very low level takes time, not to mention the uncertainties of government policies and other developments disturbing to business confidence during the New Deal era. The contraction of 1937–38 also delayed the return to full employment. The failure of monetary expansion after 1933 to achieve full employment by 1937 has been likened to the futile gesture of pushing on a limp string; but the analogy should be changed to pushing on a taut coil spring, which compresses—but not indefinitely.

In any event, the efficacy of monetary expansion in that recovery, however assessed, does not bear upon the capability of monetary factors to *deepen* contractions.

ALTERATIONS IN MONETARY INSTITUTIONS AND PRACTICES: MILD CYCLES

Although the evidence points to a crucial role of the money stock in severe business contractions, it need not follow that its role in mild cycles is equally important. For one thing, mild business contractions have none of the features of a financial disturbance. Money markets do not thrash about in panic; interest rates ease as the decline in demand for loanable funds outweighs rising liquidity preference by lenders; and banks do not take strong steps to increase their reserve ratios. Under such conditions, nonmonetary factors appear relatively important, and we do not know to what extent they are set off or aggravated by declining growth in the money stock. Although the cyclical patterns of the money series and the three determinants cannot definitely indicate the cause-and-effect relations, we may examine their behavior from the point of view of summarizing the answers they suggest to this question.

To show the contributions of the three determinants to monetary growth in a way that relates their movements to fluctuations in economic activity, Chart 23 presents reference cycle patterns for cycles with severe business contractions, and Chart 24 presents the patterns for cycles with mild contractions. This second chart shows two later cycles not included in the cyclical analyses in preceding chapters. It will help in examining these patterns to keep in mind several points noted earlier. (1) The patterns are adjusted to have an average level of zero. (2) The sign of changes in the currency and reserve ratios is reversed to show their contribution to the rate of change in the money stock. (3) These patterns are somewhat dissimilar from those for specific cycles, summarized in Chart 2, because matching stages of specific and reference cycle patterns, after the timing lead of the specific cycles is taken into account, have different time spans.[27] Specific cycle peaks often correspond in time to stage II or III of matching reference cycles, for example, and the two stages differ appreciably in the length of the periods encompassed. For this and the additional reason that rate-of-change series are highly volatile, these reference cycle patterns do not always exhibit the position of the peak and trough accurately. (Specific cycle turning points are given in Table 1.) Finally, Chart 24 reveals considerable diversity among cycles, which reflects in part the variable timing relation between the cyclical turning points in money and the corresponding reference turns. Consequently, the average patterns, presented at the bottom of the chart, have less amplitude than do most of the individual patterns, and fail to catch some of the typical movements. The averages are presented to indicate that the earlier and later subgroups are very similar for the money stock and the currency ratio, but not for high-powered money and the reserve ratio. For comparing the movements with business cycles, we should not rely exclusively on the average patterns.

On a reference cycle basis, the rate of monetary growth has a peak in stages I to III. The only exception among these nonwar mild cycles is 1888–91, for which the annual data put the peak in stage V. Following the peak, the rate falls to a trough usually in stages V and VII. (In a few cycles the trough comes earlier or later.) The rise following the trough is often broken by a decline in the last stages of the reference contraction.

The individual patterns for the growth rate of high-powered money differ considerably. Before World War I, the patterns commonly show a trough in stage III or V and little accord with respect to the peak. In the later period, by contrast, they most typically rise to a peak in stage III. The growth rate then usually declines until stage

---

[27] Also, the underlying series differ slightly (see notes to Table F-1), but this difference should not matter much.

CHART 24

Reference Cycle Patterns of the Rate of Change in the Money Stock and the Contributions of the Three Determinants, Nonwar Cycles with Mild Business Contractions, 1885–1961
(per cent per year)

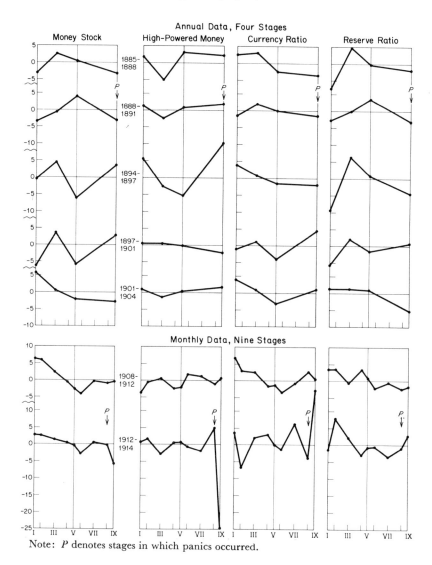

Note: *P* denotes stages in which panics occurred.

CHART 24 (*concluded*)

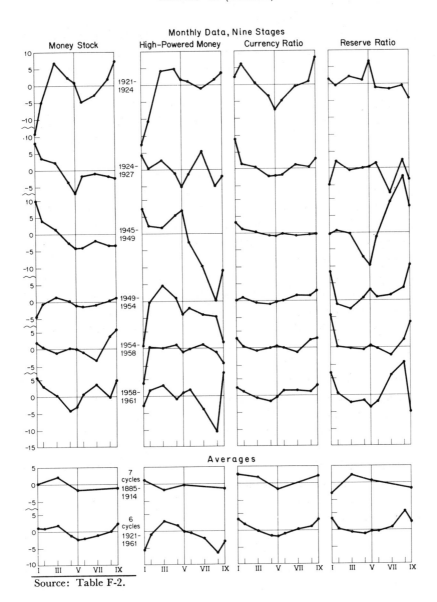

Source: Table F-2.

VII or VIII, though sometimes the decline is interrupted by a rise from stage IV or V to stage VI or VII.

The contribution of the currency ratio most often displays an inverted pattern with a trough near the reference peak. In terms of movements in the level of the ratio, this pattern reflects a diminishing rate of decline during the first part of reference cycles, in which the ratio levels off from stage IV to VII and then starts to fall again in the final stages. These movements in the level of the ratio approximate a sine curve with a trough at stage III and a peak at stage VII (see Chart 11).

The contribution of the reserve ratio has a markedly different pattern before and after World War I or even, perhaps, after the turn of the century. In the earlier period it usually rose until stage III and fell thereafter, which reflected, in terms of movements in the level of the ratio, a fall at a diminishing rate during reference expansions and a moderate rise during reference contractions. The contribution of the ratio after World War I, as shown by its average pattern at the bottom of Chart 24, is inverted, but this is mostly due to some large changes in reserve requirements, particularly in 1948–49, 1953–54, and (owing to a sharp rise in time deposits relative to demand deposits) in 1960–61. If we exclude these movements, the reserve ratio has no clearly defined cyclical pattern in the later period, which manifests a tendency, first noticeable around the turn of the century and continuing except during the 1930's, of banks to keep reserves fairly close to required amounts in all phases of the business cycle.

To describe the cyclical behavior of the money stock does not, of course, explain it. Chapters 3 to 5 analyze the evidence. It seems highly probable that cyclical fluctuations in business activity account for most of the cyclical variations in growth of the money stock, although many variations in particular years can be traced to special monetary developments largely unrelated to concurrent business conditions. The pattern of money-stock changes shown in Chart 24 can also be interpreted as supporting that explanation. The patterns may be viewed as having an inverted conformity to business cycles with approximately coincident or perhaps somewhat lagging turning points. That is, peaks in monetary growth correspond to reference troughs, and monetary troughs correspond to reference peaks. By this interpretation, business activity produces inverted cycles in monetary growth and accounts for the correspondence of turning points. On the additional assumption that changes in monetary growth affect the economy after a fairly short lag, it may be concluded that they work to *dampen* fluctuations occurring for other reasons in business activity.

The length of the lag in monetary effects is, of course, crucial to this interpretation. If the lag is long—which is not implausible in view of the institutional arrangements by which changes in the money stock work into the economy—there may also be, in addition to the inverted relation, a positive relation (Table 1) between money and business activity, with a considerable time difference between turning points. By this second interpretation, the effect of business activity on money produces an inverted pattern and, at the same time, the effect of money on business produces a leading positive pattern.

While it is difficult to measure the relative importance of these two relations and to determine whether the second effect contributes significantly to the observed association, there is some evidence suggesting that it does. First, the timing relation between turning points in the money series and reference cycles seems to show less variability on a positive than on an inverted basis.[28] In line with the foregoing argument, this suggests that the effect of money on business activity is the more consistent relation. This finding alone is not conclusive, because of the practical difficulties of dating turning points in the rate of monetary growth, and because of the fundamental pitfalls in measuring a complicated relationship between two series solely by their turning points.

Another piece of evidence is the persistence of the association over time. No significant secular change in the relative timing or amplitude of cyclical movements in the money stock and business activity is evident for the period since the 1870's, notwithstanding the considerable variability in these measures from cycle to cycle and the changes in the relative contributions and patterns of the three determinants (Chapter 2). If the direction of influence ran from economic activity to the money stock but not the other way, the association between the two ought by all odds to bear evidence of the substantial

---

[28] This evidence is presented and discussed by Friedman and Schwartz in "Trends and Cycles in the Stock of Money in the United States, 1867–1960," a National Bureau study, in preparation, Chap. 5; a preliminary presentation appears in *Forty-Fourth Annual Report*, NBER, 1964, pp. 14–18.

changes in our monetary institutions over the past seventy-five years. These changes have involved all three determinants.

(1) High-powered money has been issued over the period under radically different institutional arrangements. A new source of issue— Federal Reserve Banks—has been introduced, which apparently increased the dependence of this determinant on movements in the two ratios. Restrictions on international trade here and abroad have interfered with the operation of the gold-flow mechanism. The Treasury, from time to time, has in other ways expanded or contracted the quantity of high-powered money outstanding.

(2) Legislation has substantially altered the banking structure. The Federal Reserve Act and the Federal Deposit Insurance Act have regulated banking operations, and many other federal and state laws have in various ways restricted the money market and all its related institutions. The latter developments have touched banking directly, and also indirectly, by reducing the risk of bank defaults and by shifting the comparative advantages of deposits and other financial assets. The conformity of the money stock to business cycles is often explained by the effect of market credit demands on the reserve ratio. Yet, though such demands presumably behave the same today as before 1914, the importance of this determinant has changed considerably. Except during panics, the reserve ratio has contributed much less to cycles in the rate of change in the money stock under the Federal Reserve than under the national banking system.

(3) The behavior of the currency ratio has undoubtedly been affected, though in a manner and degree hard to determine, by various developments in the economy at large. Financial assets have taken new forms, reordering the relative advantages of the different ways in which people hold wealth. The relative amounts of money balances held by various sectors of the economy have shifted with likely effects on the aggregate demand for currency. Changes in the manner and means of making payments have altered earlier practices in the relative use of currency and deposits.

These well-known developments might have been expected to produce changes also in the response of each determinant to external influences and hence to changes in the effect of fluctuations in general activity on the money stock. And, indeed, the cyclical patterns of the three determinants before World War I are different than after it (according to the analysis, mostly the patterns of high-powered money, less so of the reserve ratio, and least of all of the currency ratio). Yet, we still observe no important change in the timing and amplitude of the money stock relative to business activity. One reason could be that the uniformity of this association over time reflects a different effect not appreciably touched by the institutional developments, the effect of changes in the money stock on business activity. Though undoubtedly altered to some degree by institutional developments, this effect has probably escaped their full force, remaining comparatively the same in form and magnitude. A reorganization of financial institutions is likely to affect the manner and means in which they supply their product and not so much the impact of changes in that supply on other sectors.

The behavior of the currency ratio is particularly relevant to this question. Its correspondence to cycles in the money series and business activity remained high over the entire period examined, and even in the cycles after 1914, when the offset produced by high-powered money appears to have increased in certain stages. If the contribution of the currency ratio was offset to a large degree, how could it continue to correspond to both the money stock and business activity? We should expect cycles in the money series to take on a different pattern and timing as a result of the offsets, and so no longer to correspond to cycles in the currency ratio, which conformed to fluctuations in business activity. One explanation of the dual correspondence is that business cycles were set in train by changes in the money stock and, in turn, produced corresponding movements in the currency ratio.

These are qualitative considerations; though relevant and suggestive so far as they go, their importance is hard to assess. We can not easily measure institutional developments or quantify the effects they might have had on the relation between money and economic activity. The evidence for the importance of monetary effects in severe cycles supports a presumption that similar effects operate during mild cycles in smaller absolute magnitude, regardless of what produces the changes in the money stock. The preceding evidence leaves open whether the magnitude of the effects in mild cycles is just as large or is smaller *relative* to the amplitude of the fluctuations in economic activity.

IMPLICATIONS OF MUTUAL DEPENDENCE

A mutual dependence between the money stock and economic activity, if it exists, has important implications for the self-generation of cycles. These implications can be explored by outlining the form of a self-generating, purely monetary business cycle suggested by the preceding analysis. The discussion will be partly hypothetical, because the preceding evidence does not firmly establish the relative importance of the two parts of the mutual dependence. The exploration may nevertheless shed light on an aspect of business fluctuations that has been largely neglected in much recent research on cycle models.

In very simple terms, the evidence examined suggests that economic activity has a lagged relation, in some undetermined form, to past rates of change in the money stock; and the past rates of change are related to economic activity, perhaps also with a lag, most likely short. An initial rise (or fall) in business activity induces a rise (fall) in the rate of change in the money stock which, after the lag period, produces a further rise (fall) in activity. For a while the mutual stimulation is reinforcing. A cyclical movement occurs because of limits to short-run expansions or contractions in the money stock, which produce turning points in its rate of change. Because of these limits, a rise (for example) in aggregate activity induces a rise in the rate of change in the money stock during the early stages of a cyclical expansion—but not indefinitely. Soon the monetary system begins to reach the end of its expansionary capabilities, and the rate of growth of the money stock slows down, even though aggregate activity continues to rise. After the lag period, the slowing down takes the steam out of the expansion in aggregate activity and eventually causes it to turn down. The sequence is similar for contractions and upturns.[29]

This model of a monetary cycle is similar to those of Hawtrey and of Mitchell[30] and many other writers. Aside from the findings presented here about the behavior and timing of turning points in the

[29] Appendix D presents a mathematical formulation of this model.

[30] See R. G. Hawtrey, "The Trade Cycle," *Readings in Business Cycle Theory*, Philadelphia, Blakiston, 1944, pp. 330–349; and Mitchell, *Business Cycles and Their Causes*, reprint, Part III of *Business Cycles*, University of California Press, 1950, especially pp. 47–52, 77–107, 137–139. For the same ideas presented in a different form, see J. R. Hicks, *A Contribution to the Theory of the Trade Cycle*, London, Oxford, 1950, Chap. XI. See also L. R. Ayres, *Turning Points in Business Cycles*, New York, 1939, pp. 144–146.

three determinants, theirs differ from the foregoing chiefly in relating activity to the level of the money stock rather than to its rate of change. If we inserted in the foregoing model "money stock" for "rate of change," the model would be identical with theirs, apart from certain details. The evidence suggests that this difference is important. If one looks at its level without adjustment for trend, the money stock seems to lag behind turns in aggregate activity, and the association between the two appears weak and irregular. With the rate of change in the money stock, however—or what is similar in practice though not in concept, deviations of the stock from its long-run trend[31]—the association appears fairly close. Hawtrey's and Mitchell's theories are not inconsistent with this form of the relation, but their emphasis on the level of the money stock led many to conclude erroneously that the association was not very close in any form.

The dimensions of the variables used in the model sketched here, whether appropriate or not, do not affect the analysis of the behavior of the three determinants. Their cyclical behavior was related to business cycles without deciding whether changes in the level or the rate of change in economic activity was more important. The choice of dimensions mainly affects the timing relation between the variables.

If one accepts the interpretation of the evidence presented here—or goes somewhat further than this evidence can justify—and designates the preceding monetary model of the cycle as a full explanation, the validity of many other models of the business cycle is not necessarily thereby denied, though the rationalizations for them would then be different in some respects. The reason is that such models can be more or less descriptively accurate even though incomplete. There is nothing in the preceding model that rules out, or even makes unlikely, cyclical relations between income, consumption, investment in plant and equipment or inventories, and other variables depicted in the well-known multiplier-accelerator model in all its versions. Indeed, the latter model seems quite consistent with the purely monetary model just described. One can make a long list of other relations that might hold for cyclical movements, whatever the initial source of instability. If the preceding monetary model is valid (in the sense of descriptive

---

[31] Clark Warburton uses this method. See his "The Misplaced Emphasis in Contemporary Business-Fluctuation Theory" in *Readings in Monetary Theory*, American Economic Association, 1951, especially pp. 296–300.

accuracy), these other models may or may not be valid; the case is in no way prejudiced. Nevertheless, given the validity of the monetary model, these other models must be incomplete—in the sense of omitting "important" elements of the cyclical process—as also the purely monetary model would be if any of the other models proved to be valid.

Business cycle research has found so many sources of instability in our economy that it would be rash indeed to suggest that money-stock changes are the main one. Aside from possible government stabilization, an industrial economy will undergo fluctuations stemming from the ubiquitous lags and rigidities, which prevent instantaneous adjustments to changes in demand. Lagged adjustments tend to be accentuated and prolonged by the interdependence of many economic variables, a process that the various "multipliers" and "accelerators" help to describe. Nevertheless, the evidence on deep depressions suggests that our largest disturbances are intensified by contractions in the money stock and otherwise would probably not have been nearly so severe. The ordinary garden variety of cyclical pest also seems to be nourished by changes in the money stock; whether and to what degree it is bred by these changes, however, cannot be clearly determined from the evidence presented here.

7

SUMMARY

THE GENERAL PROPOSITION that the stock of money depends on the behavior of the institutions that issue money and their interrelations with the rest of the economy would receive wide agreement. Beyond that, however, current theories treat monetary relationships with considerable variety, reflecting the paucity and ambiguity of the evidence. New data recently made available and supplemented here allow further examination of the record. This study has aimed at providing a broad historical analysis of monetary behavior as necessary background for further work. Many short periods have special features which such an analysis helps to place in perspective. Within this over-all objective the study was directed toward three specific tasks:

1. To describe the secular and cyclical movements in the money stock and identify the institutional channels through which they occurred.

2. To look beyond these channels, as far as is possible in a broad study, to analyze the underlying factors and relationships at work.

3. To use the findings of supply factors to clarify monetary effects on prices and output.

The analysis was facilitated by distinguishing the actions of the federal government, commercial banks, and the public. The government (including Federal Reserve Banks) is responsible for the issue of money that can serve as bank reserves, called high-powered money. During the period studied, high-powered money outstanding has consisted, at different times, of currency and gold outside the Treasury and Federal Reserve Banks, deposits of banks at Federal Reserve Banks, and national bank notes outside issuing banks. The amount outstanding is held by both the public and banks. Its division between them is jointly determined by two ratios: the fraction of total money balances the public holds in the form of currency instead of bank deposits—the currency-money ratio—and the quantity of high-powered reserves held by banks per dollar of total deposits held by the public—the reserve ratio. A simple formula allocates changes in the money stock to the part contributed by each of the three proximate determinants—high-powered money outstanding, and the two ratios. The money stock increases with an increase in high-powered money or with a decline in either of the two ratios.

A change in the money stock may be attributed to the sum of the three contributions so long as they are largely independent. Lack of independence would mean there were causal connections between the determinants or constraints on movements in the total money stock. Evidence was found of a partial dependence of high-powered money on the two ratios, attributable partly to the common effects of business cycles and partly to a constraint on the money stock produced by the gold-standard mechanism in the long run and Federal Reserve operations in the short run. Such interdependence was confined to effects on high-powered money and does not preclude a general analysis of the factors affecting each determinant.

This summary chapter brings together the major findings on the above three topics. The evidence for long and short movements is discussed separately because the factors affecting the determinants differed according to the time span.

1. Secular Movements

CONTRIBUTIONS OF THREE DETERMINANTS
TO GROWTH IN THE MONEY STOCK

The money stock as defined here—currency outside banks plus demand and time deposits at commercial banks—grew from 1875 to 1955 at an average annual rate of nearly 6 per cent, though with considerable variation. Nine-tenths of the secular growth of the money stock over the whole period was accounted for by the expansion of high-powered money, and the remaining one-tenth by declines in the currency and reserve ratios. These fractions were virtually the same after excluding the two world war periods. Most of the decline in the ratios occurred before World War I, so that high-powered money has been relatively more important in the period since then. Growth of this determinant has tended in the very long run to follow the growth of the total domestic gold stock. While the ratio of high-powered money to the total domestic gold stock has varied considerably in the short run, it was about the same in 1955 as in the 1880's (after the large increase in the gold stock which followed the resumption of specie payments in 1879). The money stock grew somewhat faster than the gold stock over the period as a whole, which is attributable entirely to the substitution of checking accounts for currency and to a decline in the reserve ratio of the banking system.

FACTORS AFFECTING THE THREE DETERMINANTS

High-Powered Money. Movements in high-powered money may be traced (1) to changes in the gold stock, (2) to Federal Reserve System operations, as indicated by changes in its monetary liabilities or, equivalently, in its credit outstanding, (3) to Treasury operations, and (4) to issues of national bank notes. This classification has the advantage of centering attention on the principal sources of change in high-powered money rather than on the particular kinds of money issued. An increase in the gold stock, for example, if not offset by Treasury or Federal Reserve operations, expands high-powered money through an addition to bank reserves or to currency in circulation, though gold itself no longer circulates and is not today a part of high-powered money outstanding.

Secular changes in high-powered money can be attributed largely to the gold stock and, after 1914, in about equal measure also to Federal Reserve operations. The latter played a conspicuous role chiefly in the rapid expansion of the money stock during the two world wars. A greater rate of growth of the money stock after 1896 reflected increased growth of the gold stock, stemming in turn from a gradual expansion of world gold production beginning in the late 1880's. Treasury operations and issues of national bank notes have been of minor importance as sources of change in high-powered money, particularly since World War I.

The Currency-Money Ratio. Currency in circulation exceeds amounts needed for retail transactions, and apparently serves also as a store of wealth. The amount demanded therefore depends not only on transaction uses affected by the volume of consumer expenditures and the cost of a checking account but also on wealth holdings affected by total private wealth and interest rates paid on substitutes—mainly savings deposits. The ratio of currency to total money holdings depends upon how the relevant demand factors affect currency and commercial bank deposits differently.

There was a secular decline in the currency-money ratio from at least the 1870's to 1930, which reflected decreasing relative demands for currency and rising relative demands for commercial bank deposits. Savings deposit rates generally fell during this period and so do not explain these demand changes, though the rates began to rise after the turn of the century and so may account for an accelerated decline in currency demand after about 1904. A variety of institutional developments in payment and saving practices accompanied the secular shift in demand from currency to deposits, for which the growth in real income and of urban centers provides a satisfactory summary explanation.

None of the aforementioned factors explains the wartime increase in currency demand, attributed here to changes of residence by workers, hoarding of U.S. currency abroad, and income-tax evasion. Since income-tax rates remained high after the war, currency holdings used for evading taxes have also remained high. The decline in currency demand since 1945 must therefore be attributed to the disappearance of the other wartime factors and to rising savings deposit rates during the 1950's. By 1960 the ratio of currency to consumer expenditures stood at about the same level as in 1939, but still considerably higher than in 1929. The explanation appears to involve a combination of partly offsetting factors. Tax evasion has added to currency demand since the early 1940's, and service charges on checking accounts, first imposed in the 1930's, have been increasing slowly since the mid-1940's. Rising savings deposit rates since the war have reduced currency demand, however, though they were still lower in 1960 than in the 1920's.

The increasing demand for commercial bank deposits (relative to national income) during the 1930's and 1940's and declining demand during the 1950's partly offset the movements in currency demand. Hence the currency-money ratio follows the movements in the currency-expenditures ratio since the 1930's, but with less amplitude.

The Reserve Ratio. The reserve ratio can be analyzed in terms of the required and the usable reserve ratios. The former shows changes in reserve requirements, which have been important mainly in certain short-run periods. The usable ratio represents reserves in excess of requirements and appears normally to be independent of the required ratio; that is, changes in the latter are usually fully transmitted to the total ratio, though the adjustment occurs with varying speeds. Over all, the required ratio has not changed greatly. Nor have shifts in the distribution of deposits among banks and between time and demand accounts affected the ratio greatly. The secular decline in the total reserve ratio reflects mainly a decline in the usable ratio. Most of the decline came before the founding of the Federal Reserve Banks and can be attributed to actions taken by the Treasury after about 1900 to assist banks and stabilize the money market. The Federal Reserve Act of a decade later formalized the government's role in these activities and induced a further, though much smaller, decline in the usable ratio. It rose temporarily in the 1930's but during World War II it came down again and by 1955 had fallen low enough almost to preclude further decline.

Since long-term interest rates started to rise shortly before 1900, it is tempting to explain the concurrent secular decline in the ratio by the inverse effect of interest-rate movements. But long-term rates were falling in the 1870's and 1880's, when the trend of the ratio was certainly not upward. Consequently, a long-run effect of this kind appears inconsistent with the behavior of the ratio.

To sum up, the long-run growth of the money stock reflects primarily growth of the world and domestic gold stocks and, since 1914, also of Federal Reserve credit outstanding. Secondarily, it reflects a decline in the reserve ratio since about 1900, owing to a more stable money market; and a decline in the currency ratio from at least the 1870's until 1930, owing to the gradual substitution of checking accounts for currency with the rise in real income.

EFFECTS OF CHANGES IN THE MONEY STOCK ON PRICES AND OUTPUT

Secular movements in money and prices, measured by their rates of change between average reference cycle standings centered at reference peaks, have a very high positive covariation, higher than can be reconciled with the view that these movements are largely unrelated. Traditional theories of monetary disturbances can be interpreted as indicating that an important line of influence runs from money, on the one side, to prices and output, on the other. Another view is that the high covariation reflects a direction of influence running primarily the other way, from prices and output to money. This study's examination of the determinants of the money stock helps to clarify the main direction of influence by showing to what extent prices and output affect the money stock and so can account for the high covariation observed. Since we find that secular variations in the rate of change in the money stock are largely due to high-powered money, effects of prices on money can account for the covariation only insofar as they occur through this determinant. Yet price changes have little effect on the nongold components of high-powered money, and the effect of prices on the gold stock is inverse. Hence, the positive covariation between money and prices cannot reflect the second direction of influence and must reflect the first, the effect of money on prices.

The evidence can be summarized in terms of correlation coefficients. The secular rate of change in prices for 18 intercyclical subperiods from 1877 to 1954 was correlated more closely with the rate of growth of the money stock than with the contributions to that growth of any of the three determinants. This supports the hypothesis that money-stock changes produced the changes in prices. Moreover, the implications of the alternative hypothesis, that the direction of influence ran from prices to money, are contradicted in two ways: (1) The secular rates of change in prices and in the gold stock were, in fact, correlated positively, not negatively, as the alternative hypothesis requires. (2) Price movements had a substantially lower correlation with all the nongold sources of change in the money stock, singly or in combination, than with changes in the total money stock.

These results do not mean that prices had no effects on the determinants, but only that the effects were not in the right direction or of sufficient importance to account for the high positive correlation with the money stock. The effect on the gold stock, as noted, should be inverse: inflation in gold-standard countries, which lowers the commodity value of gold, discourages its production and so reduces the rate of growth of the world gold stock; in addition, inflation in one country makes its prices higher relative to prices in other countries and leads to outflow of gold. Deflation has the converse effects. These adjustments, of course, take time. If they occurred immediately, price changes would set up countermovements at once in the gold and money stocks, and could not go far. Though the data show the lags to be quite long, the relationship accords with the traditional theory of a commodity standard: a rise in the money stock, for example, raises prices; this, in turn, tends eventually to reduce gold production and the annual growth of the world gold stock, thereby holding back the growth of money stocks of countries on the gold standard and counteracting the initial rise. The relatively more rapid effect of money-stock changes on prices, compared with the lagged effect of prices on the gold stock, accounts for the observed positive correlation of concurrent movements in prices and gold.

Apart from gold, the components of high-powered money are not greatly affected by price changes. Government actions have to some extent produced a weak inverse effect, because silver purchases and Federal Reserve credit outstanding have been used to offset some price movements. That these components nevertheless tend to have a positive secular correlation with prices may be attributed to their effect on prices through the money stock. Price effects on the two ratios also appear negligible; since high-powered money is by far the most important determinant of secular movements, however, the two ratios can be ignored.

Notwithstanding these results for the period as a whole, the results for the subperiod 1919–54 are not on the surface inconsistent with the alternative hypothesis that price changes produced the secular movements in the money series. For that period, prices had just as close a correlation with the nongold components of high-powered money as they had with the money stock, and also had a slight negative correlation with the gold stock. The latter result reflects primarily the large rise in the gold stock in the 1920's, when prices were relatively constant, and the large rise in the 1930's following the devaluation of the dollar, when prices barely made up for ground lost in the early 1930's and, by our measure of the secular rate of change, did not advance. Federal Reserve credit outstanding, rather than gold, has largely determined the secular movements in the money stock since 1914. That is why prices were correlated highly, not only with the money stock but also with an important source of change in high-powered money, Federal Reserve credit outstanding. These results do not, however, establish the alternative hypothesis for that subperiod. To do that would also require evidence that the effects of money on prices found for the pre-1914 period somehow no longer occurred thereafter, and that price changes had a strong positive effect on Federal Reserve credit outstanding. Neither proposition is credible. Federal Reserve policies were often intended to counteract price movements, not to reinforce them. The correlation coefficients for 1919–54 are also consistent with the first hypothesis and can be interpreted as reflecting the new importance of Federal Reserve credit on money-stock changes, and thence on prices.

The present findings suggest that long-run changes in the money stock produce corresponding, very likely proportional, changes in prices relative to what they would otherwise be. Recent theoretical work also supports these suggested links, but many writers have not been persuaded because of doubts about the empirical evidence. Our data dispel the basis for most of these doubts, at least for the period covered. Nonmonetary factors also affect prices, of course, through changes in the velocity of money. Prices do not remain in fixed ratio to the money stock, as a "crude" quantity theory is supposed to assert. Nevertheless, changes in the velocity of money were relatively unimportant in secular movements, as indicated by the high correlation found between the rates of change of money and prices. To explain secular movements in prices, therefore, we should look primarily to the money stock, and then secondarily to nonmonetary factors that may also have important influence. Changes in the money stock may, of course, reflect many different factors which, in these days of thoroughly managed monetary systems, have widely different origins. We have come a long way from a primitive commodity currency; this study indicates how varied the sources of change in the money stock have become.

Secular price movements may be related to long cycles in aggregate output and productivity, as suggested by similar movements in such series and in price indexes. Insofar as these movements are in fact related, our findings suggest that the direction of influence runs primarily from money to prices, then to output, because no evidence was found that prices and output systematically affect the money stock and come first in the chain of influence. The further question presents itself: how money and prices affect output in the long run. Some leading possibilities were reviewed, but tests of their validity are still to be made.

2. Cyclical Movements

CONTRIBUTIONS OF THREE DETERMINANTS TO CYCLES IN MONETARY GROWTH

There were 18 short-run cycles corresponding to business cycles in the rate of monetary growth from 1877 to 1954. (The few non-corresponding movements are noted in Chapter 1.) The currency ratio was the proximate source of half the variation in the rate of monetary growth during those 18 cycles. High-powered money and the reserve ratio were each responsible for about a quarter of the overall variation. The relative contributions to the two war cycles were different, but excluding them does not affect the general picture. The important role of the currency ratio reflects two factors: the comparatively large amplitude of its fluctuations, and the regularity of its cyclical pattern. High-powered money showed fluctuations nearly as large, but they were erratic and frequently contrary to movements in the ratios; hence, the average relative contribution of this determinant was quite low. The reserve ratio over the period as a whole had the greatest cyclical regularity in absolute terms, but, since it also had a small amplitude, its net influence on cycles in the rate of monetary growth was lower than that of the currency ratio.

While displaying considerable diversity, the individual cycles reveal common patterns. The peak in the monetary growth rate typically comes during the first part of business expansions. The ensuing decline in the rate during this phase reflects decreasing contributions from the currency and reserve ratios, primarily the former. (Since the two ratios each contribute *inversely* to the rate of change in the money stock, our description of their contribution takes account of this. The ratios themselves move in the opposite direction to the way their contributions are described. During business expansions, for example, the ratios generally decline at a gradually diminishing rate. This means that they make a diminishing positive contribution to the rate of change in the money stock as the expansion proceeds, and hence account for the decline in the rate.)

High-powered money behaves irregularly during business expansions, but, more often than not, its growth rate at first expands and then subsides during this phase. On net, the rate of change in the money stock falls steadily until there is a peak in business activity, or somewhat later. Then monetary growth begins to rise, reflecting an upturn in the contribution of the currency ratio and irregular contributions by the other two determinants that tend to cancel each other. Although the growth rate of high-powered money has often declined substantially during the last part of business contractions, sometimes the decline merely offset large changes in reserve requirements. Apart from such changes, the reserve ratio has no consistent pattern over business contractions. These divergent movements of the three determinants have nearly always raised the growth rate of the money stock during business contractions as a whole, but not steadily. Sometimes the rise in the rate has faltered in the final stages of business contractions, and sometimes it has accelerated. The cycles in money can be attributed to all three determinants, though most consistently for the entire period to the currency ratio, and for the later period more so to high-powered money than to the reserve ratio.

In a comparison of the periods before and after World War I, the relative contribution of the currency ratio to cycles in monetary growth was about the same. The relative contribution of the reserve ratio was much lower in the later period, chiefly because of a reduction in its amplitude of fluctuation. The reduction began earlier than World War I—around 1900—in response to a new willingness and ability of the Treasury to alleviate financial stringencies in the money market. The Federal Reserve took over this function and, except for the 1930's, has made it possible for banks to operate at all stages of the cycle with reserves barely above minimum requirements. The amplitude of cycles in monetary growth was still larger in the later period, however, owing to the increased amplitude of fluctuations in high-powered money produced by Federal Reserve credit outstanding, which more than compensated for the smaller fluctuations in the reserve ratio.

Although there was a striking difference between the sources of monetary change in business cycles before and after World War I, there was little difference between mild and severe cycles. When the cycles in monetary growth were classified according to the amplitude of the corresponding contractions in business activity, the relative contributions of the determinants were roughly the same. The contributions fluctuated with larger amplitude in those cycles corresponding to the six most severe business contractions, but with about the same relative importance and essentially the same patterns as in mild cycles. Apparently, financial panics, which have accompanied most of the six severe cycles, intensify but do not alter the pattern of cycles in monetary variables.

These findings need qualification insofar as the relative contributions of the determinants offset each other. Occasional offsets will occur by accident, but, if persistent, they suggest that the determinants are behaviorally related. To that extent the determinants are not independent, and changes in the money stock cannot be meaningfully attributed to the sum of their three contributions. It makes more sense, then, to count as contributions just those movements in each determinant that are not offset by related movements in the other two. The extent to which the determinants are related to each other is not easy to establish, but intercorrelations of their cyclical movements provide some evidence.

There is no correlation between cycles in the currency and reserve ratios. High-powered money, however, has considerable correlation with the combined contribution of the two ratios. The correlation is highest in the post-World War I cycles, from mid-expansion to the first stage of contraction of those cycles. For each of these stages separately, correlating among cycles, the contribution of high-powered money tends to be lower when that of the two ratios is higher, and conversely. The correlation reflects either unrelated parallel responses to business cycles, or a direct relation produced by Federal Reserve operations on high-powered money to offset certain movements in the two ratios.

The offsetting movements generally worked to lower the relative contribution of high-powered money, by the measure used, and to raise that of the two ratios. The measure can be adjusted to remove the main influence of offsetting movements. For the earlier cycles, the adjustment raises the relative contribution of high-powered money, though the two ratios still appear to be the major contributors by a small margin. In the later cycles, high-powered money becomes the major contributor. The adjustment is imprecise and probably overstates the relative contribution of high-powered money, but it indicates in a general way how a correction for intercorrelation affects the findings.

FACTORS AFFECTING THE THREE DETERMINANTS

High-Powered Money. Few of the findings of this study concerning secular movements help to identify the sources of short-run cycles in the money series. Cyclical movements are not only more erratic than the secular but also seem to depend on a separate set of factors, which for the most part are of little significance over long periods. The difficulties are most severe for high-powered money, partly because of our inability to disentangle foreign and domestic influences on gold flows, partly because Treasury and Federal Reserve operations reflect a hard-to-separate mixture of deliberate policy and passive response to market developments.

For the pre-1914 period, cyclical changes in high-powered money reflected gold flows and the nongold sources about equally. One of the important elements in gold flows, the balance of foreign commodity trade, generally moved inversely to domestic business activity, contributing to like fluctuations in gold flows. This reflected conforming behavior of U.S. commodity imports to business activity and in part also inverse behavior of U.S. exports. Exports usually had a trough about the time general business reached a peak, though their pattern in other stages shows considerable diversity among cycles. Business activity in foreign countries affected the demand for U.S. exports irregularly relative to the timing of U.S. business cycles.

In general, cyclical changes in high-powered money before 1914 followed the inverse pattern of the trade balance in part only, because the other sources of change in the gold stock—changes in domestic gold production, in the service balance, and in capital movements —offset the trade balance. Presumably, short-term capital movements provided most of the offset; the other items would not ordinarily respond much to cyclical developments. On this evidence, therefore, capital movements had a stabilizing influence on gold flows in the period, thus apparently reducing—though not eliminating—the domestic monetary effects of foreign trade. The question remains open whether those effects moderated or reinforced U.S. business cycles.

After 1914, cyclical changes in high-powered money reflected primarily the nongold sources—mainly Treasury and Federal Reserve operations—despite the large gold inflows during the first half of the 1920's and throughout the 1930's. The nongold sources were largely responsible for the irregular cyclical behavior of this determinant. Treasury operations had a cyclical impact—generally slight—through silver-purchase programs mainly in the 1890's, through temporary relief to banks in tight-money periods of the early 1900's, and through gold sterilization in the 1930's. Federal Reserve loans to banks and open-market operations were important in all the post-1914 cycles except the second half of the 1930's. Their loans to banks had a positive conformity to reference cycles, presumably because the incentive of banks to borrow varied with market interest rates. These loans have diminished in relative amount and no longer introduce, as they did in the 1920's, a slight direct dependence of the money stock on market credit demands and interest rates. Notwithstanding the declining importance of those loans, total Federal Reserve credit outstanding materially altered the cyclical pattern of high-powered money from what it had been before 1914.

So far as can be judged from the post-World War I business cycle patterns of the nongold sources, the Reserve Banks did not follow a uniform cyclical policy. This is true even if we exclude their loans to banks. Their behavior was governed rather by a variety of policies. Sometimes their actions supported inflation, as in the First World War, and sometimes deflation, as in 1921, or imposed restraint in a buoyant business climate, as in 1928–29, or sometimes were not motivated by cyclical developments, as in the bond-support program during and after World War II. The objectives of policy preclude simple classification at other times, as when open-market operations were countercyclical in over-all pattern but insufficient to reverse the forces carrying the money stock the other way; the 1929–33 contraction is an example. The variety of cyclical patterns discourages generalizing about Federal Reserve actions as simply "active" or "passive," responsive to the needs of trade or countercyclical.

In general, of course, the Federal Reserve has not viewed a particular growth rate of the money stock as the sole, or even the most important, goal of its actions. We should not expect to find a perfect or uniform offset. The period examined was colored by three particularly severe cycles in the interwar period which, together with the two world wars, account for the largest fluctuations in the series during the post-1914 period. Since World War II, the money stock has been unusually stable, by past standards, even allowing for the absence of severe cycles.

The Reserve Ratio. Most cyclical fluctuations in the reserve ratio may be traced to the usable reserve ratio and so reveal bank preferences with respect to their cash balances. We have seen how government actions to stabilize the money market have reduced the average level of the usable reserve ratio since about 1900; at the same time, the amplitude of its fluctuations has also declined. There has always been, and still is, a tendency for the usable ratio to rise when general business contracts and to fall when business improves, though in mild contractions the amount of rise has been small, particularly since 1914. On the other hand, when panics developed, as in most severe cycles, the reserve ratio rose steeply and continued rising for some time thereafter. Following such episodes, banks naturally sought safety in plentiful reserves until all traces of panic disappeared.

In mild cycles, fluctuations in the ratio have been widely attributed to the effect of interest rates, but the evidence justifies skepticism. Our analysis reveals no consistent relation between the size of changes in interest rates and in the total reserve ratio. Often the timing of movements in the two differed appreciably. Apparently, reserves become uncomfortably low during business expansions and, when the demand for loans slackens after a business peak, banks take the first opportunity to augment their reserves. Although the effects of a decline in loan demand and in rates are difficult to separate empirically, the analysis here suggests that movements in the ratio conform in timing and amplitude more closely to general business activity than to interest rates, insofar as the two differ. The only discernible effect of interest rates on the reserve ratio occurs indirectly: they influence the relative proportion of time and demand deposits at banks and hence affect required reserves.

The rise in the ratio in the first half of the 1930's, often attributed to the decline in interest rates and fall in loan demand, is better explained by the strain on bank solvency. By 1936, the usable ratio had risen considerably, but not above levels common before 1914, when there was no Federal Reserve System and banks had to rely on their own reserves to weather financial storms. After the experience of 1931–33, member banks apparently chose to rely on adequate usable reserves as a first line of defense. Accordingly, when reserve requirements were raised in 1936–37, member banks took steps to restore the loss of usable reserves and increased the total reserve ratio between 1936 and 1938. This interpretation is supported by the concurrent dissimilar behavior of other banking institutions and by the similar response of member banks to increases in requirements at other times. The common presumption that such increases have little effect on the total reserve ratio finds no support.

The Currency Ratio. Although the government and banks are usually the center of attention in monetary studies, the currency-money ratio has been a far more consistent source of cycles in monetary growth. It was as important as the reserve ratio before 1914, and has been more important since—contrary to the popular assumption that variations in bank reserves are the main source of monetary cycles. One long-standing theory of cyclical movements in the currency ratio relates the use of currency to the volume of retail trade. Cycles in retail trade coincide with business cycles, however, and so cannot explain the peculiar timing of movements in the currency ratio. Midway through business expansions, it levels off from a long-run downward trend. This behavior could be explained by a similar pattern of the distribution of money holdings between consumers and businesses, the currency ratio of each sector remaining the same: since the consumer sector has the higher ratio, a shift in relative money holdings to consumers would raise the aggregate currency ratio—and conversely. In recent cycles—the only ones for which data on owner-ship of the money stock are available—the distribution had the required cyclical pattern part of the time, but the amplitude of fluctuation was small enough to rule out this theory.

Another approach is to analyze cyclical movements in the currency-money ratio in terms of the ratio of currency to consumer expenditures, which the retail-trade theory implies is constant, but which apparently is largely responsible for the leading turn in the currency-money ratio. Use of currency per dollar of expenditures falls during reference expansions—that is, the velocity of currency rises just as the velocity of deposits does—but tends to level off midway through expansions. Deposit rates seem unable to account for this behavior. Currency demand apparently adjusts with a lag to changes in expenditures and wealth.

THE INTERRELATION OF CYCLES IN
MONETARY GROWTH AND BUSINESS

If money-stock changes affect prices in the long run, they must do so in the short run as well, but not necessarily to the same relative extent. Changes in the velocity of money are relatively more important in short-run cycles, and we do not know how much of the cyclical movements in prices and output, if any, would disappear if money-stock changes were somehow eliminated. The rate of monetary growth corresponds closely to cycles in business activity, but this might result solely from the effect of activity on money. Although this direction of influence was found unimportant for secular movements, it appears to be important for cyclical movements.

Short-run fluctuations in the three determinants appear to reflect cycles in business activity. The currency ratio seems to fluctuate because of differences in the cyclical behavior of the velocity of currency and of deposits, and the reserve ratio seems to fluctuate chiefly because of cyclical movements in credit demands. The gold component of high-powered money varies with both domestic and foreign business cycles through its dependence on the balance of payments. The nongold component—primarily Federal Reserve credit outstanding—seems to react to cycles in general economic activity, though not in any simple way which can be readily summarized. Interest rates, however, appear to have very minor effects on the money stock.

There could of course be other explanations for cycles in the determinants that would carry radically different implications. Some kind of interaction between financial institutions and capital markets might generate cycles in the two ratios, unrelated to concurrent cycles in commercial and industrial activity. For example, changes in the money stock might temporarily alter the distribution of money holdings and affect the currency ratio. But no evidence of such an interaction was found. If business activity is responsible for the cycles in the money series, it is difficult to assess the importance of the reverse effects of those cycles on the economy.

There is one aspect of cycles in money, however, that seems to originate in developments other than the fluctuations in business activity itself. Large declines in the rate of growth of the money stock have occurred sporadically and for a variety of reasons, each largely independent of the concurrent movement of business. Most of the declines reflected sharp increases in the currency and reserve ratios during and following panics. At such times the public rushed to withdraw bank deposits before payment was suspended, and the heavy loss of reserves threatened banks with failure. To save them-selves, banks sometimes had to suspend payments. The currency ratio as measured does not always exhibit the full effects of panics, sometimes because banks suspended and no more currency could then be withdrawn, often because currency flowed back to banks quickly after the panic subsided, and the annual data miss the point of high demand. Whether they suspended or not, banks contracted credit sharply and, for some time afterwards, sought to build up their reserves. The only exception to that response occurred in the panic of 1914, precipitated by the outbreak of war in Europe, when banks could issue unlimited amounts of emergency notes, thanks to the provisions of the Aldrich-Vreeland Act of 1908. With that effective defense, banks had no serious trouble handling the panic and did not contract credit. Two other large declines in monetary growth—in 1921 and 1937–38—reflected special factors. In both, high-powered money contracted sharply; and also, in 1937–38, the reserve ratio rose in response to the 1936–37 increases in reserve requirements.

The evidence indicates that a severe contraction in business alone will not produce extreme increases in the currency and reserve ratios— certainly not so large as occurred in panics. Panics as a rule do not reflect severe business contractions. Most panics have broken out during the first part of business downturns, following a series of dramatic bankruptcies, before general business activity declined to low depression levels. In the absence of a panic, business declines have produced only mild changes in the currency and reserve ratios, and that was true in one crucial instance, 1921, when the contraction in business became severe. There are no unexplained exceptions to this behavior. The two ratios did rise sharply well before the banking holiday in 1933, but that reflected the near-panic conditions of 1930–32, when banks were failing all over the country. The reserve ratio also rose sharply in 1937–38, and first rose and then declined in 1948–49, because of related changes in reserve requirements.

Severe depressions are, to be sure, relatively rare phenomena, and we must draw our conclusions from only a small number of cycles. Indeed, an important part of the evidence is the behavior of the two ratios when business contracts severely but no panic occurs, and 1921 provides the only clear-cut case. It may be that the two ratios are not normally so unresponsive to a severe business decline as they were in

1921. Even so, their response to panics seems exceptional. In mild cycles, business declines appear actually to increase monetary growth. In most severe cycles, the monetary upturn is considerably delayed because of other special influences and apparently only in small part because of the steepness of the business decline itself.

This evidence points to an important independent role of monetary factors in severe business contractions. The six largest declines in money were associated with severe depressions, and severe depressions have never occurred otherwise. In the six most severe business contractions since the 1880's, the declines in monetary growth became sharp generally before, and ended during, the contraction in business. Since severe contractions in business alone do not appear to produce an exceptionally large fall in monetary growth, the association of amplitudes can only be explained by an effect of money on business. Panics cannot be held solely responsible for the deep declines in both money and business. Two severe business contractions had no panic; in addition, some panics did not produce a large drop in monetary growth, and the accompanying declines in business did not become severe. The leading turning points of the money series also support the independence of its effects, since business activity can be expected to reflect and to recover from a drastic monetary deflation only after a lag.

Conceivably, one might attribute the entire decline in the money stock in 1929–33 to the contraction in activity (the two in that instance largely coincided) and argue that the suspension of payments by banks, which came at the end of the contraction, was not an independent development, as in other panics, but reflected the pressures of the prolonged deflation on the banking system. But we should not conclude even then that the monetary decline had little effect on business. If all severe cycles are considered together, the sharp declines in monetary growth occurred for a variety of reasons and cannot all be attributed to the severity of the accompanying business contractions. If the monetary decline was important in some, it was surely important in all. The consistent behavior of money in all severe depressions is too strong to be ignored. The widespread tendency, following the 1930's, to neglect the influence of money was too sweeping.

One can, of course, imagine various nonmonetary factors that might make a business decline severe and not at the same time produce a sharp drop in monetary growth. That has not happened in the period examined, and there is considerable justification for the view that sharp declines in monetary growth are not only an important contributor to severe depressions but are also responsible for them. If that is true, such calamities can be avoided so long as large declines in monetary growth do not occur—which is within the realm of possibility through prevention of panics and sharp declines in high-powered money.

In relation to mild business cycles, the rate of change in the money stock may be viewed as having an inverted pattern with lagging turns, peaks in monetary growth corresponding to business troughs, and troughs corresponding to business peaks. An inverted pattern is not the only interpretation of the fluctuations in monetary growth, however. The fluctuations may also be viewed as conforming positively to business cycles with a high correlation of amplitudes and a timing lead at turning points, peaks in monetary growth corresponding to business peaks occurring a quarter or more of a cycle later, and similarly for troughs. The conformity appears strong on either a positive or inverted comparison, which suggests a two-way relationship between money and business. By this interpretation, the inverted conformity reflects the influence of business, acting through the three determinants, on money; and the positive leading conformity reflects the lagged effects of money on business. Indeed, the timing relations show less variability when the money series is viewed positively rather than invertedly, suggesting that the positive conformity is not simply a reflection of an inverted pattern.

If large changes in the money stock produce a substantial decline in business activity, they must also have some effect in mild business cycles; the only question is one of their relative importance. Dependence of the cycles in money on business activity does not rule out the reverse effects of money on business, but a high covariation between them is no proof of the importance of monetary effects. The analysis in this study provides some indirect evidence, however, that even moderate variations in the rate of change in the money stock are important. The evidence is the persistence of their correspondence to mild business cycles, particularly the largely unaltered timing, over a long period. Some alteration in timing would be expected if this relation ran solely from business to money, but not if it ran the opposite way. Since 1875, far-reaching developments have transformed our financial institutions and markets, as shown by differing relative contributions over time of the reserve ratio and high-powered money to cycles in the money stock, and by changes in the degree of inter-dependence among the determinants. Yet, in the face of these develop-ments, the relation between the rate of monetary growth and business cycles has remained the same. We are apparently dealing not with many unrelated periods since 1875 but basically with one, differentiated by changes in monetary institutions which affected mainly the sources of variation.

Casual impressions may be a particularly poor guide to the over-all importance of money in business cycles, because its effects apparently occur with lags. Both theoretical and empirical studies point to lags, though exactly how long they are remains in dispute. It is easy to overlook factors that take hold slowly and without fanfare, and to overstress those that have a quick and dramatic impact, though the cumulative effect of the former may be vastly more important. The widely raised objections to the effectiveness of monetary policies—based in part on the alleged insensitivity of investment expenditures to changes in the supply of loanable funds and interest rates—really argue that monetary effects involve lags, not that they never occur. Lags do not necessarily or typically make an effect, once it occurs, weaker. Our analysis does not establish clearly whether or not mone-tary effects are important in mild cycles; but if they are, a lag, to-gether with the reciprocal dependence of money on business activity, supplies all the necessary ingredients for a self-generating cyclical process.

The reduction of all business cycles to one process is obviously unrealistic, since it omits the interplay of many other economic vari-ables that are involved in actual cycles. Other related processes undoubtedly occur and, so far as the limited evidence presented goes, may do so with more or less relative importance. Although the variety of cyclical experience warns against preconceived and over-simplified formulations, much of the seeming complexity of cycles may reflect our failure to include all the vital parts. If one vital part is described even roughly by a monetary process, models of a "real" cycle, which try to explain aggregate expenditures without reference to monetary factors, lack an essential element. By our results, the transmission of fluctuations in spending and output to and from the banking system merits close attention in business cycle research.

APPENDIX A

Supplementary Measures of the Relative Contributions of the Three Determinants

THIS APPENDIX presents various measures of the relative contributions of the determinants to specific cycles in the rate of change in the money stock in order to check and amplify the results in Chapter 2.

Table A-1 gives weighted averages of the relative contributions to five specific-cycle stages, where the weight for each stage is the number of cycles covered. This treats the relative contributions in each stage with equal emphasis, no matter how large or small the value of the money series in each stage. Table 4, in effect, weights the relative contributions in each stage by the amplitude of the money series.[1] It should be noted that the measure of Table A-1 for any group of cycles cannot be expressed as a weighted average of the relatives for the subgroups, as is true for Table 4 (under very general conditions). This explains why the relative contribution of the currency ratio can be lower in all nonwar cycles than in any of the subgroups, and also why the relative contributions of high-powered money and the reserve ratio can be larger in the nonwar cycles than in either the mild- or the severe-cycle group. At first sight, the figures seem to be inconsistent.

[1] The measure of Table A-1 for high-powered money can be written:

$$\sum_s \left(\frac{\bar{h}_s}{\bar{m}_s} \frac{N_s}{\sum_s N_s} \right),$$

where h and m are defined as in Chapter 2, N is the number of cycles, and the subscript s enumerates the five stages. The bar over a variable designates its average value. If we weight the relatives, not by $N_s / \sum N_s$, but by the amplitude of the money series for each stage weighted by the number of cycles for which a figure for the stage was computed, we have

$$\sum_s \left(\frac{\bar{h}_s}{\bar{m}_s} \frac{|\bar{m}_s| N_s}{\sum_s |\bar{m}_s| N_s} \right).$$

Since $|\bar{m}_s| / \bar{m}_s$ gives the sign of $\bar{m}_s$, we can write the preceding measure as

$$\frac{\sum_s \bar{h}_s N_s \, (\text{sign of } \bar{m}_s)}{\sum_s |\bar{m}_s| N_s},$$

which was used for Table 4. An identical demonstration holds for the contributions of the currency and reserve ratios.

Table A-1 reproduces the main outline of the results in Table 4. The currency ratio was responsible for one-half or more of the nonwar cycles, and the other two determinants for the remaining one-half; although, in comparison with Table 4, high-powered money was relatively more important, and the reserve ratio relatively less. The similarity between the two tables also holds for the main differences between the major subgroups of cycles. In particular, the currency ratio maintains its primacy in all, with only small

TABLE A-1

FIRST ALTERNATIVE MEASURE OF THE RELATIVE CONTRIBUTIONS
OF DETERMINANTS TO SPECIFIC CYCLES IN THE TREND-ADJUSTED
RATE OF CHANGE IN THE MONEY STOCK, 1877-1953
(per cent)

Specific Cycles	Total[a]	High-Powered Money	Currency Ratio	Reserve Ratio
16 nonwar, 1877-1953	100	32	48	19
10, 1877-1913	100	16	50	33
6, 1918-53	100	46	52	1
6 most severe, 1877-1953[b]	100	28	54	18
10 mild, 1877-1953[b]	100	17	69	14

Source: Same as for Table 3.
Note: Relative contributions of determinants computed as follows:
Averages for each of five stages of the trend-adjusted contribution of each determinant to cycles in the group were divided by the corresponding average for the money series. The ratios were then averaged for the five stages; the figures for each stage were weighted by the number of cycles used in computing the average contributions for the stage (see text footnote 1).

[a]Lines may not add exactly to total because of rounding and approximation error.

[b]Same as in Table 4.

differences between mild and severe cycles. High-powered money and the reserve ratio, as in Table 4, switch rankings in the two periods: in the pre-1913 period, high-powered money was insignificant and the reserve ratio important, whereas in the post-1918 period, the converse relationship held.

One difference between Tables A-1 and 4 is the reversal of ranking of the relatives for the two ratios between severe and mild cycles. As measured by Table 4, the relative for the currency ratio is slightly higher, and that for the reserve ratio lower, in severe than in mild cycles; while the figures in Table A-1 exhibit the opposite ranking. These differences are small, however.

The over-all similarity between Tables A-1 and 4 for the nonwar cycles suggests that the stage-by-stage variations in the average contributions of the determinants are not closely related to the amplitudes of the corresponding variations in the money series. Such a relation for any determinant, if positive, associates the larger weights with the larger relatives in the measure of Table 4 (see footnote 1). Given such an association, this measure would then exceed the corresponding measure in Table A-1, which is not weighted; and, conversely for a negative relation. Since treating the average contributions in each cycle stage equally, as in Table A-1, does not affect the over-all results, the conclusion is that the behavior inferred from Table 4 was not importantly influenced by the particular stages in which the money series typically reached its highest and lowest levels.

The chief effect of the formula used for Table A-1 as compared with that in Table 4 is to increase the relative contributions of high-powered money in all the cycle groups. The cyclical pattern of this determinant explains the difference. High-powered money, with its double-peak pattern, made its smallest contribution, in both absolute and relative terms, to the peak and trough stages of the money series. And it is these stages to which the measures of Table 4 give the heaviest weight, because the money series then reaches the extremes of its cycle.

The counterpart of the greater contribution of high-powered money shown in Table A-1 is the lesser contribution of the reserve ratio. (Such differences in the contributions of the currency ratio shown in the two tables are small and not uniform, as we might expect.) The small differences between the two tables in the contributions of the reserve ratio mean that its average contribution correlates positively over cycle stages with the average amplitude of the money series. The corresponding correlation for high-powered money is negative. The reason for these correlations is that the reserve ratio made its largest relative contributions in the trough and peak stages, when the deviation of the money series from trend was greatest; and conversely, for the relative contributions of high-powered money.

The contrasting cyclical patterns of high-powered money and the reserve ratio are brought out in another way by Table A-2, with two measures of the relative contributions to the average amplitude of contractions in the non-war cycles of the money series. Both measures automatically eliminate the trend without further adjustment. The first covers the change from peaks to troughs of specific cycles. By omitting the intraphase variations, it shows, as might be expected, that the two ratios account for virtually all the movement in the money series. High-powered money accounts for almost nothing, because its contribution in the peak and trough stages deviates very little from trend.

The second measure deals with the change from the expansion to the contraction phases of step cycles. Friedman and Schwartz derived these phases from changes in the average level of the money series, that is, they selected dates when the series "steps" noticeably to a higher or lower level. Such cycles provide meaningful intervals, if the time series approximates a step function, which cyclical fluctuations in the money series do, to some extent. Since the step phases are averages for the entire upward and the entire downward movements, they catch the major contributions of high-powered money and so, as the table shows, elevate its relative importance compared with the change of specific cycles from peaks to troughs.[2]

[2] For a further description of step cycles, see Milton Friedman and Anna Jacobson Schwartz, "Trends and Cycles in the Stock of Money in the United States, 1867–1960," a National Bureau Study, in preparation, Chap. 5.

TABLE A-2

RELATIVE CONTRIBUTIONS OF DETERMINANTS TO AMPLITUDE OF
CONTRACTIONS IN NONWAR SPECIFIC AND STEP CYCLES IN THE
RATE OF CHANGE IN THE MONEY STOCK, 1877-1953
(per cent)

	Total[a]	High-Powered Money	Currency Ratio	Reserve Ratio
Specific cycles Difference between peak and succeeding trough stage	100	1	52	46
Step cycles Difference between expansion and succeeding con- traction phase	100	29	51	20

Source: Specific cycles, Table F-1; step cycles, Table F-3.
Note: Relative contributions of the determinants computed as
follows: Averages of the difference between the contributions of
each determinant to the two stages or phases of each cycle were
divided by the corresponding average for the money series. No
weighting was necessary because every cycle has a value for these
stages or phases. No adjustment for trend was necessary, because
taking the difference between these stages or phases automatically
adjusts for intracyclical trend in the money stock.

[a]Lines may not add exactly to total because of rounding and
approximation error.

Because they average the entire movement within each phase, the step
cycles necessarily have a smaller average amplitude of variation than the
specific cycles have. In addition, the step dates differ from the peak and
trough dates of the specific cycles. Despite these differences, the step cycle
measures for nonwar specific cycles closely follow those in Table A-1. By both
measures, the currency ratio accounts for one-half the movement, the reserve
ratio for about one-fifth, and high-powered money for about one-third. The
similarity of the results justifies some confidence that they are not wholly
dependent on the particular measures of the data used here and in Chapter 2.

As a further check on the results, the relative-of-averages type of measure,
used in Tables A-1 and A-2, may be contrasted with the average-of-relatives
type, presented in Table A-3. The latter is an unweighted average of the
relative contributions over all stages of all cycles in a group. The measure
used in Table A-1 can be interpreted as a weighted average of relative contributions, where the weights are the corresponding value of the money series
relative to its average value over the same stage of all cycles in the group.[3]

[3] The unweighted average is

$$\frac{\sum\limits_{s} \sum\limits_{c} \frac{h_{sc}}{m_{sc}}}{\sum\limits_{s} N_s},$$

TABLE A-3

SECOND ALTERNATIVE MEASURE OF THE RELATIVE
CONTRIBUTIONS OF DETERMINANTS TO SPECIFIC
CYCLES IN THE TREND-ADJUSTED RATE OF CHANGE
IN THE MONEY STOCK, 1877-1953
(per cent)

Specific Cycles	Total[a]	High-Powered Money	Currency Ratio	Reserve Ratio
16 nonwar, 1877-1953	100	20	88	-10
10, 1877-1913	100	8	105	-18
6, 1918-53	100	37	64	3
6 most severe, 1877-1953[b]	100	18	66	15
10 mild, 1877-1953[b]	100	21	101	-24

Source: Same as for Table 3.
Note: Relative contributions of determinants computed as follows:
The trend-adjusted contributions of each determinant for the five stages
of each cycle in the group were divided by the corresponding value of
the money series. An unweighted average of the ratios was taken for
each determinant, covering all stages of the cycles in the group, except
some of the expansion and contraction stages of the pre-1907 cycles,
which are lacking.

[a]Lines may not add exactly to total because of rounding and approximation error.

[b]Same as for Table 4.

The measure of Table A-3, unlike the previous ones, shows the relative importance of the determinants without regard to the size of concurrent levels of the money series. Contributions of the determinants occurring with large values of the money series count equally with those occurring with small values. Because this measure is not weighted as is the measure in Table A-1, it is apt to be distorted by extreme relative contributions in particular stages and, in

where the subscript c enumerates specific cycles and the other symbols are the same as in footnote 1. The weighted average referred to in the text is

$$\frac{\sum_s \sum_c \frac{h_{sc}}{m_{sc}} \frac{m_{sc}}{\overline{m}_s}}{\sum_s \sum_c \frac{m_{sc}}{\overline{m}_s}},$$

which $\left(\text{since } \sum_c \frac{m_{sc}}{\overline{m}_s} = N_s\right)$ equals

$$\frac{\sum_s \frac{\overline{h}_s}{\overline{m}_s} N_s}{\sum_s N_s},$$

the measure used in Table A-1. An identical relation holds for the currency and reserve ratios.

that respect, may be less representative of the over-all relative contributions of the determinants than the other measures are.

From the results in Table A-3, the currency ratio appears even more important than previously indicated. Its contributions are responsible for almost nine-tenths of all nonwar cycles in the rate of change of the money stock and for over 100 per cent of the pre-1913 cycles and of the mild cycles. The over 100 per cent contribution implies that the contribution of at least one of the other determinants (and the combined contribution of the other two) is a negative one—in all cases the reserve ratio. High-powered money has a lower relative contribution than in Table A-1 but not a negative one. The major over-all difference in results of the second alternative measure is the enhanced importance of the currency ratio gained primarily at the expense of the reserve ratio.

The measure of Table A-3 can be interpreted as showing the average percentage reduction in amplitude of cycles in the money series if one of the determinants had remained constant and the others had behaved as they actually did. The negative figures mean that, had the reserve ratio been constant, the amplitude of the money-series pattern would have been increased, and the figures over 100 per cent (plus) mean that, had the currency ratio been constant, the pattern would have been inverted. (These percentage reductions are to be distinguished from the numerical amount of reduction in amplitude, discussed in Chapter 2.) While formally correct, however, such an interpretation of Table A-3 is misleading. The results do not mean that, had the currency ratio been constant, the over-all amplitude of nonwar cycles in the money series would have been reduced by nine-tenths, or that the pre-1913 cycles would have been negligible. The measure, as noted, can be abnormally affected by a few extreme values as, in fact, it was. The trend-adjusted value for the money series was typically small in stage III, and the value for the contribution of the currency ratio was high, so the figure for this determinant occasionally had extreme values in that stage. Consequently, the high average relative contribution of this determinant would be reduced if stage III were omitted. What the results mean, therefore, is that (1) while the average amplitude of the money series would be reduced greatly without the contribution of the currency ratio, much of the reduction would occur in stage III; and (2) the numerical amount of the reduction, though large *relative* to the level of the money series in that stage, would be fairly small relative to the level in other stages.

APPENDIX B

Some Evidence on Fisher's Explanation of the Gibson Paradox

ONE TEST of Fisher's explanation (Chapter 6) is to compare yields on bonds and common stocks during periods of rising or falling commodity prices. If Fisher is right, the Gibson Paradox reflects an adjustment of bond yields to allow for the expected rate of change in prices, while stock yields—which need no such adjustment—will be uncorrelated with price movements, except perhaps in short-run business cycles. Since Fisher's explanation allows for

TABLE B-1

BOND AND STOCK YIELDS AND THEIR DIFFERENTIALS:
AVERAGE REFERENCE CYCLE STANDINGS, 1873-1913
(per cent per year)

Period Between Reference Cycle Bases, Centered at Peaks	Bonds[a]	Common Stock[b] Dividends			Excess[c] over Bond Yields of Stock Dividends		
		Indus-trials	Util-ities	Rail-roads	Indus-trials	Util-ities	Rail-roads
		PERIOD OF DEFLATION					
Oct. '73 – Mar. '82	5.0	5.2	5.1	5.5	0.1	0.1	0.5
Mar. '82 – Mar. '87	4.0	5.7	6.9	5.0	1.7	2.9	1.0
Mar. '87 – July '90	3.7	4.7	5.5	3.7	1.0	1.8	0.1
July '90 – Jan. '93	3.8	5.1	5.1	3.7	1.4	1.3	0.0
Jan. '93 – Dec. '95	3.6	5.7	5.6	4.1	2.1	2.0	0.4
		PERIOD OF INFLATION					
Dec. '95 – June '99	3.3	4.8	4.1	3.4	1.4	0.7	0.1
June '99 – Sept. '02	3.2	4.3	3.9	3.2	1.1	0.7	0.0
Sept. '02 – May '07	3.5	4.5	4.5	3.6	1.0	1.0	0.1
May '07 – Jan. '10	3.7	4.8	4.8	4.9	1.1	1.1	1.2
Jan. '10 – Jan. '13	3.8	5.0	5.1	4.7	1.2	1.2	0.8

[a]Average of monthly money yields, beginning and terminal peaks weighted one-half, Macaulay's series adjusted for drift (Frederick R. Macaulay, Some Theoretical Problems Suggested by the Movements of Interest Rates, Bond Yields and Stock Prices in the United States Since 1856, New York, NBER, 1938, Table 10, col. 5).

[b]Average of prevailing dividend rates for each month divided by prices, beginning and terminal peaks weighted one-half (A. Cowles and Associates, Common-Stock Indexes 1871-1937, Bloomington, 1938, Series Y-2, Y-3, and Y-4).

[c]Numerical difference may not exactly equal difference between yields shown because of rounding.

CHART 25

Yield Differentials of Stocks over Bonds : Average Reference Cycle Standings, 1873–1913

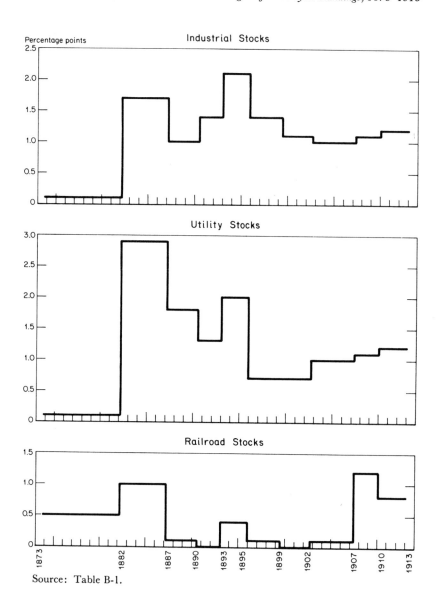

Source: Table B-1.

long-run changes common to yields on all assets, it pertains to the differential between stock and bond yields, not to their absolute levels.

Long periods of more or less continual inflation or deflation are necessary to reveal clearly whether yield differentials support or conflict with Fisher's explanation. One period satisfying this requirement in recent U.S. history is the downward and subsequent upward sweep of commodity prices from 1873 to World War I, though most of the rise ended by 1910. Since then, price trends have been either horizontal or too volatile for simple classification. The relevant figures for the pre-1913 period, presented in Table B-1, were averaged for each reference cycle to avoid so far as possible the influence of short-run fluctuations. The differentials are plotted in Chart 25. For bonds, Macaulay's yields on railroad debentures were used and, for common stocks, Cowles' dividend-price ratios for industrials, utilities, and railroads. Conceptually, earnings-price ratios might be more appropriate, but dividend data, less volatile and more reliable than earnings data, seemed preferable for comparison with bond yields. The behavior of earnings-price ratios for that period, apart from their greater volatility, was about the same as that of dividend-price ratios.

For these data, the magnitude of the movement in bond yields appears consistent with Fisher's explanation. Wholesale prices fell at an average rate of 2.4 per cent per year from 1873 to 1895, and rose 2.5 per cent per year from 1895 to 1910 (computed between reference cycle bases centered at the reference peaks). Bond yields fell and rose during those respective periods somewhat less: a fall of 1.4 percentage points in the first period (or 1.7 points allowing for the lagged upturn) and a rise of 0.1 point in the second period (or 1.0 point from their trough in 1899–1902 to a prewar high for the 1913–18 reference cycle, not shown in the table). Bond yields in money terms, therefore, seem to have accounted gradually and slowly for roughly half the average rate of initial appreciation and subsequent depreciation of money; and, the longer the movement of commodity prices in one direction, the larger was the adjustment. Furthermore, the timing of the upturn in bond yields, which came in the 1899–1902 cycle and lagged behind the upturn in prices in 1896, is consistent with Fisher's explanation; but it is incompatible with a theory which relates movements in both series to exogenous changes in aggregate demand.[1]

---

[1] David Meiselman (see "Bond Yields and the Price Level: The Gibson Paradox Regained," in *Banking and Monetary Studies*, D. Carson, ed., Irwin, 1963) has regressed interest rates on lagged changes in prices in a test similar to Fisher's but covering a longer period. Meiselman finds some support for the theory but concludes that the evidence is inconclusive.

A suggested explanation (not opposed to Fisher's theory) why bond yields do not adjust fully to the rate of change in prices is that real money balances and saving are affected. Inflation, for example, allegedly reduces the amount of real money balances demanded and thereby reduces total real wealth. Hence, real saving, which depends on real wealth, increases, reducing the real rate of interest and the amount of increase in the money rate required to adjust it to the inflation (see Robert Mundell, "Inflation

The differentials of stock over bond yields present a mixed picture. By Fisher's explanation the differentials should widen or be higher during deflation and narrow or be lower during inflation.

1. INDUSTRIALS. The differential displays such a pattern; it rose considerably during the pre-1895 period of deflation and fell moderately during the post-1895 period of inflation. The magnitudes of the movements were less than the respective average rates of price change, which would be true of lagged adjustments.

2. UTILITIES. The differential cannot be said to display the same pattern. Possibly it might, if the high yields in the 1882–87 reference cycle could be dismissed as unduly high for other reasons, though the rising trend of the differential after 1895 is still troublesome. Apart from the low yield in the 1873–82 reference cycle, which might be unduly low, the differential was apparently higher on the average before 1895 than after, which is consistent with Fisher's explanation without an adjustment lag. But by that interpretation the differentials for utilities and industrials were not consistent with each other. The pattern for utilities, therefore, is a puzzle, but it is even more of a puzzle if interpreted according to the Wicksell-Keynes explanation.

3. RAILROADS. The differential cannot be reconciled with Fisher's explanation. It fell in the pre-1895 period and rose thereafter. Railroad stock yields, therefore, fell more than bond yields did during deflation and rose more than bond yields did during inflation; this is consistent with the Wicksell-Keynes explanation, as a constant differential would be also.

Why the railroad differential displays a different pattern from the others is perplexing, and I have discovered no satisfactory explanation. One important difference between railroad and industrial stocks even accentuates the disagreement. Railroads have large amounts of bonds outstanding, the real burden of which varies inversely with the price level, so that railroad net income in money as well as real terms is affected by price movements. Industrials as a group may also be net monetary debtors and so be affected in the same way, but certainly less. The effect of changes in the real burden of bonds on net income reflects a change in the average return on a firm's previously invested equity, rather than reflecting the estimated return on new additions to equity—relevant here. Insofar as a change in prices is expected, stock market yields are adjusted to allow for the expected gains or losses resulting from a firm's indebtedness already incurred. For this reason, railroad stock yields should rise, relative to industrial stock yields, during deflation and fall during inflation, just the opposite to their actual behavior shown in

---

and Real Interest," *Journal of Political Economy*, June 1963, pp. 280–283). A more plausible argument to me along these lines would be that inflation induces people to shift from money and other assets with fixed nominal values to common stocks and real assets, raising the price and lowering the yield on the latter assets for a prolonged period until suppliers of assets adjust to the change in demand. Contrary to either argument, however, such changes in real money balances seem normally too small to have much effect on the real rate of interest.

Chart 25. Utilities, like railroads, also have large amounts of bonds outstanding, and the yield on their stock did change in the inflation and deflation in the expected manner. This might explain some of our difficulty in reconciling the pattern of utilities stock differentials over bond yields with the pattern shown by industrials.

These observations take no account of changes over time in premiums for risk. Risk premiums on widely traded assets probably have declined as the economy has matured, but whether more so on bonds than on stocks, or the reverse, is not known. In any event, a constant secular decline in risk premiums would affect yields before and after 1895 in the same direction and should not disturb the foregoing comparisons of the two periods before and after that year. Conceivably, one might explain these results by pointing to the 1890's as a period of extreme economic instability, which might have raised yields on industrial and utility stocks, but not yields on railroad stocks, higher in that decade than they would have been. But that is conjecture.

In summary, Fisher's explanation is neither firmly supported nor rejected outright by these data.[2] One may nevertheless conclude that the Gibson Paradox shows up much less clearly—if at all—in stock than in bond yields, and not solely because stock yields are more volatile. This is some slight confirmation that Fisher's explanation accounts for at least part of the paradox. Yet even this weak conclusion must be hedged. Table B-1 covers only two movements, one down and one up, which essentially give two observations in the allegedly long history of the Gibson Paradox. The subject clearly requires a good deal more careful investigation than it has so far received.[3]

[2] As Rendigs Fels also concluded from such evidence (see his *American Business Cycles, 1865–1897*, Chapel Hill, 1959, pp. 71–72).

[3] Three other explanations of the Gibson Paradox may be mentioned.

1. R. G. Hawtrey (*Good and Bad Trade*, London, 1913) denies that investors (and savers?) have any long-run expectations of price movements and so rules out an explanation of Fisher's kind. Hawtrey argues instead that price movements cause rates of return and profits to move in the same direction, because of a lag in wages. For this reason money, prices, and interest allegedly move together.

2. F. R. Macaulay (*Some Theoretical Problems Suggested by the Movements of Interest Rates, Bond Yields and Stock Prices in the United States since 1856*, New York, NBER, 1938, Chap. VI) was vehemently critical and highly skeptical of Fisher's empirical results. Macaulay's explanation of the paradox was that rising prices induce increases in investment expenditures and thereby cause interest rates to rise; and, conversely, for falling prices.

3. J. R. Hicks (*A Contribution to the Theory of the Trade Cycle*, Oxford, 1950, p. 154n) attributes the paradox to a tendency of the monetary growth rate to fluctuate more when its secular trend is higher, because banks take more risks; with greater monetary fluctuation, short-term interest rates rise more sharply in booms, which allegedly keeps long rates at a higher average level. And, conversely, for low secular trends in monetary growth.

I doubt the adequacy of all three of these explanations for long-run movements.

APPENDIX C

Four Theories of How Price Changes May Affect Output in the Long Run

SOME STUDIES have pointed to a tentative relation between long-run swings in prices and output (Chapter 6, p. 260). If such a relation does exist, it apparently runs primarily from prices to output, not the other way. The evidence is inconsistent with the second part of a connection from output to prices to money (Chapter 6), and there is no evidence of an important effect of output on money. (For short-run cyclical movements, of course, there probably are such effects.) Economists have long found it plausible that the rate of change in prices might affect the rate of change in output in the long run. Of the explanations offered, four can be distinguished and are discussed here.

1. If price movements are largely unforeseen, or at least unprepared for, business firms are said to gain from inflation, which stimulates them to expand, and to lose from deflation, which induces or forces them to curtail investment and (the rate of increase in) output. Unforeseen price rises would confer gains on business firms, and unforeseen price declines impose losses, if firms are generally net monetary debtors (that is, liabilities fixed in money terms exceed assets fixed in money terms), or if wage contracts are fixed in money terms for a fairly long time. Yet, the question remains whether such windfall profits would stimulate purchase of additional capital goods, since by hypothesis the expected rate of return on new investment need not have changed. If they did stimulate capital investment, the reasons might be that inflation redistributed income in favor of businessmen, who supposedly tend to save more than others, and that the resulting addition to the supply of loanable funds reduced rates on new borrowing. Even granting that much, there remain the two assumptions underlying the cause-and-effect relation of rising prices to gains for business: most business firms are net debtors; and wages lag behind prices. The validity of these assumptions is doubtful for recent decades and unknown for earlier periods.[1] Despite its long standing, therefore, this explanation is by no means established.

[1] See R. Kessel and A. Alchian, "The Inflation-Induced Lag of Wages," *American Economic Review*, Mar. 1960, pp. 43–66; A. Rees, *Real Wages in Manufacturing 1890–1914*, Princeton University Press for NBER, 1961, especially pp. 10–11, 13, and 125–126. A wage lag is alleged for the 1897–1913 inflation by F. Lavington (*The English Capital Market*, London, 1921, Chap. IX).

Actually, if recognized at the time, a lag in wages ought to increase the use of labor

2. A different kind of lag is reflected in the discrepancy Irving Fisher noted between the market rate of interest and the real rate, that is, adjusted for future price changes. His argument is presented in Chapter 6 as a possible explanation of the Gibson Paradox. If such a discrepancy were to affect the level of investment and so the growth of output in a way that would explain an association between output and prices, however, that would require lenders and borrowers systematically to disagree on expected price movements. Indeed, borrowers would always have to foresee future price trends more accurately than lenders would, which is difficult to rationalize. To the extent that a discrepancy between money rates and real rates of interest explains the Gibson Paradox, both lenders and borrowers would have to be slow in perceiving new price trends; but then the discrepancy cannot explain a long-run association between prices and output.

3. An association between prices and output in the long run might be created by variations in the severity of cyclical contractions. Contractions might tend to be more severe in a long-run period of falling prices than in one of constant or rising prices, even though business firms were generally not net debtors and wages did not lag behind prices. In cyclical expansions, a downward price trend will be temporarily counteracted, and prices might rise slightly or be constant, avoiding the downward pressure on inflexible wage levels and other costs. In cyclical contractions, a downward price trend will accentuate the cutback in production and employment. Successive cyclical contractions have a cumulative effect on the long-run growth of output, provided the amplitudes of contractions and expansions are not positively related (although some evidence suggests they are). A deflationary period of unusually severe contractions would then retard long-run growth compared with an inflationary period of mild contractions. This theory claims only that falling prices retard growth, not that rising prices stimulate growth.

4. A fourth explanation—more appealing to me than the others because it does not rest on lags or inflexibilities—is that changes in the rate of growth of the money stock affect the supply of loanable funds and so induce increases in investment, in periods of rising prices, and reductions, in periods of falling prices. Such an effect seems to imply that interest rates move inversely to changes in monetary growth. Because actual behavior has shown the reverse relation—the Gibson Paradox again—this explanation has often been dismissed. If we accept Fisher's hypothesis to account for the paradox, however, and formulate the argument in terms of real interest rates, it is possible that real rates do move in a direction consistent with this explanation. To be sure, our examination of stock yields in Appendix B does not clearly reveal such behavior

---

and not of capital goods. The wage lag might temporarily make employment "fuller" than it would otherwise be, but it hardly seems able to account for variations in the secular growth of output. Of course, if the lag is recognized at the time, even if only by employers, bidding for labor would remove the lag. Such a lag, therefore, presupposes that price movements are unforeseen.

(no clear-cut response of stock yields either up or down to deflation and in-flation could be established). But this might mean only that real interest rates are not very sensitive to changes in the supply of loanable funds, possibly because the investment curve is fairly elastic in the long run to interest rate changes or is highly dependent on prevailing expectations of the future state of business.

Historical variations in the growth of the money stock were sufficient to have had sizable effects on the supply of loanable funds, assuming that nearly all new money enters into circulation through bank loans. Table 28 shows that the growth rate of the money stock varied between reference cycle bases often by 2 percentage points or more. Taking into account the probable ratio of the money stock to the supply of loanable funds, we may expect such changes in monetary growth to have increased or decreased the amount of loanable funds supplied by as much as 10 per cent or more. All increases in those funds could not have been hoarded or all decreases offset by dishoarding, for, if they had been, money and prices would not have been highly correlated. Appar-ently most of the funds supplied were spent, therefore, on whatever they were borrowed to procure, presumably consumers' and producers' investment goods. Whether an increase in investment of about 10 per cent would stimulate the growth of output very much would depend upon the importance of increases in capital equipment relative to autonomous technological improvements.[2]

These are the standard rationalizations of a long-run association between prices and output. Though none of the four can be ruled out, none seems compelling either, which is one reason for doubts about the firmness of the empirical connection between the two variables. The question is of consider-able importance and merits further research.

[2] If increased growth of the money stock removed some pockets of persistent unemployment, this too would add to aggregate output. That effect on the long-run rate of growth of output, however, is limited and would be negligible, notwith-standing the exaggerated emphasis accorded the effect in recent discussions of growth.

APPENDIX D

Mathematical Analysis of a Purely Monetary Cycle

THE RELATIONS outlined in Chapter 6 (pp. 276–277) can be expressed as follows:

(1) $$Y_{t+\theta} = \phi(\dot{M}_t)$$

(2) $$\dot{M}_{t+\eta} = \Omega(\dot{Y}_t) ,$$

where Y_t is an index of economic activity and M_t, of the money stock, both measured at time t as deviations from their respective secular trends. Overhead dots signify the rate of change in the variable.

Equation 1 expresses the lagged dependence of activity on the rate of growth of the money stock, where θ is the length of the lag. The first derivative of ϕ is positive, and also assumed to be more or less constant (i.e., ϕ is linear) over the relevant range. The evidence does not clearly indicate whether the rate of change or the level of the money stock should be related to the level of economic activity. Consequently, the results of using the level of the money stock (adjusted for trend) as the argument of equation 1 will be examined later in this appendix.

Equation 2 describes the effect of economic activity on the rate of change in the money stock. The lag time η is assumed to be short and will be omitted hereafter. The argument of Ω is shown in 2 as the rate of change in economic activity, which seems plausible. Hence, by integration, the stock of money is a function of the level of economic activity. (Note that a similar model results from making $Y_{t+\theta}$ depend on M_t, and $\dot{M}_t$ depend on Y_t.)

The analysis of the behavior of $\dot{M}$ (Chapter 2, summarized in Chart 2) suggests that equation 2 has the general form shown in Figure 1. The evidence suggests that the function passes through the origin and has two turning points, one in the first and one in the third quadrant. (Remember that the variables are measured as deviations from their respective secular trends.) Otherwise, the exact shape of the function cannot be specified and, in particular, whether it is approximately symmetrical or not. For present purposes, however, such details do not seem necessary.

It should be emphasized that Figure 1 is based solely on the average behavior of $\dot{M}$ over business cycles. Besides ignoring differences among individual cycles, the diagram translates an empirical covariation into a fixed relation. The evidence of this study pertains only to the observed values of the variables

FIGURE 1

The Ω Function

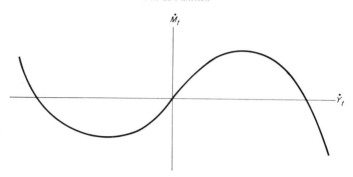

over the cycle, during which they appear to be associated in the manner shown. We cannot be certain that the value of $\dot M$ corresponding to a given $\dot Y$ on the diagram does not in fact change over time even though $\dot Y$ were to remain unchanged. (The behavior of the reserve ratio, in particular, is subject to this qualification.) What this qualification amounts to is the possibility that $\ddot M$ or higher-order derivatives rather than $\dot M$ are stable functions of (the rate of change in) economic activity. This possibility is ignored in what follows.

Combining (1) and (2) to eliminate $\dot M$ gives

(3) $$Y_{t+\theta} = \phi(\Omega[\dot Y_t]).$$

We may approximate the left-hand side at time t with the first two terms of a Taylor expansion, which gives

(4) $$Y_t + \theta \dot Y_t = \phi(\Omega[\dot Y_t]) \ .$$

(5) Letting $$\psi(\dot Y_t) = \phi(\Omega[\dot Y_t]) - \theta \dot Y_t ,$$

(6) we have $$Y_t = \psi(\dot Y_t) \ .$$

The shape of ψ can be surmised from Figure 1. If ϕ is roughly linear in the relevant range, ψ will have the shape of Ω in Figure 1 with the curve pulled progressively downwards to the right of the origin and progressively upwards to the left by the second term on the right in equation 5, and pulled in the same or the opposite direction, respectively, as the first derivative of ϕ is less or greater than unity. Hence the phase map of equation 6, which is a first-order nonlinear differential equation, may be sketched as in Figure 2.[1]

There is one equilibrium point, at the origin, but it is unstable, so that from there the movement proceeds to either A or C. Both A and C are unstable

[1] Equation 6 is similar mathematically (not in derivation) to one presented by R. M. Goodwin in his paper on nonlinear investment accelerators, and I have followed his analysis. See "The Nonlinear Accelerator and the Persistence of Business Cycles," *Econometrica*, Jan. 1951, equation 5a (with $\alpha = 0$) and Figure 5.

positions, and there is a discontinuous jump in $\dot{Y}$ to B from A and to D from C. A solution of equation 6, therefore, is a cyclical movement following the closed loop $ABCDA$. The discontinuous jump in $\dot{Y}$ at A and C is partly a consequence of neglecting higher-order terms of the Taylor expansion of $Y_{t+\theta}$ in equation 4. Equation 3 would presumably have a similar solution but with less abrupt turning points.

As noted earlier, it might be more appropriate to use M (adjusted for trend) as the argument of equation 1. If so, equation 3 becomes, if we write equation 2 as $M_t = \pi(Y_t)$,

(3a) $$Y_{t+\theta} = \phi(\pi[Y_t]) .$$

The cycle produced by equation 3a is somewhat different, and considerably easier to analyze. Whether Y moves continually in one direction or oscillates depends on whether

(7) $$\frac{dY_{t+\theta}}{dY_t} = \phi'\pi' ,$$

is positive or negative, respectively; and whether the movement is explosive or damped depends on whether

(8) $$\frac{d^2Y_{t+\theta}}{dY_t{}^2} = \phi'\pi'' + \phi''\pi'$$

is positive or negative, respectively. (The primes indicate derivatives.)

FIGURE 2

Phase Map of ψ

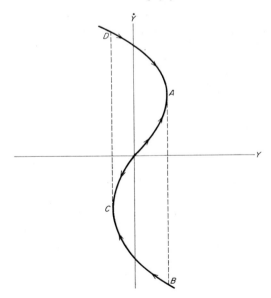

Suppose ϕ' and π' were always positive and, because of barriers that tighten gradually, ϕ'' is negative. If π'' is negative or, if positive, constant, so that the first term is gradually reduced by the decline in ϕ', equation 8 will either be always negative or eventually become negative, implying a damped, one-way movement. Equation 7, however, though at times positive, becomes negative at certain times because π' gradually turns negative after Y increases or decreases a certain amount, then becomes positive again sometime after Y turns back from either its peak or trough level.

Peaks and troughs in Y will be rounded rather than cusps (explosive) if the positive value of the second term of equation 8 (produced by negative values of π' and ϕ'') is outweighed, as seems plausible, by the negative value of the first term (produced by a negative value of π'' occurring sometime before the change in sign of π' from plus to minus).

A cusp would occur if the negative value of ϕ'' became sufficiently large. In that event the extreme levels of Y would be determined (as in the multiplier-accelerator model cited of Goodwin, for example) by physical—not monetary—barriers to further increases or decreases in output. Output would then remain at this barrier level, however, until π' declined. There is no reason for M to decline simply because Y hits a barrier. This model therefore differs from the multiplier-accelerator type in having no accelerator—that is, no relation involving the rate of change of output—whereas the first model presented above has.

It is possible to obtain a self-generating cycle from the purely monetary relations posited by equations 1 and 2 in either form. These models bear a mathematical resemblance to those describing interactions between the multiplier and accelerator. The foregoing paragraphs should be viewed only as illustrative of the statements made in Chapter 6. They hardly constitute a complete theory of cycles. Some of the as yet unknown characteristics of the functions may alter the results in important ways. In addition, the model, as presented, does not allow for changes in the demand to hold money balances, which a complete theory needs to specify.

APPENDIX E

Interest Payments and Service Charges on Bank Deposits

THIS APPENDIX brings together scattered data on deposit rates and charges from which are inferred the major secular movements in the net rate of return on deposits.

The available data on member and insured banks are presented in Table E-1. Service charges were first reported separately in 1933. It is not known when charges were first imposed, but they were not common before the 1930's. The Banking Act of 1933 prohibited interest on demand accounts at member banks, and the Banking Act of 1935 extended the prohibition to insured banks. In interpreting these data, one should bear in mind that (except interbank deposits, which are excluded from these figures) interest was paid mainly on U.S. Treasury deposits (included here until mid-1933) and other large accounts, and that charges have been levied only on small checking accounts. Table E-1 gives an average rate on deposits, on many of which no interest was paid or charges levied. The rates applicable to deposits on which interest was paid or charges levied, therefore, were higher (in absolute amount) than the average rates shown. Interest is paid on virtually all time deposits, though the rates vary. Interest payments were not reported separately for demand and time deposits before 1927.

The rates paid by mutual savings banks are presented in Table E-2. These rates and those on time deposits and savings and loan shares are graphed in Chart 18. The post-World War I data all agree in showing little change during the 1920's and a sharp decline after 1929. Thereafter, rates paid on time and savings deposits reached a trough in 1946–47 and then rose. Charges on demand deposits were roughly constant during the 1930's and 1940's and then doubled during the 1950's.

For the years before 1919, the data are much less satisfactory, consisting of only some indirect evidence on the average rate paid on total deposits at commercial banks. One relevant series is the annual rate of return received on loans and investments by national banks. That rate fell gradually from 6.5 per cent in 1890, the year such data were first reported, to 4.8 per cent in 1905 and rose to 6.2 per cent by 1913.[1] Such movements are consistent with the well-documented fall in long-term interest rates in the economy at large

---

[1] See "Trends in Rates of Bank Earnings and Expenses," *Federal Reserve Bulletin*, Feb. 1938, especially p. 103.

TABLE E-1

AVERAGE RATE OF INTEREST OR CHARGE ON DEMAND AND TIME
DEPOSITS, ANNUALLY, 1927-60
(per cent per annum)

Year	Average Rate on Demand Deposits of:		Average Rate of Interest on Time Deposits
	Interest	Charge	
1927	1.25		3.34
1928	1.28		3.36
1929	1.32		3.34
1930	1.23		3.31
1931	0.84		2.99
1932	0.69	b	2.80
1933	0.32	0.16	2.55
1934	a	.18	2.41
1935		.19	2.01
1936		.18	1.72
1937		.20	1.62
1938		.23	1.55
1939		.24	1.43
1940		.22	1.30
1941		.21	1.20
1942		.19	1.11
1943		.17	0.93
1944		.17	0.88
1945		.15	0.86
1946		.15	0.84
1947		.17	0.87
1948		.20	0.90
1949		.22	0.91
1950		.23	0.94
1951		.24	1.04
1952		.24	1.15
1953		.26	1.24
1954		.29	1.32
1955		.30	1.38
1956		.33	1.58
1957		.38	2.08
1958		.41	2.11
1959		.43	2.36
1960		.47	2.56

Source: Annual Report, Federal Deposit Insurance
Corporation (FDIC), and Banking and Monetary Statistics,
Board of Governors of the Federal Reserve System, 1943,
pp. 262-263. See also Cagan, The Demand for Currency
Relative to Total Money Supply, New York, NBER,
Occasional Paper 62, 1958, Appendix.

Demand deposits: Amounts paid and charged both
divided by the same Dec.-June-Dec. weighted average of
demand deposits to which the data on payments pertain
(see The Demand for Currency). Data are for member banks,
1927-41, and insured banks, thereafter. No deductions were
made for losses. The small federal tax levied on checks
from June 21, 1932, to Jan. 1, 1935, has been ignored.

NOTES TO TABLE E-1 (concluded)

Time deposits: Amounts paid divided by a Dec.-June-Dec. weighted average of total time deposits at member banks, 1927-33, and at insured banks, thereafter. No deductions were made for losses.

[a] No interest was paid on demand deposits at member banks after 1933.

[b] Not reported separately before 1933.

TABLE E-2

AVERAGE RATE OF INTEREST PAID BY MUTUAL SAVINGS BANKS, ANNUALLY, 1920-34 AND 1945-60
(per cent per annum)

1920	4.1	1945	1.6
1921	4.1	1946	1.6
1922	4.1	1947	1.6
1923	4.2	1948	1.7
1924	4.2	1949	1.8
1925	4.2	1950	1.9
1926	4.3	1951	2.0
1927	4.3	1952	2.3
1928	4.2	1953	2.4
1929	4.2	1954	2.5
1930	4.6	1955	2.6
1931	4.2	1956	2.8
1932	4.2	1957	2.9
1933	3.8	1958	3.1
1934	3.5	1959	3.2
		1960	3.4

Source: 1920-34: A weighted average of interest rates reported for each state, begun in 1920 and discontinued after 1934, in *Annual Report* of the Comptroller of the Currency. Earlier rates, which are comparable but not as accurate, are given in Cagan, *The Demand for Currency*, Table C.
1945-60: An average rate of interest for all mutual savings banks from The National Association of Mutual Savings Banks. (No comparable figures are available for 1935-44. Data given by the FDIC for that period are for insured banks only and are not representative.)

until the turn of the century and the rise, thereafter, until World War I. The rate paid by mutual savings banks shows the same pattern, though the magnitude of movement was smaller.[2] Commercial bank earnings were sufficient

[2] See Cagan, *The Demand for Currency Relative to Total Money Supply*, New York, NBER, Occasional Paper 62, 1958, p. 29. Fragmentary data on the rate paid by commercial banks on time and savings deposits (*ibid.*) are also consistent with this pattern though, for reasons given in footnote 5, below, these data seem unreliable.

The reserve ratio of commercial banks began a long-run decline around the turn of the century (Chapter 5), which had the small effect of raising earnings per dollar of deposits and allowing banks to pay more, but that would not have been a sufficient reason for a rise in the interest paid on deposits.

TABLE E-3

AVERAGE RATE OF INTEREST PAID ON DEPOSITS AT STATE AND
PRIVATE BANKS IN KANSAS, 1897-1927, AND AT ALL MEMBER
BANKS, 1919-26
(per cent per annum)

	Kansas Banks		Kansas Banks	Member Banks
1897	1.15[a]	1913	1.29	
1898	0.93	1914	1.49	
1899	0.77	1915	1.44	
1900	0.71	1916	1.45	
1901	0.56	1917	1.55	
1902	0.63	1918	1.53	
1903	0.63	1919	1.54	1.87
1904	0.71	1920	1.68	1.91
1905	0.73	1921	1.83	2.04
1906	0.76	1922	1.94	2.07
1907	0.79	1923	1.83	2.05
1908	0.90	1924	1.90	2.06
1909	0.86	1925	1.78	2.03
1910	0.94	1926	1.75	2.04
1911	1.05	1927	1.73	
1912	1.21			

Source: Biennial Report of the Bank Commissioner of
the State of Kansas and Banking and Monetary Statistics,
pp. 262-263.
Note: Interest rate was computed by dividing interest
paid on total deposits by a weighted average of total
deposits (including interbank deposits) on call dates.
[a]Not available before 1897.

on the average, therefore, to allow an increase in the rates paid on deposits
after 1905. The number of commercial banks increased rapidly in the decades
before and after the turn of the century and, from all indications, competition
for deposits intensified.

Confirmation is provided by data on state and private commercial banks
in Kansas, the only state that collected data on bank earnings and expenses
well before World War I (Table E-3). From 1897, when the reports started,
to 1902, the annual rate paid on all deposits fell. From 1902 to 1903, it stayed
the same and then began to rise, adding two-thirds of a percentage point by
1913 and just over a full point by 1920. For comparison, an average rate paid
on all deposits at member banks, which can be computed back to 1919, is
also shown.

The only comparable figure for earlier years is a lone statement of the
Comptroller of the Currency on the amount of interest paid by national banks
in 1870 which, divided by the total deposits of those banks, gives an average
rate of 1 per cent.[3] That is below the rate paid by member banks in the 1920's
and about equal to that paid by Kansas nonnational banks around 1897-98.

These pre-1919 data portray an uncertain picture. The Kansas data are

[3] *Annual Report*, 1870, p. xii; see also Cagan, *The Demand for Currency*, p. 24n.

not necessarily representative of all commercial banks, though they do agree fairly well in direction of change with rates paid by all member banks during the 1920's. Even if the average rate on all deposits did behave as previously described, however, there is no certainty that rates on demand deposits behaved the same way; the rates on time deposits may have produced most of the change in the total. The latter comprised only 12 per cent of total deposits at commercial banks in 1900 but grew in relative importance thereafter, reaching 30 per cent by 1915.[4] This means that the averages shown progressively understate the rate on time deposits. It is plausible but not certain that the two rates usually moved more or less together, as they did from 1927 to 1933, though they differed later partly because interest payments on demand deposits were prohibited. The evidence is admittedly hazy, therefore, and needs to be supplemented by more exact data on when and by how much the demand deposit rate rose.[5] Perhaps a more intensive search of early sources would turn up more than has so far been found. In the meantime the evidence suggests that the rate paid on time deposits (and perhaps also on large demand accounts) was constant or falling from 1890, or earlier, to around the turn of the century; and that it then rose appreciably until World War I and more slowly thereafter until 1929.

[4] See Chapter 5, sect. 1, subsect. Shifts Between Time and Demand Deposits.

[5] I have intentionally ignored one other piece of evidence: a rate of 2.35 per cent on demand deposits reported by the Comptroller of the Currency for national banks in 1910 (see *Annual Report*, 1910, p. 57). That figure is much higher than the data show for the 1920's and for 1870. (Although the 1870 rate of 1 per cent was an average for total deposits, we may assume that the demand rate was lower and the time rate, higher.) A rate of 2.35 per cent seems much too high compared with all the other data. This figure has puzzled me for a long time and I have finally concluded that it is unrepresentative and should be ignored. It seems to be an unweighted average of rates paid by reporting banks, and it very likely excludes banks or deposits that paid nothing—possibly a not inconsequential part of the total. In the Comptroller's survey (*Annual Report*, 1870), for example, one-third of the banks paid no interest. The 2.35 rate is probably typical, however, of the rate then paid on interbank deposits and large accounts.

APPENDIX F

TABLE F-1

CONTRIBUTIONS OF THE THREE DETERMINANTS TO MATCHED SPECIFIC CYCLES IN THE RATE OF CHANGE IN THE MONEY STOCK, 1877-1953
(per cent per year)

Matched Reference Cycles (trough to trough)	Specific Cycle Stage			AVERAGE RATE OF CHANGE IN MONEY STOCK Contributed by:			
	Number	Dates (end of month)		Total	High-Powered Money	Currency Ratio	Reserve Ratio
Mar. 1879-May 1885 (1)	I	Feb. 1877 - Aug. 1877		-7.5	0.6	-6.5	-1.5
	III	Aug. 1877 - Aug. 1888		7.8	8.3	0.0	-0.6
	V	Aug. 1880 - Feb. 1881		20.2	6.7	2.8	10.2
	VII	Feb. 1881 - June 1883		9.4	7.0	1.0	1.3
	IX, I }	June 1883 - June 1884		-1.7	0.4	0.0	-2.2
May 1885-Apr. 1888 (2)	III	June 1884 - June 1885		2.6	3.6	5.5	-6.2
	V	June 1885 - June 1886		8.3	-3.2	6.0	5.3
	VII	June 1886 - June 1887		6.2	5.1	0.5	0.4
	IX, I }	June 1887 - June 1888		2.5	4.0	-0.5	-0.8
Apr. 1888-May 1891 (3)	III	June 1888 - June 1889		5.3	0.7	2.8	1.7
	V	June 1889 - June 1890		9.8	3.5	0.9	5.3
	IX, I }	June 1890 - June 1891		2.8	4.8	-0.5	-1.7
May 1891-June 1894 (4)	V	June 1891 - June 1892		10.6	6.5	5.1	-0.9
	IX, I }	June 1892 - June 1893		-6.5	-1.0	-6.5	1.1
June 1894-June 1897 (5)	III	June 1893 - June 1894		0.9	3.5	5.9	-8.5
	V	June 1894 - June 1895		5.8	-4.4	2.8	7.3
	IX, I }	June 1895 - June 1896		-4.8	-7.2	0.5	1.9
June 1897-Dec. 1900 (6)	III	June 1896 - June 1898		9.3	10.4	-0.4	-0.9
	V	June 1898 - June 1899		16.1	4.8	5.6	5.6
	IX, I }	June 1899 - June 1900		5.5	7.9	-2.7	0.4
Dec. 1900-Aug. 1904 (7)	V	June 1900 - June 1901		14.0	5.7	5.5	2.5
	VII	June 1901 - June 1903		7.5	4.3	0.6	2.5
	IX, I }	June 1903 - June 1904		5.3	6.4	2.6	-3.7
Aug. 1904-June 1908 (8)	V	June 1904 - June 1905		11.4	2.7	3.4	5.4
	VII	June 1905 - Dec. 1907		3.4	8.3	-2.7	-2.1
	IX, I }	Nov. 1907 - Feb. 1908		-13.4	12.2	-8.7	-16.9
June 1908-Jan. 1912 (9)	II	Jan. 1908 - Apr. 1908		1.6	0.0	19.3	-18.0
	III	Apr. 1908 - July 1908		13.0	-3.6	11.3	5.2
	IV	July 1908 - Oct. 1908		13.4	-0.8	9.2	4.7
	V	Sept. 1908 - Dec. 1908		13.4	-0.8	3.3	10.9
	VI	Nov. 1908 - Apr. 1909		9.2	-0.7	5.5	4.3
	VII	Apr. 1909 - Oct. 1909		7.7	0.2	3.6	4.0
	VIII	Oct. 1909 - Mar. 1910		4.8	1.0	3.8	-0.2
	IX, I }	Feb. 1910 - May 1910		0.4	0.8	1.5	-1.4
Jan. 1912-Dec. 1914 (10)	II	Apr. 1910 - Oct. 1910		4.4	3.2	-1.9	2.9
	III	Oct. 1910 - Mar. 1911		4.3	4.5	5.0	-5.1
	IV	Mar. 1911 - Sept. 1911		6.5	0.2	2.9	3.2
	V	Aug. 1911 - Nov. 1911		9.9	0.8	8.5	0.5
	VI	Oct. 1911 - Apr. 1912		7.3	2.4	1.8	3.2
	VII	Apr. 1912 - Nov. 1912		5.7	1.0	1.3	3.3
	VIII	Nov. 1912 - May 1913		1.6	1.8	-2.4	2.0

(continued)

TABLE F-1 (continued)

Matched Reference Cycles (trough to trough)	Specific Cycle Stage		Total	AVERAGE RATE OF CHANGE IN MONEY STOCK Contributed by:		
	Number	Dates (end of month)		High-Powered Money	Currency Ratio	Reserve Ratio
Dec. 1914– Apr. 1919 (11)	IX } I }	Apr. 1913 – July 1913	-2.8	5.2	-0.7	-6.9
	II	June 1913 – Aug. 1914	4.3	2.9	1.7	-0.1
	III	Aug. 1914 – Sept. 1915	8.6	6.4	4.2	-1.9
	IV	Sept. 1915 – Nov. 1916	18.6	13.7	1.0	3.8
	V	Oct. 1916 – Jan. 1917	23.7	24.1	-1.1	0.6
	VI	Dec. 1916 – May 1917	15.6	23.5	-12.1	4.0
	VII	May 1917 – Nov. 1917	6.3	19.8	-12.6	-1.1
	VIII	Nov. 1917 – Apr. 1918	12.6	19.4	-6.2	-0.8
Apr. 1919– July 1921 (12)	IX } I }	Mar. 1918 – June 1918	-1.6	5.6	-13.1	5.6
	II	May 1918 – July 1918	17.7	13.6	-17.1	21.4
	III	July 1918 – Sept. 1918	31.0	44.0	-12.5	0.0
	IV	Sept. 1918 – Nov. 1918	1.2	2.4	-5.0	3.6
	V	Oct. 1918 – Jan. 1919	23.7	-13.4	20.8	16.0
	VI	Dec. 1918 – Aug. 1919	12.7	2.4	9.7	0.4
	VII	Aug. 1919 – Apr. 1920	15.0	12.8	-1.3	3.4
	VIII	Apr. 1920 – Dec. 1920	-0.8	0.6	-1.8	1.6
July 1921– July 1924 (13)	IX } I }	Nov. 1920 – Feb. 1921	-6.0	-17.2	10.3	0.7
	II	Jan. 1921 – June 1921	-11.6	-15.1	2.8	0.7
	III	June 1921 – Oct. 1921	-3.6	-14.1	9.0	1.8
	IV	Oct. 1921 – Mar. 1922	1.9	-1.4	7.5	-3.9
	V	Feb. 1922 – May 1922	14.5	7.9	8.0	-1.6
	VI	Apr. 1922 – Sept. 1922	11.7	5.5	2.7	3.4
	VII	Sept. 1922 – Jan. 1923	9.2	8.6	4.0	-3.5
	VIII	Jan. 1923 – June 1923	6.2	5.7	-5.7	6.2
July 1924– Nov. 1927 (14)	IX } I }	May 1923 – Aug. 1923	-1.2	3.2	-3.1	-1.6
	II	July 1923 – Mar. 1924	3.1	2.7	1.8	-1.3
	III	Mar. 1924 – Nov. 1924	11.1	5.0	6.8	-0.6
	IV	Nov. 1924 – July 1925	6.9	0.1	3.2	3.6
	V	June 1925 – Sept. 1925	10.3	5.0	6.5	-0.7
	VI	Aug. 1925 – Jan. 1926	3.8	3.1	0.6	0.1
	VII	Jan. 1926 – June 1926	2.9	0.7	0.7	1.1
	VIII	June 1926 – Nov. 1926	-1.7	-2.7	0.0	1.1
Nov. 1927– Mar. 1933 (15)	IX } I }	Oct. 1926 – Jan. 1927	0.0	0.0	-0.7	0.9
	II	Dec. 1926 – Mar. 1927	9.5	6.7	3.5	-0.7
	III	Mar. 1927 – July 1927	3.9	-0.6	3.7	0.7
	IV	July 1927 – Oct. 1927	2.0	-3.2	4.0	0.9
	V	Sept. 1927 – Dec. 1927	2.8	-0.8	5.7	-1.9
	VI	Nov. 1927 – Feb. 1929	1.3	-0.1	0.6	0.7
	VII	Feb. 1929 – June 1930	-1.6	-2.6	1.0	0.0
	VIII	June 1930 – Sept. 1931	-8.2	6.8	-10.6	-4.4
Mar. 1933– June 1938 (16)	IX } I }	Aug. 1931 – Nov. 1931	-31.4	4.7	-33.1	-2.6
	II	Oct. 1931 – Apr. 1933	-18.7	4.5	-15.9	-7.5
	III	Apr. 1933 – Sept. 1934	10.3	13.3	7.0	-10.2
	IV	Sept. 1934 – Mar. 1936	12.3	12.7	2.7	-3.2
	V	Feb. 1936 – May 1936	16.5	1.6	4.4	10.5
	VI	Apr. 1936 – Oct. 1936	11.1	22.8	-0.3	-11.5
	VII	Oct. 1936 – Mar. 1937	6.9	9.4	-0.2	-2.4
	VIII	Mar. 1937 – Sept. 1937	-1.6	1.8	-2.0	-1.2

(continued)

TABLE F-1 (concluded)

| Matched Reference Cycles (trough to trough) | Specific Cycle Stage | | | AVERAGE RATE OF CHANGE IN MONEY STOCK | | | |
| | | | | | Contributed by: | | |
	Number	Dates (end of month)		Total	High-Powered Money	Currency Ratio	Reserve Ratio
	IX	Aug. 1937 – Nov. 1937		-8.5	2.0	-1.8	-8.6
June 1938–	I						
Oct. 1949	II	Oct. 1937 – Aug. 1939		5.8	17.2	0.4	-11.8
(17)	III	Aug. 1939 – July 1941		12.3	12.4	-1.1	1.0
	IV	July 1941 – May 1943		17.6	11.7	-5.7	11.7
	V	Apr. 1943 – July 1943		37.4	17.6	2.0	17.7
	VI	June 1943 – Apr. 1945		17.4	18.1	-3.1	2.4
	VII	Apr. 1945 – Jan. 1947		7.8	4.1	2.1	1.5
	VIII	Jan. 1947 – Nov. 1948		0.9	3.6	1.4	-4.1
	IX	Oct. 1948 – Jan. 1949		-1.2	-5.2	0.8	2.9
Oct. 1949–	I						
Aug. 1954	II	Dec. 1948 – Oct. 1949		-0.2	-11.2	1.0	10.0
(18)	III	Oct. 1949 – Aug. 1950		3.7	0.8	2.5	0.3
	IV	Aug. 1950 – June 1951		3.1	7.6	0.1	-4.5
	V	May 1951 – Aug. 1951		8.3	6.1	0.9	0.6
	VI	July 1951 – Apr. 1952		5.7	5.6	0.4	-0.4
	VII	Apr. 1952 – Jan. 1953		4.1	3.3	-0.2	1.0
	VIII	Jan. 1953 – Oct. 1953		3.2	-0.8	0.7	3.2
	IX	Sept. 1953 – Dec. 1953		2.8	0.8	1.9	-0.2

AVERAGES

10, 1877–1913	I			-1.7	2.9	-2.1	-2.5
	III			6.2	3.9	4.3	-2.1
	V			12.0	2.2	4.4	5.2
	VII			6.7	4.3	0.7	1.6
	IX			-1.3	3.4	-1.5	-3.0
6 nonwar, 1918-53	I			-6.9	-1.5	-6.5	1.0
	II			0.0	0.2	-4.0	3.8
	III			9.4	8.1	2.8	-1.3
	IV			4.6	3.0	2.1	-0.6
	V			12.7	1.1	7.7	3.8
	VI			7.7	6.6	2.3	-1.2
	VII			6.1	5.4	0.7	-0.1
	VIII			-0.5	1.7	-3.2	1.1
	IX			-7.4	-1.1	-4.4	-1.9
6 most severe, 1877-1953	I			-5.4	3.7	-8.5	-0.5
	III			13.2	16.2	-0.4	-2.5
	V			14.2	0.6	7.0	6.6
	VII			6.6	6.9	-0.4	0.0
	IX			-11.2	0.2	-6.6	-4.8
10 mild non-war, 1877-1953	I			-2.6	-0.2	-0.8	-1.6
	III			5.2	1.2	5.4	-1.4
	V			11.0	2.5	4.8	3.6
	VII			6.2	3.3	1.5	1.3
	IX			1.0	2.6	-0.2	-1.3

NOTES TO TABLE F-1

Source: Milton Friedman and Anna Jacobson Schwartz, <u>A Monetary History of the United States, 1867-1960</u>, Princeton for NBER, 1963, Tables A-1 and B-3, except that the data here exclude from bank reserves vault cash at mutual savings banks and do not incorporate minor later revisions made in the Friedman and Schwartz estimates.

Vault cash at mutual savings banks was excluded from currency outside banks (inadvertently) and from reserves of commercial banks (correctly), whereas it is included in high-powered money (correctly). Hence the relation shown by the formula does not hold exactly, though the error on this account is small. For this reason and also because of rounding and approximation error, the total rate may not equal exactly the sum of the other three columns.

Note: Specific cycle dates and matched reference cycles: Based on an earlier version of Table 1. The differences are as follows: For Table F-1, a peak is dated in Nov. 1880 instead of May 1881, as in Table 1, a peak in Nov. 1908 instead of Oct. 1908, a trough in July 1923 instead of June 1923, a peak in Aug. 1925 instead of Aug. 1924, a trough in Dec. 1948 instead of Jan. 1949, a peak in July 1951 instead of Nov. 1951, and a trough in Nov. 1953 instead of Sept. 1953. A few of these changes are large, but over-all they would not greatly affect the tables in Chapter 2.

The nonmatched phases in Table 1 are suppressed here; that is, the Feb.-Oct. 1941 specific cycle contraction was suppressed and the period from Oct. 1937 to June 1943 was treated as one expansion matched with the 1938-45 reference expansion. (Also, there is no specific cycle to match the reference cycle, with trough in Oct. 1945 and peak in Nov. 1948. Consequently, the June 1943-Dec. 1948 specific cycle contraction was matched with a reference cycle contraction assumed to run from Feb. 1945 to Oct. 1949 by suppressing the short 1945 contraction.)

The specific cycle dates shown are for the money-stock figures used to compute the rates of change. (Table 1 gives the corresponding peak and trough dates for the rate-of-change series.) The specific cycle stages were dated by the usual National Bureau procedure. Stages II, III, and IV divide into thirds the expansion phase between the peak and trough in the rate of change; and stages VI, VII, and VIII divide into thirds the contraction phase. The rates for peak and trough stages in the monthly data are derived from the four end-of-month dates surrounding the mid-month rate-of-change peak or trough month (hence are based on the rates of change for the three months surrounding the peak or trough month) and so overlap the adjacent stages. For the annual and semiannual data, stages II, IV, VI, and VIII were omitted, and sometimes also stage III or VII, if too short to be computed satisfactorily with these data.

Rates of change: Computed by formula 2 in Chap. 2. The four differentials,

$$\frac{d\,\log_e H}{dt} \ , \ \frac{d\,\log_e H}{dt} \ , \ d\,\frac{C}{M} \ , \ d\,\frac{R}{D} \ ,$$

in the formula were approximated for finite periods by numerical changes in C/M and R/D and in the natural logarithms of M and H (hence the rates for the latter two are compounded instantaneously). The factors M/H (1-C/M) and M/H (1- R/D) were approximated by averages of the beginning and ending values of the factors for each stage.

Averages at end of table: An arithmetic average of the relevant cycles for which a figure for the stage had been computed. War cycles are numbers 11 and 17; the six severe cycles are numbers 1, 4, 8, 12, 15, and 16. These are the matched reference contractions ranked in Table 1 as the 6 most severe by an average of three indexes of business activity (see <u>Business Cycle Indicators</u>, G. H. Moore, Ed., 1961, Vol. I, p. 104). All others are mild nonwar cycles. The sixth most severe reference contraction, 1882-85, is a marginal one, but is considerably more severe by Moore's rankings than the seventh most severe, 1895-97 (and even ranks slightly ahead of the protracted 1873-79 decline).

TABLE F-2

CONTRIBUTIONS OF THE THREE DETERMINANTS TO NONWAR REFERENCE CYCLE
PATTERNS OF THE RATE OF CHANGE IN THE MONEY STOCK, 1878-1961
(per cent per year)

| | | | AVERAGE RATE OF CHANGE IN THE MONEY STOCK | | |
| | | | | Contributed by: | |
Reference Cycle Stages		Total	High-Powered Money	Currency Ratio	Reserve Ratio
			FISCAL-YEAR DATA		
1878-85	I	-12.2	-5.6	-3.7	-2.9
	II	5.0	-0.5	1.6	4.0
(1)	III	5.8	11.0	-1.3	-4.0
	IV	11.9	6.9	-0.2	5.3
	V	-3.8	-5.4	0.5	1.1
	VII	-5.0	-3.8	-0.5	-0.7
	IX	-5.6	-3.0	4.4	-7.0
Cycle Average		8.2	6.6	1.2	0.5
1885-88	I	-3.0	1.7	2.5	-7.3
	III	2.6	-5.0	3.0	4.7
(2)	V	0.5	3.1	-2.5	-0.2
	IX	-3.1	2.2	-3.5	-1.9
Cycle Average		5.7	1.9	3.0	0.8
1888-91	I	-3.4	1.2	-1.6	-3.0
	III	-0.6	-2.2	1.7	-0.1
(3)	V	3.9	0.7	-0.1	3.4
	IX	-3.2	1.9	-1.6	-3.4
Cycle Average		5.9	2.9	1.1	1.9
1891-94	I	0.8	1.6	-0.9	0.1
	III	8.7	3.2	4.7	0.7
(4)	V	-8.5	-4.2	-6.9	2.6
	IX	-1.2	0.4	5.4	-6.8
Cycle Average		2.0	3.2	0.5	-1.7
1894-97	I	-0.4	5.4	3.8	-9.5
	III	4.5	-2.5	0.7	6.3
(5)	V	-6.1	-5.3	-1.6	0.8
	IX	3.6	10.3	-2.1	-4.7
Cycle Average		1.3	-1.8	2.1	1.0
1897-1901	I	-6.3	0.5	-1.2	-5.7
	III	3.7	0.5	1.2	2.0
(6)	V	-5.7	-0.1	-4.0	-1.6
	IX	2.8	-2.2	4.3	0.8
Cycle Average		11.2	8.0	1.2	2.0
1901-04	I	5.8	0.9	3.8	1.2
	III	0.5	-1.4	0.8	1.2
(7)	V	-2.0	0.3	-3.2	0.8
	IX	-2.9	1.5	0.9	-5.3
Cycle Average		8.2	4.9	1.7	1.6
1904-08	I	-0.1	0.2	2.3	-2.6
	II	6.0	-3.6	3.0	6.6
(8)	III	2.2	0.0	-0.3	2.4
	IV	2.0	2.3	-1.0	0.7

(continued)

TABLE F-2 (continued)

| | | AVERAGE RATE OF CHANGE IN THE MONEY STOCK | | |
| | | | Contributed by: | |
Reference Cycle Stages	Total	High-Powered Money	Currency Ratio	Reserve Ratio
		MONTHLY DATA		
V	-8.1	-10.0	8.1	-6.2
VI	-12.7	-9.0	3.7	-7.5
VII	-17.8	22.1	-30.2	-9.8
VIII	-0.5	-9.4	17.4	-8.5
IX	8.2	-7.8	9.6	6.2
Cycle Average	5.4	6.2	0.4	-1.2
1908-12 I	6.2	-3.6	6.5	3.3
II	5.8	-0.5	2.9	3.4
(9) III	2.3	0.4	2.5	-0.6
IV	-0.7	-2.4	-1.7	3.3
V	-2.7	-1.8	-1.5	0.7
VI	-4.0	1.8	-3.5	-2.2
VII	-0.2	1.3	-0.9	-0.6
VIII	-0.9	-1.1	2.6	-2.4
IX	-0.5	0.8	0.2	-1.7
Cycle Average	7.3	2.1	3.5	1.7
1912-14 I	2.7	0.8	3.5	-1.6
II	2.6	1.7	-6.8	7.7
(10) III	1.3	-2.7	2.1	2.1
IV	0.5	0.5	2.9	-2.9
V	-0.4	0.6	-0.3	-0.7
VI	-2.7	-0.6	-1.5	-0.6
VII	0.5	-1.9	6.0	-3.6
VIII	-0.1	4.9	-4.0	-1.0
IX	-5.7	-24.7	16.1	2.8
Cycle Average	4.1	2.1	0.3	1.6
1919-21 I	9.8	6.2	5.8	-2.1
II	8.2	3.0	7.9	-2.7
(11) III	15.9	8.9	2.6	4.3
IV	15.3	11.5	-2.4	6.3
V	8.2	10.2	-4.8	3.0
VI	2.1	9.3	-6.6	-0.6
VII	-5.7	-3.1	-2.4	-0.3
VIII	-18.1	-18.6	2.0	-1.4
IX	-12.7	-16.5	4.0	-0.1
Cycle Average	4.3	0.4	2.0	1.9
1921-24 I	-14.2	-18.0	2.4	1.4
II	-5.1	-10.8	6.1	-0.4
(12) III	6.8	4.1	0.5	2.2
IV	2.4	4.7	-3.4	1.1
V	0.8	1.6	-7.4	6.6
VI	-4.8	1.1	-4.8	-1.1
VII	-2.9	-0.9	-0.5	-1.5
VIII	1.8	1.6	1.0	-0.7
IX	7.2	3.5	8.0	-4.2
Cycle Average	5.9	1.9	3.6	0.4

(continued)

TABLE F-2 (continued)

| | | | AVERAGE RATE OF CHANGE IN THE MONEY STOCK | | |
| | | | | Contributed by: | |
Reference Cycle Stages		Total	High-Powered Money	Currency Ratio	Reserve Ratio
			MONTHLY DATA		
1924-27	I	8.0	4.3	8.8	-4.9
	II	3.5	0.2	1.4	2.0
(13)	III	2.3	2.7	0.3	-0.7
	IV	-3.7	-1.4	-2.3	0.0
	V	-6.9	-5.3	-2.1	0.4
	VI	-1.8	-1.5	-1.9	1.5
	VII	-1.0	5.3	1.1	-7.4
	VIII	-2.0	-5.0	0.5	2.4
	IX	-2.2	-2.1	3.0	-3.3
Cycle Average		5.0	1.1	2.8	1.2
1927-33	I	9.8	-4.4	13.1	1.0
	II	7.9	-3.4	6.1	5.1
(14)	III	10.0	-4.4	11.2	3.2
	IV	6.3	-3.4	5.9	3.8
	V	10.5	-5.0	13.8	1.9
	VI	4.6	-7.6	9.9	2.4
	VII	-9.2	7.3	-11.9	-4.6
	VIII	-4.7	7.6	-8.3	-4.1
	IX	-48.4	-13.1	-32.7	-2.5
Cycle Average		-6.9	3.5	-7.3	-3.1
1933-38	I	-61.8	-19.5	-43.3	1.0
	II	2.0	-1.4	8.0	-4.7
(15)	III	6.4	4.7	0.2	1.6
	IV	2.3	1.8	-3.4	3.9
	V	-8.8	-10.6	-4.8	6.6
	VI	-6.8	-6.9	-5.4	5.4
	VII	-12.3	-8.7	-3.1	-0.5
	VIII	-8.6	3.1	-3.3	-8.4
	IX	-6.7	6.7	-3.8	-9.6
Cycle Average		6.5	9.9	3.3	-6.6
1945-49	I	9.9	7.4	3.0	-0.6
	II	3.9	2.2	1.2	0.5
(16)	III	1.4	1.7	0.2	-0.3
	IV	-2.7	5.3	-0.8	-7.3
	V	-4.2	6.8	-1.0	-9.7
	VI	-4.2	-2.7	-0.4	-1.3
	VII	-2.0	-9.8	-0.9	9.0
	VIII	-3.4	-19.8	-0.6	16.4
	IX	-3.4	-11.1	-0.5	7.9
Cycle Average		2.6	0.1	1.7	0.8

(continued)

TABLE F-2 (concluded)

Reference Cycle Stages		Total	AVERAGE RATE OF CHANGE IN THE MONEY STOCK		
			Contributed by:		
			High-Powered Money	Currency Ratio	Reserve Ratio
MONTHLY DATA					
1949–54	I	−4.7	−13.2	0.1	8.2
	II	−0.6	−0.3	0.9	−1.3
(17)	III	1.4	4.6	−0.7	−2.7
	IV	0.1	0.9	−1.1	0.6
	V	−1.2	−3.9	−0.5	3.0
	VI	−1.5	−2.3	0.0	0.9
	VII	−1.1	−4.1	1.4	1.4
	VIII	0.3	−4.7	1.4	3.6
	IX	1.0	−12.1	2.8	10.5
Cycle Average		3.8	2.3	1.1	0.5
1954–58	I	1.9	−10.2	2.9	9.5
	II	0.6	0.3	0.3	0.0
(18)	III	−1.2	0.1	−0.9	−0.3
	IV	0.2	1.0	−0.1	−0.8
	V	−0.1	−1.1	0.3	0.3
	VI	−1.0	−0.3	0.0	−0.3
	VII	−3.5	0.9	−1.5	−2.3
	VIII	3.6	−1.2	2.3	2.2
	IX	5.7	−4.4	2.6	7.7
Cycle Average		2.9	0.3	1.0	1.5
1958–61	I	5.5	−3.1	2.4	6.5
	II	3.0	1.6	1.1	0.4
(19)	III	0.1	3.1	−0.7	−2.4
	IV	−4.3	−0.9	−1.8	−1.6
	V	−3.1	0.9	−0.6	−3.7
	VI	0.6	1.8	1.3	−2.2
	VII	3.5	−4.0	1.3	5.8
	VIII	−0.1	−10.7	1.2	9.6
	IX	4.6	6.8	2.9	−5.7
Cycle Average		3.1	−0.9	1.2	2.8
AVERAGES					
7 mild	I	0.2	1.0	2.5	−3.2
cycles	III	2.0	−1.8	1.7	2.2
1878–1914	V	−1.8	−0.4	−1.9	0.5
	IX	−1.3	−1.5	2.0	−1.9
6 mild	I	1.1	−5.5	3.3	3.4
cycles	II	0.9	−1.1	1.8	0.2
1919–61	III	1.8	2.7	−0.2	−0.7
	IV	−1.3	1.6	−1.6	−1.3
	V	−2.4	−0.2	−1.9	−0.5
	VI	−2.1	−0.6	−1.0	−0.4
	VII	−1.2	−2.1	0.2	0.8
	VIII	0.0	−6.6	1.0	5.6
	IX	2.2	−3.2	3.1	2.2

NOTES TO TABLE F-2

Source: Friedman and Schwartz, <u>A Monetary History</u>, Tables A-1 and
B-3, extended to 1961. These data differ slightly from those used for
Table F-1.

Note: These patterns are numerical deviations from cycle averages.
Add the cycle average to derive the actual rates of change. Because
of rounding and approximation error, the total rate may not equal
exactly the sum of the other three columns.

Rates of change: Computed the same way as for Table F-1, except that
the rates of change were first computed for each year or month and then
averaged for the reference cycle stages. Although semiannual data are
available before 1882, cycle 1 is based on Jan. figures only, centered
on preceding Dec.

Mild cycles: Same as for Table F-1.

TABLE F-3
CONTRIBUTIONS OF THE THREE DETERMINANTS TO STEP CYCLES IN
THE RATE OF CHANGE IN THE MONEY STOCK, 1877-1954
(per cent per year)

| | | | | AVERAGE RATE OF CHANGE IN THE MONEY STOCK | | |
| | | | | | Contributed by: | |
Step Cycle Phase			Total	High-Powered Money	Currency Ratio	Reserve Ratio
Expansion	Feb.	1879 – Aug. 1881	19.3	15.7	1.2	2.1
Contraction	Aug.	1881 – June 1885	3.3	2.7	2.1	-1.4
Expansion	June	1885 – June 1887	7.2	0.9	3.3	2.8
Contraction	June	1887 – June 1888	2.5	4.0	-0.5	-0.8
Expansion	June	1888 – June 1890	7.5	2.2	1.9	3.4
Contraction	June	1890 – June 1891	2.8	4.8	-0.5	-1.7
Expansion	June	1891 – June 1892	10.6	6.5	5.1	-0.9
Contraction	June	1892 – June 1893	-6.5	-1.0	-6.5	1.1
Expansion	June	1893 – June 1895	3.3	-0.4	4.6	-0.9
Contraction	June	1895 – June 1896	-4.8	-7.2	0.5	1.9
Expansion	June	1896 – June 1899	11.5	8.5	1.6	1.3
Contraction	June	1899 – June 1900	5.5	7.9	-2.7	0.4
Expansion	June	1900 – June 1901	14.0	5.7	5.5	2.5
Contraction	June	1901 – June 1904	6.8	5.0	1.2	0.5
Expansion	June	1904 – June 1907	8.4	5.2	1.1	2.1
Contraction	June	1907 – Feb. 1908	-11.4	12.2	-9.3	-14.3
Expansion	Feb.	1908 – Aug. 1909	10.8	-0.9	9.1	2.6
Contraction	Aug.	1909 – Aug. 1910	2.6	1.3	1.0	0.2
Expansion	Aug.	1910 – June 1912	7.1	1.4	2.4	3.3
Contraction	June	1912 – July 1913[a]	2.2	2.5	0.5	-0.8
Expansion	July	1913 – May 1914[a]	6.1	3.0	3.9	-0.7
Contraction	May	1914 – Dec. 1914[a]	1.4	-3.6	-0.4	5.4
Expansion	Dec.	1914 – July 1917	15.8	15.7	-0.2	0.2
Contraction	July	1917 – Aug. 1918	7.8	18.9	-13.6	2.4
Expansion	Aug.	1918 – Mar. 1920	17.0	9.0	5.0	3.0
Contraction	Mar.	1920 – July 1921	-6.1	-7.7	0.8	0.9
Expansion	July	1921 – May 1923	7.3	1.8	4.2	1.3
Contraction	May	1923 – Feb. 1924	1.9	1.9	1.0	-1.1
Expansion	Feb.	1924 – Sept. 1925	9.3	2.5	5.2	1.6
Contraction	Sept.	1925 – Dec. 1926	0.2	0.6	-0.7	0.2
Expansion	Dec.	1926 – Apr. 1928	6.1	1.3	4.1	0.8
Contraction	Apr.	1928 – Apr. 1933	-9.0	2.3	-8.4	-3.4
Expansion	Apr.	1933 – July 1936	12.1	14.1	4.5	-6.7
Contraction	July	1936 – May 1938	0.4	8.0	-0.6	-7.0
Expansion	May	1938 – Sept. 1945	14.9	15.0	-2.5	2.4
Contraction	Sept.	1945 – Oct. 1949[a]	2.3	0.0	1.8	0.5
Expansion	Oct.	1949 – Aug. 1952	4.4	4.5	1.0	-1.1
Contraction	Aug.	1952 – June 1954	2.9	-0.4	0.8	2.6

NOTES TO TABLE F-3

Source: Step cycle dates were derived by Friedman and Schwartz (see
Table 1 of "Money and Business Cycles"). The published dates have been revised from those used above. The differences are as follows: The Aug. 1909
peak has been revised to June 1909, the Aug. 1918 trough to May 1918, the
Feb. 1924 trough to Mar. 1924, the Sept. 1945 peak to Oct. 1945, the
Oct. 1949 trough to Jan. 1950, the Aug. 1952 peak to Dec. 1952, and the June
1954 trough to April 1954.
    Rates of change were computed by the method described for Table F-1.

[a]July 1913 trough and May 1914 peak in step cycles do not correspond to
reference cycles. All others do, though there is no step cycle corresponding to a reference cycle trough in Oct. 1945 and peak in Nov. 1948.

TABLE F-4

CONTRIBUTIONS OF THE THREE DETERMINANTS TO SECULAR MOVEMENTS IN
THE MONEY STOCK, 1877-1953: AVERAGE RATE OF CHANGE BETWEEN
SPECIFIC CYCLE BASES CENTERED AT PEAKS
(per cent per year)

| | AVERAGE RATE OF CHANGE IN THE MONEY STOCK | | | |
| | | Contributed by: | | |
Period Between Specific Cycle Bases, Centered at Peaks	Total	High-Powered Money	Currency Ratio	Reserve Ratio
Nov. 1880 – Dec. 1885	6.8	4.7	2.0	0.1
Dec. 1885 – Dec. 1889	4.7	2.2	1.7	0.8
Dec. 1889 – Dec. 1891	8.1	5.3	1.8	1.0
Dec. 1891 – Dec. 1894	0.5	1.1	0.4	-1.0
Dec. 1894 – Dec. 1898	3.6	1.4	1.4	0.8
Dec. 1898 – Dec. 1900	20.7	13.3	3.1	4.3
Dec. 1900 – Dec. 1904	7.9	5.3	1.6	1.0
Dec. 1904 – Nov. 1908	3.7	3.8	1.3	-1.5
Nov. 1908 – Oct. 1911	5.6	1.0	2.8	1.8
Oct. 1911 – Dec. 1916	6.1	4.5	0.9	0.7
Dec. 1916 – Dec. 1918	23.3	25.1	-5.1	3.4
Dec. 1918 – Apr. 1922	2.4	-1.5	2.6	1.3
Apr. 1922 – Aug. 1925	5.5	2.4	2.4	0.7
Aug. 1925 – Nov. 1927	4.7	0.9	2.9	0.9
Nov. 1927 – Apr. 1936	-2.0	4.5	-2.8	-4.0
Apr. 1936 – June 1943	12.3	15.8	-1.2	-2.4
June 1943 – July 1951	6.6	5.0	-0.1	1.7

Source: Rates of change were computed by the approximation to
formula 2 in Chap. 2 (and hence are compounded continuously), between average levels of the money stock and the determinants from
the initial to the terminal trough of each matched specific cycle
and centered at the specific cycle peak. The data and specific
cycle dates are the same as for Table F-1. Total may not equal
sum of other cols. because of rounding and approximation error.
(Comparable figures on a reference cycle basis are given in
Table 28.)

TABLE F-5

SOURCES OF CHANGE IN HIGH-POWERED MONEY, FISCAL YEARS, 1876-1955
(millions of dollars)

Year Ending June 30	Total (1)	Monetary Gold Stock (2)	Federal Reserve Operations (3)	National Bank Notes (4)	SOURCES OF CHANGE IN HIGH-POWERED MONEY					
							Treasury Operations			
					Silver Purchases (5)	Total Excluding Silver (6)	Budget (7)	Public Debt (8)	Deposits at Banks (9)	Miscellaneous Accounts (10)
1876	-20	10		-24	11	-17	-29	20	-4	-4
1877	5	33		-4	12	-36	-40	-14	0	18
1878	5	44		9	20	-68	-21	-72	40	-15
1879	18	34		9	22	-47	-7	-138	161	-63
1880	159	106		10	25	18	-66	207	-200	77
1881	135	123		-6	23	-5	-100	85	4	6
1882	52	24		-3	24	7	-146	166	0	-13
1883	59	34		3	26	-4	-133	134	1	-6
1884	6	2		-17	24	-3	-104	100	1	0
1885	45	42		-25	24	4	-63	46	-3	24
1886	-41	0		-26	23	-38	-94	45	6	5
1887	68	60		-72	26	54	-103	128	7	22
1888	49	50		-15	24	-10	-111	75	35	-9
1889	9	-26		-26	25	36	-88	121	-11	14
1890	47	15		-3	27	8	-85	105	-17	5
1891	67	-53		-2	54	68	-27	101	-4	-2
1892	96	11		17	51	17	-10	24	-12	15
1893	-10	-79		13	46	10	-2	1	0	11
1894	50	28		17	9	-4	61	-50	0	-15
1895	-68	0		6	0	-74	31	-81	1	-25
1896	-102	-45		21	0	-78	14	-131	1	38
1897	126	89		-2	0	39	18	0	0	21
1898	197	163		-8	0	42	38	0	23	-19
1899	83	105		10	0	-32	89	-199	38	40
1900	122	57		66	1	-2	-46	23	22	-1
1901	116	85		53	0	-22	-63	36	1	4
1902	70	66		-9	0	13	-77	56	24	10
1903	116	55		53	0	8	-45	17	28	8
1904	145	76		39	0	30	43	18	-35	4
1905	70	28		51	0	-9	23	1	-40	7
1906	147	116		58	0	-27	-25	0	17	-19
1907	172	124		38	8	2	-87	0	88	1
1908	264	152		64	10	38	57	-6	-19	6
1909	61	24		29	3	5	89	-15	-88	19
1910	13	-6		33	1	-15	18	1	-19	-15
1911	118	117		10	1	-10	-11	-2	-4	7
1912	47	65		24	3	-45	-3	-48	2	4
1913	92	53		13	1	25	0	-2	27	0
1914	32	20		0	7	5	0	-2	9	-2
1915	178	95	11	0	6	66	63	-2	-8	13

(continued)

TABLE F-5 (concluded)

SOURCES OF CHANGE IN HIGH-POWERED MONEY

Year Ending June 30	Total (1)	Monetary Gold Stock (2)	Federal Reserve Operations (3)	National Bank Notes (4)	Treasury Operations					Miscellaneous Accounts (10)
					Silver Purchases (5)	Total Excluding Silver (6)	Budget (7)	Public Debt (8)	Deposits at Banks (9)	
1916	466	459	131	-46	7	-85	-48	-2	-21	-14
1917	919	775	296	-15	8	-145	853	-1,754	782	-26
1918	824	-57	748	21	34	78	9,032	-9,279	736	-411
1919	629	-50	955	-4	-193	-89	13,363	-13,240	-492	280
1920	677	-248	763	11	-19	169	-291	1,176	-649	-67
1921	-672	410	-1,118	16	66	-46	-509	320	145	-2
1922	-205	510	-845	22	57	51	-736	1,014	-248	21
1923	365	265	-42	-6	70	78	-713	630	147	14
1924	162	438	-283	10	20	-23	-963	1,094	-120	-34
1925	73	-128	187	-81	3	92	-717	770	-3	42
1926	173	87	86	3	5	-8	-865	844	53	-40
1927	90	140	-32	0	5	-23	-1,155	1,130	-2	4
1928	-58	-478	400	-2	4	18	-939	904	41	12
1929	-61	215	-262	0	2	-16	-734	673	101	-56
1930	-172	211	-409	3	3	20	-738	736	-76	98
1931	366	421	-4	-13	1	-39	462	-618	148	-31
1932	469	-1,037	1,409	13	1	83	2,735	-2,650	-14	12
1933	184	399	-263	78	1	-31	2,602	-3,002	425	-56
1934	1,601	1,040	332	-32	47	214	3,630	-4,311	862	33
1935	1,440	1,239	-39	-476	202	514	2,791	-1,341	-896	23
1936	968	1,551	-286	-222	396	-471	4,425	-5,282	327	59
1937	1,794	1,820	392		125	-543	2,777	-2,760	-482	-78
1938	1,142	520	-40		202	460	1,177	-799	-74	156
1939	2,688	3,188	-272		195	-423	3,862	-3,311	196	-1,170
1940	4,496	3,854	-564		122	1,084	3,918	-2,553	35	-316
1941	1,054	2,664	-882		83	-811	6,159	-6,011	-75	-884
1942	2,134	46	1,098		70	920	21,490	-23,474	1,086	1,818
1943	4,222	-360	4,076		12	494	57,420	-63,454	6,185	343
1944	6,123	-1,205	7,559		-29	-202	51,423	-64,223	11,489	1,109
1945	5,859	-900	6,741		-48	66	53,941	-56,881	4,875	-1,869
1946	2,595	47	2,376		-40	212	20,676	-11,862	-10,964	2,362
1947	221	1,076	-1,790		17	918	-754	13,143	-12,057	586
1948	952	2,323	-128		31	-1,274	-8,419	5,001	813	1,331
1949	242	897	-2,224		33	1,536	1,811	-663	124	264
1950	-2,447	-306	-1,712		37	-466	3,122	-4,468	1,497	-617
1951	3,185	-2,459	4,979		33	632	-3,510	2,110	2,531	-499
1952	2,075	1,660	419		35	-39	4,017	-3,918	-211	73
1953	1,503	-1,011	2,081		32	401	9,449	-6,963	-2,179	94
1954	-1,316	-494	-584		31	-269	3,117	-5,102	1,953	-237
1955	-264	-297	-538		32	539	4,180	-2,983	-477	-181

Note: For schematic description, see Table 9.

NOTES TO TABLE F-5

Source, by Column

(1): Change in currency outside the Treasury and Federal Reserve Banks, less national bank notes in vaults of issuing banks, plus deposits of commercial banks with Federal Reserve Banks. This series differs slightly from that in Friedman and Schwartz, A Monetary History, Table B-3, chiefly because of no seasonal adjustment and no adjustment for gold correction (see col. 2 and col. 1, c, below). The quantity of high-powered money outstanding at the beginning of each fiscal year is shown in Table F-6, col. 7, and was derived by adding:

a. National bank notes secured by lawful money (the difference between national bank notes in circulation and national bank notes secured by U.S. bonds): Historical Statistics of the United States, 1789-1945, Bureau of the Census, 1949 (Historical Statistics, 1949), Series N-165, p. 275; and Annual Report, Comptroller of the Currency, 1908, pp. 123-129; 1926, pp. 138-140; 1931, pp. 178-179; 1934, p. 176; 1935, p. 184.

b. Note liabilities of national banks: 1875-1918: Annual Report, Comptroller of the Currency, 1918, Vol. II, pp. 254 ff.; values interpolated between closest June call dates in years for which national banks did not report on June 30th. 1919-35: Historical Statistics, 1949, Series N-33, p. 263.

c. Treasury and Federal Reserve currency, i.e., the difference between money in circulation and national bank notes in circulation, 1875-1935; thereafter, money in circulation: Money in circulation is based on the published series in Banking and Monetary Statistics, Board of Governors of the Federal Reserve System, 1943, pp. 408-09, thereafter the Circulation Statement of U.S. Money in Federal Reserve Bulletin, with corrections for: lost gold 1875-1907, as estimated in Annual Report, Director of the Mint, 1907, pp. 87 and 94; fractional currency presumed lost 1875-78; subsidiary silver error 1891-1910, as estimated in ibid., 1910, p. 54. The series does not include: minor coin; an adjustment for gold presumed lost 1907-33. The original figures exclude $287 million of gold coin in circulation beginning with 1914, the amount presumed lost in 1934. In computing the change from 1913 to 1914 this amount was restored.

d. Deposits of commercial banks at Federal Reserve Banks (i.e., member bank reserves at Federal Reserve Banks less float, plus nonmember bank clearing accounts). Member bank deposits at Federal Reserve Banks less float, i.e., uncollected items less deferred availability items, excluding through April 1929 miscellaneous components not properly classified as deferred availability items (last Fri. of June 1915-21; last Wed. thereafter): 1915-16, Net deposits from Annual Report, Federal Reserve Board, 1915, p. 46 and FRB, 1916. 1917-21, FRB. 1922-41, deposits from Banking and Monetary Statistics, pp. 378-394 and float from FRB. 1942-55, deposits and float from FRB. Nonmember bank clearing accounts, beginning 1917: Figure for 1917 is for July 6, from FRB. 1918-55, straight-line estimates between Dec. 31 figures are shown on Reserve System balance sheets in Annual Report, Federal Reserve Board and, after 1935, Board of Governors, FRS, 1917-21, 1926-43, 1945-55. So derived, high-powered money excludes deposits at Federal Reserve Banks of certain government agencies (in addition to Treasury deposits, which are excluded intentionally). The first exclusion is inconsistent with the inclusion in the money stock of deposits of such agencies at commercial banks, though the quantities involved are quite small. Minor coin (nickels and pennies) is ignored because of unavailability of early data and its quantitative insignificance, though it is reported by banks in vault cash data. Silver coinage is included in high-powered money.

(2): Change in domestic monetary gold stock (i.e., all gold coin and bullion at par value outside and inside banks and the Treasury): 1875-1907, Annual Report, Mint, 1907, p. 87. 1908-13, Circulation Statement of

NOTES TO TABLE F-5 (continued)

<u>United States Money</u>. 1914-41, <u>Banking and Monetary Statistics</u>, pp. 373-77 and 536, with the corrections noted below. 1942-55, <u>FRB</u>. No adjustment was made for the premium on gold before the resumption of specie payments in 1879. For the post-1913 data, the three following corrections were made.

a. Gold in the active portion of the Exchange Equalization Fund, reported in <u>Banking and Monetary Statistics</u>, p. 526, and in <u>Report on the Finances</u>, Secretary of the Treasury, 1940, p. 789, was added to the figures shown in sources listed above, beginning 1934.

b. The official figures, beginning 1914, exclude (arbitrarily) $287 million gold coin, the amount unaccounted for when gold coin was retired in 1933. In computing the change from 1913 to 1914 that amount was restored.

c. Part of the increase in the gold stock from 1933 to 1934 in the official figures ($2,811 million) resulting from the devaluation of the dollar in 1934, was excluded in computing the change from 1933 to 1934. (The gold-stock series is shown annually in col. 1, Table F-7, with a different adjustment for lost gold.)

(3): Change in Federal Reserve currency outside Federal Reserve Banks, less all currency and gold held (here and abroad) by Federal Reserve Banks, plus deposits at Reserve Banks of the Treasury and of commercial banks, less float. The actual figures were derived as follows.

a. Federal Reserve notes and Federal Reserve Bank notes outside Federal Reserve Banks (last Fri. of June 1915-20, June 30th thereafter): 1915-36, compiled directly from <u>Annual Report</u>, Federal Reserve Board and <u>FRB</u>, or by deduction of Federal Reserve notes at other Banks from amounts in circulation. 1937-50, Federal Reserve notes outstanding minus notes held by Federal Reserve Banks and agents, from <u>Report on the Finances</u>. 1951-55, "Statement of Condition of Federal Reserve Banks," <u>FRB</u>.

b. Reserve cash, redemption fund, nonreserve cash, other cash and gold held abroad: 1915-55, <u>Annual Report</u>, FRS, and <u>FRB</u>.

c. Deposits of the Treasury at Federal Reserve Banks (last Friday of June 1915-20, end of June thereafter), <u>FRB</u>, and <u>Banking and Monetary Statistics</u>, pp. 374-77.

d. Deposits of commercial banks at Federal Reserve Banks, less float: Same series described in note to col. 1, d. Before 1923, currency holdings of Reserve Banks exclude nickels, cents, and unassorted currency which are shown in "other resources," but with only small error.

(4): Liabilities of national banks for notes in circulation: Same series described in note to col. 1, b, excluding Treasury liability for the notes (col. 1, a).

(5): Acquisition or sale by the Treasury of silver bullion (excluding U.S. coin) by cash payment, not by exchange for silver bars. This series measures net silver purchases at cost and represents increase or decrease in silver coin issued (or to be issued) or held at the Treasury as backing for silver certificates or Treasury notes of 1890. No appropriation of tax revenues was made for those purchases, which do not appear in the budget figures in col. 7. Seigniorage, when spent, was treated before 1934 as a budget receipt (see footnote 32, Chap. 3). 1934-55, purchase and sale under various acts (including lend-lease programs to cancel U.S. foreign debts) from <u>Annual Report</u>, Mint, 1955, pp. 56-84 (see 1954, pp. 36-39 for explanatory text), and amounts acquired and sold by the Exchange Equalization Fund in 1934 from <u>Report on the Finances</u>, 1940, p. 789. 1895-1933, cost of purchases (including amounts combined with gold ore purchased by the mints) from <u>Annual Report</u>, Mint, for each year. Amounts deducted were realized from sale to India in 1919 under the Pittman Act

NOTES TO TABLE F-5 (concluded)

and from open-market sales in 1920 (D.H. Leavens, <u>Silver Money</u>, Blooming-ton, 1939, pp. 147 and 152). 1878-94, cost of purchases under the Bland-Allison Act of 1878 and the Sherman Silver Purchase Act of 1890 from <u>Annual Report</u>, Mint, for each year (see also summaries in <u>ibid.</u>, 1894, pp. 16-17, and in <u>Report on the Finances</u>, 1897, pp. 192-193). The figure for 1878 includes $7.1 million purchased for fractional coinage in addi-tion to the $13.0 million purchased under the act of 1878. 1875-77, cost of purchases under the acts of 1873 and 1875 from <u>Annual Report</u>, Mint for 1875 and 1877. Since only total purchases for 1876-77 are given, that total was divided between the two fiscal years according to deposits of silver bullion at mints in each year.

(6): Sum of cols. 7-10.

(7): Fiscal year deficits or surpluses of the budget (minus signs indicate Treasury receipts, and conversely): 1875-1931, <u>Historical Statistics</u>, 1949, Series P-98, pp. 295-297. 1932-55, <u>Report on the Finances</u>, 1957, p. 332. The budget figures do not include transactions recorded in other Treasury accounts (cols. 8, 9, and 10) or net operating income of certain government agencies, such as trust funds and government corporations--the latter included here in the nongovernment sector. Budget figures for vari-ous years up to 1896 include premiums over par paid or received by the Treasury for U.S. bonds, but in inconsequential amounts (see <u>Report on the Finances</u>, 1899).

(8): Change in par value of interest-bearing and matured debt of the Treas-ury: <u>Historical Statistics</u>, 1949, Series P-134 and P-136, pp. 305-306; and <u>Report on the Finances</u>, 1955, pp. 404-405 (minus signs indicate pay-ment of high-powered money by the public to the Treasury, and conversely).

(9): Change in deposits of the Treasury and its disbursing officers at commercial banks: 1876-1918, <u>Report on the Finances</u>. 1918-47, <u>All-Bank Statistics, United States, 1896-1955</u>, Board of Governors, FRS, 1959. 1947-55, <u>FRB</u>. This series was taken from bank statements for the years after 1918 in order to omit amounts in transit between banks and the Treas-ury. For the years before 1919, since banks did not consistently report on June 30, Treasury statements were used. Transit items are excluded in the <u>Report on the Finances</u>, 1914-18.

(10): Col. 1 minus cols. 2-5 and 7-9. Figures represent changes in miscel-laneous (nonmonetary) Treasury assets and liabilities not shown in other columns. On the asset side are: disbursing officers' balances at sub-treasuries (largely warrants issued but not paid); minor coin and frac-tional currency in Treasury offices; prepaid interest on the public debt and other prepaid items; and moneys in the Treasury, received but not yet registered by the issue of warrants. On the liability side are: checks and warrants outstanding; redemption fund for Federal Reserve Bank notes (but not the 5 per cent or retirement fund for national bank notes, shown as changes in note liabilities of national banks, col. 4); and Post Office funds on deposit at the Treasury.

TABLE F-6

SOURCES OF CHANGE IN HIGH-POWERED MONEY AS PERCENTAGE OF HIGH-POWERED
MONEY, FISCAL YEARS, 1876-1955
(per cent per year)

Year Ending June 30	Total (1)	Monetary Gold Stock (2)	Federal Reserve Operations (3)	National Bank Notes (4)	Silver Purchases (5)	Total, Excluding Silver (6)	Quantity of High-Powered Money at Beginning of Fiscal Year ($ millions) (7)
						SOURCES OF CHANGE IN HIGH-POWERED MONEY	
					Treasury Operations		
1876	-2.6	1.3		-3.1	1.4	-2.2	770
1877	0.7	4.4		-0.5	1.6	-4.8	750
1878	0.7	5.8		1.2	2.6	-9.0	755
1879	2.4	4.5		1.2	2.9	-6.2	760
1880	20.4	13.6		1.3	3.2	2.3	778
1881	14.4	13.1		-0.6	2.5	-0.5	937
1882	4.9	2.2		-0.3	2.2	0.7	1,072
1883	5.2	3.0		0.3	2.3	-0.4	1,124
1884	0.5	0.2		-1.4	2.0	-0.3	1,183
1885	3.8	3.5		-2.1	2.0	0.3	1,189
1886	-3.3	0.0		-2.1	1.9	-3.1	1,234
1887	5.7	5.0		-6.0	2.2	4.5	1,193
1888	3.9	4.0		-1.2	1.9	-0.8	1,261
1889	0.7	-2.0		-2.0	1.9	2.7	1,310
1890	3.6	1.1		-0.2	2.0	0.6	1,319
1891	4.9	-3.9		-0.1	4.0	5.0	1,366
1892	6.7	0.8		1.2	3.6	1.2	1,433
1893	-0.7	-5.2		0.9	3.0	0.7	1,529
1894	3.3	1.8		1.1	0.6	-0.3	1,519
1895	-4.3	0.0		0.4	0.0	-4.7	1,569
1896	-6.8	-3.0		1.4	0.0	-5.2	1,501
1897	9.0	6.4		-0.1	0.0	2.8	1,399
1898	12.9	10.7		-0.5	0.0	2.8	1,525
1899	4.8	6.1		0.6	0.0	-1.9	1,722
1900	6.8	3.2		3.7	0.1	-0.1	1,805
1901	6.0	4.4		2.8	0.0	-1.1	1,927
1902	3.4	3.2		-0.4	0	0.6	2,043
1903	5.5	2.6		2.5	0	0.4	2,113
1904	6.5	3.4		1.7	0	1.3	2,229
1905	2.9	1.2		2.1	0	-0.4	2,374
1906	6.0	4.7		2.4	0.0	-1.1	2,444
1907	6.6	4.8		1.5	0.3	0.1	2,591
1908	9.6	5.5		2.3	0.4	1.4	2,763
1909	2.0	0.8		1.0	0.1	0.2	3,027
1910	0.4	-0.2		1.1	0.0	-0.5	3,088
1911	3.8	3.8		0.3	0.0	-0.3	3,101
1912	1.5	2.0		0.7	0.1	-1.4	3,219
1913	2.8	1.6		0.4	0.0	0.8	3,266
1914	1.0	0.6		0.0	0.2	0.1	3,358
1915	5.7	3.1	0.4	0.0	0.2	2.1	3,390
							3,103
1916	14.2	14.0	4.0	-1.4	0.2	-2.6	3,281
1917	24.5	20.7	7.9	-0.4	0.2	-3.9	3,747
1918	17.7	-1.2	16.0	0.5	0.7	1.7	4,666
1919	11.5	-0.9	17.4	-0.1	-3.5	-1.6	5,490
1920	11.1	-4.1	12.5	0.2	-0.3	2.8	6,119
1921	-9.9	6.0	-16.5	0.2	1.0	-0.7	6,796
1922	-3.3	8.3	-13.8	0.4	0.9	0.8	6,124
1923	6.2	4.5	-0.7	-0.1	1.2	1.3	5,919
1924	2.6	7.0	-4.5	0.2	0.3	-0.4	6,284
1925	1.1	-2.0	2.9	-1.3	0.0	1.4	6,446

(continued)

TABLE F-6 (concluded)

| | | SOURCES OF CHANGE IN HIGH-POWERED MONEY | | | | | Quantity of High-Powered Money at Beginning of Fiscal Year ($ millions) |
| | | | | | Treasury Operations | | |
Year Ending June 30	Total (1)	Monetary Gold Stock (2)	Federal Reserve Operations (3)	National Bank Notes (4)	Silver Purchases (5)	Total, Excluding Silver (6)	(7)
1926	2.7	1.3	1.3	0.0	0.1	-0.1	6,519
1927	1.3	2.1	-0.5	0.0	.1	-0.3	6,692
1928	-0.9	-7.0	5.9	0.0	.1	0.3	6,782
1929	-0.9	3.2	-3.9	0.0	0	-0.2	6,724
1930	-2.6	3.2	-6.1	0.0	0	0.3	6,663
1931	5.6	6.5	-0.1	-0.2	0	-0.6	6,491
1932	6.8	-15.1	20.5	0.2	0	1.2	6,857
1933	2.5	5.4	-3.6	1.1	0.0	-0.4	7,326
1934	21.3	13.8	4.4	-0.4	0.6	2.8	7,510
1935	15.8	13.6	-0.4	-5.2	2.2	5.6	9,111
1936	9.2	14.7	-2.7	-2.1	3.8	-4.5	10,551
1937	15.6	15.8	3.4		1.1	-4.7	11,519
1938	8.6	3.9	-0.3		1.5	3.5	13,313
1939	18.6	22.1	-1.9		1.3	-2.9	14,455
1940	26.2	22.5	-3.3		0.7	6.3	17,143
1941	4.9	12.3	-4.1		0.4	-3.7	21,639
1942	9.4	0.2	4.8		0.3	4.1	22,693
1943	17.0	-1.5	16.4		0.0	2.0	24,827
1944	21.1	-4.1	26.0		-0.1	-0.7	29,049
1945	16.7	-2.6	19.2		-0.1	0.2	35,172
1946	6.3	0.1	5.8		-0.1	0.5	41,031
1947	0.5	2.5	-4.1		0.0	2.1	43,626
1948	2.2	5.3	-0.3		0.1	-2.9	43,847
1949	0.5	2.0	-5.0		0.1	3.4	44,799
1950	-5.4	-0.7	-3.8		0.1	-1.0	45,041
1951	7.5	-5.8	11.7		0.1	1.5	42,594
1952	4.5	3.6	0.9		0.1	-0.1	45,779
1953	3.1	-2.1	4.3		0.1	0.8	47,854
1954	-2.7	-1.0	-1.2		0.1	-0.5	49,357
1955	-0.5	-0.6	-1.1		0.1	1.1	48,041

Source, by Column

(1)-(6): Table F-5, cols. 1-6, respectively, divided by col. 7 of Table F-6.
(7): Same series for which changes are shown in col. 1, Table F-5. The first figure for 1915 includes, and the second excludes, the $287 million presumed lost between 1907 and 1934. The figure for 1956 is $47,777 million.

Note: Detail may not add exactly to total because of rounding.

TABLE F-7

STOCK OF MONETARY GOLD, ITS RELATION TO HIGH-POWERED
MONEY, AND COMMODITY VALUE OF GOLD,
ANNUALLY, 1875-1955

Year (end of June)	Stock of Monetary Gold ($ millions)		Ratio of High-Powered Money to Gold Stock (3)	Index of Commodity Value of Gold (1926=100) (4)
	Current Par Value (1)	Pre-1934 Par Value (2)		
1875	89	a	8.65	142
1876	99		7.58	148
1877	132		5.72	144
1878	176		4.32	162
1879	210		3.70	162
1880	316		2.96	146
1881	439		2.44	142
1882	463		2.43	135
1883	497		2.38	145
1884	499		2.38	157
1885	541		2.28	172
1886	541		2.21	178
1887	601		2.10	172
1888	651		2.01	170
1889	625		2.11	180
1890	640		2.13	178
1891	587		2.44	179
1892	598		2.56	192
1893	519		2.93	187
1894	547		2.87	209
1895	547		2.74	205
1896	502		2.79	215
1897	591		2.58	215
1898	754		2.28	206
1899	859		2.10	192
1900	916		2.10	178
1901	1,001		2.04	181
1902	1,067		1.98	170
1903	1,122		1.99	168
1904	1,198		1.98	168
1905	1,226		1.99	166
1906	1,342		1.93	162
1907	1,466		1.88	153
1908	1,607		1.88	159
1909	1,620		1.89	148
1910	1,603		1.91	142
1911	1,709		1.86	154
1912	1,763		1.82	145
1913	1,805	a	1.82	143
1914	1,814		1.83	147
1915	1,898		1.83	144
1916	2,346		1.68	117
1917	3,110		1.56	85
1918	3,041		1.86	76
1919	2,980		2.11	72
1920	2,721		2.55	65

(continued)

TABLE F-7 (continued)

Year (end of June)	Stock of Monetary Gold ($ millions)		Ratio of High-Powered Money to Gold Stock (3)	Index of Commodity Value of Gold (1926=100) (4)
	Current Par Value (1)	Pre-1934 Par Value (2)		
1921	3,120		2.01	102
1922	3,619		1.67	103
1923	3,873		1.65	99
1924	4,300		1.52	102
1925	4,161		1.59	97
1926	4,237		1.60	100
1927	4,366		1.57	105
1928	3,877		1.75	103
1929	4,081		1.64	105
1930	4,281		1.52	116
1931	4,691		1.47	137
1932	3,643		2.01	154
1933	4,031		1.86	194
1934	7,877	4,652	1.16	225
1935	9,116	5,384	1.16	212
1936	10,667	6,300	1.08	210
1937	12,487	7,375	1.07	196
1938	13,007	7,682	1.11	215
1939	16,195	9,565	1.06	220
1940	20,049	11,841	1.08	215
1941	22,713	13,414	1.00	194
1942	22,759	13,441	1.09	171
1943	22,399	13,229	1.30	164
1944	21,194	12,517	1.66	163
1945	20,294	11,986	2.02	160
1946	20,341	12,013	2.15	140
1947	21,417	12,649	2.05	114
1948	23,740	14,021	1.89	105
1949	24,637	14,551	1.83	111
1950	24,331	14,370	1.75	107
1951	21,872	12,918	2.09	96
1952	23,532	13,898	2.03	99
1953	22,521	13,301	2.19	100
1954	22,027	13,009	2.18	100
1955	21,730	12,834	2.20	99

[a]Not shown, because same as col. 1, through 1933.

Source, by Column

(1): Same as for Table F-5, col. 2, except that instead of corrections
under (C) for lost gold in the notes to that table the following
adjustment was made: The $287 million gold coin presumed lost was
distributed over the period 1908-33; that is, $11.05 million was
deducted from each of those years, on the assumption that the estimates of the Director of the Mint for the period before 1908
allow for lost coin. This seems preferable to assigning the entire
loss to one arbitrary year.

(2): 1934-55: Col. 1 times the ratio of the old to the new dollar value,
$20.67/$35 or $0.5906.

(3): Table F-6, col. 7, for the end of the corresponding fiscal year,
adjusted for gold coin presumed lost (see correction for gold stock
figures in col. 1) divided by col. 1.

(4): Index of average monthly wholesale prices due to Warren and Pearson
1875-89 and Bureau of Labor Statistics thereafter (Historical
Statistics, 1949, Series App. 23-24, p. 344), adjusted for monthly
variations in the dollar price of gold, 1875-78 (from W. C.
Mitchell, Gold Prices Under the Greenback Standard, Berkeley, 1908),
and 1933-34 (from G. F. Warren and F. A. Pearson, Gold and Prices,
New York, 1935, p. 154), and for the devaluation of the dollar in
1934.

TABLE F-8

DEPOSITS AND RESERVES AT COMMERCIAL BANKS, ANNUALLY AND SEMIANNUALLY, 1875-1955

(million dollars)

Date (end of month)	National Banks			Other Commercial Banks		All Commercial Banks		
	Deposits (1)	Net Due to Nonnational Banks (2)	Reserves (3)	Deposits (4)	Reserves (5)	Deposits (6)	Reserves (7)	Due to Mutual Savings Banks (8)
1875								
Aug.	575	38	167	610	74	1,185	242	29
1876								
Feb.	560	43	156	598	71	1,158	227	29
Aug.	549	36	160	603	71	1,152	230	29
1877								
Feb.	577	36	158	589	71	1,166	229	30
Aug.	529	35	150	563	71	1,092	221	30
1878								
Feb.	532	32	155	521	69	1,053	225	29
Aug.	525	30	152	501	74	1,026	226	28
1879								
Feb.	533	33	152	490	69	1,023	221	28
Aug.	674	38	157	527	76	1,201	233	31
1880								
Feb.	699	51	174	596	86	1,295	261	29
Aug.	715	60	198	665	99	1,380	297	30
1881								
Feb.	808	55	184	737	95	1,545	279	33
Aug.	837	70	208	865	96	1,702	304	38

(continued)

TABLE F-8 (continued)

Date (end of month)	National Banks			Other Commercial Banks		All Commercial Banks		
	Deposits (1)	Net Due to Nonnational Banks (2)	Reserves (3)	Deposits (4)	Reserves (5)	Deposits (6)	Reserves (7)	Due to Mutual Savings Banks (8)
			(million dollars)					
1882 June	894	68	208	893	97	1,787	305	38
1883 June	943	65	223	1,012	94	1,955	317	40
1884 June	900	56	216	1,023	120	1,922	336	43
1885 June	982	70	293	1,074	146	2,057	438	41
1886 June	1,059	73	265	1,270	163	2,330	428	44
1887 June	1,142	73	278	1,344	174	2,486	452	50
1888 June	1,209	87	298	1,332	175	2,541	473	51
1889 June	1,330	105	314	1,394	170	2,724	484	52
1890 June	1,422	108	297	1,598	166	3,020	463	53
1891 June	1,443	110	325	1,655	173	3,098	498	57

(continued)

TABLE F-8 (continued)

Date (end of month)	National Banks			Other Commercial Banks		All Commercial Banks		
	Deposits (1)	Net Due to Nonnational Banks (2)	Reserves (3)	Deposits (4)	Reserves (5)	Deposits (6)	Reserves (7)	Due to Mutual Savings Banks (8)
	(million dollars)							
1892 June	1,650	155	382	1,891	202	3,541	584	67
1893 June	1,436	99	308	1,767	204	3,203	512	71
1894 June	1,602	155	460	1,739	208	3,341	668	71
1895 June	1,642	159	392	1,954	211	3,596	603	73
1896 June	1,582	134	360	1,852	189	3,434	549	73
1897 June	1,671	175	433	1,939	201	3,609	634	81
1898 June	1,914	209	482	2,205	205	4,120	687	97
1899 June	2,301	277	503	2,665	218	4,966	721	99
1900 June	2,279	397	520	2,908	225	5,187	745	102
1901 June	2,617	454	560	3,487	261	6,104	821	107

(continued)

TABLE F-8 (continued)

(million dollars)

Date (end of month)	National Banks			Other Commercial Banks		All Commercial Banks		
	Deposits (1)	Net Due to Nonnational Banks (2)	Reserves (3)	Deposits (4)	Reserves (5)	Deposits (6)	Reserves (7)	Due to Mutual Savings Banks (8)
1902								
June	2,831	502	585	3,898	262	6,729	847	107
1903								
June	2,952	461	561	4,171	281	7,123	842	105
1904								
June	3,140	584	661	4,440	324	7,580	985	118
1905								
June	3,488	607	656	5,108	321	8,596	977	116
1906								
June	3,711	585	672	5,567	354	9,278	1,026	116
1907								
June	4,054	603	714	5,823	383	9,877	1,097	120
Dec.	3,901	610	758	5,246	430	9,147	1,188	129
1908								
June	4,093	747	864	5,370	479	9,463	1,343	138
Dec.	4,390	864	895	5,839	478	10,229	1,373	139
1909								
June	4,564	876	895	6,279	543	10,843	1,438	139
Dec.	4,751	771	860	6,495	550	11,246	1,410	137

(continued)

TABLE F-8 (continued)

Date (end of month)	National Banks			Other Commercial Banks		All Commercial Banks		
	Deposits (1)	Net Due to Nonnational Banks (2)	Reserves (3)	Deposits (4)	Reserves (5)	Deposits (6)	Reserves (7)	Due to Mutual Savings Banks (8)
			(million dollars)					
1910								
June	4,806	809	848	6,551	587	11,357	1,435	135
Dec.	4,917	821	915	6,792	551	11,709	1,466	144
1911								
June	5,147	877	942	7,023	582	12,170	1,524	154
Dec.	5,291	885	970	7,427	614	12,718	1,584	152
1912								
June	5,539	878	953	7,596	532	13,135	1,485	150
Dec.	5,676	853	949	7,809	601	13,485	1,550	153
1913								
June	5,649	865	937	7,847	581	13,496	1,518	155
Dec.	5,794	904	1,034	8,136	554	13,930	1,588	163
1914								
June	5,986	934	1,006	8,313	625	14,299	1,631	172

(continued)

TABLE F-8 (continued)

Date (end of month)	Member Banks			Other Commercial Banks		All Commercial Banks		
	Deposits (1)	Net Due to Nonmember Banks (2)	Reserves (3)	Deposits (4)	Reserves (5)	Deposits (6)	Reserves (7)	Due to Mutual Savings Banks (8)
			(million dollars)					
1914								
Dec.	5,986	681	1,003	8,457	617	14,443	1,620	177
1915								
June	6,445	977	1,128	8,811	620	15,256	1,748	182
Dec.	7,155	1,143	1,307	9,855	637	17,010	1,944	196
1916								
June	7,904	1,228	1,278	10,285	671	18,189	1,949	211
Dec.	8,625	1,364	1,574	11,667	842	20,292	2,416	212
1917								
June	9,558	1,465	1,723	11,758	676	21,316	2,399	212
Dec.	13,534	1,441	1,923	9,104	503	22,638	2,426	205
1918								
June	14,528	1,435	1,835	7,834	427	22,362	2,262	199
Dec.	15,729	1,526	2,018	9,168	391	24,897	2,409	198
1919								
June	17,234	1,549	2,095	9,228	421	26,462	2,516	197
Dec.	19,027	1,548	2,182	10,316	428	29,343	2,610	197
1920								
June	19,514	1,662	2,224	10,949	436	30,463	2,660	196
Dec.	19,441	1,463	2,303	10,584	404	30,025	2,707	189

(continued)

TABLE F-8 (continued)

(million dollars)

Date (end of month)	Member Banks			Other Commercial Banks		All Commercial Banks		
	Deposits (1)	Net Due to Nonmember Banks (2)	Reserves (3)	Deposits (4)	Reserves (5)	Deposits (6)	Reserves (7)	Due to Mutual Savings Banks (8)
1921								
June	18,451	1,354	2,041	9,839	379	28,290	2,420	182
Dec.	18,726	1,364	2,089	9,434	359	28,160	2,448	188
1922								
June	20,389	1,499	2,236	9,756	367	30,145	2,603	194
Dec.	21,648	1,622	2,248	10,288	393	31,936	2,641	191
1923								
June	21,751	1,612	2,245	10,817	378	32,568	2,623	188
Dec.	22,035	1,627	2,373	11,043	401	33,078	2,774	202
1924								
June	22,893	1,908	2,446	11,303	399	34,196	2,845	216
Dec.	24,349	2,133	2,679	11,722	418	36,071	3,097	213
1925								
June	25,560	1,990	2,640	12,363	412	37,923	3,052	209
Dec.	25,874	1,984	2,757	13,183	428	39,057	3,185	209
1926								
June	26,930	1,984	2,694	12,799	414	39,729	3,108	208
Dec.	26,441	1,908	2,698	12,621	399	39,062	3,097	215
1927								
June	27,828	2,135	2,842	12,777	405	40,605	3,247	223
Dec.	28,282	2,297	2,907	12,872	403	41,154	3,310	214

(continued)

TABLE F-8 (continued)

(million dollars)

Date (end of month)	Member Banks			Other Commercial Banks		All Commercial Banks		
	Deposits (1)	Net Due to Nonmember Banks (2)	Reserves (3)	Deposits (4)	Reserves (5)	Deposits (6)	Reserves (7)	Due to Mutual Savings Banks (8)
1928								
June	29,088	2,000	2,803	13,018	387	42,106	3,190	206
Dec.	29,442	2,151	2,854	13,359	406	42,801	3,260	196
1929								
June	29,076	1,829	2,761	13,108	375	42,184	3,136	186
Dec.	29,152	2,110	2,777	12,989	365	42,141	3,142	218
1930								
June	29,090	2,344	2,878	12,677	344	41,767	3,222	255
Dec.	28,857	2,274	2,978	11,590	339	40,447	3,317	298
1931								
June	28,174	2,302	2,883	10,737	326	38,911	3,209	348
Dec.	24,448	1,633	2,787	8,842	313	33,290	3,100	364
1932								
June	22,611	1,409	2,507	7,592	270	30,203	2,777	381
Dec.	22,793	1,501	2,901	7,198	241	29,991	3,142	371
1933								
June	20,682	1,303	2,790	5,437	234	26,119	3,024	361
Dec.	21,664	1,306	3,234	5,219	245	26,883	3,479	406
1934								
June	23,704	1,619	4,290	5,504	255	29,208	4,495	457
Dec.	25,064	1,682	4,590	5,948	280	31,010	4,870	465

(continued)

TABLE F-8 (continued)

Date (end of month)	Member Banks			Other Commercial Banks		All Commercial Banks		
	Deposits (1)	Net Due to Nonmember Banks (2)	Reserves (3)	Deposits (4)	Reserves (5)	Deposits (6)	Reserves (7)	Due to Mutual Savings Banks (8)
			(million dollars)					
1935								
June	27,377	2,027	5,393	6,375	296	33,752	5,689	473
Dec.	28,864	2,481	6,282	6,839	322	35,701	6,604	495
1936								
June	31,280	2,704	6,167	7,043	358	38,323	6,525	488
Dec.	32,184	2,883	7,333	7,427	378	39,611	7,711	503
1937								
June	32,306	2,887	7,377	7,536	382	39,842	7,759	482
Dec.	31,213	2,575	7,707	7,317	350	38,530	8,057	481
1938								
June	31,588	2,516	8,605	7,227	378	38,815	8,983	514
Dec.	33,579	2,869	9,497	7,444	375	41,023	9,872	512
1939								
June	34,306	3,220	10,691	7,528	410	41,834	11,101	626
Dec.	37,278	3,845	12,531	7,764	438	45,042	12,969	729
1940								
June	39,876	3,998	14,297	7,916	562	47,792	14,859	890
Dec.	42,265	4,174	14,832	8,111	658	50,376	15,490	866
1941								
June	44,744	4,205	14,055	8,443	672	53,187	14,727	875
Dec.	45,675	4,215	13,325	8,822	635	54,497	13,960	691

(continued)

TABLE F-8 (continued)

Date (end of month)	Member Banks			Other Commercial Banks		All Commercial Banks		
	Deposits (1)	Net Due to Nonmember Banks (2)	Reserves (3)	Deposits (4)	Reserves (5)	Deposits (6)	Reserves (7)	Due to Mutual Savings Banks (8)
			(million dollars)					
1942								
June	49,413	4,264	13,057	8,586	560	57,999	13,617	660
Dec.	55,022	4,779	13,316	10,021	469	65,043	13,785	561
1943								
June	63,278	6,052	12,904	11,253	534	74,531	13,438	630
Dec.	67,881	5,029	13,130	12,409	503	80,290	13,633	699
1944								
June	70,382	5,182	13,969	13,292	544	83,674	14,513	449
Dec.	76,343	5,447	14,570	15,169	554	91,512	15,124	487
1945								
June	83,323	5,831	15,627	16,179	563	99,502	16,190	495
Dec.	88,110	6,425	16,353	18,158	593	106,268	16,937	504
	($bill.)		($bill.)	($bill.)		($bill.)	($bill.)	
1946								
June	93.6	6,120	16.56	18.5	654	112.1	17.20	645
Dec.	95.7	6,031	17.05	19.6	675	115.3	17.73	706
1947								
June	97.4	5,851	17.15	20.1	709	117.5	17.86	738
Dec.	100.1	5,765	18.89	20.4	695	120.5	19.60	762

(continued)

TABLE F-8 (concluded)

Date (end of month)	Member Banks			Other Commercial Banks		All Commercial Banks		
	Deposits (1)	Net Due to Nonmember Banks (2)	Reserves (3)	Deposits (4)	Reserves (5)	Deposits (6)	Reserves (7)	Due to Mutual Savings Banks (8)
	($bill.)		($bill.)	($bill.)		($bill.)	($bill.)	
1948								
June	99.9	5,739	18.75	19.7	694	119.6	19.46	722
Dec.	98.9	5,609	21.39	20.2	748	119.1	22.14	749
1949								
June	99.6	5,628	19.54	19.9	728	119.5	20.27	683
Dec.	99.7	5,549	17.61	20.5	762	120.2	18.37	738
1950								
June	102.9	5,694	17.41	20.4	763	123.3	18.17	710
Dec.	104.6	6,184	17.96	21.3	788	125.9	18.74	658
1951								
June	106.4	6,127	20.08	21.0	811	127.4	20.88	722
Dec.	110.4	6,544	20.95	21.8	811	132.1	21.76	728
1952								
June	113.2	6,721	21.39	23.2	809	136.3	22.20	826
Dec.	115.0	6,805	20.88	23.5	761	138.5	21.64	763
1953								
June	116.9	6,948	21.13	23.8	815	140.7	21.94	729
Dec.	118.6	7,159	21.05	24.3	845	142.9	21.90	819
1954								
June	120.7	8,131	20.47	24.6	814	145.2	21.29	836
Dec.	124.3	7,868	20.4	25.2	863	149.5	21.26	852
1955								
June	127.1	8,223	20.1	25.3	904	152.3	21.00	831
Dec.	127.8	7,759	19.8	26.1	959	153.9	20.76	887

NOTES TO TABLE F-8

Note: Semiannual figures are seasonally adjusted.

Source, by Column

(1): Deposits of the public less float and (beginning June 1911) of the postal savings system at national member banks.

1875-June 1914: For annual data and, for semiannual data, call-date figures from Annual Report, Comptroller, nearest to June 30 seasonally adjusted and interpolated arithmetically to end-of-month dates.

Dec. 1914-55: Call-date figures from Banking and Monetary Statistics and FRB, seasonally adjusted.

Deposits of the public at national banks are individual deposits and dividends unpaid; and at member banks are time and demand deposits, letters of credit, and certified, cashiers', travelers' checks.

Deposits of the postal savings system were estimated for some earlier years (for which they were not reported separately from U.S. deposits) to be the total held at all banks given in Banking and Monetary Statistics (assuming that amounts held at nonmember banks were zero before June 1921 and at nonnational banks were zero before June 1912).

(2) 1875-June 1914: Due to nonnational banks less due from the same, including the net amount owed on clearing house loan certificates. 1875-1906, for annual data, call-date figures from Annual Report, Comptroller, nearest June 30; for semiannual data, call-date figures seasonally adjusted and interpolated arithmetically to end-of-month dates. June 1907-14, call-date figures from Annual Report, Comptroller, seasonally adjusted and interpolated arithmetically to end-of-month dates.

Dec. 1914-55: Due to all banks less due from the same. Call-date figures from Banking and Monetary Statistics and FRB seasonally adjusted. "Due from" excludes foreign banks after 1919. This series includes "due to less due from" member banks, which may not equal zero because of items in transit.

(3): Vault cash, plus (Dec. 1914 and after) deposits less float of member banks at Federal Reserve Banks.

Annual data, 1882-1906: Vault cash (all currency and coin on hand).

Semiannual data, 1875-81 and 1907-June 1919: Call-date figures nearest June 30, from Annual Report, Comptroller. Call-date figures, from ibid., and Banking and Monetary Statistics, adjusted for daily and monthly seasonal variations and interpolated arithmetically to end-of-month dates.

Dec. 1919-55: Wed. figures nearest end of June and Dec. (except before June 1921 when it is Fri.) from FRB, adjusted for daily and monthly seasonal variations.

Federal Reserve member bank balances less float (i.e., uncollected items less deferred availability items): Dec. 1914-55 Federal Reserve Bank reports from Banking and Monetary Statistics and FRB for Wed. nearest June 30 and last Wed. in Dec., except June 1915-Dec.1920, when it is Fri.; Dec. 1914, for which only an end-of-month figure is available; and June 1930-36, for which only end-of-month figures are available for float. All are seasonally adjusted. In 1933 the figures include special deposits of member banks not recorded in their reserve accounts (FRB, 1933 and 1934). (This series is the same as that used to derive high-powered money for Table F-5 except that the latter series contains minor adjustments of reported Federal Reserve float.)

(4): Deposits less float of the public and postal savings system deposits at other commercial banks.

1875-95: Centered annual and semiannual averages from David I. Fand, "Non-National Banks Estimates: 1867-1896," unpublished Ph.D. dissertation, University of Chicago, 1954.

1896-1906: Call-date figures nearest June 30 for each state from All-Bank Statistics, Board of Governors, FRS, 1943.

June 1914-Dec. 1955: Seasonally adjusted estimates from Friedman and Schwartz, A Monetary History, worksheets underlying Table A-1, col. 4.

NOTES TO TABLE F-8 (concluded)

(5): Vault cash plus (Dec. 1914 and after) balances of nonmember commercial banks at Federal Reserve Banks.

Vault cash of nonnational commercial banks.

1875-95: Centered annual and semiannual averages from Fand, "Non-National Banks Estimates."

1896-1906: Call-date figures nearest June 30, for each state, from All-Bank Statistics.

1907-42: Vault cash of nonmember commercial and mutual savings banks seasonally adjusted from Friedman and Schwartz worksheets, less vault cash of mutual savings banks on June 30 from All-Bank Statistics and, for Dec., an arithmetic interpolation of June figures. (Vault cash data for the two classes of banks are not available separately in Friedman and Schwartz estimates.)

1943-1955: Call-date figures from FRB, seasonally adjusted (including a small amount of vault cash in banks in U.S. possessions, excluded from the other series).

Balances at Federal Reserve Banks.

Dec. 1914-55: Balances of nonmember banks at year's end from Annual Report, Federal Reserve Board and Board of Governors, FRS, and FRB, partly estimated for certain years and, for June, an arithmetic interpolation of Dec. figures, less balances of mutual savings banks at Federal Reserve Banks from Annual Report, Federal Deposit Insurance Corporation since Dec. 1947, and assumed zero earlier.

(6): Deposits at banks of the public and the postal savings system less float. Col. 1 plus col. 4. This series differs slightly from that in Friedman and Schwartz, A Monetary History, Table A-1, col. 4. The differences are due to later revisions made in the latter.

(7): Col. 3 plus col. 4 before rounding. (The vault cash component of this series is the same as estimates of total vault cash in Friedman and Schwartz, A Monetary History, Table A-2, except for the exclusion here of mutual savings banks vault cash and for minor differences in seasonal adjustment.

(8) 1875-1887: Cash assets of mutual savings banks (5.2 per cent of deposits, which is the corresponding average percentage for 1888-92) less their vault cash from Fand, "Non-National Banks Estimates."

1888-95: Balances of mutual savings banks in each state at commercial banks from Annual Report, Comptroller, interpolated logarithmically to June 30, totaled, and raised by 10 per cent (10 per cent is the average understatement of the uncorrected figures in 1896-97, based on a comparison with the subsequent, more accurate source).

1896-1934: Balances of mutual savings banks at banks for June 30, from All-Bank Statistics, and interpolated logarithmically for Dec.

1935-46: Total cash assets of mutual savings banks excluding cash items (Table F-17, col. 2), less their vault cash for June from All-Bank Statistics, and interpolated arithmetically for Dec.

1947-55: Balances of mutual savings banks at banks, excluding Federal Reserve Banks, from Annual Report, FDIC, seasonally adjusted.

TABLE F-9

PERCENTAGE OF COMMERCIAL BANK DEPOSITS CREATED BY
NATIONAL OR MEMBER BANKS, ANNUALLY AND SEMIANNUALLY,
1875-1955

Year	Month	%	Year	Month	%	Year	Month	%
1875	Aug.	49.8	1911	June	43.0	1933	June	79.5
1876	Feb.	49.6		Dec.	42.3		Dec.	80.9
	Aug.	48.9	1912	June	42.8	1934	June	81.4
1877	Feb.	50.8		Dec.	42.7		Dec.	81.1
	Aug.	49.8	1913	June	42.5	1935	June	81.4
1878	Feb.	51.8		Dec.	42.3		Dec.	81.1
	Aug.	52.5	1914	June	42.6	1936	June	81.9
1879	Feb.	53.4		Dec.	42.2		Dec.	81.5
	Aug.	57.2	1915	June	42.9	1937	June	81.3
1880	Feb.	55.0		Dec.	42.7		Dec.	81.2
	Aug.	52.8	1916	June	44.1	1938	June	81.6
1881	Feb.	53.3		Dec.	43.1		Dec.	82.1
	Aug.	50.3	1917	June	45.4	1939	June	82.3
1882	June	51.1		Dec.	60.1		Dec.	83.0
1883	June	49.3	1918	June	65.3	1940	June	83.7
1884	June	48.0		Dec.	63.5		Dec.	84.2
1885	June	48.8	1919	June	65.4	1941	June	84.4
1886	June	46.4		Dec.	65.1		Dec.	84.0
1887	June	47.0	1920	June	64.3	1942	June	85.4
1888	June	48.6		Dec.	65.0		Dec.	84.7
1889	June	49.8	1921	June	65.4	1943	June	85.0
1890	June	48.0		Dec.	66.7		Dec.	84.7
1891	June	47.5	1922	June	67.8	1944	June	84.2
1892	June	47.6		Dec.	68.0		Dec.	83.5
1893	June	46.0	1923	June	67.0	1945	June	83.8
1894	June	49.0		Dec.	66.8		Dec.	83.0
1895	June	46.7	1924	June	67.2	1946	June	83.6
1896	June	47.2		Dec.	67.7		Dec.	83.1
1897	June	47.5	1925	June	67.6	1947	June	83.0
1898	June	47.7		Dec.	66.4		Dec.	83.2
1899	June	47.4	1926	June	68.0	1948	June	83.6
1900	June	45.0		Dec.	67.9		Dec.	83.2
1901	June	43.9	1927	June	68.7	1949	June	83.5
1902	June	43.0		Dec.	68.9		Dec.	83.0
1903	June	42.3	1928	June	69.2	1950	June	83.5
1904	June	42.3		Dec.	68.9		Dec.	83.2
1905	June	41.4	1929	June	69.1	1951	June	83.6
1906	June	40.7		Dec.	69.3		Dec.	83.6
1907	June	41.8	1930	June	69.8	1952	June	83.1
	Dec.	43.4		Dec.	71.6		Dec.	83.1
1908	June	44.1	1931	June	72.7	1953	June	83.2
	Dec.	43.7		Dec.	73.7		Dec.	83.1
1909	June	42.8	1932	June	75.2	1954	June	83.2
	Dec.	42.9		Dec.	76.3		Dec.	83.2
1910	June	43.0				1955	June	83.5
	Dec.	42.7					Dec.	83.1

Semiannual figures are seasonally adjusted.

Sum of Table F-8, cols. 1 and 8, divided by sum of cols. 6 and 8, before
rounding. These figures are too high (at most, by a percentage point or two)
because col. 8 includes mutual savings bank balances at other commercial
banks, which cannot be excluded. The amount of this overstatement is not the
same from year to year but probably varies with the relative importance of
other commercial banks; hence it is probably smaller for more recent years
than earlier.

TABLE F-10

RESERVE RATIOS OF COMMERCIAL BANKS, ANNUALLY AND SEMIANNUALLY, 1875-1955
(per cent)

Date (end of month)		National Banks, Net Due to Nonnational Banks		Other Commercial Banks	All Commercial Banks
		Included (1)	Excluded (2)	(3)	(4)
1875	Aug.	27.2	27.6	12.1	19.9
1876	Feb.	25.9	26.5	11.9	19.1
	Aug.	27.4	27.7	11.8	19.5
1877	Feb.	25.8	26.0	12.1	19.1
	Aug.	26.6	26.8	12.6	19.7
1878	Feb.	27.5	27.6	13.2	20.8
	Aug.	27.4	27.5	14.8	21.4
1879	Feb.	26.9	27.1	14.1	21.0
	Aug.	22.1	22.3	14.4	18.9
1880	Feb.	23.2	23.9	14.4	19.7
	Aug.	25.5	26.6	14.9	21.1
1881	Feb.	21.3	21.9	12.9	17.7
	Aug.	22.9	23.8	11.1	17.5
1882	June	21.6	22.3	10.9	16.7
1883	June	22.1	22.7	9.3	15.9
1884	June	22.6	22.9	11.7	17.1
1885	June	27.8	28.6	13.6	20.9
1886	June	23.4	24.0	12.8	18.0
1887	June	22.9	23.3	12.9	17.8
1888	June	23.0	23.7	13.1	18.2
1889	June	21.9	22.7	12.2	17.4
1890	June	19.4	20.1	10.4	15.1
1891	June	20.9	21.7	10.4	15.8
1892	June	21.2	22.2	10.7	16.2
1893	June	20.1	20.4	11.5	15.6
1894	June	26.2	27.5	12.0	19.6
1895	June	21.8	22.9	10.8	16.4
1896	June	21.0	21.8	10.2	15.7
1897	June	23.5	24.7	10.4	17.2
1898	June	22.7	24.0	9.3	16.3
1899	June	19.5	21.0	8.2	14.2
1900	June	19.4	21.8	7.7	14.1
1901	June	18.2	20.6	7.5	13.2
1902	June	17.6	19.9	6.7	12.4
1903	June	16.4	18.4	6.7	11.6
1904	June	17.7	20.3	7.3	12.8
1905	June	16.0	18.2	6.3	11.2
1906	June	15.6	17.6	6.4	10.9
1907	June	15.3	17.1	6.6	11.0
	Dec.	16.8	18.8	8.2	12.8
1908	June	17.9	20.4	8.9	14.0
	Dec.	17.0	19.8	8.2	13.2
1909	June	16.5	19.0	8.6	13.1
	Dec.	15.6	17.6	8.5	12.4
1910	June	15.1	17.2	9.0	12.5
	Dec.	15.9	18.1	8.1	12.4
1911	June	15.6	17.8	8.3	12.4
	Dec.	15.7	17.8	8.3	12.3
1912	June	14.9	16.8	7.0	11.2
	Dec.	14.5	16.3	7.7	11.4
1913	June	14.4	16.1	7.4	11.1
	Dec.	15.4	17.4	6.8	11.3
1914	June	14.5	16.3	7.5	11.3

(continued)

TABLE F-10 (continued)

Date (end of month)		Member Banks Net Due to Nonmember Banks		Other Commercial Banks (3)	All Commercial Banks (4)
		Included (1)	Excluded (2)		
1914	Dec.	15.0	16.3	7.3	11.1
1915	June	15.2	17.0	7.3	11.3
	Dec.	15.8	17.8	6.5	11.3
1916	June	14.0	15.7	6.5	10.6
	Dec.	15.8	17.8	7.2	11.8
1917	June	15.6	17.6	5.7	11.1
	Dec.	12.8	14.0	5.5	10.6
1918	June	11.5	12.5	5.5	10.0
	Dec.	11.7	12.7	4.3	9.6
1919	June	11.2	12.0	4.6	9.4
	Dec.	10.6	11.4	4.1	8.8
1920	June	10.5	11.3	4.0	8.7
	Dec.	11.0	11.7	3.8	9.0
1921	June	10.3	11.0	3.9	8.5
	Dec.	10.4	11.0	3.8	8.6
1922	June	10.2	10.9	3.8	8.6
	Dec.	9.7	10.3	3.8	8.2
1923	June	9.6	10.2	3.5	8.0
	Dec.	10.0	10.7	3.6	8.3
1924	June	9.9	10.6	3.5	8.3
	Dec.	10.1	10.9	3.6	8.5
1925	June	9.6	10.2	3.3	8.0
	Dec.	9.9	10.6	3.2	8.1
1926	June	9.3	9.9	3.2	7.8
	Dec.	9.5	10.1	3.2	7.9
1927	June	9.5	10.1	3.2	8.0
	Dec.	9.5	10.2	3.1	8.0
1928	June	9.0	9.6	3.0	7.5
	Dec.	9.0	9.6	3.0	7.6
1929	June	8.9	9.4	2.9	7.4
	Dec.	8.9	9.5	2.8	7.4
1930	June	9.2	9.8	2.7	7.7
	Dec.	9.6	10.2	2.9	8.1
1931	June	9.5	10.1	3.0	8.2
	Dec.	10.7	11.2	3.5	9.2
1932	June	10.4	10.9	3.6	9.1
	Dec.	11.9	12.5	3.3	10.3
1933	June	12.7	13.3	4.3	11.4
	Dec.	14.1	14.7	4.7	12.7
1934	June	16.9	17.8	4.6	15.2
	Dec.	17.2	18.0	4.7	15.5
1935	June	18.3	19.4	4.6	16.6
	Dec.	20.0	21.4	4.7	18.2
1936	June	18.1	19.4	5.1	16.8
	Dec.	20.9	22.4	5.1	19.2
1937	June	21.0	22.5	5.1	19.2
	Dec.	22.8	24.3	4.8	20.7
1938	June	25.2	26.8	5.2	22.8
	Dec.	26.1	27.9	5.0	23.8

(continued)

TABLE F-10 (concluded)

Date (end of month)		Member Banks, Net Due to Nonmember Banks		Other Commercial Banks (3)	All Commercial Banks (4)
		Included (1)	Excluded (2)		
1939	June	28.5	30.6	5.4	26.1
	Dec.	30.5	33.0	5.6	28.3
1940	June	32.6	35.1	7.1	30.5
	Dec.	31.9	34.4	8.1	30.2
1941	June	28.7	30.8	8.0	27.2
	Dec.	26.7	28.7	7.2	25.3
1942	June	24.3	26.1	6.5	23.2
	Dec.	22.3	24.0	4.7	21.0
1943	June	18.6	20.2	4.7	17.9
	Dec.	18.0	19.1	4.1	16.8
1944	June	18.5	19.7	4.1	17.3
	Dec.	17.8	19.0	3.7	16.4
1945	June	17.5	18.6	3.5	16.2
	Dec.	17.3	18.5	3.3	15.9
1946	June	16.6	17.6	3.5	15.3
	Dec.	16.8	17.7	3.5	15.3
1947	June	16.6	17.5	3.5	15.1
	Dec.	17.8	18.7	3.4	16.2
1948	June	17.7	18.6	3.5	16.2
	Dec.	20.5	21.5	3.7	18.5
1949	June	18.6	19.5	3.7	16.9
	Dec.	16.7	17.5	3.7	15.2
1950	June	16.0	16.8	3.7	14.7
	Dec.	16.2	17.1	3.7	14.8
1951	June	17.8	18.7	3.9	16.3
	Dec.	17.9	18.9	3.7	16.4
1952	June	17.8	18.8	3.5	16.2
	Dec.	17.1	18.0	3.2	15.5
1953	June	17.1	18.0	3.4	15.5
	Dec.	16.7	17.6	3.5	15.2
1954	June	15.9	16.9	3.3	14.6
	Dec.	15.4	16.3	3.4	14.1
1955	June	14.8	15.7	3.6	13.7
	Dec.	14.6	15.4	3.6	13.4

Source by Column

(1): Col. 3 divided by sum of cols. 1 and 2, Table F-8.

(2): Col. 3 divided by cols. 1 and 8, Table F-8. These figures are slightly too low because col. 8 includes mutual savings bank balances at other commercial banks, which cannot be excluded.

(3): Col. 5 divided by col. 4, Table F-8.

(4): Col. 7 divided by sum of cols. 6 and 8, Table F-8.

All computations were made before rounding the data from Table F-8. Semi-annual figures are seasonally adjusted.

TABLE F-11

RESERVE RATIOS OF NATIONAL BANKS, BY CLASS OF BANK, ANNUALLY, 1875-1917
(per cent)

Year	Central Reserve City Banks			Reserve City Banks			Country Banks			All National Banks		
	Total (1)	Required (2)	Usable (3)	Total (4)	Required (5)	Usable (6)	Total (7)	Required (8)	Usable (9)	Total (10)	Required (11)	Usable (12)
1875	42.6	34.3	8.3	24.2	13.0	11.2	16.6	2.4	14.2	25.0	13.1	11.9
1876	43.8	34.9	8.9	26.2	13.4	12.8	16.1	2.5	13.6	25.7	13.4	12.3
1877	38.7	34.0	4.7	25.9	13.1	12.8	17.0	2.5	14.5	24.5	12.7	11.8
1878	41.3	37.1	4.2	26.6	13.3	13.3	18.4	2.3	16.1	25.9	13.3	12.6
1879	38.5	37.1	1.4	26.2	13.5	12.7	17.0	2.8	14.2	24.4	13.4	11.0
1880	41.7	38.1	3.6	24.5	13.7	10.8	15.7	3.4	12.3	23.9	13.9	10.0
1881	35.3	36.5	-1.2	22.1	13.9	8.2	14.0	3.9	10.1	20.5	13.1	7.4
1882	36.2	34.8	1.4	21.7	13.7	8.0	14.1	4.1	10.0	20.3	12.5	7.8
1883	39.0	35.7	3.3	22.9	13.6	9.3	14.0	4.2	9.8	21.0	12.5	8.5
1884	48.9	33.4	15.5	26.9	13.6	13.3	16.0	4.3	11.7	25.5	12.6	12.9
1885	52.7	34.7	18.0	27.4	14.0	13.4	16.1	4.4	11.7	26.8	13.4	13.4
1886	39.5	35.4	4.1	23.5	14.0	9.5	15.5	4.8	10.7	22.0	12.8	9.2
1887	39.8	33.9	5.9	22.1	14.2	7.9	14.7	5.1	9.6	21.8	13.4	8.4
1888	40.9	35.1	5.8	21.5	14.7	6.8	14.1	5.4	8.7	21.9	14.3	7.6
1889	38.5	35.8	2.7	19.6	14.8	4.8	13.1	5.5	7.6	20.0	14.1	5.9
1890	38.4	34.1	4.3	18.2	14.4	3.8	12.6	5.5	7.1	19.4	13.7	5.7
1891	38.2	33.7	4.5	20.6	14.2	6.4	13.2	5.5	7.7	20.3	13.6	6.7
1892	37.1	34.3	2.8	19.3	14.4	4.9	12.5	5.5	7.0	19.4	13.8	5.6
1893	48.8	31.8	17.0	23.0	13.7	9.3	17.4	5.2	12.2	25.8	13.2	12.6
1894	46.6	33.3	13.3	19.5	14.2	5.3	13.8	5.3	8.5	23.7	14.8	8.9
1895	37.8	32.8	5.0	17.9	13.8	4.1	12.7	5.4	7.3	20.1	14.1	6.0
1896	38.6	32.1	6.5	21.1	13.6	7.5	15.7	5.2	10.5	22.3	13.5	8.8
1897	40.3	34.8	5.5	19.9	14.4	5.5	13.1	5.3	7.8	21.5	14.8	6.7
1898	39.4	36.7	2.7	19.6	14.6	5.0	12.5	5.4	7.1	20.9	15.5	5.4
1899	36.9	36.4	0.5	17.4	15.2	2.2	11.1	5.5	5.6	19.1	15.7	3.4
1900	41.0	36.5	4.5	17.7	15.2	2.5	10.3	5.4	4.9	19.8	15.7	4.1
1901	36.6	34.7	1.9	16.2	15.2	1.0	9.6	5.4	4.2	18.1	15.3	2.8
1902	34.6	35.6	-1.0	15.3	15.1	0.2	8.8	5.5	3.3	16.2	14.6	1.6
1903	35.3	32.8	2.5	16.3	14.3	2.0	9.3	5.3	4.0	16.9	13.7	3.2
1904	36.4	33.0	3.4	16.0	14.5	1.5	8.8	5.3	3.6	17.8	14.8	3.0

(continued)

TABLE F-11 (concluded)

Year	Central Reserve City Banks			Reserve City Banks			Country Banks			All National Banks		
	Total (1)	Required (2)	Usable (3)	Total (4)	Required (5)	Usable (6)	Total (7)	Required (8)	Usable (9)	Total (10)	Required (11)	Usable (12)
1905	34.5	33.4	1.1	16.0	14.6	1.4	8.6	5.3	3.3	16.7	14.3	2.4
1906	34.5	35.1	-0.6	15.1	14.4	0.7	8.2	5.3	3.0	15.0	13.3	1.7
1907	35.9	33.9	2.0	16.5	14.3	2.2	8.4	5.3	3.1	15.6	12.9	2.7
1908	37.9	33.7	4.2	17.5	14.1	3.4	9.3	5.2	4.1	18.0	14.0	4.0
1909	34.0	33.1	0.9	16.2	14.1	2.1	8.7	5.3	3.4	16.2	13.7	2.5
1910	35.5	33.1	2.4	15.9	13.9	2.0	8.5	5.3	3.2	15.9	13.1	2.8
1911	34.6	33.0	1.6	15.8	13.9	1.9	8.2	5.3	2.9	15.6	13.2	2.4
1912	33.1	33.1	0.0	15.2	13.9	1.3	8.0	5.3	2.7	14.7	12.9	1.8
1913	33.8	31.4	2.4	15.5	14.0	1.5	7.7	5.5	2.2	14.6	12.5	2.1
1914	31.9	30.7	1.2	16.1	13.8	2.3	8.3	5.9	2.4	15.1b	13.0	1.8
1915	37.6	a	a	13.4	a	a	8.7	a	a	16.4	a	a
1916	26.3			14.7			10.1			15.0		
1917	21.2			15.1			10.4			14.2		

Source: Ratio of reserves to deposits for call date nearest Oct. 1st from Annual Report, Comptroller, and National Bank Call Report. The usable ratio is the difference between the total and the required ratios. Cols. 10, 11, and 12 are presented back to 1865 in Table 24.

Deposits (all cols.): 1875–1914, Individual deposits and dividends unpaid (and deposits of postal savings system first shown separately in 1913–14) less float; and due to less due from state banks, trust companies, and savings banks. 1915–17, Demand deposits (excluding Treasury balances, which are shown for all banks only and so were distributed one-third to each class) less float, time deposits including postal savings, dividends unpaid (shown separately 1915–16); and due to less due from nonnational banks (estimated 1915–16 for each class of banks by multiplying "due to banks" of the class by the ratio for all national banks of "net due to banks" to "gross due to banks").

High-powered reserves (cols. 1, 4, 7, and 10): All currency and coin on hand (including clearing house loan certificates in 1885 and 1914) and (beginning 1915) balances at Federal Reserve Banks.

Required high-powered reserves (cols. 2, 5, 8, and 11): Requirements in effect times net amount of deposits subject to requirements reported in Annual Report, Comptroller, less (1875–1913) the 5 per cent redemption fund for national bank notes, which counted toward reserve requirements until 1914.

aNot computed for years after 1914 (see Table F-12 for all national banks).

bFigure for December 1914 (just after Federal Reserve Act came into effect) is 14.8.

TABLE F-12

REQUIRED AND USABLE RESERVE RATIOS OF MEMBER BANKS,
SEMIANNUALLY, 1914-55
(per cent)

Date (end of month)	Reserve Ratio Required (1)	Reserve Ratio Usable (2)	Date (end of month)	Reserve Ratio Required (1)	Reserve Ratio Usable (2)
1914 June	13.3	1.2	1935 June	8.9	9.4
Dec.	10.3	4.7	Dec.	8.6	11.4
1915 June	10.3	4.9	1936 June	8.7	9.4
Dec.	11.9	3.9	Dec.	13.0	7.9
1916 June	11.6	2.4	1937 June	17.5	3.5
Dec.	12.4	3.4	Dec.	16.9	5.9
1917 June	13.4	2.2	1938 June	15.3	9.9
Dec.	8.9	3.9	Dec.	14.9	11.2
1918 June	8.6	2.9	1939 June	15.9	12.6
Dec.	9.0	2.7	Dec.	15.4	15.1
1919 June	8.9	2.3	1940 June	16.1	16.5
Dec.	8.7	1.9	Dec.	15.6	16.3
1920 June	8.8	1.7	1941 June	16.3	12.4
Dec.	8.1	2.9	Dec.	18.4	8.3
1921 June	8.4	1.9	1942 June	18.8	5.5
Dec.	8.1	2.3	Dec.	18.3	4.0
1922 June	8.3	1.9	1943 June	16.0	2.6
Dec.	7.9	1.8	Dec.	15.8	2.2
1923 June	8.1	1.5	1944 June	15.8	2.7
Dec.	7.8	2.2	Dec.	15.3	2.5
1924 June	8.1	1.8	1945 June	15.2	2.3
Dec.	8.0	2.1	Dec.	15.1	2.2
1925 June	8.0	1.6	1946 June	15.3	1.3
Dec.	8.0	1.9	Dec.	15.2	1.6
1926 June	7.8	1.5	1947 June	15.1	1.5
Dec.	7.8	1.7	Dec.	15.3	2.5
1927 June	7.9	1.6	1948 June	15.9	1.8
Dec.	7.8	1.7	Dec.	18.2	2.3
1928 June	7.7	1.3	1949 June	16.7	1.9
Dec.	7.5	1.5	Dec.	14.5	2.2
1929 June	7.7	1.2	1950 June	14.4	1.6
Dec.	7.6	1.3	Dec.	14.7	1.5
1930 June	7.8	1.4	1951 June	16.6	1.2
Dec.	7.5	2.1	Dec.	16.7	1.2
1931 June	7.7	1.8	1952 June	16.9	0.9
Dec.	7.5	3.2	Dec.	16.6	0.5
1932 June	7.6	2.8	1953 June	15.6	1.5
Dec.	7.8	4.1	Dec.	15.2	1.5
1933 June	8.3	4.4	1954 June	14.4	1.5
Dec.	8.1	6.0	Dec.	13.9	1.5
1934 June	8.4	8.5	1955 June	13.5	1.3
Dec.	8.4	8.8	Dec.	13.7	0.9

Source

1914-June 1917, National Banks Only, by Column

(1): Ratio of required reserves to deposits. Denominator is deposits of the
public and postal savings system, less float and due to less due from
nonnational banks, for call dates nearest end of June and Dec. from
Banking and Monetary Statistics, seasonally adjusted. This series is
the same as the sum of cols. 1 and 2, Table F-8, except for the exclusion of state member banks.

NOTES TO TABLE F-12 (concluded)

The latter banks were unimportant during that period, and their exclusion has little effect on the figures. Numerator is the required reserves of national banks on corresponding call dates from <u>Annual Report</u>, Comptroller, Vol. II, 1917, pp. 244-48, seasonally adjusted.

(2): Ratio of usable reserves to deposits. Denominator is the same as for col. 1. Numerator is high-powered reserves minus required reserves used for col. 1. High-powered reserves are the same as col. 3, Table F-8, except for the exclusion of state member banks.

Dec. 1917-55, All Member Banks, by Column

(1): Ratio of required reserves to deposits. Denominator is the sum of cols. 1 and 2, Table F-8. Numerator is member bank reserve balances (excluding excess reserves) at Federal Reserve Banks, for Wed. nearest end of June and Dec., from <u>Banking and Monetary Statistics</u> and <u>FRB</u> seasonally adjusted.

(2): Col. 1 subtracted from col. 1, Table F-10.

Note: Figures are seasonally adjusted. The corresponding total reserve ratio (sum of cols. 1 and 2) is given in Table F-10, col. 1.

TABLE F-13

RESERVE RATIOS OF MEMBER BANKS, BY CLASS OF BANK,
ANNUALLY, 1918-55
(per cent)

Year	Central Reserve City Banks (1)	Reserve City Banks (2)	Country Banks (3)	All Member Banks (4)	Year	Central Reserve City Banks (1)	Reserve City Banks (2)	Country Banks (3)	All Member Banks (4)
1918	20.4	12.6	9.5	13.9	1938	46.5	22.0	13.9	26.5
1919	17.5	12.2	9.4	12.6	1939	52.1	24.0	14.3	29.7
1920	15.9	11.2	9.0	11.5	1940	55.7	28.8	16.0	34.5
1921	14.8	10.6	8.5	10.8	1941	43.5	28.3	16.2	29.9
1922	15.7[a]	10.1	8.2	10.8	1942	33.3	24.5	16.9	25.0
1923	16.5	10.2[a]	7.8	10.5	1943	21.7	21.0	16.0	19.6
1924	18.9	10.1	8.1	11.0	1944	21.6	20.3	15.5	18.9
1925	18.7	10.1	8.1	10.9	1945	22.0	19.8	14.7	18.4
1926	17.8	9.7	7.9	10.5	1946	21.3	18.5	13.4	17.2
1927	17.0	9.3	7.7	10.2	1947	21.0	18.0	13.4	16.9
1928	15.2	9.0	7.1	9.6	1948	25.1	18.5	13.9	18.2
1929	15.4	9.0	7.1	9.6	1949	24.9	19.2	14.5	18.7
1930	18.2	8.9	7.5	10.2	1950	22.4	16.7	11.9	16.1
1931	17.0	9.0	7.7	10.3	1951	25.9	19.1	13.4	18.3
1932	17.6	8.9	8.0	10.7	1952	25.7	17.9	13.7	17.9
1933	18.9	11.1	9.1	12.7	1953	25.9	17.5	13.2	17.5
1934	26.9	15.5	11.6	17.5	1954	22.5	17.1	12.8	16.5
1935	30.3	16.1	12.2	19.3	1955	20.3	15.7	11.6	15.0
1936	30.7	18.3	12.3	20.1					
1937	34.9	20.5	14.4	22.6					

Source: Ratio of high-powered reserves to deposits for call dates nearest June 30, from Banking and Monetary Statistics and Member Bank Call Report.

Deposits: Demand deposits (including certified, cashiers', and travelers' checks listed separately 1919-22) less float; time deposits including postal savings (except 1942, when they are not separated from U.S. time deposits); and due to non-member banks less due from (estimated by multiplying "due to banks" of each class by the ratio for all member banks of "net due to banks" to "gross due to banks"). "Due from banks" excludes foreign banks except in 1918 and excludes reciprocal bank balances after 1941. "Due to banks" excludes foreign banks, foreign branches of domestic banks, and reciprocal bank balances after 1941.

High-powered reserves: All currency and coin on hand and balances at Federal Reserve Banks.

[a] St. Louis was a central reserve city until 1922; its reserve city status begins with the 1923 figure.

TABLE F-14

HYPOTHETICAL RESERVE RATIO OF NATIONAL OR MEMBER BANKS,
BASED ON 1914 DISTRIBUTION OF DEPOSITS AMONG BANKS,
ANNUALLY, 1875-1955
(per cent)

Year	Hypothetical Ratio (1)	Actual Ratio Minus Hypothetical Ratio (2)	Year	Hypothetical Ratio (1)	Actual Ratio Minus Hypothetical Ratio (2)
1875	23.9	1.1	1916	14.6	0.4
1876	24.3	1.4	1917	13.8	0.4
1877	23.7	0.8	1918	12.5	1.4
1878	25.2	.7	1919	11.8	0.8
1879	23.8	.6	1920	11.0	0.5
1880	23.3	.6	1921	10.4	0.4
1881	20.4	0.1	1922	10.2	0.6
1882	20.6	-0.3	1923	10.2	0.3
1883	21.4	-0.4	1924	10.8	0.2
1884	25.5	0.0	1925	10.8	0.1
1885	26.5	0.3	1926	10.4	0.1
1886	22.5	-0.5	1927	10.0	0.2
1887	21.7	0.1	1928	9.2	0.3
1888	21.5	.4	1929	9.3	0.4
1889	19.9	.1	1930	10.0	0.2
1890	19.3	.1	1931	10.0	0.3
1891	20.2	.1	1932	10.2	0.5
1892	19.3	.1	1933	11.6	1.1
1893	25.2	0.6	1934	15.7	1.8
1894	21.9	1.8	1935	16.9	2.4
1895	19.1	1.0	1936	17.6	2.5
1896	21.8	0.5	1937	20.1	2.5
1897	20.4	1.1	1938	22.6	3.9
1898	19.8	1.1	1939	24.5	5.2
1899	18.0	1.1	1940	27.4	7.1
1900	18.5	1.3	1941	24.9	5.0
1901	16.8	1.3	1942	22.2	2.8
1902	15.7	0.5	1943	18.5	1.1
1903	16.4	0.5	1944	18.0	0.9
1904	16.3	1.5	1945	17.5	0.9
1905	15.8	0.9	1946	16.3	0.9
1906	15.4	-0.4	1947	16.1	0.8
1907	16.1	-0.5	1948	17.4	0.8
1908	17.2	0.8	1949	17.8	0.9
1909	15.8	0.4	1950	15.3	0.8
1910	15.9	0.0	1951	17.4	0.9
1911	15.5	0.1	1952	17.2	0.7
1912	15.0	-0.3	1953	16.9	0.6
1913	15.0	-0.4	1954	15.9	0.6
1914	15.1	0.0	1955	14.4	0.6
1915	15.8	0.6			

Source, by Column

(1): Weighted average of reserve ratios for three classes of national or
member banks (Table F-11, cols. 1, 4, and 7; and Table F-13, cols. 1,
2, and 3), where the weights are the proportionate amount of deposits
at each class in 1914: central reserve city banks, 20.3 per cent;
reserve city banks, 26.0 per cent; and country banks, 53.7 per cent.

NOTES TO TABLE F-14 (concluded)

(2): Table F-11, col. 1 subtracted from col. 10 (1875-1917) and Table F-13, col. 4 (1918-55).

An algebraic expression for col. 2 is derived as follows: Let R^i_t, represent the reserve ratio for the i class of banks at time t, and w^i_t, the amount of deposits at this class as a fraction of those at all classes at time t. The operator Δ signifies the change in a variable over the period t-1 to t. Then the actual ratio R^a_t and the hypothetical ratio R^h_t are given by

$$R^a_t = R^1_t w^1_t + R^2_t w^2_t + R^3_t w^3_t$$
$$R^h_t = R^1_t w^1_{1914} + R^2_t w^2_{1914} + R^3_t w^3_{1914}.$$

The difference between them is

$$R^a_t - R^h_t = R^1_t(w^1_t - w^1_{1914}) + R^2_t(w^2_t - w^2_{1914}) + R^3_t(w^3_t - w^3_{1914}). \qquad (1)$$

We may similarly express the total change in R^a as

$$\Delta R^a_t = \overset{3}{\underset{1}{\Sigma}}\Delta(R^i_t w^i_t). \qquad (2)$$

Expanding and rearranging terms, we get:

$$\Delta R^a_t = \overset{3}{\underset{1}{\Sigma}} R^i_t \Delta w^i_t + \overset{3}{\underset{1}{\Sigma}} w^i_t \Delta R^i_t - \Sigma \Delta R^i_t \Delta w^i_t. \qquad (3)$$

This divides the total into three subchanges: one representing the change in weights, one, the change in reserve ratios, and one, the interaction between the two subchanges, respectively.

The change in $R^a - R^h$, using (1), is

$$\Delta(R^a_t - R^h_t) = \overset{3}{\underset{1}{\Sigma}}\Delta(R^i_t w^i_t) - \overset{3}{\underset{1}{\Sigma}} w^i_{1914} \; \Delta R^i_t, \text{ since } \Delta w^i_{1914} = 0.$$

Collecting terms and using (3), we get:

$$\Delta(R^a_t - R^h_t) = \overset{3}{\underset{1}{\Sigma}} R^i_t \Delta w^i_t + \overset{3}{\underset{1}{\Sigma}} (w^i_t - w^i_{1914}) \Delta R^i_t - \overset{3}{\underset{1}{\Sigma}} \Delta R^i_t \Delta w^i_t. \qquad (4)$$

In most periods the absolute difference between Δw^i_t and $(w^i_t - w^i_{1914})$, that is, $w^i_{t-1} - w^i_{1914}$, is small, since the weights in fact have small year-to-year changes and no trend. Consequently, the second term on the right side approximates in magnitude the interaction (last) term, and the two tend to cancel each other. Hence, changes in the difference between the actual and the hypothetical ratio reflect mainly changes in the weights.

TABLE F-15

TOTAL CASH RESERVE RATIO OF NATIONAL OR MEMBER BANKS,
BY CLASS OF BANK, ANNUALLY, 1875-1955
(per cent)

Year	Central Reserve City Banks (1)	Reserve City Banks (2)	Country Banks (3)	All National or Member Banks (4)
1875	35.8	40.7	40.7	39.3
1876	37.1	42.5	41.8	40.7
1877	34.8	39.9	40.4	38.7
1878	33.6	42.4	44.7	40.9
1879	29.9	43.1	45.3	40.4
1880	31.7	43.0	43.7	40.1
1881	30.2	36.5	39.6	36.3
1882	32.0	34.9	34.3	34.0
1883	32.4	38.1	33.7	34.7
1884	40.9	39.7	35.9	38.2
1885	42.0	40.9	38.7	40.2
1886	32.8	36.9	36.4	35.7
1887	36.2	37.1	34.1	35.4
1888	36.1	38.7	35.1	36.3
1889	35.0	37.1	34.9	35.5
1890	36.3	35.3	32.3	34.1
1891	36.0	37.3	32.8	34.8
1892	34.5	36.8	33.9	34.8
1893	44.3	39.6	34.5	38.5
1894	40.7	38.6	36.0	38.2
1895	35.0	36.5	32.9	34.5
1896	36.9	38.9	33.9	36.1
1897	36.4	41.1	37.5	38.1
1898	35.4	39.8	36.7	37.1
1899	33.0	38.5	37.8	36.6
1900	36.0	40.9	36.0	37.4
1901	34.7	38.7	33.3	35.2
1902	33.5	37.5	31.2	33.6
1903	35.0	38.3	29.8	33.5
1904	34.3	41.6	30.8	34.8
1905	32.7	39.6	31.1	33.9
1906	32.6	37.4	29.4	32.5
1907	33.6	37.1	28.1	31.9
1908	34.5	41.1	29.9	34.3
1909	31.9	38.2	28.2	32.1
1910	33.7	37.8	26.2	31.4
1911	33.2	37.3	26.3	31.2
1912	32.9	37.5	26.4	31.2
1913	33.0	36.9	24.8	30.1
1914	32.9	34.5	24.1	29.1
1915	33.6	34.9	24.0	29.7
1916	26.6	33.2	26.5	28.4
1917	20.8	24.1	23.1	22.8
1918	24.6	26.4	20.8	23.7
1919	22.1	23.3	20.3	21.8
1920	18.1	20.0	17.7	18.5
1921	16.8	17.6	15.4	16.5
1922	17.1	18.4	16.3	17.2
1923	17.7	17.4	15.3	16.6

(continued)

TABLE F-15 (concluded)

Year	Central Reserve City Banks (1)	Reserve City Banks (2)	Country Banks (3)	All National or Member Banks (4)
1924	19.9	19.2	16.1	18.0
1925	20.2	17.6	16.2	17.6
1926	18.7	17.2	15.5	16.8
1927	18.0	16.2	15.2	16.2
1928	16.4	15.7	13.8	15.1
1929	17.4	15.8	13.3	15.2
1930	19.5	18.2	14.9	17.2
1931	18.4	18.4	16.4	17.7
1932	19.0	17.8	14.7	17.0
1933	20.4	22.1	18.5	20.4
1934	25.7	27.6	24.1	25.9
1935	29.0	28.1	26.4	27.9
1936	27.9	30.9	27.9	29.0
1937	32.1	29.0	27.3	29.4
1938	40.8	33.8	29.2	34.6
1939	45.1	36.1	31.3	37.7
1940	47.8	41.3	36.0	42.3
1941	38.1	39.6	36.6	38.2
1942	30.5[a]	32.2[a]	34.7[a]	32.3[a]
1943	20.5	25.7	30.7	25.7
1944	20.3	24.8	28.8	24.8
1945	20.7	23.7	27.2	24.1
1946	20.3	21.9	22.6	21.8
1947	20.1	21.4	21.7	21.2
1948	23.8	21.8	21.7	22.2
1949	23.7	22.3	21.8	22.4
1950	21.2	19.7	20.0	20.2
1951	24.5	22.0	21.1	22.2
1952	24.2	21.0	22.0	22.2
1953	24.3	20.7	21.0	21.6
1954	21.2	20.4	21.1	20.9
1955	19.3	18.8	19.1	19.0

Source: 1875-1917: Call date nearest Oct. for national banks from *Annual Report*, Comptroller; and *National Bank Call Report*.
1918-55: Call date nearest June 30 for member banks from *Member Bank Call Report*.

Denominator is the same as for Tables F-11 and F-13 except that interbank deposits are treated differently: gross (not net) amounts due to all (not just other commercial) banks are included (except that deposits of foreign banks and reciprocal balances were excluded when available separately).

Numerator is high-powered reserves used in Tables F-11 and F-13 plus amounts due from all banks (excluding deposits of foreign banks and reciprocal balances when available separately).

These reserve ratios represent a combination of banks without cancellation of interbank deposits in contrast to all the ratios used elsewhere in this study, in which the banking system is consolidated and interbank deposits cancel out.

The cash reserve ratio is high-powered reserves and amounts due from other banks divided by deposits of the public and amounts due to banks.

[a]Exclude reciprocal balances beginning 1942 (see notes to table). Ratios for 1942, including these balances, are, reading left to right: 30.8, 33.6, 34.9, and 33.1.

TABLE F-16

TOTAL CASH RESERVE RATIO OF OTHER COMMERCIAL BANKS,
ANNUALLY AND SEMIANNUALLY, 1896-1955
(per cent)

1896	June	24.6	1924	June	16.2	1943	June	32.4
1897	June	27.8	1925	June	17.2		Dec.	28.8
1898	June	27.0	1926	June	16.4	1944	June	28.9
1899	June	25.7	1927	June	16.3		Dec.	26.5
1900	June	25.3	1928	June	14.4	1945	June	27.2
1901	June	23.5	1929	June	13.5		Dec.	25.2
1902	June	22.6	1930	June	14.3	1946	June	23.6
1903	June	21.9	1931	June	16.3		Dec.	21.0
1904	June	25.3	1932	June	16.4	1947	June	20.7
1905	June	21.8	1933	June	19.8		Dec.	20.2
1906	June	21.2	1934	June	23.8	1948	June	20.1
1907	June	21.7		Dec.	25.4		Dec.	19.3
1908	June	25.6	1935	June	26.0	1949	June	19.6
1909	June	24.2		Dec.	27.0		Dec.	18.7
1910	June	22.9	1936	June	28.1	1950	June	19.9
1911	June	24.0		Dec.	28.9		Dec.	20.2
1912	June	22.5	1937	June	26.1	1951	June	20.8
1913	June	22.0		Dec.	25.6		Dec.	22.0
1914	June	22.2	1938	June	27.3	1952	June	20.5
1915	June	23.3		Dec.	27.0		Dec.	20.0
1916	June	22.6	1939	June	28.3	1953	June	20.0
1917	June	22.6		Dec.	30.8		Dec.	19.9
1918	June	21.9	1940	June	33.9	1954	June	19.9
1919	June	20.3		Dec.	34.6		Dec.	19.2
1920	June	17.8	1941	June	35.5	1955	June	18.9
1921	June	16.1		Dec.	35.0		Dec.	18.4
1922	June	17.0	1942	June	35.6			
1923	June	16.7		Dec.	34.6			

Source: This series is the same as Table F-10, col. 3, except for the inclusion here in the numerator of the amount due from banks and inclusion here
in the denominator of the amount due to banks from All-Bank Statistics, FRB,
and Annual Report, FDIC, seasonally adjusted after 1933. This series is comparable to the national or member bank ratio shown in Table F-15.
Note: Semiannual figures are seasonally adjusted; not available before
1896.

TABLE F-17

DEPOSITS, RESERVES, AND RESERVE RATIO OF MUTUAL SAVINGS BANKS,
ANNUALLY AND SEMIANNUALLY, 1875-1955

Date (end of month)	Deposits ($ millions) (1)	Reserves ($ millions) (2)	Reserve Ratio (per cent) (3)
1875 Aug.	837		
1876 Feb.	842		
Aug.	847		
1877 Feb.	841		
Aug.	818		
1878 Feb.	797		
Aug.	772		
1879 Feb.	751		
Aug.	744		
1880 Feb.	787		
Aug.	829		
1881 Feb.	867		
Aug.	957		
1882 June	952		
1883 June	1,004		
1884 June	1,034		
1885 June	1,068		
1886 June	1,125		
1887 June	1,183		
1888 June	1,237	66	5.3
1889 June	1,300	68	5.2
1890 June	1,373	68	5.0
1891 June	1,427	71	5.0
1892 June	1,517	83	5.5
1893 June	1,546	88	5.7
1894 June	1,571	89	5.7
1895 June	1,650	91	5.5
1896 June	1,693	91	5.4
1897 June	1,784	98	5.5
1898 June	1,869	114	6.1
1899 June	1,999	116	5.8
1900 June	2,128	120	5.6
1901 June	2,260	124	5.5
1902 June	2,389	123	5.1
1903 June	2,504	121	4.8
1904 June	2,601	135	5.2
1905 June	2,743	133	4.8
1906 June	2,911	132	4.5
1907 June	3,011	141	4.7
Dec.	3,017	149	4.9
1908 June	3,000	157	5.2
Dec.	3,055	157	5.1
1909 June	3,133	157	5.0
Dec.	3,221	156	4.8
1910 June	3,290	155	4.7
Dec.	3,356	162	4.8
1911 June	3,429	169	4.9
Dec.	3,501	168	4.8
1912 June	3,587	166	4.6
Dec.	3,658	169	4.6

(continued)

TABLE F-17 (continued)

Date (end of month)		Deposits ($ millions) (1)	Reserves ($ millions) (2)	Reserve Ratio (per cent) (3)
1913	June	3,732	171	4.6
	Dec.	3,786	181	4.8
1914	June	3,841	193	5.0
	Dec.	3,862	199	5.2
1915	June	3,873	205	5.3
	Dec.	3,986	220	5.5
1916	June	4,103	236	5.8
	Dec.	4,277	238	5.6
1917	June	4,342	238	5.5
	Dec.	4,359	229	5.3
1918	June	4,344	222	5.1
	Dec.	4,498	222	4.9
1919	June	4,715	222	4.7
	Dec.	4,926	223	4.5
1920	June	5,146	222	4.3
	Dec.	5,362	213	4.0
1921	June	5,492	205	3.7
	Dec.	5,572	215	3.9
1922	June	5,683	225	4.0
	Dec.	5,919	220	3.7
1923	June	6,189	215	3.5
	Dec.	6,416	229	3.6
1924	June	6,582	243	3.7
	Dec.	6,819	240	3.5
1925	June	7,033	236	3.4
	Dec.	7,218	235	3.3
1926	June	7,424	234	3.2
	Dec.	7,678	242	3.2
1927	June	7,953	251	3.2
	Dec.	8,264	242	2.9
1928	June	8,508	234	2.8
	Dec.	8,752	225	2.6
1929	June	8,836	216	2.4
	Dec.	8,794	249	2.8
1930	June	9,050	287	3.2
	Dec.	9,387	332	3.5
1931	June	9,854	383	3.9
	Dec.	9,940	407	4.1
1932	June	9,880	432	4.4
	Dec.	9,871	426	4.3
1933	June	9,576	420	4.4
	Dec.	9,503	460	4.8
1934	June	9,638	506	5.3
	Dec.	9,702	511	5.3
1935	June	9,777	516	5.3
	Dec.	9,839	541	5.5
1936	June	9,918	536	5.4
	Dec.	10,018	553	5.5
1937	June	10,094	533	5.3
	Dec.	10,129	535	5.3
1938	June	10,155	570	5.6
	Dec.	10,238	572	5.6

(continued)

TABLE F-17 (concluded)

Date (end of month)	Deposits ($ millions) (1)	Reserves ($ millions) (2)	Reserve Ratio (per cent) (3)
1939 June	10,377	690	6.6
Dec.	10,481	799	7.6
1940 June	10,573	967	9.1
Dec.	10,615	944	8.9
1941 June	10,595	955	9.0
Dec.	10,500	771	7.3
1942 June	10,344	741	7.2
Dec.	10,637	641	6.0
1943 June	11,070	709	6.4
Dec.	11,678	776	6.6
1944 June	12,390	524	4.2
Dec.	13,297	563	4.2
1945 June	14,331	572	4.0
Dec.	15,295	585	3.8
1946 June	16,172	730	4.5
Dec.	16,769	790	4.7
1947 June	17,500	822	4.7
Dec.	17,700	858	4.8
1948 June	18,100	815	4.5
Dec.	18,400	841	4.6
1949 June	18,800	781	4.2
Dec.	19,300	834	4.3
1950 June	19,800	801	4.0
Dec.	20,000	754	3.8
1951 June	20,300	822	4.0
Dec.	20,900	836	4.0
1952 June	21,700	928	4.3
Dec.	22,600	872	3.9
1953 June	23,500	838	3.6
Dec.	24,400	928	3.8
1954 June	25,300	955	3.8
Dec.	26,300	967	3.7
1955 June	27,200	951	3.5
Dec.	28,100	904	3.2

Source, by Column

(1): Deposits of the public: Estimates of Friedman and Schwartz, A Monetary History, Table A-1, col. 5, not incorporating minor later revisions in the latter.

(2): Vault cash; and balances at commercial banks, not available before 1888. (For the purposes of Table F-8, col. 8, balances at commercial banks were estimated indirectly by extrapolating later reserve ratios back in time, which is not appropriate here.)
1888-95: Balances of mutual savings banks in each state at commercial banks from Annual Report, Comptroller, interpolated logarithmically to June 30, totaled, and raised by 10 per cent (which is the average understatement of this series in 1896-97, based on a comparison with the subsequent, more accurate source) plus vault cash from Fand, "Nonnational Banks Estimates."
1896-1934: Total cash assets, excluding cash items in process of collection, for June from All-Bank Statistics and interpolated logarithmically for Dec.

NOTES TO TABLE F-17 (concluded)

1935-46: Total cash assets from <u>Annual Report</u>, FDIC, for 1935-38 and <u>FRB</u> for 1939-46, seasonally adjusted, less cash items, for June from <u>All-Bank Statistics</u>, and for Dec. an arithmetic interpolation of June figures.
1947-55: Total cash assets excluding cash items and balances at Federal Reserve Banks from <u>Annual Report</u>, FDIC, seasonally adjusted.

This series, less balances at commercial banks, shown in Table F-8, col. 8, equals vault cash of mutual savings banks.

Note: Semiannual figures are seasonally adjusted.

TABLE F-18

RATIO OF CURRENCY TO CONSUMER EXPENDITURES,
DECENNIALLY AND ANNUALLY, 1869-1960
(per cent)

1869-78	9.0[a]	1911	5.9	1936	8.3
1879-88	8.7[a]	1912	5.7	1937	8.2
1889	8.4	1913	5.6	1938	8.5
1890	9.3	1914	5.6	1939	8.8
1891	9.1	1915	5.6	1940	9.3
1892	9.1	1916	5.2	1941	10.2
1893	9.4	1917	5.6	1942	12.8
1894	9.4	1918	6.7	1943	16.2
1895	8.5	1919	7.0	1944	19.2
1896	8.3	1920	6.7	1945	20.7
1897	8.0	1921	6.4	1946	17.9
1898	9.0	1922	5.9	1947	15.8
1899	8.3	1923	5.7	1948	14.4
1900	8.7	1924	5.4	1949	13.8
1901	8.1	1925	5.4	1950	12.6
1902	8.0	1926	5.1	1951	12.0
1903	8.2	1927	5.0	1952	12.0
1904	8.0	1928	4.8	1953	11.7
1905	7.8	1929	4.5	1954	11.3
1906	7.5	1930	4.8	1955	10.5
1907	7.6	1931	6.3	1956	10.2
1908	7.9	1932	9.3	1957	9.7
1909	6.5	1933	10.2	1958	9.5
1910	6.2	1934	8.8	1959	9.0
		1935	8.4	1960	8.6

Source: Currency outside banks from Friedman and Schwartz, <u>A Monetary History</u>, Table A-1. Annual and semiannual data before 1907, for dates near the middle of year; thereafter, averages of monthly data. Currency includes state bank notes 1869-75.

Consumer expenditures from John W. Kendrick, <u>Productivity Trends in the United States</u>, Princeton for NBER, 1961, pp. 296-297, extended with Department of Commerce figures.

[a]Ten-year averages of annual figures.

AUTHOR INDEX

Abramovitz, Moses, 260n
Alchian, A., 310n
Andrew, A. Piatt, 182n
Angell, James W., 2
Ayres, L. R., 276n

Bloomfield, Arthur I., 53n, 109n
Brechling, Frank, 122n
Brockie, M. D., 199n
Brown, E. H. Phelps, 254n
Brunner, Karl, 199n
Burgess, W. R., 166n
Burns, Arthur F., 260n
Busschau, W. J., 67n

Cagan, P., 128, 319n, 320n
Cairnes, John E., 249n
Cannon, J. G., 139n
Cassel, Gustav, 250n
Christ, C. F., 173n
Creamer, Daniel, 145n
Currie, Lauchlin, 2, 253n

Dewey, D. R., 76n

Fand, David I., xx
Fels, Rendigs, 309n
Fisher, Irving, 171n, 256, 257, 258, 305, 307–309, 311
French, D. R., 172n
Freund, W. C., 174n
Friedman, Milton, 150n
Friedman, Milton, and Schwartz, A. J., xx, 1, 2, 9n, 13, 21, 54n, 69n, 76n, 82n, 84n, 90n, 97, 120n, 169, 174n, 199n

Garvy, G., 166n
Gibson, A. H., 252n.
    See also Gibson Paradox, Subject Index
Goldsmith, Raymond, 169
Goodwin, R. M., 314n, 316
Gurley, John G., 259n

Harding, W. P. G., 183n
Harris, Seymour, 210n

Harrod, R., 65n
Hartzel, Elmer, 172n
Hawtrey, R. G., 143, 145, 276, 277
Hayek, F., 249n
Hicks, J. R., 276n, 309n
Higgonet, René, 250n
Horwich, G., 199n
Hotelling, Harold, 240

Jeffreys, J. B., 128n
Jevons, W. Stanley, 249
Johnson, G. G., 65n, 79n

Kahn, C. Harry, 131n
Kemmerer, E. W., 76n, 215, 218n
Kessel, R., 310n
Keynes, J. M., 172n, 252–258, 308
Kindahl, James, 82n
Kitchen, Joseph, 59n
Knox, John Jay, 90n

Lavington, F., 143n, 310n
Leavens, D. H., 79n
Lock, Alfred G., 60n

Macaulay, F. R., 78n, 209, 307, 309n
Meade, Edward S., 60n, 61n
Meade, J. E., 12n
Meiselman, David, 307n
Mintz, Ilse, 105n, 107, 107n, 110n
Mitchell, Wesley C., 143, 145, 260n, 276, 277
Morgenstern, Oskar, 110n, 244n
Morrison, George R., 200n
Mundel, Robert, 307n
Myers, Margaret G., 84n, 213n

Noyes, A. D., 74n, 83n

Ohlin, B., 254n
Ozga, S. A., 254n
Paris, J. D., 94n
Pearson, F., 59n, 67n
Persons, W. M., 233n
Phinney, J. T., 250n
Polak, J. J., 143n, 233n

SUBJECT INDEX

(Page numbers in **boldface** refer to charts)